MICHAEL TAYLOR

Michael Taylor is a historian of the British Empire and the British Isles in the eighteenth and nineteenth centuries. He graduated with a double first in history from the University of Cambridge, where he earned his PhD – and also won *University Challenge*. He has since been Lecturer in Modern British History at Balliol College, Oxford, and a Visiting Fellow at the British Library's Eccles Centre for American Studies.

Praise for *The Interest*:

'Scintillating ... compulsively readable ... As this timely, sobering book reminds us, British abolition cannot be celebrated as an inevitable or precocious national triumph. It was not the end, but only the beginning'

Guardian

'One achievement of Taylor's fascinating book is that, for the first time in a book about abolition, it gives equal weight to the force of pro-slavery ... Taylor's political analysis is first-rate and riveting ... Above all, he reminds us of the role of those who have been unsung in this story – of Mary Prince, S⸻ ⸻nd Quamina'

'Those seeking a catalogue of the country's old iniquities need look no further'
The Telegraph Books of the Year

'A magnificent book ... riveting'
Evening Standard

'Powerful ... engrossing ... Taylor's potent book shows why slavery took root as an essential part of British national life'
Independent

'Taylor can tell a story superbly and has a fine eye for detail ... His argument is a potent and necessary corrective to a cosy national myth'
Economist

'Superbly brings to life all the intrigue, machinations, heavy-lifting, rigmarole and chance of the tortuous path to abolition'
Literary Review

'Impressively researched and engagingly written'
Sunday Times

'Tells a compelling story, graced with anecdotes but driven by argument, that moves the reader to and fro between London and the Caribbean, and between aristocratic houses and anti-slavery rallies ... The writing of British history must encompass slave-power, not just sea-power – as Taylor's scorching book makes clear'
New Statesman

MICHAEL TAYLOR

The Interest

VINTAGE

1 3 5 7 9 10 8 6 4 2

Vintage is part of the Penguin Random House
group of companies whose addresses can be found at
global.penguinrandomhouse.com

Penguin
Random House
UK

First published in Vintage in 2021
First published in hardback by The Bodley Head in 2020

penguin.co.uk/vintage

A CIP catalogue record for this book is available from the
British Library

ISBN 9781529110982

Printed and bound in Great Britain by Clays Ltd, Elcograf S.p.A.

The authorised representative in the EEA is Penguin Random House
Ireland, Morrison Chambers, 32 Nassau Street, Dublin D02 YH68.

Penguin Random House is committed to a sustainable future for our
business, our readers and our planet. This book is made from Forest
Stewardship Council® certified paper.

MIX
Paper from
responsible sources
FSC
www.fsc.org
FSC® C018179

To my parents, Hubert and Geraldine.

Contents

List of Maps

Preface

Shortly before 4.00 p.m. on 29 September 2015, the private plane carrying David Cameron and his retinue touched down at Norman Manley International Airport outside Kingston, Jamaica. As the prime minister disembarked, he was greeted with a red carpet, a ceremonial guard of honour, and a military brass band playing 'God Save the Queen'. In the shadow of a canopy on the runway, Cameron shook hands with his Jamaican counterpart, Portia Simpson-Miller, and several members of her Cabinet. It was the first prime ministerial visit to this former British colony since 2001, and Cameron had been invited to address a joint sitting of Jamaica's Houses of Parliament on the following day. In keeping with his commitment to spend 0.7 per cent of British GDP on international aid, he was expected to announce £300 million of investment in Caribbean infrastructure; accordingly, a press release from Downing Street gave details of a new fund that would 'invest in roads, bridges and ports to help drive economic growth and development across the region'. The British prime minister was also expected to say something about slavery.[2]

For almost 200 years, Jamaica had been the largest and most valuable slave colony in the British Empire, and by the early nineteenth century there were more enslaved people in Jamaica – over 300,000 – than there were people of any description in any British city except London. Some of the legacies of this history are obvious. Jamaica's three counties are Surrey, Middlesex, and Cornwall, while the island's parishes include Manchester and Westmoreland; Sabina Park in Kingston is one of the great crucibles of cricket; and the tripartite structure of the Jamaican government is modelled on Westminster. There are also pointed, personal aspects to these shared histories, for many Jamaicans of the present day are descended from the Africans whom the British had enslaved and trafficked across the Atlantic, their surnames often taken from the slaveholders who once 'owned' their ancestors. At the same time, many Britons have ancestors among those slaveholders, and Cameron's visit had brought one in particular to public attention. Sir James Duff was an army officer and MP who, as the trustee of a Jamaican estate, had received compensation for 202 enslaved people. Duff was also Cameron's first cousin six times removed.[3]

In the weeks and months before Cameron went to Jamaica, he had faced mounting calls to 'atone [and] apologise personally and on behalf of his country' for the horrors of colonial slavery. The Barbadian historian Sir Hilary Beckles asked him 'to acknowledge responsibility for your share of this situation and ... to contribute in a joint programme of rehabilitation and renewal'. Earlier that year the Jamaican Parliament had unanimously passed a motion which stated that the country was entitled to reparations for colonial slavery, and now Professor Verene Shepherd, the chair of Jamaica's National Commission on Reparations, declared that 'nothing short of an unambiguous apology' would suffice. Then, shortly after Cameron's plane touched down at Kingston, Portia Simpson-Miller raised the issues of slavery and reparatory justice during their bilateral talks. It followed that, on 30 September, when Cameron finally addressed the assembled dignitaries in the Jamaican Parliament, he would indeed speak of slavery and 'the long, dark shadow' that it cast over the Caribbean. But he did not say sorry.[4]

Instead, Cameron appeared to represent Britain as a fellow *victim* of slavery. Describing Britons and Jamaicans as 'friends who have gone through so much together since those darkest of times', he urged his audience to 'move on from this painful legacy and continue to build for the future'. And while Cameron allowed that slavery was 'abhorrent in all its forms' and without a 'place whatsoever in any civilised society', the traditional, triumphalist account of Britain's connection to colonial slavery shone through. 'Britain is proud', he told the descendants of the very people whom the British had enslaved, 'to have eventually led the way in its abolition.'[5]

The lack of apology should not have been surprising. On the day before Cameron's speech, Downing Street had defended the British government's stubborn refusal to discuss reparations. Slavery was 'centuries old', a spokesman said, and it happened 'under a different government'. It therefore remained official policy that 'the right approach' did not encompass reparations. On the contrary, the 'right' approach appeared to involve spending £25 million on a new prison outside Kingston for the purpose of incarcerating Jamaican nationals who had been convicted of crimes in Britain. Downing Street promptly issued another press release: 'UK signs deal', ran the headline, 'to send Jamaican prisoners home'. Notably, all this occurred while Theresa May's Home Office was aggressively pursuing the deportation of *Windrush*-generation West Indians.[6]

In his 732-page memoir, *For the Record*, David Cameron found no space for his 2015 trip to Jamaica, or the issue of historical slavery more generally. However, the *abolition* of slavery had long been central to his ideas about Britishness. In a 2014 *Mail on Sunday* article on 'British Values' he had written: 'This is the country that helped ... abolish slavery'. Nine years previously, as the shadow Education Secretary, he had pressed for a policy of 'ensuring that all children are taught to be proud of Britain, our history and our values'. Among the 'proud achievements' in British history, he alighted on 'Britain's role in ending slavery', but there was no mention of Britain's prior role in developing and then exploiting colonial slavery and the slave trade.[7]

Of course, Cameron is not alone in perpetuating this brand of unthinking, self-congratulatory nationalism. The mythology of Britain as the champion of liberty and the enemy of slavery has a long-standing tradition, and abolition has figured as the triumph of British justice and morality since the early decades of the nineteenth century. The halcyon days of these beliefs were probably between the wars and, in 1935, the historian Reginald Coupland proclaimed that

> [Abolition was] not after all a romantic illusion ... It may be that politics ... is often no more than a mask for the strife of rival interests, but the lives and work of Wilberforce and the [anti-slavery campaigners known as the] Saints are certain proof that not merely individuals but the common will, the State itself, can rise on occasion to the heights of pure unselfishness.

Somehow, the myth that Britain was really an *anti-slavery* nation survived the trauma of decolonization in the 1950s and 1960s. Somehow, the myth also survived Britain's secret war in Oman in the late 1960s, when the Foreign Office turned a blind eye to the slavery there that it rationalised as 'the local equivalent of the welfare state'. By the time of the bicentennial anniversary of the abolition of the slave trade in 2007, the celebrations were described by the activist Toyin Agbetu, who interrupted a commemorative ceremony at Westminster Abbey, as a mere 'Wilber-fest'. (Strangely, in December 2019, Boris Johnson's government could not find the money for a bronze memorial to the *victims* of British slavery that was proposed for Hyde Park.)[8]

The idea that abolition was the triumph of British Christianity is equally commonplace. I grew up in the Northern Irish heartland of the Democratic Unionist Party and the intellectual culture of this staunchly conservative part of the United Kingdom was often informed by an unyielding, fundamentalist Christianity. When I was sixteen, one DUP councillor reacted to the midnight sale of a Harry Potter book with the words, 'These cults with their stories about witches are damaging, especially to young people who would be better off saying their prayers'. Later that year, another DUP councillor declared that Hurricane Katrina had been sent by God to punish New Orleans for its gay-friendly Mardi Gras. In this world, it was assumed knowledge that Wilberforce and Britain's Christians had 'freed the slaves'. Yet as I searched the Bible for the verses that could explain how Christian faith alone had enabled Britain to sweep away slavery, I searched in vain.[9]

By the age of twenty-two, beguiled by eighteenth- and nineteenth-century history, I secured funding for doctoral research into the Bible's role in historical slavery. Really, I wanted to answer two questions. First, how and why do intelligent people defend the indefensible? The last five years of Anglo-American politics have been fascinating. Second, if abolishing slavery was a great achievement – and it *was* – then who and what were the necessarily 'great' obstacles in the way? While there is voluminous scholarship on slavery, there was a relative dearth of work about British *opposition* to abolition. But as my PhD expanded into a wider history of the British defence of slavery, I uncovered hundreds of pro-slavery documents that had been 'forgotten'. Building on the work of historians such as Lowell J. Ragatz, Elsa Goveia, Lillian Penson, Christer Petley, Nick Draper, David Lambert, Katie Donington, among others, this book is based in part upon that research.'[10]

These sources reveal a clear and troubling picture of widespread and fervent British support for colonial slavery and, although recent scholarship has demurred, I have no difficulty in describing their authors as 'pro-slavery', not as 'anti-abolitionist'. In truth, the choice over ending slavery was binary: Britons of the 1820s or 1830s could choose to preserve slavery or to abolish it; and by opposing abolition an MP, financier, or journalist in fact supported the persistence of slavery. Indeed, it is worth considering whether the equivocal person, who prefaced arguments against abolition with professions of hating slavery 'in the abstract', committed the more grievous offence: the person who defended slavery *on the merits of slavery* did something evil, but the person who defended slavery, despite knowing that slavery was wrong, did something even worse.[11]

The realities of British colonial slavery and abolition were strikingly different from the sweeping, sentimental accounts which prevail in the popular imagination. When Parliament abolished the British slave trade in 1807, it did *not* abolish colonial slavery; and when the last slave ship dropped anchor, more than 700,000 people remained in bondage in the British Caribbean. For these men, women, and children, the abolition of the trade made no difference whatsoever to their lives. They were still enslaved, and abolition did nothing to diminish the pain, cruelty, and violence that British slaveholders continued to inflict upon them. In fact, the campaign to abolish colonial slavery did not even *begin* for another sixteen years until, on a cold London night in January 1823, a few dozen committed radicals founded the Anti-Slavery Society. In the meantime, much of Latin America, the northern US states, and the free black republic of Haiti had already abolished slavery on their own terms: the idea that Britain was 'first' to do so is bogus nonsense.

The ensuing, belated campaign for slave emancipation was no mere coda to the campaign against the slave trade. It was waged by different people with different ideas against different enemies in a different context. Moreover, there was absolutely nothing inevitable about its success. When the anti-slavery campaigners made their first move, they were confronted by stupendously wealthy planters and merchants whose fortunes depended on the enslavement of Africans, by intellectuals and publishers who deplored the very idea of 'colonial reform', and by government ministers who dared not endanger the future of colonies which had provided Britain with economic and strategic security for centuries. Together these men formed the West India Interest, the 'Interest' of this book's title, and rolled national politics as one of the most fearsome lobbies ever known to British history. Indeed, as these men corralled the national press, the City of London, and the Tory government of the day into the *pro*-slavery ranks, it became clear that the West India Interest did not simply have connections to the British establishment; it *was* the British establishment.

The fight to eradicate slavery – and to overturn widely held assumptions about the merits of it – is one of Britian's defining moral and political battles. This book tells that story. While there are some broadly thematic chapters and analytical sections, it is nonetheless framed as a narrative. If history is about anything, it is probably about 'how' and 'why'. And if one purpose of this book is to explain how and why Britain transformed itself from a slaveholding superpower into a supposedly 'anti-slavery nation', that story needs to be told in chronological order. To do otherwise and to write about slavery from the perspective of 'freedom' would risk entrenching the dangerous idea that the abolition of slavery was a *fait accompli*.

This has not been an easy book to write. For one thing, there is blood in these pages because the history of slavery cannot be told without it. To sanitise the story would not only understate the role that shocking imagery played in slavery-related materials; it would also – and less excusably – minimise the atrocities that the British perpetrated against millions of Africans over hundreds of years across oceans, islands, and continents. For another, there is terminology here that would be unforgivable if it were used today, but where historical figures have used racist language, I have reproduced it in full. This is not gratuitous. These *were* the terms of debate.

There is a further problem with sources. From the advent of the anti-slavery campaign in 1823, Britons wrote thousands of letters, articles, pamphlets, and books about slavery, but almost nobody did so from a position of neutrality. Almost everything which entered the public domain was crafted as propaganda, and the challenges for the historian are obvious. Nonetheless, this is the first narrative history of British colonial slavery which gives equal space to the pro-slavery figures who finished on the 'wrong side' of history. There are plenty of good reasons *not* to memorialise these people, but there is every good reason to remember them: if we are to understand how and why Britain abolished slavery, we also need to understand how and why Britons fought to preserve it. I have also sought, where possible, to give expression to voices that are often excluded from histories of the early nineteenth century, principally those belonging to women and people of colour. I have not always succeeded, in the main because the historical record is skewed towards the educated white men who monopolised political and literary power at the time.

On that point, a note about myself. I am a white man who was born into a middle-class family. I went to a grammar school and then to Cambridge; I have taught at Cambridge and Oxford; and I now work in the corporate world. As such, some readers might think that I am exactly the wrong person to write a book about slavery, and perhaps there is some merit in that argument; indeed, if this were a book about the black experience of enslavement, it might not be 'my' story to tell. However, even if this book must and does include elements of that experience, that is not the history I have chosen to write; rather, this book is primarily a history of how white Britons have thought, written, and acted about slavery. To that end, it is worth remembering that just as slavery was always something *done to* people, it was also something *done by* people – and almost always, in the British case, by educated white men. It follows that this book, which narrates and seeks to explain that history of exploitation, necessarily focuses on those historical figures.

For the past two hundred years, the authors of Britain's 'national story' and the smiths of British 'national values' have placed *opposition* to slavery at the core of their constructions. I have never been persuaded. As this book will show, the British 'nation' was in fact deeply implicated in and violently supportive of colonial slavery. If this book achieves anything, I hope it encourages readers to interrogate the myths of British history, to question Britain's troubling role in the shaping of the modern world, and to think about what should happen next. Perhaps most relevantly, this book poses the question: Should criminals ever celebrate the end of their own criminality?

Introduction: Demerara, 1823

The valuable Colony of Demerara is very imperfectly known to Europeans ... Executing a work of this kind ... requires an extent and variety of reading, and acquirements ... and a patience of investigation, and soundness of judgment, which ... are rarely to be found in the works of travellers. Indeed, these histories are, in general, very defective, and surprisingly inaccurate.[1]

Joshua Bryant, *Account of an Insurrection* (1824)

Shortly after dawn, between the hours of six and seven on Monday, 18 August 1823, Joseph Packwood raised the alarm. Waking his manager with the blast of a bugle, he reported a plot among the enslaved of Demerara. The plan had been fixed the night before at the Bethel Chapel and, that morning, across the fields and farmyards of the colony, they would rise to seize their freedom. Packwood's manager was John Simpson, the supervisor of the Reduit plantation and the captain of a local troop of cavalry. Simpson knew his duty. He rose, dressed, mounted his horse, and rode the five miles west to Georgetown, the capital of the colony. The governor needed to know. In the words of Joshua Bryant, a local artist who became the first historian of the Demerara Rebellion, this was 'a ramified Conspiracy, [a] formidable Insurrection', and 'a crisis, agitating and perilous beyond all previous example'.[2]

Stretching along the northern coast of South America, Demerara was the tropical frontier of the British Empire. Founded by the Dutch in the 1740s and later captured by the French, the colony had 'become' British only in 1814, but these delta-lands had long inspired European dreams of lucre. In the 1590s, Sir Walter Raleigh had been commissioned to explore the region and, more sensationally, to find the mythical city of El Dorado, which supposedly lay on the upper reaches of the Orinoco River. Of course, that expedition failed: the quest for the Lost City of Gold was scuppered by yellow fever, dense jungle, and crocodile attacks, but also by the inconvenient fact that El Dorado did not exist. By the 1820s, however, Demerara was giving its name to the crisp, golden-brown sugar that grew in its fields, and the colony was famed for its fertility. Whereas the soils of older, smaller British colonies were tiring, the land in Demerara was fresh and rich. There was plenty of it, too: if the jungle, swamp, and savannah were cleared to the south, sugar could be grown deep into the continent. All this was a boon for the planters, but a curse upon the enslaved people who actually performed the work of draining swamps, cutting down trees, and planting cane. With heavy rain, stifling heat, and stagnant water making the colony a 'reaper's garden', death stalked every man and woman: every year, thousands died painfully from malaria, cholera, and dehydration.[3]

The promise of bountiful harvests drove Demeraran planters to unusual degrees of cruelty. One Christian missionary observed that they extracted 'a most immoderate quantity of work' from the enslaved, 'not excepting women far advanced in pregnancy'. The crack of the whip was the sound of plantation life and, 'from ½ past 6' in the morning 'until ½ past 9' at night, people's ears were 'pain'd' by it. The same missionary wondered whether the sins of this regime would 'awaken the vengeance of a merciful God' and, on that Monday in 1823, it seemed such wrath had come.[4]

By mid-morning, John Simpson had reached Georgetown. Built on the eastern bank of the Demerara River and once known to the Dutch as Stabroek, the colony's capital represented the idyll which had drawn so many Europeans to the Caribbean. As the historian Emilia Viotta da Costa has described, it was a place of white-painted wooden mansions in the shade of palm trees, imposing warehouses and wharves, verges of oleander and hibiscus that rustled in the breeze, and gardens of orange, lemon, and banana trees. On most days it was a scene of bustling markets, handsome black carriages racing along red-dirt streets, and taverns dispensing liberal volumes of rum. When a white immigrant stepped off the ship after six weeks on board, the Demeraran capital must have looked like paradise. Yet when the drums beat to arms in 1823, Georgetown surrendered to a state of panic, 'to the miseries of war'. It was placed under martial law.[5]

The long-serving governor of Demerara was the Irish-born soldier and slaveholder John Murray and, by early afternoon that Monday, he had made his plans. First, all those who had not rebelled would be confined to their houses. Second, all free 'Persons, without distinction, capable of bearing Arms, [were] required to enrol themselves in some Troop or Company of the Georgetown Brigade of Militia'. The Marine Battalion, composed of Georgetown's sailors, was placed under the command of a naval captain by the name of Muddle. Nearly six hundred men, many of them teenagers and tradesmen, came together in the Provisional Battalion; they took the Presbyterian church for their base and placed cannon on the roads leading into town. Georgetown also hosted barracks of professional soldiers, so Governor Murray ordered out the 21st North British Fusiliers and the 1st West India Regiment, both of whom readied for the fight. The ladies of the capital meanwhile hastened onto boats on the river, seeking sanctuary from 'scenes of horror too shocking to think on'. The rest of Georgetown fell into silence. 'All the stores were shut up', noted Bryant, and 'not a negro was to be seen on the streets ... If it had not been for the hurrying backwards and forwards of all classes to the guard-houses for arms, a solemn silence would have pervaded the whole capital – awful and impressive.'[6]

The reaction of the colonists was far from alarmist. In the Caribbean they feared nothing, not even a hurricane, more than a slave rebellion. Part of this was practised and pragmatic, for even mild unrest could cripple a colonial economy. The greater part of it, though, was primal and visceral, and colonial folk memory was filled with horrific tales of the violence done to planters during uprisings. There had been Tacky's War in Jamaica and the 1816 rebellion in Barbados, but in the colonial imagination the worst tales came from the French colony of Saint Domingue, present-day Haiti'. Spread over the western half of Hispaniola, Saint Domingue had once been the most productive colony in the world: in the 1780s, it produced 30 per cent of the world's sugar and more than half of its coffee. Pitt the Younger even called it 'the Eden of the Western World', but the enslaved people of the colony did not share in his admiration: some French planters put tin muzzles on their slaves to stop them eating sugar cane; others encouraged 'slow punishments' that would 'make a greater impression'; and one French colonist crafted a party trick which involved placing an orange on a slave's head before inviting his guests to shoot at the fruit with a pistol.[7]

The French thus slept 'at the foot of Vesuvius' until 1791 when, at the signal of the Vodou priest Dutty Boukman, the slaves of Saint Domingue rebelled. The next thirteen years of the Haitian Revolution witnessed ferocious fighting between the rebels led by Toussaint Louverture, various French forces, and the British, who invaded on the grounds of 'security' but really in the hope of re-enslaving the rebels and seizing Saint Domingue for themselves. By 1804, when the free black republic of Haiti proclaimed its independence, stories of atrocity were legion. After one battle a French commander burned five hundred Haitian prisoners alive, while Napoleon's brother-in-law created the first known gas chamber by setting fire to barrels of sulphur in the holds of ships packed with Haitian prisoners. British colonists, however, remembered the deeds of the Haitian rebels: white carpenters had been sawn in half; French women were given a choice between forced marriage and death; and one member of the slave-catching militia was nailed to the gate of his plantation before his limbs were chopped off. The rivulets of Haitian towns ran red, and the assassin Jean Zombi became the eponymous inspiration for all 'zombies' thereafter.[8]

This was the kind of rebellion that the Demeraran colonists feared, but at first they did not know which kind of rebellion they faced. John Simpson's report had come from Le Reduit, just five miles from Georgetown, yet the colony stretched for thirty miles more to Mahaica Creek. This meant they knew nothing about dozens of plantations and thousands of potential rebels to the east. Nor was there any safe, reliable means of acquiring intelligence from the field. There was no telephone, no telegraph, and the estates along the shore were connected by roads and canals that, if seized by the

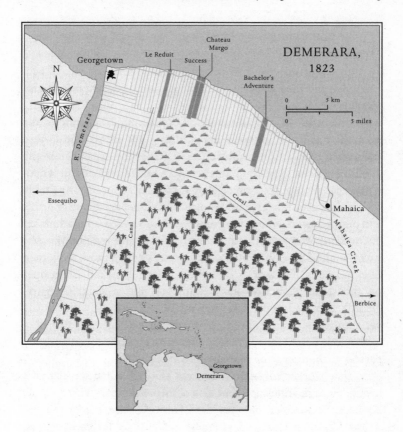

rebels, the British could not use. Only the sight of smoke could signal insurgency from afar: if the rebels refrained from arson, the rebellion could proceed undetected.

As Georgetown prepared for war, John Simpson was sent back into the countryside, riding with his cavalrymen to Le Reduit. En route he called at each plantation, urging the whites to secure their weaponry. By mid-afternoon, Simpson had been joined by Governor Murray, a handful of colonial officials, and a detachment of regular soldiers. At Le Reduit, they set upon Joseph Packwood, the servant who had first alerted Simpson to the trouble: What more did he know? Under interrogation, Packwood gave up the names of two ringleaders from the Vryheid estate, Mars and Cato, who in turn identified two men as the instigators of the whole uprising. Those men were Quamina and Jack, a father and son from the Success plantation owned by John Gladstone, the 'self-made Liverpool merchant prince' who had made and then grown a West Indian fortune despite never once visiting the colonies.

At the time of the insurrection, Quamina Gladstone – the surname had been imposed upon him – was in his mid-forties. Born on the Gold Coast and trafficked across the ocean before the abolition of the slave trade in 1807, he had been trained in wood-work, rising to the position of head carpenter at Success. As Emilia Viotta da Costa relates, he was also a 'well-behaved, trustworthy, and pious deacon' within the colony's Methodist congregation. Yet if Quamina was a dignified 'man of reason' and religion, his son was a 'man of passion' whose attention was drawn more to women than to books of prayer. A skilled artisan who worked as a cooper on the same plantation, Jack Gladstone was a striking figure. Described as 'handsome' and 'well made' and credited with a 'lively yet thoughtful countenance', he stood at six feet two inches, a remarkable height for any man in the 1820s, let alone for an enslaved person at the mercy of malnutrition.[9]

As they worked together at Success, the father and son shared a loving, close relationship – but also a deep and bitter hatred of the bondage they suffered. For the elder Gladstone, slavery was an affront to the Christian tenets of kindness and justice; for the younger, restless Gladstone, slavery was a cage. Yet beyond the cruelties inflicted daily upon all prisoners of the slave colonies, both men had more personal cause for grievance. In October 1822, Quamina had been forbidden from tending to his seriously ill wife, Peggy; forced instead to work a thirteen-hour shift, he came home only 'an hour after Peggy had breathed her last'. In the summer of 1823, when strange murmurings of freedom reached Demerara, no two men were more anxious to seize the moment. Assuming that Parliament had already abolished slavery, Quamina and Jack begged a missionary to 'fetch up the new Law' from Georgetown that they believed would set them free. When they were rebuked for foolish dreaming, they settled on a new approach.[10]

Before Governor Murray and his military party could apprehend Jack and Quamina, they spotted smoke in the distance. Success would have to wait. As the fire drew the soldiers east in the gloaming, they were ambushed by a band of rebels brandishing cutlasses. 'We have them!' cried the rebels. 'We have them!' Murray demanded their terms, and the reply was simple: 'Our rights', by which they meant the liberties that Parliament had supposedly conferred upon them. Murray refused to yield. He would not talk until the rebels laid down their arms. A few obliged and offered to negotiate, but their moderation was drowned out by the sound of conch-shells. In Demerara, these shells were used to signal the start and the end of the working day, but now they were the sirens of rebellion. The noise grew and grew until the soldiers intervened, firing their muskets into the sky and dispersing the rebels. This early skirmish established a pattern of cagey, almost reluctant fighting that would define the insurrection. On the one hand, the rebels knew they outnumbered the British, but they were outgunned: most of them carried only axes, cutlasses, or at best the unwieldy shotguns known as fowling-pieces. On the other hand, the British knew they had superior firepower but a numerical disadvantage. Moreover, they could not shoot too many rebels without endangering the future prosperity of the colony, and the militia would have to answer to the planters for the destruction of their 'property'.[11]

By the time that Murray and his men made camp for the night, estates all along the Demeraran coast had fallen to the rebels. At the Walrond estate of Nabaclis, the whites had grabbed what ammunition they could before taking refuge in the plantation house. Within ten minutes of barricading the doors, the rebel 'war-whoops', described by Joshua Bryant as 'a most dreadful yell', went up around the house's yard. Hiding upstairs, Mrs Walrond fell into 'the most acute distress from the noisy turbulence of the revolters below'. When she leaned out of her bedroom window, she got shot in the arm. Downstairs in the hallway, the estate's overseer, Mr Tucker, took the fight to the rebels. He edged towards the front door of the house and shot through it, down into the yard. When the rebels fired back, they struck Tucker in the chest. His last words were to the point: 'O, Christ! I am shot!' With only Mr Walrond and one other man left fighting, the rebels stormed the house. Dragged down the steps, Walrond begged for his life. 'Will you murder me in this barbarous manner?' he pleaded. His captors' mercy was unexpected. 'You are a good man,' he was told, and 'you love God'. All that Walrond suffered was the ignominy of the stocks, with his wounded wife shown similar clemency: 'We intend you no harm,' a rebel explained. 'We are only determined to have our freedom.'

Another siege was unfolding at Mon Repos, where the plantation manager and his men, taking cover behind the house's window-frames, engaged the rebels in a gunfight. At Bachelor's Adventure, the black bookkeeper, Mr Rogers, was woken in the night by insurgents demanding 'guns, powder, ball, [and] iron'. When Rogers refused, they beat down his door and took what they wanted; the next wave of rebels seized Rogers himself. These scenes were repeated on almost forty plantations from Plaisance, just four miles from Georgetown, along the coast to Clonbrook.

The morning after his encounter with the rebels, Governor Murray returned to Georgetown, leaving command in the field to Colonel John Thomas Leahy, a stern and ruthless veteran of the Napoleonic Wars. Camping at night and travelling by day, Leahy and his men pushed from west to east, trying to clear the road of rebels and to open a line from Georgetown to Mahaica. Progress was not straight-forward: 'to impede the march of the military', the rebels had burned or broken the bridges that spanned the colony's canals and trenches. Where they could, the soldiers used timber from the sundered bridges and, in one case, from the roof of a plantation's turtle pool to jerry-rig new paths across the water. At each estate, the British strove to free the captured colonists, disarm the rebels, and return the land to white control. These 'liberating missions' led to wildly differing outcomes. At Success, the British were humiliated. When the rebels stepped out from the main house to encounter the redcoats, the cavalry panicked and fled. Some rode for a mile before pausing; some did not rest until they met with reinforcements; and others fell from their steeds into the canal that marked the planta-tion's boundary.

At Bachelor's Adventure, however, the British struck a decisive blow. This estate had become the effective headquarters of the rebellion and, by the Wednesday, hundreds of insurgents had gathered on its grounds: as the military later reported, 'an immense body of negroes had secreted themselves [there] ... for the purpose of attacking us'. The British detachment which approached Bachelor's Adventure was led by Leahy himself. Now moving at night, the troops took cover in the cane fields, but always close enough that pistol shot would reach the rebels. As day broke, Leahy revealed himself. Walking calmly towards the rebels with just a handful of men around him, the British colonel demanded their surrender. He was met with scorn and laughter: What could these few soldiers do? One of the insurgents proposed that they shoot Leahy and be done with him, but instead the rebels presented their demands: they would surrender *only* when granted three days' holiday per week and the right to attend church each Sunday.

For British troops reared on outrageous stories of 'slave atrocity', this must have been stunning. Here, having inflicted precious little violence on the people and property of Demerara, and having heard rumours from London of proposals to reform slavery, the rebels were insisting simply upon the extension of their rights. They were not threatening to march upon Georgetown, to burn the crops, or to massacre the whites; they were not even demanding their immediate emancipation. Joseph Bryant would write about 'lawless outrages' and 'dreadful rencontres', but all that these rebels wanted was more time off work and permission to worship freely on the Sabbath.

Leahy was unmoved. In his eyes, the enemy were rebels against the Crown, and nothing could redeem them. Once more, he demanded their surrender and, as the rebels debated their choices, the rest of his troops looped round to outflank them. With his foes now trapped between the soldiers and the cane fields, Leahy ordered a volley of shots. Some of the insurgents fled into the fields, but most held their ground. One last chance for surrender was spurned and this was the cue for bloodshed. The British troops fired at will, cutting down hundreds and scattering the rest. Later reports put a gloss on the killing. 'The Lieutenant-Colonel having in vain attempted to convince these deluded people of their error', it was recorded, 'and every attempt to induce them to lay down their arms having failed, he made his dispositions, charged the [slaves] ... and dispersed them with the loss of 100 to 150.' On the British side, just one rifleman was injured.

News of the rout travelled quickly by the back roads and dirt tracks and the rebels' spirit soon broke. By Friday morning, British soldiers were marching freely along the coast, 'liberating' the plantations and visiting 'justice' upon the subdued insurgents. It was at many places a tour of execution. A white flag was raised at Resouvenir but the conspirators were shot dead on the spot. At Drogerie, when two rebels wore pieces of white cloth as a sign of peace, they were tied to a cabbage tree and executed. At Clonbrook, when one rebel volunteered to give up Quamina and Jack, he was chastised by an elder called Beard, who said that he would rather die than betray his friends. Overheard by Colonel Leahy, Beard was given the chance to prove the courage of his convictions, and when his word held true, he too was killed. Back at the Walrond estate, the rebels Caleb and Sloane were held accountable for the murder of the overseer, Mr Tucker. Both were shot. Joseph, the driver on the estate, was forced to saw the heads off their corpses.

As the British military served its swift and brutal retribution in the fields, and as the planters of Demerara resumed control of their estates, a more formal vengeance was exacted in the government buildings of Georgetown. Eight days after the rebellion had broken out, the courts-martial began. Their president was Stephen Goodman, the commander of the Georgetown Militia, and Goodman's aide-de-camp acted as the court's interpreter, translating the charges, questions, and evidence into 'the negro dialect' for the benefit of the accused; in turn, the aide-de-camp interpreted the rebels' evidence for the prosecution, the judges, and the public gallery. One might wonder how much was lost, and lost deliberately, in translation. The first two defendants were called Natty and Louis; inevitably, they were the first to be convicted. At five o'clock on the day of their hearing, they were marched through Georgetown to the rhythm of a dead march played by a military band. There was not time to construct the gallows, so Natty and Louis were shot.

Joshua Bryant's history of the insurrection records that over seventy rebels were tried by the Georgetown courts-martial. Only one, Dick, was acquitted. Ten were hanged then decapitated, their heads fixed on spikes as a deterrent to many of the older Africans who believed they could not be 're-born' in their homeland if their bodies were not whole. A handful more rebels had their sentences respited and one of them, Trim, was pardoned because he informed on a friend. The courts might have considered this justice, but it was more likely a calculated decision: the execution of all seventy men would have dealt a significant economic blow to the planters. Moreover, sending back the conspirators, scarred and broken, would impress the fate prescribed to traitors upon the minds of would-be rebels. Some of them were given months in solitary confinement, but the common penalty was whipping. In the British army, 175 lashes were known to put a strong man in hospital for weeks; one rebel in Demerara received 1,000 lashes.

Yet as many insurgents were rounded up, Jack and Quamina remained at large. They were thought to have fled into the jungle to the south of the plantations and, for two reasons, the need to capture them was acute. First, if they remained free, the pair would be a symbol of hidden hope for those who remained in slavery. Second, if they could endure in the swamps and savannah, there beckoned months and maybe years of guerrilla-style attacks on the colony. Decades of combat against the free Maroons of Jamaica were a stark reminder of this problem.

Governor Murray now placed a thousand-guilder bounty on the heads of Jack and Quamina, but the British would look for them too. The next Friday, eleven days after the rebellion had broken out, a hunting party mustered at dawn by the back-dam of the Lusignan estate. Marching along the canal trenches, a detachment of militiamen led by two redcoat officers and a posse of Indian guides drove deep into the South American wilderness. The expedition met with calamity. The British had taken only small rations of pork and biscuit with them and, wading through waist-high waters that were festering in the late summer heat, they were abandoned by their guides. Lost, exhausted, and defeated by the land, the soldiers turned back and retreated to Georgetown. Thus ended, wrote Joshua Bryant, 'the most harassing and dreary march'.

By the first Saturday in September, the British had readied another mission. At five o'clock that afternoon, with new Indian guides and

better supplies, they were ready to depart from the military post at
Felicity. Yet now, by chance, an enslaved man called Frank approached
the soldiers. Tempted by the thousand-guilder bounty, he offered
intelligence that Jack Gladstone was hiding with his wife Susannah at
the Chateau Margo estate. Reconnaissance proved the truth of Frank's
report and, at one o'clock the next morning, the British crept onto
the plantation. For hours they waited in the darkness, encircling the
house where Jack Gladstone slept. At last, at half past five, they moved:
Jack was found sleeping on the floor, and Susannah on the roof.

Quamina, however, was nowhere to be seen; by lunchtime, the
bush expedition had readied again. Scouring the backs of the plantations, the soldiers came upon clusters of crude sheds that the fugitives
had built and then abandoned. The soldiers passed another week in
failure and stress, suffering the 'grievous hardships and fatigues [that
were] necessarily inflicted upon all who range those wild forests'.
Their only break came on the next Saturday, when fresh intelligence
revived their hunt and a newly captured fugitive offered up Quamina's
location in exchange for his life. Now, the chase began in earnest. The
British soon caught sight of the rebel leader, but this did not mean
they could catch him: Quamina knew the country better than the
British, and he was faster. Indeed, he was on the verge of disappearing
into the bush, perhaps for ever, when the Indian scout Skillikelly took
aim: Quamina was shot in the temple and the torso, and he was killed.
But death alone did not satisfy the British soldiers. They dragged
Quamina's body back to the coast, erected a gibbet, and strung up
his corpse, leaving it to rot in the late summer heat. A local merchant
later noted that a 'colony of wasps ... built a nest in the cavity of the
stomach and were flying in and out of the jaws which hung frightfully
open'. The defilement of Quamina's body was an ultimate declaration:
the rebellion was over.[12]

For some British observers, the rebellion had brought Demerara to
the brink of destruction. Although the rebels had by and large refrained
from maiming or killing the whites, and although it was only plantation buildings with symbolic importance that bore 'the lamentable
marks of the destructive fury of savage dissipation', one colonist wrote
to the *Morning Chronicle*, a leading London newspaper, that 'it was

only divine Providence that saved us. A few more hours and Demerara would have been a second St Domingo'. Yet with the supposed guidance of the Almighty to thank, the colonists had restored what they saw as the 'proper' way of things. In three weeks, the rebellion had been quashed, its leaders killed or convicted, and the colony returned to peace.[13]

It would be a fleeting victory. The colonists could not have known it at the time, but the Demerara Rebellion of 1823 was a critical milestone in the history and downfall of slavery in the British Empire. Over the previous decades, the chains which bound the enslaved had been rattling across the Atlantic world. As the Latin American revolutionary Simón Bolívar and the *libertadores* carved new republics out of the crumbling Spanish Empire, they damned slavery as 'the daughter of darkness' and decreed that children born to enslaved women would live free. In the United States, most northern states had already abolished slavery within their own borders and the Compromise of 1820 had brokered a constitutional truce by creating the free state of Maine as a counterweight to the new slave state of Missouri, although the intractable problem of American slavery was given violent expression two years later by Denmark Vesey's thwarted rebellion in South Carolina. All the while, notwithstanding its own internal crises, the free black nation of Haiti figured as a beguiling, provocative example of self-liberation.[14]

It was in this context of growing tension, seven months before the outbreak of the Demerara Rebellion, that the humanitarian campaigners who had secured the abolition of the British slave trade in 1807 regrouped to form the Anti-Slavery Society. In May 1823, their parliamentary leader, Thomas Fowell Buxton, had proposed the reform and the gradual eradication of colonial slavery. Whispered, half-accurate reports of those proposals and the Demeraran planters' supposed refusal to enact them had been the source of the rebels' demands for their 'rights'. Over the following decade slavery became the defining moral issue in British public life. At public lectures attended by thousands, in newspapers and magazines, in the City and Parliament, in universities and churches, and in royal palaces too, the supposed rights and wrongs of slavery would be debated with a ferocity that split political parties, communities, and families. On one side, the Anti-Slavery Society argued

for emancipation. On the other, the powerful West India Interest –
backed by leading politicians, publishers, and intellectuals – insisted on
the preservation of colonial slavery. This is the story of that decade:
of conspiracy, espionage, rebels, and radicals; intrigue and backdoor
deals; upheaval in politics, religion, and society; and the ultimate victory
of radical campaigners and Caribbean rebels over the might of the
British establishment.

I.

An Evil of Our Own Creation

At the end of six or seven months after I had been kidnapped, I arrived at the sea coast ... The first object which saluted my eyes ... was the sea, and a slave-ship, which was then riding at anchor, and waiting for its cargo. These filled me with astonishment, which was soon converted into terror, which I am yet at a loss to describe ... I was now persuaded that I had gotten into a world of bad spirits, and that they were going to kill me.[1]

Olaudah Equiano, *The Interesting Narrative* (1789)

English involvement in the slave trade began as a simple matter of jealousy. In the mid-sixteenth century, as Spain and Portugal were colonising the western hemisphere, the Spanish and Portuguese sailors who trafficked African people across the Atlantic were being paid in American gold, and the English had a basic, piratical desire to share in the spoils. John Hawkins, a naval captain from Plymouth, was the first to break the Iberian monopoly when, in 1562, he hijacked a Portuguese ship off the coast of western Africa and sold its cargo of 301 people to the planters of Hispaniola. Two years later, when he was sent back to sea on the orders of the Elizabethan court, Hawkins embarked on 'The Good Ship Jesus' and took with him his cousin, Francis Drake. Besides supplying enslaved labour to other empires, the English began to seize swathes of the New World as their own. The colonists at Roanoke in present-day North Carolina might have disappeared, lost into legend, but Jamestown in Virginia and the Pilgrim settlement on Massachusetts Bay soon figured as key settlements in a colonial domain stretching along the American seaboard. In 1627, Barbados became the first English colony in the Caribbean.

Initially 'discovered' by the Spanish and Portuguese, who named it after the island's bearded fig trees, Barbados was strategically vital: the most easterly of the Antilles, it was the gateway to the West Indies. Early settlers such as the Draxes and Codringtons stamped their names on the island, as did the Lascelles family, who in time used their colonial riches to build Harewood House outside Leeds.[2]

Further expeditions seized Saint Kitts, Antigua, Nevis, and the Bahamas for the English Crown, but the jewel was Jamaica. First claimed by the Spanish, the island fell to the English in the 1650s when Oliver Cromwell instructed his commanders in the Caribbean, Admiral William Penn and General Robert Venables, to open a new front in the Anglo-Spanish War. Having failed to make inroads on the sugar island of Hispaniola, Penn and Venables landed an invasion force – 'our souldiers in number 7000' – on the southern coast of Jamaica in 1655. They came upon Spanish forts that were 'very strong and cannon proofe' and defended by 'very greate murderers', but it was only days before Venables observed 'a Spaniard with a white flagg comming to our outguards, desiring a treaty was conducted'. The Spaniards were expelled.[3]

By the late seventeenth century, more than simple greed informed these imperial ventures; they were now a matter of complex market economics, of supply and demand. The first major colonial crop had been tobacco, but European fashion soon embraced coffee, sugar, and cotton. Coffee houses were prime locations for political discussion, intellectual debate, and polite socialising, and coffee was a source of cachet as much as caffeine. Sugar sweetened the coffee, as well as the tea that was becoming a staple of the English diet. Cotton was meanwhile the fabric *du jour* – cheap, colourful, and easily washable. The voracious demand for these products soon outstripped supply. Coffee, cotton, and sugar cane grew best in warm, wet climates and tropical soils, and though English colonists could settle the Caribbean islands and the coastal plains of the Americas, they could not sustain the plantation economy. The diseases of the New World ravaged the bodies of English workers, who also struggled to adapt to the heat and humidity of the climate. More seriously, the work was brutally hard. Few Englishmen emigrated to the Caribbean if they had another choice and, with Irish indentured servants often leaving Barbados and Jamaica when their terms of service expired, the English found themselves with land but not the labour.

The chosen solution to this problem was slavery: where European colonists could not or would not perform the work that was needed to grow sugar, they compelled others to toil on their behalf. The most frequent victims of this enslavement were black Africans, who had been ascribed an inherent inferiority ever since self-justifying theories of racial hierarchy had emerged in the Spanish and Portuguese slaving markets of the sixteenth century. It was by associating white and lighter skin colours with Christian concepts of 'goodness' and purity, and by linking black skin with darkness and evil, that early European colonists had rationalised African slavery to themselves. During the initial process of enslavement on the coastal plains of western Africa, local people were captured by raiding parties or sold by their enemies in exchange for guns, metal, and alcohol. They were marched for miles to the shoreline, far from home, to the stone forts where the slaving captains took their pick. Then, the European sailors loaded their captives into the vast wooden ships that lay at anchor in the water. In this way, between the sixteenth and nineteenth centuries, some twelve million people were stolen, enslaved, and shipped from Africa to the New World. Two million died before even seeing the Americas, victims of the horrific 'Middle Passage' where cramped and suffocating conditions beneath deck allowed dysentery and typhus to spread. Those who succumbed were dumped into the ocean and written off by British traders as bad investments.[4]

In the early eighteenth century, as England and Scotland united under the same crown, the British slave trade thrived. Merchants and financiers commissioned hundreds of ships to ferry human freight from Africa to the colonies. If they survived the Atlantic voyage, the Africans were transferred to local slave markets and, in return, the British ships were laden with the tropical crops that sold for huge profits at home and in Europe. With cash banked, these ships sailed again for Africa, and the cycle continued. Historians such as Eric Williams and Joseph Inikori have argued that this triangular trade was integral to Britain's industrial development. Glasgow grew rich on American tobacco. London's banking houses, not least Lloyds and Barings, could not have flourished without financing these ventures. And slavery reached into every alley and corner of Liverpool, with one local historian observing that 'almost every order of people is interested in a Guinea cargo ... Many of the small vessels that import a hundred slaves are fitted out by attorneys, drapers, ropers, grocers, tallow-chandlers, barbers, [and] tailors'. The 'sugar barons', as the planters were known, became a byword for preposterous wealth. Even George III was stunned by the splendour of West Indian riches. 'Sugar, sugar, eh?' the King marvelled upon seeing the finery of a planter's carriage. 'All that sugar!'[5]

All the while, Acts of Parliament encouraged and protected the slave trade, and the opinions of the judiciary gave legal sanction to the odious commerce. In 1729, the Attorney General, Sir Philip Yorke, responded to a petition from West Indian planters by pronouncing that 'a Slave, by coming from the West-Indies to Great Britain or Ireland ... doth not become free, and ... Baptism doth not bestow Freedom on him'. Twenty years later, Yorke, who had since become the Lord Chancellor, used a High Court judgment to confirm his opinion that 'a Negro slave ... is as much property as anything else'. Content with the import revenues that swelled the coffers of the government, as well as with the strategic advantages of a Caribbean empire, eighteenth-century Britain accepted the slave trade and slavery as facts of national life.[6]

It was not until the 1770s that the morality and policy of the slave trade were widely questioned by Britons. Since the Glorious Revolution of 1688, the British had been engaged in almost continuous war with Catholic France. Besides commercial and strategic concerns, those conflicts had been framed as part of a universal battle between parliamentary democracy and absolutist tyranny. Whenever Britain won these wars, and it was undefeated between 1688 and 1763, the triumph belonged not just to the British, but to liberty and justice too. The American Revolution undermined this moral certainty. Beginning with the midnight ride of Paul Revere in 1775 and concluding with the Treaty of Paris in 1783, this was a conflict with fellow Protestants and free-born British subjects who now claimed moral superiority over the motherland: Who was the enemy here? When Britain lost, nobody could remember the last defeat. At the same time, new branches of Christianity were changing the way that Britons thought about the world. Methodism had been founded by the Wesley brothers in the 1730s; Quakers were increasingly vocal about political causes; and low-church Evangelicalism had caused a spiritual awakening within the Church of England. Together, these factors of military humiliation and religious activism induced growing numbers of Britons to question

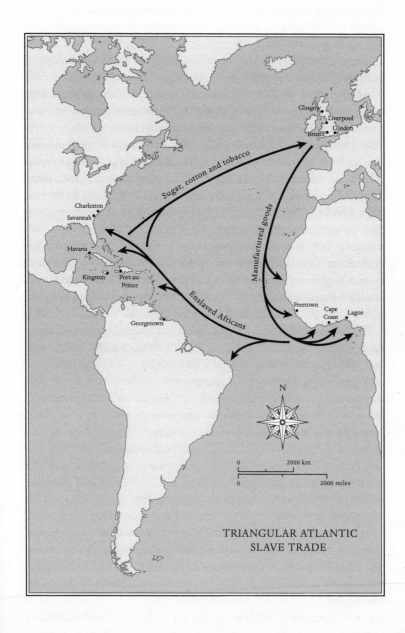

TRIANGULAR ATLANTIC
SLAVE TRADE

the ethics and principles of imperial government. The British had lost their American colonies, so had they deserved to lose them? Was British rule in India, where abuse and corruption were endemic, any better? What else was the Empire getting 'wrong'?[7]

Some Britons had already identified the slave trade as the obvious example. Granville Sharp was the son of a Northumbrian deacon and a member of a musical family which gave public concerts as they sailed their barge, the *Apollo*, along the Thames; Sharp himself was one of the best bass singers in England, often signing his name as 'G#' on the treble clef. As a young man, Sharp was a draper's apprentice and he worked briefly as a clerk, but fighting the slave trade became his vocation. Sharp's interest in the matter began in 1765, when he found a teenage African, Jonathan Strong, lying badly beaten on the cobbles of Mincing Lane: 'The boy,' said Sharp, 'seemed ready to die.' Learning that Strong's master had brought him to Britain from Barbados before pistol-whipping him, Sharp took pity. He paid for Strong's medical bills, found him work and lodgings, and two years later, when Strong's former master spotted him on the street and 'sold' him to a Jamaican planter, it was Sharp who rescued Strong from the bowels of a West Indian ship.[8]

Five years later, in 1772, Sharp was more famously involved in the case of James Somerset. The plaintiff, Somerset, was an African who had been purchased at Boston and then taken to England, where he fled from his master only to be seized and – just like Jonathan Strong – imprisoned on a slave ship bound for Jamaica. When sympathisers sued for Somerset's freedom, the case went before the Lord Chief Justice, Lord Mansfield. Following a lengthy, dramatic hearing that captured the public imagination, with the courtroom gallery packed out for weeks on end, Mansfield handed down a judgment that the *Morning Chronicle* described as 'guarded, cautious, and concise'. Mansfield found for the plaintiff, declaring that 'the black must be discharged', but this was *not* the signal victory that many have supposed. Although Mansfield held that 'the state of slavery is of such a nature that ... it must take its rise from *positive law*', and though slavery was not 'allowed or approved by the law of England', he confined his judgment to the narrow principle that Jamaican laws could not be 'imported' into England to justify the re-enslavement of a person. As events would prove, neither the slave trade nor slavery itself had been outlawed.[9]

In late 1781, the Liverpool ship *Zong* sailed for Jamaica from the Gold Coast. In the custody of seventeen white sailors were four hundred and forty-two Africans. At São Tomé, an island off the coast of present-day Gabon, the crew of the *Zong* filled dozens of sturdy wooden casks to the brim with drinking water in preparation for the Atlantic crossing. In the weeks ahead, sixty Africans perished from the febrile horrors of the Middle Passage, but shipowners considered such deaths as nothing more than the natural 'wastage' for which they allowed. Yet when the ship's captain fell ill, and when a power struggle broke out between the first mate and the rest of the crew, chaos ensued. First, the *Zong* failed to call at Tobago to replenish its stocks of water. Then, and more seriously, the ship's navigator mistook Jamaica for a more easterly island, and it was not for another 300 miles that they realised the error. By now, however, with Jamaica nearly a fortnight in the opposite direction, only four days' worth of drinking water remained. The *Zong* was in crisis.[10]

But for the *Zong*'s owners – the Gregson shipping syndicate of Liverpool – this crisis was not human; it was commercial. They had taken out the customary insurance on the survival of their human cargo so that, if the ship was wrecked, or if pirates attacked, their losses would be covered. Yet if the enslaved died a 'natural death' from dehydration, the insurers would not pay. The *Zong*'s leadership therefore alighted on the principle of 'general average', which provided that when part of a ship's cargo was jettisoned to save the remainder, shipowners could claim for *that* loss. The crew of the *Zong* turned this principle into practice. To conserve rations of water, fifty-four women and children were dragged from their berths and thrown into the deep of the Caribbean. The next day, forty-two men followed them down. Within a week, one hundred and thirty-two people had been drowned, not including ten defiant souls who, rather than die at the hands of their captors, jumped overboard.

The Gregsons duly made a claim for compensation and instructed the Solicitor General, John Lee, as their barrister. Granville Sharp lambasted Lee as 'the advocate for Liverpool iniquity', but the Gregsons won decisively. Only a few years after the Jamaican-born historian Edward Long had compared Africans to orang-utans, the British courts entertained 'no doubt ... that the Case of Slaves was the same as if Horses had been thrown overboard'. When the insurers appealed, the Gregsons repeated the argument that the enslaved had 'perished just as a Cargo of Goods [would perish]'. But this time new evidence arose. Although the captain's log had mysteriously disappeared, the ship's first mate testified that rain had fallen steadily *before* the final killings. In fact, when the *Zong* docked at last in Jamaica, it had 420 gallons of fresh drinking water on board. The crew had drowned the last Africans for the money. The shipowners were humiliated, the crew was disgraced, and Lord Mansfield absolved the insurers of liability, but that was the limit of justice: Granville Sharp tried in vain to bring charges of murder against the crew of the *Zong*.

Yet only a few years later, in 1787, Sharp led a group of Evangelicals and like-minded Quakers in founding the Society for Effecting the Abolition of the Slave Trade. Rooted in the 'sect' that was growing around the Holy Trinity Church in Clapham, the Society found its political leader in William Wilberforce MP, who until a Damascene moment in the Swiss Alps had been known more for his biting wit and gambling debts than Christian devotion. The early years of this campaign were defined by massive petitions and public meetings which engaged Britain's emerging middle classes, but also by the work of the Sons of Africa Society and former and working slaves.

Chief among these black leaders was Olaudah Equiano, a polymath whose life was just as remarkable as any picaresque hero of the eighteenth century. According to his autobiography, Equiano was enslaved as a child in what is now Nigeria and trafficked to Barbados and then Virginia, where he was purchased by a British sailor who renamed him after the Swedish king Gustavus Vasa. After serving in the Royal Navy and eventually earning enough money from sales of fruit and crockery to buy his own freedom, he joined a daring expedition to find an Arctic path to India before settling in London. And then, having drawn the attention of his friend Granville Sharp to the *Zong* massacre, Equiano made his lasting mark by writing the *Interesting Narrative* of his own life. It was a publishing sensation which raced through nine English editions. Translated into five other languages, it did more than any other work of the 1780s to draw public attention to the evils of the slave trade.[11]

Equiano was joined in this fight by Ottobah Cugoano, a former Grenadian slave who had been freed during a trip to Britain when his master misinterpreted Lord Mansfield's judgment in *Somerset*. Finding work with the renowned miniaturist Richard Cosway, Cugoano learned to read and write and, with the encouragement of Equiano, produced an autobiographical polemic against the slave trade. Published in 1787, *Thoughts and Sentiments on the Evil and Wicked Traffic of the Slavery and Commerce of the Human Species* detailed the 'dreadful sense of misery and cruelty' that pervaded life on a slave plantation. It was so popular that George III was said to have owned a copy.[12]

In spite of all this and the friendship of the prime minister, the younger William Pitt, the abolitionists made little progress. Their first bill for abolishing the slave trade was defeated in the Commons in 1791. The second bill passed the Commons in 1792, but was defeated in the Lords. The third, in February 1793, was voted down again and within weeks the abolitionist movement stalled entirely. With France's revolutionary Convention executing Louis XVI and then declaring 'total war' on Britain, reactionary conservatism swept the country. Under the repressive rule of Pitt's Tories, anything which threatened the social order and the safety of property was now damned as a Trojan horse for Jacobin anarchy. 'What [else] does the abolition of the slave trade mean,' asked the Earl of Abingdon, '... than liberty and equality?' Parliament refused to reconsider abolition until 'mankind may be restored to their Senses'. The abolitionists stopped meeting.[13]

But if the political context had overwhelmed abolitionism in 1794, context revived it in 1805. Napoleon might have been dominant across a war-torn Europe, but Nelson's victory at Trafalgar had confirmed British supremacy at sea. Moreover, neither France *nor Britain* had been able to subdue and re-enslave the rebels of Saint Domingue, which was now the free black republic of Haiti, and this had encouraged Napoleon to sell the vast Louisiana Territory to the United States. France was no longer a credible slaveowning, sugar-growing rival to the British West Indies, and so abolishing the British slave trade would no longer jeopardise the relative prosperity of the British colonies. Perhaps more importantly, there was an opportunity for self-righteous one-upmanship. Napoleon had sought to restore slavery in Haiti, so which patriotic Briton would not seek the moral high ground over the French? With Lord Grenville leading the liberal coalition known as the Ministry of All the Talents at Westminster, the abolitionists tried again.

This time, as imperial realpolitik collided with a belated humanitarian impulse, they won. On 23 February 1807, after twenty years of campaigning, Parliament passed the Act for Abolishing the Slave Trade. The final vote in the House of Commons was a landslide – two hundred and eighty-three Ayes, sixteen Noes – and the British slave trade, an evil which had lasted centuries, was abolished on 1 January 1808.

Curiously, given the fierce resistance that Wilberforce had faced for twenty years, abolition was celebrated as the triumph of the *whole* British nation. The Duke of Norfolk hailed abolition as 'the most humane and merciful Act which was ever passed by any Legislature in the world', and the artists who commemorated abolition sought to share in the glory too. One medallion bore the image of Wilberforce, 'the Friend of Africa'. On its reverse was Britannia, the serene and glorious personification of the nation, commanding the slave trade to cease; above her soared an angel bearing a cross and a crown; beneath her was a throne bearing the words 'I have heard their cry'. At the same time, the engraver Joseph Collyer depicted *Britannia Trampling on the Emblems of Slavery*. Here she was again, flanked by 'Lady Justice' and 'Religion'. Behind them all was a British ship, laden with skulls and flying the 'standard of slavery' but now at anchor for eternity. By their side was a bust of Wilberforce, his countenance brightened by rays of light from heaven.[14]

From 1 January 1808, British ships were banned from carrying on the slave trade and British colonists were forbidden from importing 'new blood' from Africa. Yet what Britons failed to consider then – and fail to remember now – is that abolition made precious little difference to the 700,000 men, women, and children who remained in bondage in the West Indies. On the day of abolition, enslaved people rose before dawn and worked in the fields, mills, and boiling-houses of the Caribbean. They felt the same aches and the same exhaustion as before. They felt the same pain of the whip upon their backs. They suffered the same incalculable cruelty that is done to a person when they are owned by another. No matter how joyously abolition was celebrated in the motherland, it had no impact upon the existence of slavery or the day-to-day lives of the enslaved, nor would it prevent Britain acquiring further slave colonies such as Demerara and Berbice.

Emancipation had never been the avowed goal of the abolitionists. Speaking in the Commons in 1805, Wilberforce had denied any intention to free the enslaved. In the racist and patronising language

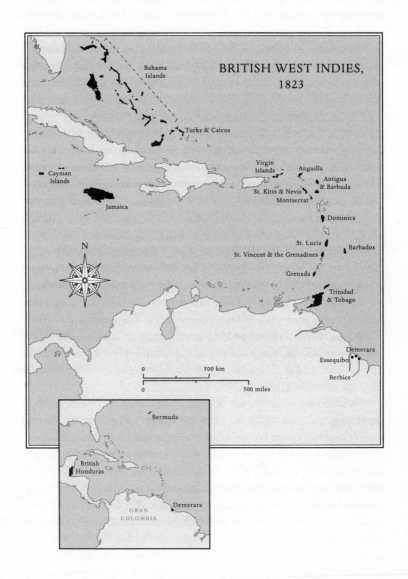

BRITISH WEST INDIES, 1823

Bahama Islands

Turks & Caicos

Cayman Islands

Jamaica

Virgin Islands

Anguilla

Antigua & Barbuda

St. Kitts & Nevis

Montserrat

Dominica

St. Lucia

Barbados

St. Vincent & the Grenadines

Grenada

Trinidad & Tobago

Demerara

Essequibo

Berbice

N

0   500 km

0   500 miles

Bermuda

British Honduras

GRAN COLOMBIA

Demerara

that characterised so much abolitionist rhetoric, he told Parliament that 'before [the slaves] could be fit to receive freedom, it would be madness to attempt to give it to them'. He was consistent on this point too. A young Robert Peel, the future prime minister, observed that Wilberforce 'disavowed the wish that freedom should be communicated to the slaves', while one historian has observed that 'the idea of pressing for clean "emancipation"' did not appear in Wilberforce's private journal for more than a decade after abolition.[15]

Striking at the trade which supplied the plantations, and not at slavery itself, was a deliberate policy. In part it was tactical, since the campaigners worried that attempting to bring about abolition *and* emancipation 'would be to aim at too much'. Class and property were at stake as well, since most abolitionists were members of the patriarchal elite who dominated British society, and Caribbean planters were of the same ilk. Wilberforce, for one, believed that 'the owners of West Indian estates [are] men of more than common kindness ... utterly unacquainted with the true nature ... of the system with which they have the misfortune to be connected.' Indeed, Wilberforce was good friends with the Barbadian slaveholder the Earl of Harewood, allying with him during the 1807 election for Yorkshire, a contest so fierce and expensive that it became known as 'the Austerlitz of electioneering'. Slave *traders*, however, were a rougher breed of harsh and uncouth men who, instead of managing landed property, as the plantations were, had consciously committed the original sin of wrenching Africans from their homeland.[16]

It was nonetheless hoped, though never admitted publicly, that abolishing the slave trade was the precursor to eradicating slavery itself. The abolitionists believed that slavery was unsustainable: Africans were shipped in, worked to death, and then replaced. They reasoned that if planters were forbidden from importing new slaves then, as older generations died off, plantation workforces would dwindle and the institution of slavery would collapse. Or that planters would be forced to treat their workers so much better that slavery, by imperceptible degrees, would transform into free labour. In this way, the abolitionists anticipated that ending the slave trade really meant 'laying the axe at the very root' of the tree of evil, and that slave emancipation would, 'like a beautiful plant in its due season, rise out of the ashes' of the trade.[17]

From 1808, the campaigners turned to other endeavours such as policing abolition and the chauvinist task of 'civilizing' Africa. The British colony of Sierra Leone had been founded in 1787 as a refuge for 'liberated Africans' who would pay off their 'debt of freedom' by growing crops and cutting roads under British supervision. This experiment in free labour was administered by the Sierra Leone Company, which was charged with building a Christian settlement from which British examples of industry and piety would flow across Africa. While some of the Company's directors focused on developing commercial ties with the colonial capital of Freetown, most were sincere and devoted believers in this 'civilizing' mission. Yet by 1807 they had failed on practically every count: the Company was dissolved and its duties were delegated to the African Institution, whose first report settled on a plan 'to introduce the blessings of civilized society among a people sunk in ignorance and barbarism'. Paternalism and racism were not the exclusive preserve of the planters.[18]

The abolitionists also took aim at the slave trade of European rivals such as France, Spain, and Portugal. By 1814, France had surrendered to the Sixth Coalition, Napoleon was in exile on Elba, and the British Foreign Secretary, Lord Castlereagh, had gone to Paris to negotiate the terms of peace. When Castlereagh returned to London with a deal that restored several Caribbean islands to France and gave French merchants five years to restock them with enslaved Africans, abolitionist fury was unleashed. Petitions flooded the Commons, sympathetic editors condemned the iniquity of the government, and the most splendid censure was reserved for Castlereagh himself when Wilberforce reduced the supposed diplomatic triumph at Paris into a cause for national shame. 'Calling to mind the arrangements made in it respecting the slave trade,' he said, 'I cannot but conceive that I behold in [the Foreign Secretary's] hand the death warrant of a multitude of innocent victims, men, women, and children, whom I had fondly indulged the hope of having myself rescued from destruction.' Stung by the venom that the abolitionists dispensed, Castlereagh was sent to the Congress of Vienna to press for the universal abolition of the trade. A 'Declaration of the Powers' was all that followed, but the French were sufficiently impressed that Louis XVIII's prime minister, the Duc de Richelieu, later subscribed to 'the entire and definitive abolition of a commerce so odious and so strongly condemned by the laws of religion and of nature'.[19]

The other major project of the 1810s involved the creation of a 'slave registry'. This was a database detailing the name, age, sex, origin, and occupation of every enslaved person in the British colonies; not coincidentally, the first census of Britain had taken place in 1801. The logic behind the registry was simple: if the authorities knew how many enslaved people were on each estate, and if each birth and death was recorded, any unexpected increase in population would expose the illicit importation of new slaves. At the time it was first mooted, in 1812, the registry was a sensible administrative solution to the problem of slave-smuggling: the Navy was preoccupied with Napoleonic France, not to mention the War of 1812 with the United States, so it could hardly spare the ships to monitor Caribbean commerce. Yet when Wilberforce proposed the registry in Parliament in 1815, the political impact was explosive. In the older colonies such as Jamaica, which self-governed through local assemblies, the planters condemned the registry as an illegal intrusion into colonial business. In the West Indies, as in the former American colonies, distinction was drawn between internal and external affairs. Even though the Americans had grudgingly tolerated London's regulation of trade with the motherland as an 'external' affair, they had refused to countenance interference in the 'internal' matter of direct taxation. In the same way, even if the West Indians recognised Parliament's power to levy tariffs on sugar, any decision to police the internal workings of the slave system by establishing a central registry would usurp the powers of the colonial assemblies and provoke the same resistance that the Stamp Act had caused in America. However, if Parliament decided to police the *internal* workings of the slave system by establishing a central registry, that would usurp the powers of the colonial assemblies and provoke the same resistance that direct taxation had caused in America. The registry proposal would even cause the same result of rebellion, but this time the rebels were not white colonists: they were the enslaved people of Barbados.[20]

Whenever news from Britain crossed the Atlantic, it was never just the colonists who received it. If Barbadian planters wanted slaves to serve them at the dinner table, they could hardly expect their waiters not to hear political chatter; and if the planters taught a few slaves to read and write so they could perform clerical tasks, they should not have been surprised if the slaves gleaned something from colonial newspapers. But in 1816 reports about the registry were misunderstood: instead of interpreting the registry as a simple census, black Barbadians believed that Parliament had ordered their liberation. Concluding that the planters were withholding freedom, they plotted rebellion at a series of meetings over Lent. The plans were confirmed at a festive dance on Good Friday and, as Christ rose at Easter, so too would the Barbadian rebels.

Just after dusk on 14 April 1816, fires lit the sky and the ash from burning sugar cane fell in a thick layer across the island. The militiamen scrambled into their regiments and prepared to confront 400 rebels led by the matriarch Nanny Grigg and the ranger Bussa, who directed a scorched-earth, guerrilla campaign under the knowingly provocative banner of a black man embracing a white woman. One British colonel reported that the parishes of St Philip and Christ Church were 'involved in a general flame, whilst household furniture of every description, Rum, Sugar, Wine, Corn, and every species of food ... were promiscuously scattered in the Roads and Fields ... with a destruction that evinced the fury of the insurgents'. Critically, however, the rebels lacked weaponry. Having failed to storm the British armouries, only a few carried muskets, the rest bearing 'machetes and billhooks, cudgels and axes'. Nor could they inspire the black soldiers of the West India Regiment to abandon the British. They were outgunned and, within three days, the rebellion was quelled.[21]

The colonial reaction was just as violent as the insurgency. The British punished the conspirators viciously and often fatally: some were shot, some were hanged, and some were tortured in public to dampen any residual enthusiasm for revolution. Across the rest of the British Caribbean, the authorities issued stark warnings: 'Should the contagion of this mad insurrection spread,' declared one governor, 'I will be among you like an arrow from the bow to execute an instant and terrible justice on the guilty.' In Britain, where the blame attached to the slave registry, the abolitionists suffered a fearsome backlash. Chastened and afraid for the political future of the movement, Wilberforce withdrew the registry proposal and even sponsored an address to the Prince Regent 'deploring the outbreak and disavowing slave emancipation'. Although the West Indians soon deigned to establish the slave registries of their own accord, the continuation of slavery appeared to have been confirmed by the abolitionist leader himself.[22]

Even without the shock from Barbados, the domestic politics of the late 1810s made the reform of slavery unlikely. As thousands of soldiers returned from Europe to find only unemployment, Britain sank into social and economic distress. Groups of Luddites were destroying the textile machinery they blamed for the demise of traditional labour, and mass protests in Islington against hunger and poverty sparked bouts of rioting. The Prince Regent survived an attempt on his life in January 1817 and, five months later, the Pentrich Rising saw 300 men march on Nottingham in a forlorn attempt to ignite a national revolution. The conspirators of Cato Street even plotted to assassinate the prime minister, Lord Liverpool, and his Cabinet. Most notoriously, in August 1819, the sabres of the Manchester and Salford Yeomanry tore through a massive but peaceful rally in support of parliamentary reform, an incident remembered ever since as the Peterloo Massacre. Wilberforce and his allies voted for legislation to suppress this unrest and by supporting the Six Acts, which allowed the government to crack down on dissent and public unrest, the abolitionists gave the lie to the notion that charity begins at home. Few men were now brave enough to inveigh against a slave system that seemed as vital as ever to the stability of the Empire. It appeared that abolition had become a fair-weather cause.

These were the fallow years of the anti-slavery movement. Wilberforce and his colleagues had been sustained through long periods of inaction by the secretly cherished hope that abolition would lead to the improved conditions and eventual freedom of the enslaved, but there was little evidence that any such 'improvement' had occurred. Reports coming back to Britain still told of cruelty and depravity and even if enslaved populations in the older colonies had declined slightly since 1808, it appeared that the planters had adapted and that slavery had somehow become sustainable. Indeed, in light of the annexation of the slave colonies of Demerara and Berbice towards the end of the Napoleonic Wars, it was arguable that British colonial slavery was expanding.

It was not until 1822 that the winds began to shift. The conservative Liverpool ministry remained in office but a younger generation of statesmen were pushing the politics of what came to be called 'liberal Toryism'. For the first time since the outbreak of the French Revolution, mainstream political figures were debating electoral reform; and as the rights of Catholics and dissenting Protestants came into focus, politicians were questioning the supremacy of the Church of England. Sympathy for liberal causes crossed borders, too. Thousands of British soldiers volunteered to fight in Latin America under Simón Bolívar, whose revolutionary republicanism had embraced abolitionism. Those of a Romantic disposition were obsessed by the Greek struggle for independence from the Ottomans, and Lord Byron was so taken with the idea of Hellenic freedom that he gave his life for the cause, contracting a deadly fever while planning an assault on the Ottoman fort at Lepanto. Encouraged by this apparent desire for reform, and despairing of the lack of progress in the West Indies, British abolitionists were emboldened.

The Liverpool merchant James Cropper made the first move. The Quaker son of a Lancashire farmer, Cropper had made a fortune importing textiles and spices from the East. Now, approaching the age of fifty, he was deploying his wealth to philanthropic ends. The Irish peasantry, north-western orphans, and the sons of farmers eventually became the objects of his charity, but in the 1820s Cropper concerned himself with slavery. When it came to undermining slavery, his preferred methods were economic. Under a system known as 'imperial preference', slave-grown sugar from the Caribbean was taxed at a much lower rate than sugar from India that, despite being cultivated under the tyranny of the East India Company, was not technically 'slave-grown'. (West Indian slaveholders would frequently, and hypocritically, draw the public's attention to the objective barbarity of working conditions in India.) Cropper reasoned that if tariffs were levelled across the board, the supposedly lower costs of 'free labour' in the East – where the East India Company did not pay for the upkeep of the sugar-croppers – would undercut slave-grown produce and drive the West Indies into economic freefall. 'Enlightened views,' he wrote, 'have almost universally condemned systems of restriction and prohibition in commerce.'[23]

Cropper was a gifted advocate – 'Give him pen and ink,' marvelled one colleague, 'and he will demonstrate that white is black' – but he knew that such a narrow campaign about economics and tariffs would have limited impact in the wider political arena. 'I am quite prepared to expect that the public papers would be all shut against us,' he wrote, 'and ... I have little expectation that many of them will notice my letters.' Cropper also anticipated accusations that he decried West Indian slavery only to advance his own commercial interests in British India, and one Cheshire newspaper duly scorned 'the holy humbug – the East Indian *Saint* and *Sugar* alliance'. Cropper therefore needed help and in July 1822 he pleaded with old friends to revive their dormant abolitionist networks. 'If you can form an association if ever so small in London,' he wrote, 'it will be a very great help to me, but I know it is difficult to make a beginning.'[24]

As Cropper wrote, William Wilberforce was pained by the stagnant state of the abolitionist movement. 'My conscience reproaches me,' he wrote, 'with having too long suffered this horrible evil to go on.' Now, nearly four decades after they founded their first society, and fifteen years since they had struck down the slave trade, the abolitionists stirred again. This time, they would pursue the final and total extinction of colonial slavery: 'We must now call upon all good men throughout the kingdom,' wrote Wilberforce, 'to join us in abolishing this wicked system.' But of what did slavery itself, which Wilberforce damned as 'an evil of our own creation', *really* consist?[25]

2.

Hell and Paradise

In front is a view of the sea, and the harbours of Kingston, Port Royal, Port Henderson, &c. full of ships of war and vessels great and small ... The plain, from the Liguanea mountains, covered with sugar estates, penns, negro settlements, &c ... [is] all so mixed with trees of different sorts, and all so new to a European eye, that it seemed like a Paradise.[1]

Lady Maria Nugent, September 1801

They will have work – work – work, night and day, sick or well, till we are quite done up; and we must not speak up nor look amiss, however much we be abused. And then when we are quite done up, who cares for us, more than for a lame horse? This is slavery.[2]

Mary Prince, *The History of Mary Prince*, 1831

Before Samuel Morse tapped out 'what hath God wrought' on the telegraph, and long before Alexander Graham Bell asked Mr Watson to come hither, news took time to travel. In the 1820s, it took weeks – if not months – to cover the 4,700 miles that lay between London and Spanish Town, the colonial capital of Jamaica. Letters, papers, decrees, and contracts that were bound for the West Indies often left on the ships of the Falmouth packet, an Admiralty-run postal service which embarked from quays to the north of Pendennis Castle in Cornwall. Fast and light, designed for speed, the packet ships sailed south past Brittany and the port of Brest, skimming the Bay of Biscay and Galicia before catching the current that ran along the coast of Saharan Africa. This was the same route that British sailors had taken to the slaving markets of Guinea; these were the same waters that had claimed the

Medusa, the French frigate whose shipwreck – and whose crew's descent into cannibalism – had become an international sensation. The packet ships veered west at Cape Verde and then began a long, dangerous slog across the Atlantic. Once, this could have been a drag race against Spanish pirates or French warships; now, the chief villain was the caprice of the wind. Good luck or a skilful captain who caught the trade winds could shave days off the voyage; bad luck or bad choices could leave a crew marooned in the doldrums, 'stuck, nor breath nor motion', as Coleridge put it. The return leg of the journey was no less dangerous. Sailing north along the American seaboard, or towards Bermuda, skippers sought the North Atlantic current to propel them home through colder, rougher waters, but it still took weeks to reach Europe.

Yet more than posing dangers to the souls who braved the crossing, and more than causing delays to correspondence, the distance between Britain and the West Indies meant that domestic opinions on the colonies were often based on second-hand evidence, not personal experience. Besides the sailors who manned the ships, the soldiers who were stationed there, and the young men who looked to make or mend their fortunes in sugar, Britons rarely went to the Caribbean. Instead, information was gleaned from newspapers, books, and hearsay; for many Britons of the early nineteenth century, this was a remote and 'imagined' empire.

This was why Thomas Clarkson's 'box' had been so important to the campaign against the slave trade. A tall, strong, red-haired, and deeply serious deacon from East Anglia, Clarkson had converted to abolitionism upon writing a prize-winning essay at Cambridge on the enslavement of 'the unconsenting'. In 1785, as he rode from the university to London, Clarkson was taken by a thought that he could not shake: 'If the contents of [my] Essay were true,' he reasoned, 'it was time some person should see these calamities to their end.' At a spot near Wadesmill in Hertfordshire, Clarkson dismounted, sat on the grass by the roadside, and swore a silent oath to devote his life to abolishing slavery. And as he toured Great Britain in the late 1780s and 1790s, speaking to thousands of people at hundreds of meetings, Clarkson took with him a strong, two-handled mahogany box. Three of the box's four 'divisions' contained polished woods, ivory and musk, spices, cloths, and gold jewellery – all from Africa, all calculated to help Clarkson's audience 'make a proper estimation of the genius and talents of the natives'. The fourth 'division' contained the worst and most appalling artefacts of the slave trade. There were iron shackles and handcuffs used to restrain the Africans, iron bits that were forced deep into their mouths to gag them, and thumbscrews used to crush and crack their digits. These were 'objects of gruesome fascination, to be held, fingered and fantasised in the hands of leading parliamentarians' and by such means Clarkson made the atrocity of the slave trade comprehensible to ordinary men and women who had never left their parish, let alone seen the coast of Africa.[3]

Slavery itself, however, was a different beast. Whereas the slave trade was a discrete and identifiable offence, a sin that was practised from port to port, slavery was inextricable from colonial life in general. Economically, it was the lifeblood of the West Indies. Enslaved people worked in farmyards, kitchens, and houses, in shops and on wharves, and of course they ploughed and harvested the fields of cane, cotton, and coffee. Slavery was politically vital to colonial life, since it was only by exploiting slave-generated wealth that absentee planters could exert influence over policy at Westminster. Slavery played an equally important role in the social structure of the colonies. For the poor white Britons who had fled from the lowest ranks of a class-riven society, the colonial hierarchy which placed enslaved Africans beneath them was a paramount source of status: as one slaveholder wrote, 'pre-eminence and distinction' were in the colonies 'necessarily attached ... to the complexion of a White Man'. In these ways, slavery was essential to daily life in the West Indies. And so, even if Britons at home drank the coffee, ate the sugar, and wore the cotton from the colonies, white West Indians maintained that understanding the 'true' nature of slavery required a personal understanding of colonial society – an understanding that only *they* possessed, since only *they* had led the colonial life. The slaveholders and their allies complained bitterly that abolitionists, many of whom had never been to the West Indies, were engaged in visionary schemes that Dickens would describe as 'telescopic philanthropy'. Indeed, in the most infamous pro-slavery cartoon of the 1820s, *John Bull Taking a Clear View of the Negro Question*, the illustrator George Cruikshank would depict gullible Britons peering through telescopes only for the abolitionists to obscure their view with fake images of slavery. Cruikshank and the West Indians were

adamant that abolitionist representations of the slave colonies bore
little resemblance to reality.[4]

As European demand for sugar boomed in the eighteenth century,
the economies of British colonies had flourished, none more so than
Jamaica's. In pamphlets and 'histories' that were effectively brochures
designed to attract investment, the planters extolled 'their' island as
a tropical paradise. In his sprawling history of the West Indies, the
slaveholding MP Bryan Edwards riffed on the idyllic climate. Discussing
the subtle changes of season, Edwards marvelled at how, in the spring,
'the foliage of the trees ... becomes more vivid, and the parched
savannas begin to change their russet hue'. The tropical summer then
'reign[ed] in full glory. Not a cloud is to be perceived; and the sky
blazes with irresistible fierceness', but the heat was cooled by sweet
sea zephyrs. Summer nights were 'transcendently beautiful. The clear-
ness and brilliancy of the heavens, the serenity of the air, and the
soft tranquillity in which Nature reposes, contribute to harmonize
the mind, and produce the most calm and delightful sensations'.
Tropical rainclouds might 'pour down cataracts', the islands might
endure 'hurricanes, those dreadful visitations of the Almighty', but
on balance this was infinitely preferable to the cold, grey inclemencies
of Britain.[5]

New arrivals were enthralled by the Jamaica's 'beauty and enchanting
scenery'. Maria Nugent was the wife of the colony's governor general
and, in 1801, she did not especially want to be in the Caribbean, writing
in her journal that 'I should greatly have preferred remaining [in
Ireland], instead of playing the Governor's lady to the blackies'. Yet
even she was charmed by Jamaica's natural majesty. Looking out from
the foothills of the Blue Mountains, she saw in one direction hills
rising over hills, 'some clothed in wood, some in canes'. In the other,
looking down into the parish of Saint Thomas, there was 'a rich vale,
full of sugar estates, the works of which look like so many little
villages'. Broadening out beneath her, 'the soft bright green of the
canes' looked like velvet, a verdant carpet dappled by the brown of
'Guinea-corn fields' and coconut trees. Wending through it all was
the Plantain Garden River, a shallow, slow-paced stream which lost
itself in the azure sea that was foaming over the shoals and rocks of
the coastline.[6]

In scenes that repeated across the Caribbean, towns of wood, brick, and stone punctuated the green and blue, most often at river mouths and harbours. The typical building in Spanish Town was 'constructed of wood or lathe-and-plaster with broad eaves, verandas, and latticed "jalousey" windows'. In Kingston, just a few miles to the east, military engineers planned for houses 'all of brick and the same height and design', with 'glass windows just as in Europe'. The streets were laid out 'wide, and more regular, to face the Sea-Breezes' that flowed between the buildings and chilled the wilting colonists. Above all else rose the stone churches and civic mansions, and while they might have paled in comparison to the grandeur of Georgian London, where Nash and Adam were creating the West End, these buildings were 'prudent and cool, able to ride out ... earthquakes', and made of tropical hardwood that was 'resistant to rot and less prone to fire'.[7]

In the world they made, the colonists ached for and aped the refinement of the motherland. Charles Leslie, the first Englishman to write a history of Jamaica, was struck by 'the number of Coaches and Chariots which are perpetually plying, besides those which belong to private Persons: They have frequent Balls, and lately have got a Play-house, where they retain a Set of extraordinary good Actors'. The colony's lending libraries were stocked with the novels of Fielding, the plays of Dryden, and the histories of Hume and Gibbon, while the *Jamaica Magazine* 'contributed to inspire a correct and elegant literary taste'. Even by imposing names such as Mars and Cato on their slaves, the colonists mimicked the fashion of the motherland, where naming pets and servants after Classical figures had been in vogue for years. The wealthier colonists who owned land, ships, and slaves lived 'as happily as if they were within the Verge of the British Court'.[8]

Affecting the genteel habits of the British nobility, the colonists enjoyed horse-riding and shooting in the cool of the morning. The afternoon heat confined them 'to sedentary Diversions at Home; as Cards, Dice, Tables, [and] Quoits', but there was cricket all the same. The sport did not truly thrive until the mid-nineteenth century, but reports from the 1800s give details of clubs and games, and the Barbados 'cricket buckle', a brass engraving which depicts a shackled slave with bat in hand, was fashioned as early as the 1780s. As for the ladies, of whom there were many fewer than the men, it was said that 'in no part of the globe is the virtue of hospitality more generally prevalent' and Maria Nugent recorded countless dinners, soirées, and dances in her diaries. Indeed, the ladies of the white West Indies would not be deterred from dancing: the doctor William Hillary warned the women of Barbados that 'dancing is too violent an Exercise in this hot Climate, and many do greatly injure their Health by it', and he duly despaired that 'most of the Ladies are so excessive fond of it, that say what I will they will dance on'.[9]

On the older islands of Jamaica and Barbados, where the colonists enjoyed a significant degree of political autonomy, there prevailed 'a fondness for dignified situations and high-sounding titles'. Here, domestic affairs were governed by local assemblies to which the colonial electorate – white, male, and qualified by property – appointed delegates by public vote. At a lower level, each parish was administered by magistrates and vestrymen, who were led by a civil official known as a 'custos'. When it came to security, barracks of imperial soldiers were supported by local regiments of militia, a system which gave the colonists another chance to acquire the office and rank that were often denied to them in Britain. This sense of self-dependence was reinforced by the colonial press, with publications such as The Barbadian, Jamaica's Royal Gazette, and Antigua's Free Press helping to craft local identities and civic pride. Even so, each colony played host to a governor who represented London's authority, advised colonists on ministerial policy, and – in the newer colonies without assemblies – enforced direct rule from Westminster.[10]

Away from the towns and ports, colonial life centred on the plantations. Some grew coffee, some grew cotton, but the vast majority of estates – about 85 per cent on Jamaica – grew sugar. On the average plantation, 200 enslaved people cultivated 600 acres in a yearly cycle of ploughing, digging, planting, tending, and harvesting. It was enormously difficult to grow sugar cane. First, cane stalks were thrust deep into the ground and fertilised with a manure that lent a putrid smell to planting season. Weeds, rats, and the wind could plague a crop, but if the cane survived and ripened it was cut by scythe and machete during a dry season that usually began in January. Cane juice spoiled quickly after cutting, so planters hastened their crops to wind- or water-powered mills where rollers squeezed the juice, coloured green by the cane, into vast receptacles. Before the juice could ferment, it was taken to an adjacent boiling house where, in huge copper kettles erected over burning fires, impurities were removed from the crystallising sugar. Moving from kettle to kettle, the sugar became hotter, browner, and thicker until, at the vital moment, the mixture was cooled and the sugar was ladled into a cistern. Laid out to dry in earthen pots, the crisp brown sugar was packed into 1,500-pound barrels known as hogsheads; the sticky, viscous liquid that drained away was sold as the black treacle of molasses, which was also distilled into rum. This was an intense, unforgiving industry whose demand for cane verged on the unsustainable: one visitor to the colonies predicted an 'eventual ruin [that] must entail by the over-working of the soil'.[11]

Within sight of the mills and boiling houses were those grand symbols of white colonial supremacy, the plantation houses. The verandas, pitched roofs, and gables of the typical house conveyed all of the tropical elegance for which the West Indies were known. Inside, the wealth of the sugar barons was opulent. The enslaved polished silverware, laundered fine clothes, and cooked rich meats for their masters; others stood ready to swat away the flies from the dinner tables around which the 'plantocracy' conducted business. The Jamaican planter Simon Taylor, whose estate was worth almost £90 million in today's money, stocked his 'capital mansion' at Prospect Pen with all 'the symbols of civilization'. The house had a ballroom, a dining room, a drawing room, and six bedrooms; there was mahogany furniture, Oriental porcelain, paintings, telescopes, and Madeira wine. In the white West Indian imagination, Taylor and his fellow planters – living in pastoral palaces, delighting in the tropes of high culture, and surrounded by an agrarian workforce – were no different from the landowners of Yorkshire or Norfolk.[12]

Like the cottages of British farmers, slave-houses were dotted about this alleged paradise. One pro-slavery magazine described the houses on Barbados as 'generally of stone, with a thatched roof'; in St Lucia they were 'wattled, plastered, and whitewashed, presenting to the view a neat and comfortable dwelling'. The typical house was described to British readers as a 'cottage with two or sometimes three rooms ... shaded by the guava and the calabash trees ... with the green and spreading leaves of the plantain and the banana, all uniting to secure a shady retreat from the influence of a meridian sun'. For one planter, they were 'as comfortable as our mansions'.[13]

In the white West Indian version of events, the slaves were also well-nourished, even gluttonous. According to one planter, Africans in Demerara received 'on average, from two to four pounds weekly of good salt fishes, chiefly Newfoundland cod or salted mackerel ... fresh from the weekly arrivals'. There was, besides, 'an abundance of plantains, yams, bananas, and other vegetable productions' and 'occasional supplies of rice'. On Barbados, the slaves enjoyed 'ample daily rations from the storehouses of Plantations', while absentee planters in London celebrated their own liberality in dispensing 'indulgencies' such as syrup and ginger-tea. The slaves procured a further feast of meats, fruits, and vegetables from the provision-grounds that were allotted to them. One Jamaican reported that his slaves raised 'large supplies of hogs, goats, and poultry'; on another plantation the slaves' favourite meal was a soup of peas, beans, yams, and sweet potatoes boiled up with beef, pork, and cod, all 'highly seasoned with capsicums and pimento'.[14]

As with food, so with clothing. For work, the slave was 'clothed at his master's cost' and in 'materials that would be quite pleasing to an English labourer'. When slaves traded surplus food for fabric and dye, they were apparently able to dress themselves in style. In one account, slaves appeared 'at church on Sunday in habiliments of the utmost neatness and comfort, and not a little cost sometimes'. They wore 'shoes and stockings, muslin gowns, and ornaments of the precious metals'. Among the women there was 'a passion for finery' and, where the slaves were skilled in needlework, they 'commonly appear[ed] in ... coats and jackets of broad cloth, or else flannel or fancy stripes'. White West Indians reported similar scenes at Sunday markets: the male slaves wore 'good coats, short jackets, or white smock frocks and trowsers, and a smart hat, with a pair of good shoes'; the women had 'printed cotton gowns, and ... black or white beaver hats'.[15]

And what of those who fell sick? William Sells, a doctor in Jamaica, exalted the care for the poorly and for pregnant women. Another pamphleteer praised the planters for receiving the unwell 'into the wards of a hospital built purposely for them', for 'send[ing] for the same apothecary that attends [his] own family; and ... call[ing] in without hesitation the best Surgeon or Physician in the island'. As for infant slaves, one traveller in Barbados described an extensive nursery. 'It is a large open room with the floor covered with wooden trays, and in each tray a naked niggerling. There they are, from the atom born to-day, up to eight or nine months of age, from the small black pudding up to a respectable sucking pig ... The venerable nurse sits placidly in the middle, and administers pap to the young gentlemen.' And with the elderly allegedly being treated with reverence as 'reward' for years of service, the West Indians represented the plantation as 'nursery for [Africans] in their youth, and an asylum in [old] age'.[16]

In the reports that West Indians sent back to Britain, slaves were characterised as healthy, well-fed, well-housed, and well-clothed. 'In our colonies,' declared one pro-colonist magazine, 'the slaves are generally happy.' The Jamaican planter John Stewart agreed that Caribbean slaves were 'a contented and happy people, uniformly treated with a mildness and humanity, and enjoying comforts beyond even those of the British peasant'. If this was slavery, the planters 'could not conceive [of] a situation more comfortable for a human being who has never tasted freedom, and whose mind is uncultivated, than that of negroes under British masters'. So content were the slaves, so munificent were the planters, that slavery, at least according to the slaveholders, was preferable to black liberty. 'Cases frequently occur,' it was reported, 'wherein the slave refuses to be made free.' Why, the West Indians asked, would anyone wish to interfere with this?[17]

Of course, the West Indians presented a grossly sanitised view of life in the slave colonies. In the 1780s, Mary Prince was born into slavery in Bermuda, from where she was sold to Grand Turk and then to Antigua, before being taken to London. Here, in the capital of Britain's slaveholding empire, Prince was abandoned by her master without any legal title to liberty. Her autobiography, which was published in 1831 with the assistance of the abolitionists, remains the most stirring, vivid narrative of the life of an enslaved person in the West Indian colonies. 'She wished it be done,' declared her editor, so that 'good people in England might hear from a slave what a slave had felt and suffered.' As a biography 'taken down from Mary's own lips', *The*

History of Mary Prince was radically different from the accounts of slavery that were produced by white West Indians.[18]

There was no sumptuous menu. Instead, Mary survived on a meagre diet of boiled corn for breakfast, corn soup for lunch, and raw corn for supper, all cooked by the enslaved themselves. She disputed the planters' accounts of accommodation. 'We slept in a long shed,' she protested, 'divided into narrow slips, like the stalls used for cattle. Boards fixed upon slates, driven into the ground, without mat or covering, were our only beds.' She dispelled the fiction that planters cared properly for the sick, too. 'When we were ill,' she recalled, 'our complaint be what it might, the only medicine given to us was a great bowl of hot salt water.' Indeed, when she came down with St Anthony's Fire – the convulsive, gangrenous disease known as ergotism – Mary was not shown tenderness, but quarantined to 'a little out-house that was swarming with bugs and other vermin'. It was another lie that the elderly lived out their lives in dignity. Mary recalled that one old man called Daniel, who was 'lame in the hip', was often 'stripped and laid down, and ... beaten till his skin was quite red and raw'. Daniel's white tormentor would 'call for a bucket of salt, and fling it upon the raw flesh till the man writhed on the ground like a worm, and screamed aloud in agony'. The old man's wounds never healed, and Mary often saw them 'full of maggots'.[19]

With every word that she wrote, Mary undermined the planters' pretence that the enslaved were a contented peasantry. Their work did *not* constitute an honest day's labour: it was cruel and achingly difficult, and performed without shade under the beating sun. In Jamaica, they could toil in the fields for nineteen hours in the day; even during quiet periods, fourteen-hour shifts were not uncommon. 'I saw how the field negroes are worked in Antigua,' Mary related. 'They are worked very hard and fed but scantily. They are called out to work before daybreak, and come home after dark; and then each has to heave his bundle of grass for the cattle in the pen.' At the salt works on Grand Turk, work began at four o'clock each morning, when the enslaved were given a 'half barrel and a shovel'. With only the shortest of breaks at nine o'clock and lunch, they worked 'through the heat of the day; the sun flaming on our heads like fire, and raising salt blisters'. Their feet and legs 'became full of dreadful boils, which cut down in some cases to the very bone'.[20]

It was a hellish, miserable existence and the slaveholders' efforts to suggest otherwise were satirised adroitly by an abolitionist poster which called for white workers to leave Britain:

Wanted Immediately
MANUFACTURING LABOURERS
To go out to the West Indies

3000 Manufacturing Labourers, who will engage to go out to the West Indies, will receive of course NO WAGES but all the kind attention, treatment, comfort, indulgences and privileges, etc, etc. … with the addition of a LARGE CART WHIP, frequently and powerfully to their bare bones.[21]

As that poster suggested, the enslaved were subjected to draconian punishment if they failed or refused to do their work. Although most colonies had laws which in theory regulated the discipline of the enslaved – in Barbados, someone could receive thirty-nine lashes for swearing or moving faster than walking pace – each plantation was really a law unto itself. Mary Prince related how accidentally cracking an earthen pot earned her a beating and two floggings, an ordeal that was concluded only when a seismic tremor caused the collapse of a nearby roof. She bemoaned that 'to hang me up by the wrists and lay my flesh upon with the cow-skin, was an ordinary punishment for even a slight offence'. Mary's master, John Ingham, was even more vicious in chastising a pregnant woman called Hetty: when she was blamed for a cow getting loose and eating the shoots of Ingham's sweet potatoes, Hetty was stripped naked and tied to a tree. Ingham whipped her until 'she was all over streaming with blood', stopping only when *he* was exhausted. On recovering his breath Ingham renewed his assault and Hetty was soon 'delivered after severe labour of a dead child'. After several more floggings, the bereaved mother's 'body and limbs swelled to a great size'. Hetty lay down on a mat in the plantation's kitchen 'till the water burst out of her body' and she died.[22]

But of all the white colonists who terrorised Africans in the West Indies, few could have been more sadistic than Thomas Thistlewood. The son of a Lincolnshire farmer, Thistlewood had arrived in Jamaica in 1750 and, finding work on the 'Egypt' plantation, he developed a predilection for dehumanising violence. In the summer of 1756, vexed by one enslaved man who was allegedly prone to stealing and eating sugar cane, Thistlewood designed the most degrading punishment in the arsenal of West Indian slavery. First, the man was flogged, his skin flayed off by the rough, coarse leather of the plantation whip. Second, he was 'pickled', which meant rubbing an acerbic cocktail of 'salt pickle, lime juice & bird pepper' into his raw, bleeding wounds. Next, and worst, another enslaved man was forced to 'shit in his mouth' before he was 'put in a gag whilst his mouth was full' and made to wear the gag for at least four hours. Named after the man who first suffered it, this was 'Derby's Dose'. Other punishments devised by Thistlewood were scarcely less appalling. Another man called Hector was whipped for 'losing his hoe' before 'New Negro Joe' was made to 'piss in his eyes & mouth'. When a runaway was returned to Egypt after four months on the run, he was gagged, locked into iron shackles, rubbed with molasses, and exposed all night to the mosquitoes.[23]

None of this surpassed the horror to which Thomas Thistlewood subjected enslaved women. Between his arrival in Jamaica in 1750 and his death in 1787, Thistlewood committed 3,852 sexual assaults on 138 different women. He raped black women against trees, in libraries, in farmyards, near duck ponds, and on plantation furniture. He spared neither old nor young, with at least seven slaves falling victim to him either during or before puberty. He would not spare expectant mothers either, with one woman losing her child in 1776, eight days after Thistlewood raped her. There is no doubt that all this was rape, or that some women were terrified into submission lest they be 'whipped for refusal'. And there was gang rape. In 1755, Thistlewood recorded that four white men, all attached to local plantations, became 'heartily drunk [and] haw'led Eve separately into the Water Room and were Concern'd with her'. Adding to the perversity of it all, Thistlewood made a report of each assault in schoolboy-level Latin. Not once did he even attempt to sleep with a white woman who might, as a free person, resist his advances without fear of reprisal. He was, in the words of his modern biographer, 'the quintessential sexual predator'.[24]

But Thistlewood was not the only one. Britons at home knew that 'miscegenation' – that is, interracial sexual relations – was commonplace in the Caribbean, with one periodical observing that white colonists would 'receive those services from a coloured woman which, in this country, it would be unusual, degrading, and perhaps cruel to look for from a wife'. John Newton, the author of 'Amazing Grace' and a former captain of slave ships, recalled how, 'when the women and girls are taken on board a ship, naked, trembling, terrified ... they are exposed to the wanton rudeness of white savages'. He regretted in particular how one of his sailors 'seduced a slave down into the room and lay with her brutelike in view of the whole quarter deck'. The former slave Olaudah Equiano had also witnessed sailors 'gratify[ing] their brutal passions with females not ten years old'. Mary Prince did not escape this tyranny. She recalled how her master on Grand Turk had 'an ugly fashion of stripping himself quite naked, and ordering me then to wash him in a tub of water'. For Mary, this was 'worse ... than all the licks' of the whip.[25]

The white colonist could even interpose in sexual relations *among* the enslaved. In 1773, Thomas Thistlewood flogged a woman called Maria 'for cuckolding' a man called Solon and again, the next year, 'for running to her sweetheart'. This was perhaps the gravest index of the legal status of enslaved people: the men were bought for field work, the women for domestic work and 'reproductive labour', and those obligations would not be suborned to love. As such, whatever fleeting intimacy that might have blossomed among the enslaved was 'every moment at the mercy of events'. At any time, an enslaved person could be sold without notice and transported to a new plantation, separated from family and friends. Mary Prince was moved from Bermuda to Grand Turk to Antigua and it was, for her, 'but going from one butcher to another'. Worst was the childhood separation from her mother and siblings. Trussed up in dresses made from coarse osnaburg cloth, the children were taken to the Bermudian slave market and lined up, 'our backs to the wall and our arms folded across our breasts'. Mary was led into the street and forced to pirouette as 'strange men ... examined and handled [her] in the same manner that a butcher would a calf or lamb he was about to purchase'. She was sold for £57, her sisters for less, and their 'poor mammy went home with nothing'. Prince wept at the memory: 'All that we love [is] taken away from us ... Oh, it is sad, sad! And sore to be born!'[26]

The advertisements that planters placed in local newspapers – and that abolitionists reprinted in Britain – were proof that Mary's story was not unique, and proof also that *internal* slave markets had only grown after the end of the slave trade in 1807. In the early 1820s, the *Royal Gazette* of Jamaica publicised the sale of '15 valuable young Negroes, together or singly, to suit purchasers' and of 'Creole' women, meaning Africans who were born in the colonies, who were 'accustomed to all sorts of work' and 'levied upon for taxes due'. Besides these were advertisements for 'Quasheba, a Black, a drudge' and 'William, a Black, a waiting boy, aged 8 years'.[27]

When at last she came to England and told her story, Mary Prince railed against the credulity of the British public. 'They believe,' she lamented, the planters 'who deceive them and say slaves are happy ... How can slaves be happy,' she asked, 'when they have the halter round their neck and the whip upon their back and [are] thought no more of than beasts – and are separated from their mothers, and husbands, and children, and sisters, just as cattle are sold and separated?' Only the abolitionists had seen through the colonial charade. For William Wilberforce, plantation slavery was 'a system of the grossest injustice, of the most heathenish irreligion and immorality, of the most unprecedented degradation, and unrelenting cruelty'. Writing in 1823, another abolitionist despaired that slaves could be 'ill-fed, hard-worked, ill-used, and wantonly and barbarously punished ... tortured, nay even deliberately and intentionally killed without the means of redress, or the punishment of the aggressor'. *This* was the reality of slavery; *this* was the hell from which enslaved rebels fought to free themselves; and *this* was the evil that British abolitionists now, in 1823, sought to abolish.[28]

3.

For All the Blood Spilt

He sees the mother of his children stripped naked before the gang ...
and flogged unmercifully; he sees his children sent to market to be
sold at the best price they will fetch; he sees in himself, not a man, but
a thing – by West Indian law, a chattel ... Will any man tell me that
the [slave], with all this staring him in the face ... never dreams that
there is an injustice in such treatment till he sits himself down to the
perusal of an English newspaper?[1]

Thomas Fowell Buxton, House of Commons, 15 May 1823

At just over one hundred yards in length, Poultry is one of the shorter
streets in London. Even on busy pavements, a person can walk from
one end to the other in sixty seconds. To the west of Poultry is
Cheapside, the former trading artery of the City that was the birthplace
of John Milton and a childhood home of Chaucer; it is still the site of
'Bow Bells'. To the east is Mansion House, the stately Palladian residence of the lord mayor of London. A few steps further on are the
underground maze of Bank station and the Old Lady of Threadneedle
Street herself. Number 1 Poultry is a looming tower of grey-blue glass
and pink-and-yellow limestone. At 27 begins the Ned, a five-star hotel
which occupies the building designed by Lutyens for the old Midland
Bank. Other tenants of the street include a pharmacist, an Italian tailor,
and a travel agency.

Number 25 Poultry is an address that no longer exists, but for years
it was home to a storied tavern. Originally known as the Rose, it is
first mentioned in the mid-sixteenth century, when the bailiff Master
Cobham, assisted by 'divers gentlemen and serving-men', arrested an
indebted rogue on the premises. By 1660, with Charles Stuart returning

from exile, the Rose had been renamed the King's Head by its royalist
landlord, William King.[2]

The landlord's wife, the formidable Mistress Rebecca, was no less
ardent in her sympathies. Despite going into labour on the day of
Charles's return to London, she had insisted on 'seeing the King pass
the tavern, or matters might go cross with her'. Left without a choice,
her husband dutifully constructed an arbour in the doorway of the
tavern, a maternal throne of 'green boughs and flowers, hung round
with tapestry and garnished with silver plate'. Rebecca's display drew
admiration from even the highest ranks. The Duke of Buckingham,
who rode with the new king, observed the pregnant lady in her splendour: 'Your Majesty's return,' he remarked, 'is here welcomed even
by a subject as yet unborn.' Struck by this devotion, Charles turned
towards the tavern, kissed his hand, and bowed to Mistress Rebecca.
She promptly fainted.[3]

Rebuilt after the Great Fire of 1666, the King's Head flourished
anew. Noted for its 'unsophisticated wines, [and] honest measures',
the tavern was also one of London's principal depots for turtles. As
patrons ate, drank, hid from bailiffs, and remembered when the King
paid homage to the mistress of the house, they were surrounded by
exotic reptiles in huge glass tanks of water. Today, the King's Head
leaves no mark on the street. There is no monument, no statue, and
no blue plaque. There should be, but not because of Charles II, or
the turtles, or even the blessed memory of Mistress Rebecca. Instead,
this long-lost pub on Poultry should be remembered because it was
here, on 31 January 1823, that the Anti-Slavery Society was founded.

The men who met at the King's Head knew each other well. They
were old friends, colleagues in the abolitionist movement, and
members of the African Institution which had 'taken over' Sierra
Leone. As the minutes record, they were 'impressed with the magnitude and number of the evils attached to the system of slavery' and,
having watched the slave system survive and even thrive since 1807,
they resolved at last to pursue its destruction. They accepted that this
could not be done quickly; indeed, the formal title of their association
was the 'London Society for Mitigating and Gradually Abolishing the
State of Slavery throughout the British Dominions'. Even so, they had
determined to begin their work. A four-page manifesto outlined the

structure, ethos, and objectives of the new Society. Its centrepiece was an impassioned attack on the obstinacy of the slaveholders: 'The time … is at length arrived, when they will no longer be permitted to impede the progress of civilisation, to set the bounds to the glory and prosperity of the Empire, to stain the character of our country, and to outrage the Holy Religion by which we [are] guided.'[4]

Among the two dozen men who gathered that night in central London, a number emerged as leaders of the new movement. Zachary Macaulay, fifty-four, was a dour and humourless Scotsman whose white hair was swept back from an often-furrowed brow. The son of a Presbyterian minister, Macaulay was one of the few campaigners who had direct experience of slavery. At the age of sixteen, having taught himself Latin and Greek, but lost in what he called a 'labyrinth' of alcoholic dissipation, the young Macaulay removed himself to Jamaica, where he found work as a plantation bookkeeper. In other colonies bookkeepers were accountants, but in Jamaica they were tasked with 'supervising the enslaved in the fields, keeping the keys for the stores, and attending the boiling house and distillery in the crop season'. Although disgusted by the violence that marked life in the tropics, and finding his work 'laborious, irksome, and degrading', Macaulay became inured to slavery's horrors. It was only much later, having returned to England, that an epiphany brought him to Evangelicalism and, with it, the anti-slavery cause. After one more spell abroad, this time as governor of Sierra Leone, Macaulay became a pillar of the abolitionist network. Possessed of an iron constitution and incomparable resilience, he rose at four o'clock each morning and completed his work on Sierra Leone before most had eaten breakfast. His day was then dedicated to the work of abolition and he became the fount of anti-slavery knowledge: when information was required, Wilberforce simply told others to 'Look it up in Macaulay'.[5]

The only other man in the King's Head who had seen the West Indies was James Stephen, a sixty-four-year-old clerk in the Court of Chancery. As a young journalist, Stephen had reported on some of the most sensational stories of the early 1780s, including the treason trial of the anti-Catholic rioter George Gordon. But when he tired of Grub Street, Stephen had retrained as a barrister and departed for the West Indies. En route to St Kitts, he stopped at Barbados, where a visit to the local courthouse changed his life for ever. Four enslaved men – 'filthily-clad, frightened . . . their wrists painfully bound together' – had been accused of murder. There was only one witness, a young girl, and every reason to believe that a white colonist was the killer, but the judge was hell-bent on convicting the accused. Terrified and crying, the witness was browbeaten into testifying against the accused, all of whom were found guilty. Two of the four were absolved by their masters, who provided alibis to preserve their 'property', but the two remaining men were sentenced to death on the same spurious evidence. With the blessing of the colony's governor, they were burned alive in public. Stephen was 'overpowered by disgust and indignation' and the injustice was seared into his conscience. He promptly became the abolitionist lobby's 'man on the spot', funnelling evidence of cruelty back to Wilberforce. Upon returning to Britain, Stephen began writing abolitionist articles for the *Morning Chronicle*; he even married, to Wilberforce's sister.[6]

Macaulay and Stephen were joined by the Whig lawyer Henry Brougham, the legal scholar Stephen Lushington, and the wealthy Quaker Henry Gurney. The Liverpool merchant James Cropper, who had kickstarted the campaign by raising the issue of sugar duties, was also present. William Wilberforce was at the King's Head, too; he could hardly not be. Now in his sixties, he was in poor and worsening health. Hunched and frail, Wilberforce wore a steel corset to keep himself upright and, never blessed with good eyesight, he was now close to blind. Suffering further from bowel and heart problems, he knew that the end of his time as a public force was nigh. He would leave this fight to younger men, but his successor had been hand-picked: in the autumn of 1822, he and Macaulay had travelled from London to Cromer Hall on the north Norfolk coast to persuade Thomas Fowell Buxton to assume leadership of the anti-slavery campaign.

A physically commanding man known as 'the Elephant', Buxton's sharp nose, spectacles, and widow's peak gave him a forceful, serious appearance. He was the thirty-six-year-old son of an East Anglian squire, but his formative influences were female: his mother was a Quaker, his wife was a Quaker, and his sister-in-law was the Quaker prison reformer Elizabeth Fry. Having graduated from Trinity College, Dublin, and deciding that he could not afford a political career, he had taken a position with Truman's brewery in the East End of London. Surrounded there by crime-ridden slums, and surrounded at home by a family whose first instinct was to help, Buxton was a tireless campaigner for social and legal reform: the silk-weavers of Spitalfields, who fell into the hardest of times in the post-war depression, were the common objects of his charity. By the late 1810s, Buxton's reputation had grown nationally and his inquiry into the treatment of Newgate Prison inmates went through five editions. His political patrons therefore determined – as such things were often determined – that he should at last become an MP and, though he lived and worked in London, he was given the Dorset constituency of Weymouth. Buxton would prove that the iniquities of the old electoral system did not always lead to further corruption, for he used this new station to champion moral causes as an independent member of the Commons. Then, in 1821, when he declaimed the inaction of the African Institution, he emerged as a rare bright spark of the moribund abolitionist movement. Indeed, Buxton's hatred of slavery was unyielding: 'I wonder when I see an honest man,' he wrote, 'who does not hate it as I do, who does not long for the opportunity of giving it a death-blow.' Wilberforce, who knew something about intransigence, compared Buxton to a dray horse: when settled on a course of action, nothing could shake him from it. Another abolitionist believed that three words could describe Buxton 'both morally and physically: he was a *tower of strength*'. In the coming years, he would need all that strength.[7]

The abolitionist leaders knew that, by proposing the end of slavery, they had effectively declared war on one of the most powerful political groups in British history. In 1823, there were no political parties in Great Britain, at least not in the modern sense. Robert Jenkinson, Lord Liverpool, might have led a 'Tory' government, but there was no Tory Party; the Whigs were in opposition, but there was no Whig Party. Rather, the 'Tories' and the 'Whigs' were loose coalitions of politicians who shared generally similar attitudes. Put crudely, the Tories were the conservative friends of the Crown and the Church of England who glorified the memory of Pitt the Younger; the Whigs were the friends of trade, finance, and nonconformist religion, cautious advocates of parliamentary reform, and the political descendants of Pitt's great rival, Charles James Fox.

The political landscape was more sharply defined by 'connexions' and 'interests'. Connexions were rooted in personal loyalty. Some were formed when electoral magnates such as the Duke of Newcastle dictated the votes of the MPs, and this was part of the 'Old Corruption' against which reformers railed. Others emerged when statesmen inspired loyalty among the backbenchers: through his insouciant brilliance, George Canning, the Foreign Secretary, had a following of 'Canningites'. In contrast, 'interests' comprised disparate figures – not just MPs, but financiers, clergymen, intellectuals, and publishers – who were united by specific anxieties. Members of the landed interest, whether Whig or Tory, united behind the Corn Laws that protected British farmers even while the same issue split the Cabinet. Likewise, the cause of Catholic Emancipation brought together religious liberals, Irish nationalists, and pragmatic imperialists who otherwise agreed on nothing. In this way, the interest was the nineteenth-century equivalent of a political lobby and, without serious competition from the wider public – only one in twenty Britons could vote – it was the formidable political unit of the age.

Few interests were as wealthy and powerful as the West India Interest, which sought to protect and promote the British Caribbean. Since the late eighteenth century, the concerns of the Interest had ranged widely. Its leadership lobbied Westminster for military defence, financial aid in the wake of hurricanes, and protection from foreign sugar. Between 1787 and 1807, the Interest's priority was resisting abolition; from 1823, from the very moment that the abolitionists met in the King's Head, it was resisting slave emancipation. It was a truly national organisation, too, with fearsome strength in the three Atlantic 'out-ports' of Liverpool, Bristol, and Glasgow.[8]

Ships from Liverpool had once carried 40 per cent of the European slave trade and the city's political leaders had been synonymous with slavery. In 1787 all but four of the city's forty councillors had ties to the Caribbean, while over the next two decades all twenty of Liverpool's mayors were slaveholders. Isaac Gascoyne, a retired general of the West India Regiment, served from 1796 as one of Liverpool's two MPs. Unbeloved by many of his constituents, who called him 'Hopper-Arsed Isaac', Gascoyne was ferociously conservative and highlights of his political career included the defence of bull-baiting and securing a better mess allowance for military officers. For part of his tenure in the Commons, Gascoyne was joined by Banastre Tarleton, a major slaveholder and more notoriously the 'Butcher' whose unrepentant violence had made him the bogeyman of American independence. Together, they formed the 'Old Guard' of West Indian slavery. In 1823, Liverpool's West India Association was led by Charles Horsfall, a pioneering dealer in African palm oil and yet another slaveholder who served as the city's mayor.[9]

The West Indies were no less important to Bristol, where the Old Vic Theatre and the colourful houses of Redcliffe Parade and Queen Square were built with slave money, and where the statue of the slave trader Edward Colston once stood as a controversial monument to a municipal past mired in slavery. In the 1820s the city's West India Association was dominated by two families. The first was the Miles dynasty: the grandfather was Bristol's first West Indian chairman; the father owned thousands of slaves; and the son sat in Parliament while moving in conservative circles. The second was the Bright–Meyler connexion led by Henry Bright, an MP who received the dedication of at least one pro-slavery pamphlet. With politics and slavery thus intertwined, Bristol was an obviously West Indian city: *Felix Farley's Bristol Journal* was 'always open to any Article in favour of the Colonial Interest', while the American abolitionist William Lloyd Garrison regarded Bristol and nearby Bath as 'the strong holds of the pro-slavery party'.[10]

The third major 'out-port' was Glasgow, where the docks and slipways of the Clyde had long been animated by colonial produce, especially tobacco from Virginia and the Carolinas. American independence had caused 'decay' in Glaswegian fortunes, but the city's merchants had taken quickly to trading in Demeraran sugar. The local West India Association was peopled with Glasgow's most prominent businessmen, among them the stupendously wealthy Colin Campbell of Colgrain and the banker James Ewing, whose mansion stood on the site of Queen Street Station. Glasgow's most notorious 'West Indian', however, was James MacQueen. An irascible, rough-hewn, middle-aged merchant who also owned the *Glasgow Courier* newspaper, MacQueen's ranting, hellfire-and-brimstone denunciations of the Anti-Slavery Society unnerved the patrician leaders of the Interest but earned him a reputation as 'the Goliath of the Colonial Host' nonetheless.[11]

The core of the Interest, and the body to which the provincial associations deferred, was the London Society of West India Planters and Merchants. Until the 1820s, Interest meetings were split between the City of London, where the merchant-princes reigned, and the West End, where the absentee planters made their fashionable homes; the fight over emancipation swung this feud in favour of the West End, since it now made sense to operate closer to Westminster. The Thatch'd House and the Crown & Anchor taverns on the Strand played host occasionally but most meetings took place at the West India Club House at 60 St James's Street, off Piccadilly, which was a leisurely fifteen-minute stroll from the Audley Square residence of the Interest's chairman, Charles Rose Ellis. The heir to five planta-tions, Ellis had studied briefly at Oxford before entering Parliament at the age of twenty-two: barely old enough to vote, he paid £200,000 in today's money for the seat of Heytesbury. Although a limited speaker and never a serious candidate for front-bench business, Ellis was a respected operative who excelled in the personal politics of favour and patronage. It also helped that he was the best friend of George Canning, who was probably the most influential figure in British politics. Indeed, Ellis was one of the few 'who at any moment could enter Canning's private room', and this friendship was invalu-able to the Interest.[12]

The Anti-Slavery Society set up headquarters at 18 Aldermanbury, a stone's throw from the London Guildhall. Its central committee would be chaired by William Smith, a radical MP and long-time member of the Clapham Sect – the reformist Christian community to which Macaulay, Stephen, and Wilberforce belonged – but subcom-mittees conducted the main part of the Society's business. While nobody used the word, a three-pronged 'strategy' emerged. The Home Correspondence Committee took charge of the first front of this war on slavery, contacting 'known friends of the cause' to encourage the formation of local chapters of the parent Society. In modern parlance, this was the anti-slavery 'ground game': resurrecting old networks, and energising activists. Dublin, Belfast, and Neath became regional hubs of the network, while committees in Liverpool and Manchester took command of the north-west and Yorkshire. Too many places, however, fell between London's and Liverpool's spheres of influence,

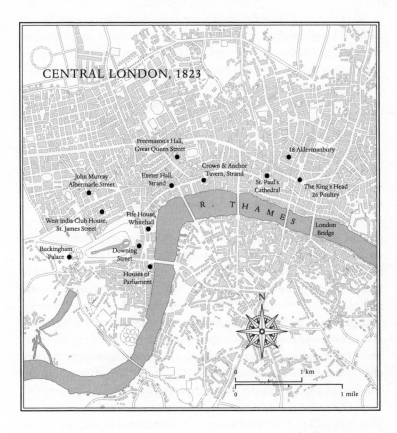

CENTRAL LONDON, 1823

Freemason's Hall, Great Queen Street

18 Aldermanbury

Crown & Anchor Tavern, Strand

John Murray Albermarle Street

Exeter Hall, Strand

St. Paul's Cathedral

The King's Head 26 Poultry

R. THAMES

West India Club House, St. James Street

Fife House, Whitehall

London Bridge

Buckingham Palace

Downing Street

Houses of Parliament

N

0   1 km

0   1 mile

and so James Cropper suggested sending forth an emissary to serve as a lightning rod for anti-slavery sentiment. Cropper pledged £500 to finance such a tour and he declared that only one man could fulfil this mission: Thomas Clarkson. The organisational heartbeat of the earlier campaign against the slave trade, Clarkson had not been at the King's Head, but he was immediately invited to join the Society. 'We have put thy name on the Committee,' a friend told him, 'in the midst of those, with whom thou hast always delighted to work.' Despite being sixty-three, infirm, and short-sighted, Clarkson answered Cropper's call. Working with Macaulay, he made a list of 597 potential contacts in the provinces, hauled himself onto a horse, and set off across Britain.[13]

At each stop, Clarkson followed a simple, repetitive routine. Before all else, he sought out the first person on Macaulay's list. Should he prove dissatisfied with the 'quality' of that person – in Carlisle, he feared that one man would put the campaign into 'low hands' – Clarkson worked his way down the list until he anointed a chairman. He then sought out local grandees, 'half a dozen Persons of Responsibility', with whom he could organise an anti-slavery meeting. Such persons were often lawyers, bankers, doctors, clergymen, and industrialists and, by means of their own networks, Clarkson promoted that meeting: newspapers carried advertisements; friends cajoled friends into attending; and the Quakers of Birmingham used their stewardship of the municipal music festival to publicise Clarkson's mission.[14]

The great weapon on this front was the petition, a declaration on parchment to which hundreds and often thousands of people put their names. In the first year of the campaign, 777 petitions from every British county were laid before Parliament and, for Clarkson, this was the essential aspect of the whole movement. 'Will not an uninterrupted Chain of Petitions,' he asked, 'show Ministers that [the slaves] will not be forsaken ... will not the voice of the Nation, thus displayed, show the Planters the impossibility of a successful resistance, and will they not therefore be more inclined to submit?' Proof that petitions mattered was found in the irritation they caused to West Indians and their allies: one pro-slavery newspaper in Macclesfield raged that the abolitionists had 'converted a most useful engine of influential control over the government into a mere fool's bauble, which any impudent mountebank may shake at his pleasure'.[15]

Not everything went smoothly on Clarkson's travels. He knew that the Interest was 'labouring to frighten the Government and to deter it' from taking action and he beseeched colleagues 'against yielding too easily ... to the Clamours ... of the West Indian opposition'. There were also local, but serious, difficulties. In Lincolnshire, Clarkson found that Whigs were willing allies but Tories were not. In Cheshire, the Tory vicar of Middlewich refused to join the local association because too many Whigs were involved. And from Lichfield, Clarkson made the 'sad report of the Cathedral & its influence on the Inhabitants, so that none will stir [in favour of abolition] till they know the Minds of the Cathedral'. Yet after months of constant touring – of strange beds, backaches, and cold rides along potholed roads – Clarkson had helped to form more than 150 anti-slavery chapters in the provinces. It was the making of a formidable political machine: 'Give us another year,' Clarkson wrote, 'and the whole Kingdom will be roused.'[16]

The second anti-slavery front, supervised by the Publications and Periodical Press committees, was literary. In the early nineteenth century, the printed page – more than the hustings or the rally – was the dominant forum for public debate. And true debate there was. While some publications catered to political whims, the absence of formal political parties and the primacy of interest-based politics meant that few Britons read within an ideological bubble. The educated British reader, who in most cases was the British voter, was open to persuasion. The critical vehicle for this debate was the periodical, a monthly or quarterly journal which distilled complex arguments into punchy, digestible articles, and its role in shaping opinion cannot be underplayed. 'The Periodical Press of Great Britain,' it was written, 'is the most powerful moral machine in the world, and exercises a greater influence over the manners and opinions of civilized society than the united eloquence of the bar, the senate, and the pulpit.' Anti-slavery articles found homes in the *Edinburgh Review* and the *Westminster Review*, the two most prominent liberal periodicals. There would also be pamphlets, often in the form of dialogues which spelt out key arguments for the layman, and in his last polemic Wilberforce appealed to the 'religion, justice, and humanity' of Britons on 'behalf of the Negro Slaves'. There were specialist tomes, too, in which intellectual heavyweights built lengthy but compelling cases for slave freedom. James Stephen published a 'delineation' of West Indian slavery which served as an 'admirable text-book' for advocates of emancipation, while Zachary Macaulay's *Negro Slavery* gave readers 'a view of the more prominent features' of slave society.[17]

This propaganda was vital to the growth of the anti-slavery campaign. Clarkson might have been rebuilding the abolitionist network, but this meant preaching to the converted, and beyond the abolitionist faithful there was in fact shocking ignorance about colonial affairs: the *Wakefield and Halifax Journal* reported despairingly of the popular opinion 'that slavery had [already] ceased'. Equally significantly, Britons of the day could distinguish the slave trade from slavery itself: for instance, the Bible appeared to outlaw slave trading but not slave*holding*, so there was no guarantee that an abolitionist in 1807 would be anti-slavery in 1823. To address these problems and to galvanise latent sympathy into an active movement, the Society set about publishing as much material as possible. It was 'highly important', observed Macaulay, 'to raise the public mind'.[18]

But just as Clarkson and Macaulay sought to enlist British readers onto the side of the angels, the West Indians strove to manipulate the reading public into sympathising with the slaveholders, not the enslaved. The fulcrum of this pro-slavery campaign was the Interest's Literary Committee, established in June 1823 to do all that was necessary to protect 'the West India Colonies through the Press'. Funded by the 'pro-slavery rent', a private impost of sixpence that the Interest levied on every cask of sugar, coffee, and rum that came into Britain, the Literary Committee had an annual budget of up to £20,000. Described by their abolitionist foes as 'a kind of secret service money', this was a war chest of almost £1.8 million in today's money.[19]

The tactics of the Literary Committee varied widely. They distributed huge volumes of short pro-slavery tracts, printing a thousand copies, for instance, of a vicious open letter from the journalist William Cobbett to William Wilberforce. There were a thousand copies more of a pro-slavery letter from the government of the Bahamas, which *The Times* praised as 'worth a serious perusal'. In advance of key votes at Westminster, the West Indians took literature straight to the doors of politicians, with copies of a pamphlet by the apostate abolitionist Joseph Sandars being 'left at the Houses of all the Members of both Houses of Parliament'. Even so, the critical West Indian mission was getting pro-slavery material into Britain's leading periodicals. Their key man here was the Mancunian lawyer James Heywood Markland, who was both the literary representative of pro-slavery authors such as Henry Nelson Coleridge, the nephew of the poet, and a founding member of the Roxburghe Club, an exclusive bibliophilic society where Markland rubbed shoulders with dukes, earls, baronets, and Sir Walter Scott. By these means, Markland became the West Indian point of contact with Britain's two foremost conservative publishers, both of whom opened their pages to pro-slavery material: John Murray and William Blackwood.[20]

From Princes Street premises in Edinburgh, William Blackwood had launched his eponymous magazine as a conservative alternative to the liberal *Edinburgh Review*. Combining politics, fiction, economics, and satire, *Blackwood's* was caustic, polemical, and essential reading for Tories and Romantics, attracting submissions from Scott and Coleridge among others. The most reactionary of Britain's major periodicals, *Blackwood's* was a natural ally of the Interest and, from 1823, it was a bastion of the pro-slavery resistance. The Glaswegian merchant James MacQueen was Blackwood's most notorious hack, but the first of his cabal to write about slavery was John Gibson Lockhart. The son-in-law of Walter Scott and a refined man of letters, Lockhart used four articles on 'the West India controversy' to argue that slavery was raising Africans out of 'barbarism' and that the colonies required urgent defence from 'these Wilberforces and Buxtons [who would] ruin the whole body of West Indian proprietors'. Should the Anti-Slavery Society succeed, Lockhart warned that the slaves, whom he claimed were not 'suffering anything like the ... thousandth part of that misery which these people delight in describing', would become 'lawless banditti, revelling in blood'. These four articles are some of the most strident pro-slavery apologetics ever published and they were written sincerely, too: Lockhart refused to submit early copy, telling Blackwood that he 'must have more material, ere I would commit you on a question of such very great moment'. The Interest knew it had a friend in Blackwood: MacQueen told him that 'the West India Gentlemen in London speak highly of your efforts in their cause', while Charles Ellis expressed his 'greatest admiration' of *Blackwood's* and 'how much good' it had done them. It also helped that *Blackwood's* had 'a great circulation in the Colonies', and the Literary Committee rejoiced that its popularity had been 'rendered ... useful to th[e] Interest'.[21]

Pro-slavery arguments were equally welcome in the *Quarterly Review*, the flagship publication of John Murray, who was probably the most influential publisher in the English-speaking world. Byron, Coleridge, Scott, Austen, Irving, and Goethe were on Murray's list and, from 1823, from his Albemarle Street offices in Mayfair, the *Quarterly* 'buffeted' the abolitionists, who duly despised it as 'one of the most effective and mischievous props of the system of West-India

Slavery'. Some of the *Quarterly*'s most explicitly pro-slavery articles were penned by Charles Ellis, the statistical economist Joseph Lowe, and the jurists John Miller and John Taylor Coleridge, the last of whom was another member of the Coleridge clan. The 1825 appointment of a new editor, poached from *Blackwood's*, only entrenched the *Quarterly*'s position: it was none other than John Gibson Lockhart. Besides curating the *Quarterly* towards pro-slavery ends, Murray was a regular publisher of West Indian books, and his correspondence with the Literary Committee confirms this close relationship. For instance, when James Markland negotiated the inclusion of Henry Nelson Coleridge's *Six Months in the West Indies* into Murray's 'Family Library' series, the Jamaican slaveholder and geologist Henry de la Beche offered free illustrations for 'the embellishment of that edition'. Indeed, the Literary Committee held substantial accounts with Murray, and one pro-slavery writer awaited the day that the *Quarterly* would 'destroy ... the [anti-slavery] Parliament of Aldermanbury'. The abolitionists were not blind to Murray's predilection: they attacked his publishing house as 'the great colonial mart in Albemarle Street'.[22]

There was further backing from one of the great institutions of Anglophone culture, the *Gentleman's Magazine*. The first employer of Samuel Johnson and the first publication to call itself a 'magazine', the *Gentleman's* might have been 'open to the Abolitionists', but it was equally receptive to pro-slavery articles: 'It is but fair that those who view their attempts with alarm or distrust', the magazine reasoned, 'should also be heard'. In the decade from 1823 the *Gentleman's* published at least eighteen pro-slavery articles, many of which focused on the supposed 'intellectual and cultural gap between Europeans and Africans' and the 'argument warning Britain against her total economic ruin'. In such national publications, the position of the West India Interest was secure. At a time when ideas were debated seriously, and where column inches were essential to cultivating support, the advantages held by the slaveholders were staggering: in most of Britain's major publications it was slavery, not emancipation, that was preferred. 'I am prepared for a poor report in the newspapers,' lamented Buxton, 'for ... the reporters sympathize with the House in detestation of [anti-] slavery questions.' The abolitionists were also left to wonder 'how many more Journals [were] kept silent by the insidious influence of the 'pro-slavery' rent'.[23]

The third but most important front of the anti-slavery campaign was political: 'the promotion of Parliamentary discussion and investigation, with a view to legislative remedies'. Here, at Westminster, the Society would deploy whatever means it could to promote 'colonial reform'. On the face of things, James Stephen's thirty-four-year-old son, an equally devout abolitionist also called James, was best placed to influence policy: as legal counsel to the Colonial Office, he was privy to all the decisions that would affect the West Indies. Indeed, when a Cabinet minister warned the governor of Jamaica about 'Individuals who bear no good-will to the West India Colonies', the junior Stephen could not have been far from his mind. Stephen, however, was often constrained by the imperative for bureaucratic impartiality: 'The less I have to do with enthusiasts in places of public resort,' he explained to Macaulay, 'the more useful I can really be in private.' Instead, Westminster would be Buxton's domain, but not before Wilberforce raised the standard.[24]

On 18 March 1823, when MPs had finished debating marriage laws and the punishment of mutineers, Wilberforce stood. He held out a petition, signed by British Quakers, which prayed 'for the Abolition of Slavery', and he told the House that it was unconscionable for Great Britain, 'the freest nation that ever existed', to 'allow slavery in any place under its control'. Was it only distance that allowed Britons to tolerate slavery? Wilberforce thought so. 'The sufferance of evil,' he mourned, had endured only 'in consequence of its being removed out of sight.' Disavowing the old spoof that emancipation was not the goal, Wilberforce allowed himself the honour of laying 'the first stone of an edifice which would flourish, at some future period, [as] an ornament to the land'. The petition was read to the House and Wilberforce sat down. His work was done.[25]

Two months later, on 15 May, Buxton took up the reins. A lesser man could have buckled, because in 1823 the House of Commons was home ground for the Interest. Indeed, there were dozens of MPs who were connected to the slave colonies. The 'Jamaican' lobby included the Tory slaveholder Alexander Cray Grant, the Wiltshire playwright

George Watson Taylor, and the pro-slavery polemicist John Rock Grossett; they were joined in the House by the leading jurist Edward Hyde East, the art collector Ralph Bernal, and Charles Long, the grandson of the racist historian Edward Long. Demerara's leading agent was a coarse and foul-mouthed Irishman, William 'Black Billy' Holmes, who as the government's chief whip had curated an intimate knowledge of the 'tastes, wishes, idiosyncrasies, weaknesses, and family connections' of other MPs. The eastern 'Spice Isle' of Grenada was represented by Joseph Marryat, 'a forceful and innovative chairman' of Lloyd's and, as Wilberforce put it, a pro-slavery 'fanatic'. Antiguan MPs included Thomas Byam Martin, a future Admiral of the Fleet, and George Henry Rose, a diplomat whose missions included Berlin and Washington. As for Barbados, there was William Lascelles, the brother of the Earl of Harewood, while St Kitts connected two major financial figures: William Manning, a former governor of the Bank of England, and Alexander Baring, a senior partner in the eponymous bank. Family ties to Trinidad drew the radical Joseph Hume into the fight over slavery, while Tobago was represented by Lord William Douglas, the Lord Commissioner of the Admiralty. It was a dizzying, daunting roster of pro-slavery politicians: these men were leading landowners, bankers, businessmen, sailors, judges, lawyers, and intellectuals, and they were but a portion of the Interest. Their presence in Parliament, combined with West Indian connections in the press, made the political strength of the slaveholders painfully clear.[26]

That night in May, as Buxton stepped out of Wilberforce's shadow, he took aim at the source of these men's wealth and status by laying out a plan for 'ameliorating' and then freeing the enslaved population of the West Indies. Touching on the Haitian Revolution, the corruption of the colonial judiciary, and the strategic threat posed by the United States, Buxton urged the House to atone 'for all the blood spilt in African wars fomented by English capital'. As he neared his crescendo, his language was ever more emotive; even the text of *Hansard* is peppered with exclamation marks. 'The State of Slavery,' he moved at last, 'is repugnant to the principles of the British constitution, and of the Christian religion ... It ought to be gradually abolished throughout the British colonies.'[27]

The government's response was led by the Foreign Secretary, George Canning. The son of an actress and a failed entrepreneur – a parentage that rivals used against him – Canning was the face and the heart of the British government. Having owed his political breakthrough to violent denunciations of the French Revolution in the *Anti-Jacobin Review*, he emerged as a figurehead of British conservatism after the death of Pitt the Younger in 1806. Foreign affairs were Canning's natural ambit and his antagonism towards Lord Castlereagh was the defining political rivalry of the era. Indeed, their 1809 dispute over troop movements led to the most notorious duel in British history: when the two men met at dawn on Putney Heath, Canning – whose second was Charles Ellis – had never before fired a gun, whereas Castlereagh was an accomplished marksman. Canning missed by a distance, and Castlereagh shot Canning in the leg. After spending the 1810s in political exile, Canning was restored to the front bench only by the death of his rival. By August 1822, Castlereagh was overworked, unhappy, and facing allegations – which turned out to be false – of soliciting male prostitutes; when his wife confiscated his razor blades, he slit his own throat with a penknife.[28]

Nine months later, on that momentous night at Westminster, Canning's reply to Buxton was encouraging, at least at first. The Foreign Secretary agreed that it was 'expedient to adopt effectual and decisive measures for ameliorating the condition' of the slaves. He appeared to be amenable to emancipation itself, proposing three of his own resolutions in favour of slave freedom. 'This House looks forward,' read one of them, 'to a progressive improvement in the character of the slave population, such as may prepare them for participation in those civil rights and privileges which are enjoyed by other classes of His Majesty's subjects.' Canning even urged MPs to vote for 'the accomplishment of this purpose, at the earliest period' and stated that, if the House were willing, he would take the proposals to the King at once. This could have been the immediate triumph of the anti-slavery movement, but Buxton had walked into a trap. Most damagingly, Canning had attached impossibly restrictive caveats to his resolutions: even though Buxton himself had been cautious, suggesting that reform should occur only gradually, Canning stipulated that emancipation could happen only if 'compatible with ... the safety of the colonies, and with a fair and equitable consideration of *the interests of private property*'. It was a vague, impossible test, and a mantra that West Indian planters would repeat for a decade.[29]

Buxton knew he had been outmanoeuvred and in private he would 'anathematise' Canning's resolutions in such a way that his friends 'challenge[d] his Quaker descent'. That night, however, he tried to pin Canning down on the question of when emancipation might ever be 'safe'. The Foreign Secretary responded with classic political evasion. 'If I am asked whether I can maintain the proposition that the progeny of slaves must be eternally slaves ... I am not at liberty to throw out a hasty opinion upon that ... most important question.' Exasperated and exhausted, Buxton loosed one last arrow by demanding Canning's thoughts on *how*, not when, emancipation could be achieved. Ever nimble, Canning ducked again. 'I abjure the principle of perpetual slavery,' he proclaimed, 'but I am not prepared now to state in what way I would set about the accomplishment of the object.' Defeated for the evening, Buxton withdrew his motion, and the House adopted Canning's resolutions unanimously.[30]

Historians have paid scant attention to this chapter of Canning's career, but his opposition to emancipation was deep-seated. He 'never read Anti-Slavery pamphlets'; he rubbished abolitionist attacks on the government; and he discussed slavery in the language of racial contempt: 'I send you,' he wrote to the Colonial Office, 'a plan for ameliorating niggers.' Moreover, the West Indians knew he was their champion: when Canning's resolutions were put to the House that night in May 1823, even slaveholders voted for them because the 'enemies of emancipation [knew] ... they were worse than unmeaning'. The government might have undertaken to do *something* about slavery, but the West Indians understood that Canning had paid only lip service to Buxton's ideas: if nothing could be done about slavery, nothing now *would* be done. In fact, Canning had planned carefully to prevent the abolitionists from instigating 'measures of Colonial reform' by 'taking the business out of [their] hands', and the colonial agent for Jamaica purred that Canning had 'subverted, in a Masterly manner, the arguments advanced by Mr Buxton'.[31]

Explaining Canning's contempt for the anti-slavery movement is another matter. It is possible that, by ambushing Buxton, he was simply defending his former constituents: until January 1823, he had been MP for the 'West Indian' city of Liverpool, where his major political patron was the Demeraran slaveholder John Gladstone. It is equally possible that Canning was concerned by the potential collapse of British influence in the Caribbean, something that he could not risk in the context of American expansion and rampant French imperialism. Perhaps Canning's position on emancipation was also the product of a world where entrenched concepts of deference and hierarchy made slavery acceptable. Or perhaps Lord Liverpool's ministry simply needed the dozens of West Indian votes in the House of Commons to bolster its majority. Whatever the reasons for Canning's hostility – and a fellow Cabinet minister believed there were 'no extant documents to prove his definite views on the subject' – the abolitionists knew what it meant: if they were going to achieve anything, they had to get past Canning first.

4.

The Ghosts of Bunker Hill

The people here are beginning to get alarmed from the debates of the Parliament at home regarding the emancipation of the slaves, which if it should take place will be a sad thing ... But I hardly think the British Government can sanction anything of the kind. If she does, she will lose the whole of the islands.[1]

John Watt, Jamaica, to his father, September 1823

The colonial interests of the British Empire are about to be immolated on the altars of folly ... surrendered to the fanaticism of a thousand Wilberforces.[2]

Robert James Turnbull, South Carolina, 1824

George Canning's resolutions were calculated to forestall any serious reform of the colonies, and they did not have the force of law – they were not a bill – but in May 1823 the British government had nonetheless committed to do *something* towards slave 'amelioration'. It therefore fell to the Colonial Office and to Lord Bathurst, the sixty-year-old Colonial Secretary who was 'greatly averse to changes', to draft a series of measures for the 'improvement' of the enslaved. In the summer of 1823, he announced eight ameliorative proposals. The first two concerned Christianity: there should be better provision for the religious instruction of the slaves, while Sunday markets should be abolished so that the enslaved could attend church. The next two concerned discipline, regulating the punishment of enslaved men and forbidding the flogging of enslaved women altogether. The fifth proposal, which came too late for Mary Prince, recommended that parents and children, and spouses, should not be separated. Proposals six and seven concerned the legal recognition of the property of the enslaved and the admission of their evidence against white colonists in court. The final proposal encouraged the manumission of those who could afford to buy their own freedom. The West Indian slaveholders who were resident in London declared themselves quite content with the proposals, and so they should have been. They wrote them.[3]

In a chilling demonstration of its influence, the Interest had taken control of the drafting process. Even before Buxton had put his motion before the Commons, the Interest and its 'Committee of 25 April' had started working on measures that would stymie the abolitionist movement politically by *appearing* to make wide-sweeping reforms, but that would in fact cause minimal disruption to the business of sugar cultivation. The Interest was acquiescing in amelioration purely to 'conciliate publick opinion in England' and to 'resist the interference of Parliament'. Even worse, there was no guarantee of the ameliorative policies ever being enacted: when Lord Bathurst issued these measures to the colonies in a circular of 9 July 1823, he merely *recommended* their implementation. Today, we might call this 'regulatory capture': as Lord Bathurst confessed, his 'Instructions contain[ed] nothing but what the Committee of West India Planters <u>authorized me to believe was fit & right to be done</u>'.[4]

In the summer of 1823, the political atmosphere in the Caribbean was febrile, for news of the anti-slavery campaign and the very *discussion* of emancipation had provoked the fury of the colonists. The Speaker of the Dominican Assembly had written to his counterpart in Tobago to urge coordinated resistance. 'Let us ... combine our Efforts and ... mark our firm Determination', he begged, 'never to consent to kiss the rod ... but with one voice denounce in the face of the World the blind fanaticism of "the [anti-slavery] Saints"'. In June, parroting the same messages of defiance and disgust, the *Jamaica Journal* launched a withering attack on London's politicians, praying that MPs would 'cleanse their consciences, which are corrupt [and] break with their false allies, who are the Saints'. The *Colonial Register* soon concluded that the colonists would never submit to 'the degradation of having our internal interests regulated by the Commons of Great Britain'.[5]

The August packet, which delivered Bathurst's circular into this bear pit, alerted the resident colonists to something even more 'sinister': the London Interest, which had failed to explain the disingenuous nature of the ameliorative measures, now appeared to be colluding with Parliament to jeopardise colonial liberties. Riding into Spanish Town from their parishes, the members of the Jamaican House of Assembly declared that 'the blood which flows in their veins is British blood' and that they would resist 'every encroachment of despotic power'. Accordingly, the House threatened that Jamaica could soon be 'as lost to the Mother-Country, as St Domingo is to France'. Twelve assemblymen even voted to impeach Lord Bathurst, whom they ridiculed as 'a nursery-lamp' in comparison to the shining lights of great British statesmen. Holding their ground in the countryside, the men of St Ann were equally combative, 'bound by every law, human and divine, to assert th[eir] rights' as free-born Britons. They wrote to George Hibbert, their agent in London, and demanded an explanation of the Interest's conduct.[6]

Hibbert was a sixty-six-year-old merchant who had entered West Indian affairs through his family's firm in Manchester. He had since served as the chairman of the West India Dock Company, securing the construction of the colonial quays on the Isle of Dogs, and as the colonial agent for Jamaica. Appointed by colonies to promote their interests in Britain, colonial agents were diplomats, negotiators, journalists, and spies all at once. They played crucial roles in setting terms of trade, arranging military protection, or gutting hostile legislation, and Hibbert – a bibliophile and a founding patron of what became the Royal National Lifeboat Institution – was a master of these arts. In the summer of 1823, Hibbert worked with Charles Ellis to allay the resident slaveholders' fears and he conveyed the party line – and, indeed, the truth – that there was no 'disposition to compromise with Mr Buxton'. But few colonists were convinced, and the Interest's Standing Committee was informed that 'there exists among our friends in Jamaica, a feeling of dissatisfaction and jealousy with respect to the course pursued'. Lord Bathurst meanwhile observed 'a very strong party against Charles Ellis'. Ignorant of Ellis's tactics, the white West Indians were 'dissatisfied with [him] for not fighting a better battle with Canning for them'.[7]

As they continued to ignore – or to misunderstand – the London Interest's plans, a growing number of colonists began to think that, if they could not keep their slaves *within* the British Empire, they should keep them *without*. From Barbados in the east to Jamaica in the west, talk turned to the prospect of seceding from the Empire. And when the packet ships sailed back to Britain – north along the American seaboard, east across the Atlantic – they carried ever-swelling rumours of rebellion. The *Barbadian*, one of the more bellicose colonial newspapers, proclaimed: 'WE CANNOT BE GOVERNED BY TYRANNY ... Your propert[y] must be held sacred ... DEFEND IT WITH YOUR LATEST BREATH!' The *Dominica Chronicle* was no less excitable. 'Rally in defence of your Laws, your properties, and your rights,' it later demanded: 'Sacrifice on the altar of Patriotism all private disputes and animosities!'[8]

In language and sentiment, the echoes of the American Revolution were unmistakable, and these West Indian complaints would rumble on. The journalist William Cobbett, who had spent almost a decade in the United States, reflected that 'the question [in 1823 was] very much like the question of 1776', and the Jamaican absentee Frederick Smyth chose his words precisely when he warned that West Indians would never 'make a voluntary surrender of rights they consider inalienable'. And while the magistrate Anthony Davis conceded that Parliament had not yet 'hit exactly upon a Stamp Act nor a Tea Duty', he believed that Britain had imposed ten times the hardship on the Caribbean than on America. Indeed, as amelioration was debated, pro-slavery writers counselled that another colonial revolution would be the likely consequence of Parliament's 'folly'. The conservative magazine *John Bull* warned that, rather 'than surrender their rights', the colonists would prefer 'a Bunker's Hill' – one of the bloodiest battles of the American Revolution – 'in every colony in the Tropics'. Even a Caribbean Congress was mooted, with the *Barbadian* asking, 'Why are not patriotic associations formed of private individuals, that some energetic, combined effort may be made?' Charles Ellis and the Interest had concocted insincere plans for amelioration as a means of staving off parliamentary interference in the West Indies, but they had seriously misjudged their colonial brethren. 'The flag of England,' warned one of them, 'will not wave another year over a single island in the Western world.'[9]

At other times, British authorities might have paid little heed to this sound and fury. There had been similar threats in the 1780s and '90s over the abolition of the slave trade but, with the colonies so dependent on the Navy for protection from the French, rebellion was always unlikely. Yet by the mid-1820s things had changed; most significantly, the Spanish Empire had collapsed. Initially because of political convulsions in Madrid, and then because of Simón Bolívar's liberating crusades, several Latin American countries – Mexico, Venezuela, New Granada (present-day Colombia), and Ecuador – had declared their independence. The disintegration of Spanish America was especially welcome in Washington, DC, for it allowed John Quincy Adams to negotiate the United States' acquisition of Florida, as well as Spain's retreat from vast swathes of North America. Yet when the restored French monarchy spied the chance to steal the crumbs from Spain's table, the United States stepped brazenly into the breach. In December 1823, acting on a proposal from George Canning, President James Monroe would use the State of the Union Address to warn Europe that the Americas were 'not to be considered as subjects for future colonization by any European powers'. More pointedly, if a European colony decided to cast off the shackles of empire, the United States would take a very dim view of any subsequent efforts to reimpose European control. In other words – and this was an accidental consequence of Canning's original proposal – the American republic was more than a successful example for the would-be revolutionaries of the West Indies; it had also emerged as a potential guardian.[10]

Pro-slavery lobbyists were convinced that the United States was a natural ally. Archibald Alison was a Scottish historian whose later works on the French Revolution rivalled Thomas Carlyle for popularity, and he wrote in *Blackwood's* that the American 'master of the Gulf of Mexico' was waiting for the British West Indies to fall into its hands. James Franklin was a failed merchant who preyed on the generosity of the Interest's Literary Committee, and he warned that the American eagle was ready to 'snatch from the crown of England one of its brightest gems' before replacing the Union Jack with the Star-Spangled Banner. 'Driven to despair at this moment,' reasoned John Gibson Lockhart, 'the thing is not improbable. Jamaica is 5000 miles from Britain, but not 500 from Florida.' A few key figures took the risk of West Indian revolution seriously. The financier Alexander Baring warned the House of Commons of the Caribbean's 'natural connexion with America'. The Duke of Wellington, still the most senior figure in the British military, was urged to consider 'the event of war between the United States and Britain', while General George Walpole – who had suppressed an enslaved uprising in Jamaica in the 1790s – noted both the Americans' designs on Cuba and the urgent need 'to cover the vulnerable side of Jamaica'.[11]

More commonly, the Interest argued that emancipation would cripple the security of the Empire and the Royal Navy in particular. The Caribbean was regarded as the nursery of British sailors and if ships no longer sailed to the slave colonies, what would become of British maritime supremacy? John Barrow, the Admiralty Secretary who wrote the classic account of the *Mutiny on the Bounty*, believed that emancipation would be 'the death-blow of our shipping interest'. The anti-slavery *Edinburgh Review* thought that all this was nonsense and that the Navy would be just as strong 'though we had not a single merchant ship', but the West Indians had a trump card: Horatio Nelson. From the decks of the *Victory*, in the year of his glory at Trafalgar, Nelson had professed himself 'a firm friend' to the colonies. 'I was bred … in the good old school,' he wrote, 'and taught to appreciate the value of our West India possessions, and neither in the field, nor in the Senate, shall their rights be infringed, while I have an arm to fight in their defence, or a tongue to launch my voice against the damnable cruel doctrine of Wilberforce, and his hypocritical allies.'[12]

In the late summer and early autumn of 1823, even though Canning had hijacked their plans, the abolitionists persisted in their pursuit of emancipation. The anti-slavery campaign's parliamentary leader Thomas Fowell Buxton was glad-handing key figures in the House of Commons; the young lawyer James Stephen was exerting influence where he could at the Colonial Office; the stern Scottish businessman Zachary Macaulay was editing a stream of anti-slavery publications; and despite his age and creaking back, Thomas Clarkson was rallying grass-roots campaigners in the provinces. Four thousand miles away, as they refused to tolerate even the most superficial commitment to amelioration, white West Indians stood in defiance of the government *and* their representatives in London. Instead of making minor, inexpensive changes to the slave system, they were calling for violent resistance; and if Britain interfered any further with their 'domestic' concerns, they promised to reprise the scenes of Yorktown and Saratoga across the Caribbean. The powder keg was full. And then came the news from Demerara.

At first, with only sketchy details available, many observers feared a revolt on the scale of Saint Domingue: 'The next intelligence,' noted *The Times*, 'is expected with much anxiety.' And when full accounts arrived, the abolitionists read them in horror. In 1816, rumours about the slave registry had provoked rebellion on Barbados; earlier in 1823, as he prepared his motion for Parliament, Buxton had worried that proposing emancipation could provoke a similar crisis. 'If a servile war should break out, and 50,000 perish,' he asked, 'how should I like that?' Now, with evidence mounting that the Demeraran rebels had been provoked by 'loose talk' about freedom, Buxton knew that the West Indians would depict even the most moderate plan for emancipation as incompatible, in the words of Canning's resolutions, 'with the safety of the colonies'.[13]

The abolitionists therefore tried desperately to downplay the extent of the rebellion. The *Edinburgh Review* described it as 'a slight commotion ... among the Negroes'. The *Christian Observer*, an evangelical magazine edited by Zachary Macaulay, compared the insurrection to a strike by Cornish miners, Welsh ironworkers, Lancashire weavers, or 'the keel men of the Tyne'. The *Hull Advertiser*, which Thomas Clarkson had brought into the abolitionist fold, argued that slavery in Demerara was harsh enough 'to goad any human being into resistance', while in York the Revd James Parsons proclaimed that the blame lay 'with the planters themselves, [with] the iron hand of oppression being ever raised against the negroes'.[14]

Of course, the Interest's friends in the conservative press narrated the rebellion as a near-disaster, and they knew exactly who to blame. It was a simple case of cause and effect: if Buxton had not agitated the issue, there would not have been a rebellion. Consequently, and perversely, the West Indians delighted in the reports of bloodshed and distress. The Jamaican agent George Hibbert reflected that the news from the South American shoreline was making 'a useful impression [in London] upon a very respectable portion of the Public [who were now] sensible of the error of giving way to these restless innovations [regarding slavery]'. As the anger spread, the abolitionists were decried as traitors to the Empire and condemned as if they had led the rebellion themselves. Wilberforce received an anonymous letter consisting of only three words: 'Thou vile hypocrite'. Thomas Clarkson, who had been traversing Britain, now charged back to London to defend the Anti-Slavery Society from charges of infamy. Even friends began to doubt the wisdom of the abolitionist leadership. Aghast at the ruin into which his plans were falling, Buxton questioned whether there was 'a more unpopular individual than myself in the House'.[15]

The effects on high politics were equally chilling. The Duke of Wellington thought the Rebellion was 'the most serious event, in relation to our military force, that has occurred for a great length of time' and for this he blamed 'the temper in which the question of emancipation has avowedly put all the negroes'. Moreover, at the very moment that Wilberforce was pleading with Canning to enforce amelioration in the colonies, the Foreign Secretary received the official report of the rebellion, 'which was very formidable in appearance'. Canning was briefed that the cry of the rebels was 'immediate unqualified freedom' and now, more than ever, he was dissuaded of the propriety of emancipation. 'I am sure you do not doubt my sincerity as to the good of the Blacks,' he told Wilberforce, 'but I confess I am not prepared to sacrifice all my white fellow countrymen to that object.' Canning's belief in abolitionist guilt was reinforced by his private secretary, Augustus Stapleton, who believed that 'the insurrection in Demerara had been instigated by Wilberforce, Buxton, and co[mpany]', and Wilberforce lamented to Macaulay that 'Canning is becoming more our enemy than formerly'. The Rebellion also outed another Cabinet minister as an enemy to slave emancipation. This was William Huskisson, the fifty-three-year-old President of the Board of Trade who had succeeded Canning as MP for Liverpool.[16]

A member of the Midlands minor gentry, Huskisson had received an unusual education at the hands of his great-uncle, a polymath who counted Benjamin Franklin, Thomas Jefferson, and the French philosopher Baron d'Holbach among his friends. These stimulating formative years set Huskisson apart from his rivals, and an aptitude for economics made him the Tories' expert on paper money, tariffs, sinking funds, and the gold standard. Technocratic brilliance, however, did not guarantee progress: Canning regarded Huskisson as the 'best practical man of business in England', but he was incapable of the machinations and compromise required of top-level politicians. It took until 1823 for Huskisson's abilities to win through, when he was appointed to the Board of Trade, an office with authority over imperial economics, overseas commerce, and duties. Given the obvious relevance of that department to the West Indies, it was crucial for the slaveholders to have a sympathetic minister in charge of it, and Huskisson was their man.[17]

A letter written to John Gladstone in the aftermath of the Demerara Rebellion gives the clearest evidence of Huskisson's opinions. First, he affirmed that the ministry had tried to stop emancipation ever becoming a parliamentary issue, telling Gladstone that 'the Govt did everything in its power to prevent Buxton's Motion altogether'. Second, he condemned the idea of immediate emancipation as madness. 'It is only by gradual amelioration,' Huskisson reasoned, 'by moral and religious improvement ... by imperceptibly creating better domestic habits and feelings among the Slaves' that freedom would ever be practical. Third, he absolved the Demerarans of blame; rather, it was 'the fault, and a heavy one it is, of Wilberforce and his associates'. This letter attained unwanted fame. Although it had been sent privately, Gladstone had shown it to confidants who secretly transmitted copies to Jamaica. Those copies then made their way back to England, where the letter was printed in *The Times*. The affair mortified Gladstone, embarrassed Huskisson – who had tried to construct a facade of neutrality – and enraged the abolitionists. The Interest, however, was delighted, and it rallied around Huskisson. The *Dominica Chronicle* would meanwhile hail him as 'perhaps the most important, and the most useful Member of the British legislature'.[18]

Huskisson's scepticism towards emancipation was given further expression in an October 1823 letter to the Liverpool merchant John Bolton in which he discussed the 'evil' that had informed the 'rebellious Conspiracy'. The next week, Huskisson joined Canning in resigning his honorary office with the African Institution, explaining to Zachary Macaulay that simply because a man's name stood among 'the List of Governors of an Institution', it did not imply 'any participation in their labours, nor an unqualified adoption of all their sentiments'. Indeed, he told Canning that he needed to 'get out as soon as [I] can', and there were further declarations in January 1824, when

Huskisson told the abolitionist Joseph Sandars that only a 'bold Philanthropist' could ever risk all the 'deplorable consequences' that would arise from 'impatient interference to obtain that Emancipation'. Huskisson's liberal economics might well have threatened West Indian trade, for he was determined to 'wean' the planters off their tariffs, but he was no friend to freedom.[19]

As Demeraran officials were mopping up the remnants of the rebellion, they too had blamed the Anti-Slavery Society. But the colonial authorities had also identified a local cause, and only days after the outbreak of the rebellion they had arrested a young English missionary, John Smith. Sent to Demerara by the London Missionary Society (the LMS), his mission was simple: to convert the enslaved of the colony to Christianity. Preaching on Sundays at the Bethel Chapel, Smith was wildly popular among the enslaved: within months, he had a congregation of eighty and he ministered to hundreds more during the week. His welcome from the colonial authorities was somewhat cooler. Across the British West Indies, most missionaries were regarded as dangerous, as threats to the colonial order: should they teach the enslaved to read or write, or should they preach about a liberating Christian justice, discontent was thought to follow. Upon presenting his papers to Governor Murray, Smith was therefore warned *not* to interfere between master and slave, an instruction which accorded with his orders from the LMS: 'Not a word must escape you in public or private which might render the slaves displeased with their masters or dissatisfied with their station'. Suspicion of Smith endured nonetheless and he made special enemies of military men who despised the fondness that Smith felt for the enslaved. So, when it emerged that some of the leading rebels were among his black congregation, the vengeful authorities wasted no time in throwing Smith into the Georgetown jail.[20]

Smith's court martial began two months later. It was a carefully managed affair that lasted twenty-seven days, and it was a sham. Although Smith was given legal representation, his lawyer was frequently absent and he was often obliged to conduct his own defence. He was charged with promoting 'discontent and dissatisfaction in the minds of the negro slaves', with inciting them to rebel 'against the peace', and with advising Quamina Gladstone on the plans for rebellion. (The colonial authorities simply could not fathom that the enslaved might have planned their own uprising.) Smith pleaded not guilty, but that would not matter. Over the course of the next four weeks, the prosecution produced dozens of pardoned rebels who now, as a condition of their release, testified that Smith had abused his influence as a missionary to encourage revolution.[21]

The star witness for the prosecution was none other than Jack Gladstone, Quamina's son. Following his capture at Chateau Margo, Jack had spent months in a Georgetown jail-cell, stewing over his choices. On the one hand, he could testify truthfully and exonerate Smith, but condemn himself to execution; on the other, he could commit perjury and risk whatever 'mercy' the British might show him. Before the court martial, Jack sacrificed Smith's life for his own. According to his testimony, the lessons and Scriptural readings in Smith's chapel were designed to render the rebels 'dissatisfied with our situations as slaves'. Had there been 'no Methodists' in Demerara, he explained, 'there would have been no revolt'; the court ignored the fact that Smith was *not* a Methodist. For more than a year afterwards, the Colonial Office debated 'what is to be done with that slave'. It was not until 1825 that John Gladstone, Jack's owner, received word that 'the Slave Jack . . . ha[d] been removed from Demerara and enrolled as a Military Labourer in St Lucia'.[22]

Several more rebels confirmed the 'truth' of Jack Gladstone's evidence. Bristol, a deacon at the Methodist chapel, absolved Quamina of guilt by declaring that the elder Gladstone had wished for the rebels only to 'lay down their tools', but he had no doubt about Smith's guilt. Recalling that Smith preached frequently about how Moses had delivered the Israelites 'from the hands of Pharaoh', Bristol testified that his fellow rebels talked at length about 'the fighting of the Israelites when they go to war'. The rebels of Demerara had straightforwardly 'applied the story of the Israelites and the Jews, and put it on themselves'. For the white colonists, the case against Smith could not have been plainer, but if the court required further proof it was furnished by Quamina's corpse. When the British hunting party had killed the rebel leader, they claimed to have found a Bible on his person that was marked at Joshua 8:1: 'Fear not, neither be thou dismayed; take all the people of war with you, and rise'. Smith was convicted and sentenced to death. While awaiting execution, and pending an appeal to London, he died in his cell of 'consumption'.[23]

Back in Britain, the pro-slavery press lauded the Demeraran authorities for their conduct. They argued that Smith's revolutionary rhetoric, encouraged by his anti-slavery masters in London, had been the sole and root cause of the Rebellion. Evoking images of the English Civil War, and conflating anti-slavery agitation with political fanaticism, Buxton and his brethren were damned as the architects of a 'GRAND PURITAN SCHEME'. Nor could the pro-slavery press discern a problem with Smith's court martial. The *Barbados Mercury* reported that 'this unfortunate man had the utmost attention and kindness shown to him by the humane keeper of the prison ... His apartment was airy and commodious, and he had always at his command every comfort which his taste fancied'. Even Cabinet ministers signalled their approval. Although William Huskisson believed that Smith's death was 'most embarrassing' for the Demerarans, he maintained that, 'after reading attentively the Minutes and Proceedings of the Court Martial ... there were circumstances of suspicion against Mr Smith quite sufficient to warrant his being put on trial'.[24]

Yet what the Demeraran officials had failed to grasp was that, by pinning the blame on Smith, they had in fact created the first white martyr of the abolitionist campaign. Early reports of Smith's arrest had piqued the British public interest and updates from Demerara were sought urgently. In London, Derby, Leicester, Leeds, and Manchester, Smith's persecution fuelled impassioned debate in parlours, pubs, and council chambers, but especially in church halls. In order to defend Smith's honour, the LMS published hundreds of documents from the trial, exposing the corruption of the colonial courts to a furious public readership. Two hundred petitions protesting Smith's treatment were generated in eleven days and, when news broke of his death in prison, there was fury: 'The day of reckoning,' wrote Wilberforce, 'will come.'[25]

Months later, in one of the great anti-slavery speeches, Henry Brougham declared to the House of Commons that Smith's trial had seen more illegality and more violation of justice 'in substance and in form, than in the whole history of modern times'. At the time, Brougham was forty-five and a liberal, almost radical Whig MP. He was priggish, self-righteous, and often unlikeable: as the essayist William Hazlitt described him, Brougham was 'overcome by no false modesty, no deference to others'. Even so, thanks to his tireless work at the *Edinburgh Review* and in Parliament, not to mention his stirring defence of Queen Caroline from the boorish George IV, Brougham had become one of Britain's leading 'progressive' voices. He had been there in the King's Head at the founding of the Anti-Slavery Society, and he knew the importance of the moment. Now, 'the nation … began to awaken to the truth, and … the religious public in England was strongly enlisted on behalf of the oppressed missionaries and [the slaves]'.[26]

Abolitionist leaders accepted that Smith's cause célèbre had done more to bring slavery to widespread attention than any pamphlet or parliamentary manoeuvre ever could. Thomas Clarkson believed that 'this single case of a persecuted individual … produced an impression far more general and more deep than all that had ever been written or declaimed against the system of West India slavery', while one historian has suggested that Smith's death in prison was 'fatal to Slavery in the West Indies in the same degree as the execution of [the abolitionist] John Brown was its deathblow in the United States'. Yet by the same token, this new alliance between Dissenting Christians and the Anti-Slavery Society would create unintended, unbearable difficulties for those missionaries who remained at work in the colonies.[27]

5.

Deliver Us from Evil

If it be meant that in the Christian religion there is a special denun-
ciation against slavery, that slavery and Christianity cannot exist
together – I think the hon. gentleman himself must admit that the
proposition is historically false ... One peculiar characteristic of the
Christian dispensation, if I must venture in this place upon such a
theme, is, that it has accommodated itself to all states of society ... If
it has added lustre to the sceptre of the sovereign, it has equally been
the consolation of the slave.[1]

George Canning, House of Commons, 1823

William Shrewsbury grew up in Kent among the lower 'middling
sorts' of the early nineteenth century. His mother was a domestic
servant, his father was a grocer and tailor, and this was an aspirational
family which at first did not blink at paying for William's schooling.
Yet when a downturn in fortunes curtailed his formal education, the
ten-year-old William elected to teach himself. He learned Hebrew and
Greek and, by devouring the collected works of John Wesley, he
immersed himself in nonconformist religion. So keen was William's
thirst for knowledge that he embarked on a regimen of sleeping just
two hours a night on hard floorboards so that rest and sloth would
not impede his study; he gave up this experiment after three exhausting
weeks. The works of Wesley nonetheless made a lasting impression,
instilling a fierce religious vigour in the young man. Shrewsbury lay
awake at night, 'thinking of divine objects, and breathing out [his]
desires to God, till [his] his eyes overflowed with tears'. After converting
his parents to Methodism, Shrewsbury became an established figure
on the itinerant preaching circuit of south-east England and, by 1815,

he had secured an appointment as a Methodist missionary to Tortola, one of the Virgin Islands between Puerto Rico and Anguilla. Five years later, he arrived in Barbados, charged with ministering to the spiritual needs of the colony's white *and* black inhabitants.[2]

Barbados was known in Methodist circles as difficult terrain. The dominant Christian institution on the island was the Anglican and deeply conservative Codrington College, which had been endowed by the estate of a major slaveholder. The college was now governed by the Society for the Propagation of the Gospel, which found no hypocrisy in preaching the Gospel whilst owning more than 400 slaves. Moreover, the enslaved of Barbados – Shrewsbury's likely flock – were reputed to be blind to the light. Thomas Coke, the first Methodist to visit the island, had complained in 1788 that 'the Negroes of Barbados are much less prepared for the reception of genuine religion than those of any other island in the West Indies'. Despite these inauspicious circumstances, Shrewsbury worked wonders. When he arrived in Barbados in 1820 there had been only forty Methodists; by 1823, there were ninety full members of his congregation and two hundred more occasional worshippers. They were free *and* slave, black *and* white.[3]

As across the Caribbean, what Christianity 'meant' to enslaved people among Shrewsbury's congregation varied enormously: some took keenly to the liberating, redemptive precepts of Christian teaching; others adapted elements and rituals of African belief systems into a 'syncretic' form of worship; others still ignored the trappings of Christianity altogether, preferring to develop spiritual practices such as obeah, which colonial authorities often persecuted as a form of witchcraft. Among Shrewsbury's white congregants were a local architect and his teenage daughter, Hilaria, whom Shrewsbury married on New Year's Day, 1823. Shrewsbury also put an end to the practice of itineracy. Where missionaries once roamed across colonies, he now gave the Methodist mission a permanent presence by erecting a chapel on land donated by Sarah Ann Gill, a free person of colour. By 1823, at the age of twenty-eight, Shrewsbury had earned a reputation for industry, honesty, and charity. One planter in Grenada would commend him as 'a superior man, who would do honour to any church or society of Christians'.[4]

Shrewsbury still suffered the petty bigotries that were the lot of Dissenting missionaries. Anglican planters were apt to throw open his chapel doors and ruin hymnal melodies by whistling out of tune, or by drumming loudly against the pews. And as news of the nascent anti-slavery campaign arrived in Barbados, and as it became clear that Dissenting churches in Britain *supported* emancipation, Shrewsbury was subjected to ever more serious reproach. He was confronted in the street, attacked in the local newspapers, and accused 'as a villain ... by the great vulgar-merchants' from their shopfronts. The rumour abounded that Shrewsbury was 'an enemy of slavery', and that under a 'garb of sanctity' he was 'undermining the West-India Interest'.[5]

Shrewsbury's standing fell further when his enemies publicised excerpts of a letter that he had written to the *Methodist Magazine* shortly after arriving in Barbados. Here, he had complained that free black Barbadians were 'exceedingly given to profanity' and that 'Swearing, Drunkenness, Fornication, and every other species of immorality, like an overwhelming torrent, overspreads [the island]'. Then there was the condition of the enslaved people on the island, with Shrewsbury lamenting that 'hundreds of them have never heard a single word of religious instruction in their whole lives; and many of them were never in a place of worship; they seem to have no thought of God'. Although Shrewsbury made the full letter available to prove that he did not intend to insult the 'good character' of *white* Barbadians, this episode destroyed whatever remained of his reputation. On an Anglican island, the Methodist was now without friends. But worse was yet to come. When the alleged conspiracies of John Smith were reported in the Barbadian press, this latent vitriol segued into wanton violence. With his fellow missionary accused of inciting the Demeraran rebels, Shrewsbury became the target of a pro-slavery campaign of terror.[6]

On the first Sunday of October 1823, when Shrewsbury's congregation gathered for the evening service, dozens of bloodthirsty Barbadians surrounded his chapel. These were not ruffians or hired muscle: they were merchants, planters, bankers, and lawyers. There were chemists, too, since they had armed themselves with vials of oil, stink bombs, and jars of nitric acid. These weapons had been chosen for the weather: in the sweltering heat, the shuttered windows of the chapel had been left open and now, as the prayers began, the pro-slavery mob began to pelt the congregation. Shrewsbury avoided injury only by ducking; the man standing behind him was not so lucky. One black woman was scarred badly when a corrosive missile exploded on her chest. As part of the congregation fled into the night, and as the rest took cover, Shrewsbury rushed his pregnant wife Hilaria to safety at the back of the chapel. He then returned to the arena. Ordering the worshippers up from their hiding places, and bidding them close the shutters, Shrewsbury finished his sermon over the noise of rocks and glass smashing against the chapel's walls.

This was but the start of things. The next day, when Shrewsbury walked into the colonial capital of Bridgetown to offer £30 as reward for information, he overheard raucous conversations: 'Serve the fellow right!' Nor was help forthcoming from the island's authorities, with one of the magistrates who served on the island's governing Council instead encouraging the vigilantes to return to the chapel and finish the job. On the following Friday, as Shrewsbury prepared to commemorate the hurricane that had devastated Barbados in 1780, he was warned that 'while you are preaching of the storm within doors, you shall have a storm without'.

Though he braced himself, Shrewsbury was taken aback by what awaited him on the following Sunday evening. Lining the length of the street to the chapel was 'an immense concourse of people'. Some were muttering 'threat[s] and slaughters', others wanted blood. The vanguard of the mob, some twenty or thirty men who were 'ready for any mischief', had infiltrated the chapel itself. This time, Hilaria would not hide. She planted herself at the foot of the pulpit and resolved that 'no one would touch the preacher without first trampling her under foot'. As her husband began to preach, the offensive began. Two masked men on horseback came racing towards the chapel, each of them brandishing a sword and a pistol. They planned to launch firecrackers into the chapel, especially 'amongst the females, to set their clothes on fire', but when they found the shutters closed, the masked horsemen resorted to shooting at the chapel's walls.[7]

Shrewsbury survived that second Sunday, but his plight now descended into nightmare. When the magistrate Mr Justice Moore concluded that 'the disturbance [had begun] to wear an alarming aspect' and summoned Shrewsbury to his offices, the missionary was at first relieved by the prospect of judicial protection. But when Moore construed the trouble as *Shrewsbury*'s fault, accusing him of treason, he was thrown into despair. Turning to the governor of Barbados, the soldier Henry Warde, Shrewsbury pleaded: 'The mob are bearing me down!' Warde was sympathetic and 'extremely sorry', but he would not help: farcically, the governor pointed Shrewsbury back towards the magistrates. 'There can be no use in applying to [them],' the young missionary protested. 'They are among the bitterest of my enemies here.'[8]

As Shrewsbury ran from pillar to post, his enemies continued to conspire. That coming Friday, twelve days after the first assault on the chapel, a 'Secret Committee' convened to plan the final defeat of the Methodist. Given that an eyewitness described the Committee as 'a thousand head-strong fools', one may wonder about the degree of secrecy it attained, but that did not matter: this was a very public war. On Sunday 19 October, the Secret Committee marched on Shrewsbury's chapel and, as the Lord rested, the slaveholders of Barbados tore down His house. They broke open the chapel's windows and doors. They tore up the benches and pews. They smashed the pulpit and set fire to the books and bibles that Shrewsbury had used to teach the enslaved. Redirecting their anger towards Shrewsbury's home, they destroyed his furniture, ripped the slate from the roof, and made his linen into flags that were waved in triumph. Exhausted by midnight, they returned in daytime to complete their demolition. The Methodist chapel was compared to 'the temple of Jerusalem – not one stone [was] left upon another'.[9]

Informed by his congregants that the mob had planned on hanging him, Shrewsbury was already in hiding, claiming sanctuary in the house of an Anglican clergyman who at last felt pity. His final escape from the mob was a close-run thing. On the Sunday evening, as he cowered in the dark beneath the window-frame, armed horsemen galloped up to the walls of his shelter, shouting 'Down with all the Methodists!' His pregnant wife Hilaria had hidden in the hut of an enslaved Methodist and, when dawn broke the next morning, she and William took flight. Scrambling down to the coast at Carlisle Bay, they were smuggled onto a boat bound for St Vincent. Hilaria went into labour while at sea. 'I could do nothing but cry to God,' she recalled, 'for no human help could possibly be obtained.' Three hours after they made landfall on St Vincent, she gave birth to a son. 'In remembrance of my sorrows,' Shrewsbury wrote, 'we designed to name him Jeremiah.'[10]

Back on Barbados, the destruction of the chapel was praised in a pair of handbills as 'High-handed work'. The pro-slavery mob acclaimed the attacks as a 'great and signal triumph over Methodism' and as justified retaliation for Shrewsbury's 'unmerited and unprovoked attacks ... upon the community'. Following an inquiry into events, the Councilmen of Barbados agreed: even if the Demerara Rebellion had heightened tensions, Shrewsbury's letter of 1820, where he had given 'a false and calumnious representation' of Barbados, was at root '*highly culpable*'. It followed that nobody was convicted for Shrewsbury's persecution, not even after Governor Warde offered a reward of £100. Perhaps the colonists approved of the vandals, who claimed they were 'supported by ... nine-tenths of the community'. Or perhaps the pro-slavery mob scared witnesses into silence: public notices explained that anyone brave enough to come forward would 'receive that punishment which their crimes will justly deserve'. This was mob rule.[11]

For missionaries, surviving in the West Indies was now a case of walking a tightrope. The Wesleyan Missionary Society instructed its emissaries that 'your only business is to promote the moral and religious improvement of the slaves without ... interfering with their civil condition'. Talking or writing about slavery was off-limits. Yet when neutrality did not secure their safety, the Wesleyan missionaries in Jamaica printed some carefully worded resolutions in the island's *Royal Gazette*, denying that slavery was 'incompatible' with Christianity and proclaiming that emancipation 'would be a general calamity'. It seems they went too far. At an emergency meeting at Hatton Garden, their superiors in the Wesleyan Society denounced those resolutions as 'unguarded and improper'. The chairman and secretary of the Jamaican mission were recalled in disgrace.[12]

Other missionaries could not stomach the deceit of neutrality. William Knibb was an impulsive young man from the Midlands who had often followed in the footsteps of his elder brother, Thomas. When William was twelve, he and Thomas had left their home in Kettering to work as apprentices to a printer in Bristol. Thomas also set William an example of Christian devotion, being such a pious child that he bought his own candles to illuminate the scriptural study that he undertook from four o'clock each morning. And when William sailed for Jamaica under the auspices of the Baptist Missionary Society, he followed his brother's lead for the last time: Thomas had died in Jamaica while serving as a pastor, and William was his replacement.[13]

That William Knibb ever made it to the colonies was something of a miracle. His ship was nearly wrecked in the English Channel, where the sea was 'boiling with the most tremendous fury': the captain was ready to cut away the masts and rigging, Knibb wrote in his journal, 'when a breeze sprang up from the west and saved us'. The rest of the voyage was blessed with good weather, but it was not without drama. In one terrifying episode, a pitch kettle boiled over, caught fire, and threatened to engulf the ship before being extinguished. And fire was not the last threat to safe passage. As they neared the Caribbean, the preacher spent time 'painting the guns' that the crew were 'getting in readiness ... should the pirates bear down upon us, who much infest the coast, and commit dreadful depredations, generally murdering all they happen to board'. For once, Knibb was not content to trust in divine providence: 'We are well armed,' he recorded, 'having eight guns, and a quantity of muskets, swords, sabres, and boarding-pikes.'[14]

When he reached Jamaica, Knibb enjoyed a 'hearty reception' from the island's six resident Baptists and he rejoiced in their fellowship, but the honeymoon was brief. Knibb had long loathed the *idea* of slavery and, en route to Jamaica, he had fought with a pro-slavery passenger whom he damned as 'an odious picture of the brutalizing and immoral tendency of this execrable system'. Afterwards, he prayed to God that he would 'never view with indifference a system of so infernal a nature', and he never would. In fact, life in Jamaica only kindled Knibb's hatred of slavery. Weeks after settling near Kingston, where he taught at a school, he wrote to his mother that 'the cursed blast of slavery, has, like a pestilence, withered almost every moral bloom' in Jamaica. He could not understand 'how any person can feel a union with ... such a child of hell' and he looked upon slavery 'as one of the most odious monsters that ever disgraced the earth'.[15]

Even if the colonists aspired to imitate genteel British society, Knibb was sickened by the apparent depravity of Jamaican life. Colonial predilections for liquor and promiscuity appalled him, and he wrote that Jamaica was 'the land of sin, disease, and death, where Satan reigns with awful power': the people were wicked, and the Sabbath was 'violated'. As the historian Catherine Hall has put it, Knibb and other missionaries had sought to build 'a new Jerusalem in Jamaica', a Christian society built around 'a chapel, a mission school, and a mission house'. What they *found*, however, despite the foundation of the Anglican dioceses of Barbados and Jamaica, was a tropical Gomorrah: if the Puritans had emigrated to America to establish a godly realm on earth, it appeared that Caribbean colonists had left Britain to escape God altogether.[16]

More urgently, Knibb had arrived in a world where Dissenting missionaries were despised and, in the cases of Smith and Shrewsbury, treated with outright violence. Historians have often treated missionaries as *agents* of the British Empire, as men and women whose evangelisation of non-white, indigenous peoples created the psychological conditions in which economic and military dominion could be established. In that way, missionaries were the first half of the famous formulation, 'the Bible and the Flag'. In the West Indies, however, at least in the 1820s, sectarian missionaries were often regarded as the *enemies* of empire. William Knibb recognised this immediately. White Jamaicans would rejoice, he wrote, 'if all the servants of God were banished out of the land'. And on those occasions when Knibb did not suffer this prejudice personally, he would read about it in the press: the *Jamaica Courant* condemned missionaries as men who 'pretend[ed] to preach and teach the mild and benign doctrines of our Saviour to our slaves, but whose souls are bent upon the destruction of the fairest portion of the British Empire'.[17]

Still, it would be wrong to think that slaveholders and the Interest at home were inimical to *all* religion. In an historical context where Christian virtue was essential to political respectability, slaveholders were stung by the allegations of ungodly conduct. This was why 1823's phantom measures of amelioration had referred to 'the indispensable necessity of religious instruction' and of appropriating the Sabbath 'to the purposes of rest'. This was why Jamaican colonists such as Alexander Barclay were 'outraged' by allegations of indecency: 'Little more than 20 years ago,' he protested, 'the churches were so ill attended that in some of the country parishes the doors frequently were not even opened on Sunday,' whereas by the 1820s the number of Jamaican churches had 'doubled, nay trebled'. And this was why senior members of the Interest such as Charles Ellis, George Hibbert, and James Markland had installed themselves on the governing board of the Society for the Conversion and Religious Instruction and Education of the Negro Slaves, an Anglican body which pursued 'the Advancement or Propagation of the Christian Religion amongst Infidels'. The Bishop of London commended their liberal contributions to the Society's funds as being made 'in the spirit of enlightened humanity'.[18]

Accordingly, *conservative* clergymen were most welcome in the slave colonies. The Moravian Church, for instance, was noted for its institutional ambivalence towards slavery and for their missionaries' long-standing instructions 'not to play any part in party politics'. Unsurprisingly, the Interest's Literary Committee was 'most cordially disposed to encourage the Moravian Missions' and even proposed to form a fund for their benefit. The slaveholding geologist Henry de la Beche would meanwhile describe the Moravians' establishments in Jamaica as 'highly useful'. Recent scholarship has also explored how, in formerly Spanish colonies such as Trinidad, 'collaboration between the Catholic Church and the British state ... was extensive', driven by 'a mutual desire to assert control over colonies with large non-white and non-British Catholic populations'.[19]

Most welcome of all was George Wilson Bridges, an odious Oxford graduate and the Anglican rector of several parishes in north-western Jamaica. From 1823, Revd Bridges reacted to the abolitionist campaign with a series of venomous pro-slavery texts that have prompted historians to characterise him as 'a bigot' and 'a lunatic'. He deserves these epithets. Bridges' first publication was a pamphlet, *A Voice from Jamaica*, which sought to rebut Wilberforce's *Appeal*. He followed this with *Dreams of Dulocracy*, a diatribe which condemned the Saints for their 'puritanical' enthusiasm and the gullible British public for believing the abolitionists. The *Barbadian* reprinted that work in full, noting that 'we should be doing the Reverend a manifest injustice, were we to quote scantily from his book'. The magnum opus of Bridges' literary career was yet to come. Published in London by John Murray, *The Annals of Jamaica* was a sprawling history of the island in which Bridges sounded forth on the merits of slaveholding. Jamaica's *Royal Gazette* previewed the *Annals* as 'replete with new and interesting matter' and the island's House of Assembly gave £700 as a reward for the 'qualifications and talents' on display.[20]

It followed that a wide range of often irreconcilable attitudes towards slavery prevailed among Christian ministers. Some of them, like William Knibb, went to the Caribbean to undermine the foundations of slavery by addressing the relative ignorance that it foisted upon the enslaved. Others were content to ignore the worst of the slave system and to work within the constraints that the colonial authorities imposed. Others still, like George Wilson Bridges, used Christianity to bind the chains forced upon the enslaved. Yet all these men would call themselves Christians. This was because biblical pronouncements on slavery were subject to ferocious debate and, in the war over emancipation, few battlegrounds were more important. In the 1820s, the Bible was a prime authority on political, intellectual, and moral questions; Christianity was essential to British national identity; belief in the divine was sincere, not yet undermined by science or secularism; and churches and chapels were the focal points of local communities. In this context, when Thomas Fowell Buxton told the House of Commons that 'Slavery is repugnant ... to the principles of Christian virtue', the abolitionists had claimed a monopoly of Christian virtue. Confronted with such moral certainty, the Interest was compelled to undercut the abolitionists by proving that the Bible in fact condoned slavery; if they succeeded, the moral imperative to free the enslaved would be removed and the Anti-Slavery Society would be deprived of its most persuasive argument.

British slaveholders did not argue that *trading* slaves was consonant with true religion. Such commerce had been outlawed by Exodus 21:16, which ordained that 'he that stealeth a man, and selleth him ... shall surely be put to death'. This approach had been confirmed in the New Testament by 1 Timothy, which explained that Christian law was made for 'the lawless and disobedient, for the ungodly and for sinners', among whom were 'men-stealers'. It appeared, however, that 'man-stealing' was distinct from slave*holding*. The former was 'expressly forbidden to Christians' but Richard Watson, the Anglican bishop of Llandaff, had explained that 'the Greek word rendered men-stealers in the New Testament does not ... mean the same as *men-buyers*', and so that 'buying men is [not] the same thing as stealing them'. This twisted logic held that slave*holding* was legitimate in the sight of the

Lord, and if the Interest wanted further biblical authority it did not have to look very far.[21]

Slavery was there from the beginning. In Genesis 9, after the flood-waters had receded, Noah drank too much of his own wine and fell asleep, naked. When his son, Ham, happened upon his father's drunken nudity and failed to cover up Noah's modesty, he was punished severely: Ham would see his own son, Canaan, condemned as 'a servant of servants unto his brethren'. For the West Indians, this 'Curse of Ham' was proof that the Almighty had sanctioned slavery. 'It was God himself,' declared the *Imperial Magazine*, 'who doomed the posterity of Ham and Canaan to the degradation of slavery.' Indeed, for the Jamaican clergyman Cynric Williams, any inquiry into Christianity's relationship with slavery could stop here: 'Have they never read of the curses pronounced on Canaan?' The Curse of Ham was also thought to justify the specific enslavement of Africans, who were regarded as the sons of Canaan. Although nothing in the Bible defined Ham's progeny by their skin colour, certain genealogies traced Ham's eldest son, Cush, to the Kingdom of Cush in ancient Ethiopia. The word 'cush' also meant 'black'.[22]

The Old Testament did not just sanction slavery as a punishment; Exodus 21 and Leviticus 25 also provided for its regulation. The former chapter, which followed on from the Ten Commandments, framed laws for the enslavement and redemption of Hebrews; there was also helpful guidance on how to sell one's own daughter into slavery. The latter chapter laid down rules for acquiring and inheriting foreign slaves, telling godly slaveholders that 'thy bondmen and thy bondmaids ... shall be of the heathen that are round about you', that 'ye shall buy ... the children of the strangers that do sojourn among you', and that 'they shall be your bondmen for ever'. For white West Indians, these lessons were clear: they could make slaves of foreigners; the children of those people would be their property; and all those people were legitimate parts of their estate. Naturally, they interpreted 'the strangers that do sojourn among you' as referring to Africans.

These passages were invaluable ammunition for slavery's apologists. The future prime minister, William Gladstone, whose family's planta-tion in Demerara had been the wellspring of the 1823 Rebellion, used his first speech as an MP to discuss these rules on slavery. He reasoned that, if slavery had been offensive to the Lord, He would have condemned it, but He did not. In fact, the Lord had explained how to *manage* slavery. 'Were the matter absolutely and necessarily *sinful*', the young Gladstone explained, then the 'paramount authority' of Scripture would not have 'regulate[d] the matter'. Such rules were thought to reflect the nature of God himself. To this end, a late Anglican bishop had composed a syllogism beloved by West Indians:

1. God cannot authorise injustice;
2. But he did authorise slavery amongst the Jews;
3. Therefore, slavery is not opposite to justice.[23]

The next 'proof' adduced from the Old Testament was slaveholding among the Patriarchs. The West Indians noted that Abraham had spoken of 'the souls that they had gotten in Haran', meaning slaves 'bought with money', but that the Lord did not rebuke Abraham for this. On the contrary, He 'directed Abraham to admit [the slaves] into the Church of God ... and did not direct him to liberate them'. Moreover, there were 318 such slaves, which was 'about the number on most sugar estates'. Abraham's wife, Sarah, then took one of those 318, Hagar, as a 'bondswoman' and 'a perfect and perpetual slave'; and when Hagar fled from Sarah, the angel of the Lord commanded her to 'Return to thy mistress, and submit thyself under her hands'. The later history of the Israelites provided further debating points. The book of Joshua showed that the Gibeonites fell 'into perpetual bondage' and were made 'hewers of wood and drawers of water'. When the Ammonites, Hittites, and Jebusites were defeated by the Lord's armies, they too had a 'tribute of bond service' levied upon them. The spoils of the Midianite Wars were virgin slaves, and even King Solomon 'brought up negroes [from Ophir] for the service of [his] Temple'. All this was alleged proof that Jehovah tolerated slavery 'from the very earliest periods of human society'.[24]

The enslavement of major biblical figures was supposedly even more significant. Joseph was sold by his brothers into slavery under the Ishmaelites and then re-sold to Potiphar, the captain of the Pharaoh's guard, and it did not escape the *Barbadian* that, when Joseph later advised the starving Egyptians to sell themselves into slavery under the Pharaoh, 'God was pleased with Joseph in all that he did'. There was also the captivity of the Israelites in Babylon. 'Slavery,' wrote George Wilson Bridges, 'fell most heavily upon the Jews them-selves. Two of their tribes ... were oppressed beneath the iron yoke of the Babylonians; and three others [taken] captive by Salmanazar.' Thus had the Lord had seen fit to condemn His own people to bondage. How, the West Indians asked, if slavery was not beneath the dignity of the Israelites, was it beneath Africans?[25]

It may be tempting to dismiss these arguments as the sort of unthinking literalism that Enlightenment rationalism had discredited. Before the mid-nineteenth century, however, few Britons seriously doubted that the Old Testament was the infallible word of God. As the historian David Brion Davis has observed, this debate 'occurred at a time when Protestant literalism still prevailed and when most Englishmen read both Old and New Testaments as a miraculously unified whole'. Few Britons dared to argue that Mosaic laws were appropriate only to their time and place, or that moral lessons in Genesis were irrelevant to the 1820s. 'What constituted in his sight MORAL GUILT in the days of ADAM,' declared James MacQueen, 'constitutes IT NOW.' Slavery had been righteous in Genesis, and so it was righteous for all time; approval of slavery under Moses implied approval for eternity. Who were the abolitionists to reform divine law?[26]

In all this, only one caveat was allowed: if the New Testament undid the Old, biblical approval of slavery could be annulled. The abolition-ists therefore built their house on the New Testament and Richard Bickell, a Jamaican curate who lived dangerously by expressly anti-slavery sentiments, argued that 'the Levitical law [was] completely annulled by Christ': the God of the *New* Testament, unlike that of the Old, respected 'not the persons or colours of men, and made of the same blood all nations of the earth'. Naturally, the West Indians disagreed. 'The New Testament and the Old,' wrote MacQueen, 'are inseparably connected.'[27]

First, Christ had not criticised slavery. Jesus entered a world of iniquity, corruption, and oppression and, wherever He found sin, He chastised the sinner: gamblers, liars, hypocrites, the greedy, and the faithless were rebuked. Christ had also entered a world in which slavery – of Jews, Africans, and tribes conquered by the Romans – was endemic. Yet slaveholders had never once been reproached. One West Indian was sufficiently confident to declare that the Almighty had never 'by his Prophets, nor our Saviour, nor his Apostles, ever reprove[d] the masters for holding slaves *as a possession*'. According to Archibald Alison, there was 'never a more mistaken idea' that Christianity made it 'wrong ... to retain any portion of our subjects in a state of servitude'. Moreover, since Christ never shied away from correcting what was wrong, the absence of criticism implied approval: if slavery was evil, Jesus would have said so, but He did not.[28]

The West Indians aimed a second blow at abolition by arguing that the Golden Rule – that of doing unto others – was inapplicable to relations between master and slave. They argued that it was no more the planter's duty to free his slaves than it was the duty of Britain's elite 'to elevate the labouring class above their present sphere'. Buxton was also reminded that the Rule applied to *slaves* as well as to masters, so that slaves were obliged to consider their masters' wishes. The Rule was even turned back on the abolitionists, who were asked to imagine what they would want *if they were slaveholders*. William Copeland, a City of London alderman, suggested that such hypothetical desires would include the avoidance of 'undue excitement' about emancipation.[29]

After this, West Indian focus turned to the letters of St Paul and his proclamations that 'servants' should obey their masters. There was some controversy here about how the operative Greek word '*doulos*' should be translated: the abolitionists thought it meant 'hired servant', but the West Indians insisted on the meaning of 'domestic slave', so that 'when our Saviour and the Apostles addressed themselves to *servants*' they were talking to *slaves*. On that basis, several Pauline letters were brought to the forefront of the debate, not least 1 Corinthians, where the seventh chapter enjoined 'every man [to] abide in the same calling wherein he was called'. For opponents of emancipation, the letter clearly meant that slaves should be content to be slaves, since God had made them so; their consolation would be spiritual freedom through Christ, not freedom from their masters. For the *Quarterly Review*, it was a passage from which 'no Wilberforce nor Stephen ever quoted, ... from which ... no [John] Smith ever took his text, when addressing the poor ignorant negroes of the British colonies'. On the pro-slavery interpretation, how could they? With similar appeals found in Colossians 3, Ephesians 6, 1 Timothy 6 and Titus 2, it appeared that Pauline teaching urged submission and obedience; emancipation was contrary to the creed.[30]

The most 'popular' book of the New Testament, however, was the shortest of them all, Philemon. Here, the runaway slave Onesimus had gone to Paul at Rome, where the apostle converted the fugitive to Christianity before sending him back to his master at Colossae. This letter encapsulated almost everything supportive of the West Indian case. By returning the fugitive to slavery, Paul had refused to endorse freedom: Onesimus was far from his Greek master and he could have started a new life in liberty, but Paul sent him back. Moreover, the letter made clear that conversion to Christianity did not loosen a slave's chains, and the Wesleyan missionary Robert Young made this point explicitly: 'The case of Onesimus,' he preached in Jamaica, 'shews that Christianity does not interfere with [slaves'] *civil state*, but produces [only] the most happy change in their *moral condition*.' Philemon was further proof that Paul found nothing *wrong* with slavery, since he did not criticise it. For Henry Duncan, the Scottish minister who founded the savings bank that became TSB, the arrival of Onesimus at Rome was 'an opportunity which could not have been passed over, of laying down an authoritative precept as to the unlawfulness of slavery'. Yet Paul 'did no such thing'; instead, 'he avowed the authority of the master over his slave'.[31]

During the debate over slavery, a former minister at the Colonial Office concluded that the notion of Christianity being incompatible with slavery was 'a silly sounding, worn-out falsehood'. Based on a literal reading of the Bible, he was not wrong. Dozens of biblical verses *do* condone or encourage slavery, and there is a striking absence of explicit scriptural criticism of slaveholding. The abolitionists knew this, and they knew they would find only limited support from the Church of England: 'The whole bench of bishops deemed it no degradation of their sacred calling', it was recalled, 'to hold a property in men … and the pulpits, too, were closed … taking their cue from the episcopal bench'. Of course, Christianity was a broad church: as the slaveholders sat at one end, abolitionists such as Buxton and Macaulay were motivated by sincere Christian sentiment at the other. Besides, Christianity was the source of Buxton's resolve: the darker entries in his journals are replete with prayers for wisdom and courage and, in the years ahead, he would need both.[32]

6.

Two Roads Diverging

I trust that the pointed and strong admonition on the subject of West India Slavery which forms the concluding part of the King's Speech will ... moderate the Zeal of those who ... were disposed to go all lengths with Buxton and his party last session ... They will be satisfied not to interfere further but to leave the concern in the hands of Government.[1]

William Huskisson to John Gladstone, February 1824

In early 1824, Lord Liverpool's Tory government could identify three major parties to the fight over slavery, and all three had reason to be unhappy. First, although the West India Interest was delighted that Canning had wrested parliamentary control of the matter from Buxton, and though it had drafted the toothless terms of amelioration, the death of John Smith had proved a political disaster. Second, although the Anti-Slavery Society could exploit Smith's martyrdom, it knew that amelioration was a shibboleth and that neither Whitehall nor the colonists had any intention of taking decisive action. Third, the resident colonists of the Caribbean appeared to be on the brink of rebellion: even if amelioration was a dead letter, they were promising violent resistance to any further interference in their internal affairs. (Of the 'moral improvement of the Negroes', which was the pretended purpose of amelioration, the Tories cared little, if anything.)

For these reasons, the King's Speech of 3 February 1824 – written by the government and delivered by the Lord Chancellor, Lord Eldon, since George IV was 'indisposed' – begged the patience of all concerned. As Eldon read the speech to Parliament, he first asked the gathered politicians to 'treat this whole subject with the calmness and discretion which it demands. It is a subject perplexed with difficulties, which no sudden effort can disentangle'. Yet if Eldon's audience wondered where the government's sympathies really lay, that soon became clear. Making implicit reference to the Demerara Rebellion, he warned that 'to excite exaggerated expectations in those who are the objects of your benevolence, would be as fatal to their welfare as to that of their employers'. The message to Buxton and his colleagues was not subtle, though there were kinder words for the white West Indians. Adverting to 'the fortunes and the safety of large classes of his majesty's subjects' and the 'considerations of justice', he assured them that, in order 'to avoid aggravation of evil ... caution shall temper zeal'.[2]

There was much else to occupy Liverpool, Canning, and the Cabinet. Over the following six weeks the House of Commons debated foreign policy towards France and Spain, political instability in Latin America, the silk trade, the 'education of the Catholic poor in Ireland', the rights of artisanal labourers, judicial reform, and the Bank of England. Even so, two things kept bringing the government back to slavery: that honouring the resolution to do *something* towards amelioration was the best means of tempering abolitionist zeal; and perhaps more urgently, that the violent rhetoric of the West Indian colonists required attention. In February and March 1824, the government therefore considered three solutions to 'the West India Question'.

The first was to crack down on the colonies and to 'crush them by the application of direct force'. Canning declared that 'nothing ... would be easier [than] to put an end to the dispute at once, by overwhelming power', but this was mere rhetoric. There was no stomach for another fight with British colonists and 'no feeling of wounded pride, no motive of questionable expediency, nothing short of real and demonstrable necessity' would induce Canning to invoke 'the transcendental power of Parliament over every dependency of the British Crown'. The government was desperate to avoid repeating the mistakes made in North America, and Canning much preferred to pacify the would-be rebels of the Caribbean. 'Superior strength disarms the spirit of resentment,' he explained: 'I could revenge, but I would much rather reclaim. I prefer that moral self-restraint, so beautifully expressed by the poet, when he represents Neptune as allaying the wild waters, instead of rebuking the winds which had put them in a roar.' He therefore told the House of Commons that, 'if there be any gentleman in the Jamaica House of Assembly who ... is preparing himself for his contemplated career, by conning over the speeches of Washington and Franklin, we shall act most judiciously, by taking from him all lofty grounds of quarrel'. The West Indians' flirtation with the United States had achieved the desired effect.[3]

The second option was to let the colonial assemblies reform slavery at their own pace, which in practice meant that nothing would be done. Abolitionists had long warned that 'no trust or hope should be invested in voluntary action by the colonial legislatures'; indeed, in 1799, Canning himself had cautioned Parliament against trusting 'the masters of slaves in what concerns legislation for slavery'. By February 1824, however, Buxton feared this would be the government's chosen approach. Despite the reputational damage that persecuting John Smith had caused the West Indians, and despite the weight of the Dissenting churches swinging behind the Anti-Slavery Society, the needle had not moved in high politics. That month, Buxton noted that Canning 'seems very cold to me, and the report is [that] he will join the West Indians', and so Buxton was ready to 'go to war with him in earnest'. Following 'a very unsatisfactory interview' with Canning a few days later, he was certain that the government meant 'to forfeit their pledge, and to do next to nothing'; Canning then told Buxton that he had 'determined to yield to the West Indian clamour'. Not without reason would Buxton's son describe the abolitionists as 'discouraged and depressed'.[4]

But the government would not do nothing. The third option, the via media, involved putting Lord Bathurst's recommendations for amelioration into an Order in Council, an executive decree which carried the force of law. And while such an Order could not be implemented in the 'chartered', self-governing colonies without risking rebellion, there was a second class of colonies where amelioration could be enforced. These were the newer, 'crown colonies' that were administered by a governor and effectively controlled from London. Of the Crown colonies in the Caribbean, St Lucia was too small and Demerara still too volatile, so it fell to Trinidad, wrested from the Spanish in 1802, to serve as the laboratory for this imperial experiment.

The governor of Trinidad, and the man who would oversee the Order's implementation, was Sir Ralph Woodford. The son of a diplomat, Woodford has been described as 'a refined, elegant, and very handsome man, dignified [and] with a strong personality', but this charm did not save him from the slander of the slaveholders. Joseph Marryat, the MP and agent to Grenada, was especially hostile to Woodford, whom he regarded as a spineless stooge of the Anti-Slavery Society. In one sense, Marryat's fears might have been justified. Woodford's letters to the Colonial Office reveal him to be a nervous, worried man who sought constant approval: 'I hope some occasion will occur,' he wrote, 'in which Lord Bathurst may have an opportunity of shewing that he is satisfied with my conduct.' Woodford also worried about his reputation more generally. Fearing 'from the tenor of the Public letters' that he 'was in disgrace', he pleaded with friends to not 'for a moment give credit to any of Mr Marryat's representations', which he described as 'full of statements maliciously false'. This is *not* to say that Woodford was an anti-slavery angel. He would complain that 'Negroes are a provoking Race and they have no Shame & very little if any gratitude', and he pushed back on the proposed abolition of flogging enslaved women: 'You cannot do better,' he protested, 'than [to] allow them to feel the Cat [o' nine tails] on their shoulders.' Even so, anxious to please his masters at Whitehall, Woodford would do their bidding.[5]

The Trinidad Order in Council was laid before the House of Commons on 16 March 1824. Introduced and explained by Canning, the Order was justified as a measure of compromise. Henceforth on Trinidad, punishing enslaved women by whipping would be forbidden, as would whipping men 'as a stimulus to labour'. Planters would be obliged 'to provide the means of religious instruction and worship' and to assist in widening 'the basis of the Ecclesiastical Establishment in the West Indies'. The Order further provided for 'those charities of life [that] religion promotes and sanctifies', by which Canning meant marriage; moreover, care would now be taken that 'in transferring slaves from one property to another ... husband and wife ... and parent and child, shall not be severed from each other'. Enslaved people's property would be protected and, where possible, lodged in special banks. By three further clauses, the evidence of enslaved people would be admitted in Trinidad's courts, Sunday markets abolished, and Sunday labour prohibited. 'By this process, and by these degrees,' said Canning, 'may the slaves be gradually fitted for the last grand consummation of benefit, the power of acquiring his freedom.'[6]

The planters of Trinidad were appalled. The wealthiest of them, William Hardin Burnley, told Woodford that 'if the Order in Council is carried out ... the Colony is ruined'. But Burnley was mistaken: the Order did not represent anything like a serious commitment to the reform of slavery. In fact, Canning had used his speech to reaffirm his contempt for emancipation. As he told the House, 'If I am asked which I would prefer, permanent slavery, or immediate abolition ... I would prefer things remaining as they are.' Indeed, when discussing the potential freedom of Trinidad's slaves, Canning talked of 'the brute state ... of the mass of the negro population' and its 'barbarism'. He ridiculed any idea that the current generation of enslaved people would ever be fit to live freely: 'To let in the full light of freedom on eyes scarcely unsealed, eyes from which the scales of bondage have not yet been purged away, would indeed be a perilous experiment.'⁷

The crux of Canning's speech is too shocking not to reprint in full. 'In dealing with the negro,' he told the House, 'we must remember that we are dealing with a being possessing the form and strength of a man, but the intellect only of a child. To turn him loose in the manhood of his physical strength, in the maturity of his physical passions, but in the infancy of his uninstructed reason, would be to raise up a creature resembling the splendid fiction of a recent romance; the hero of which constructs a human form, with all the corporeal capabilities of man, and with the thews and sinews of a giant; but being unable to impart to the work of his hands a percep-tion of right and wrong, he finds too late that he has only created a more than mortal power of doing mischief, and himself recoils from the monster he has made.' The 'recent romance' of which Canning spoke was Mary Shelley's *Frankenstein*, which had been published in 1818. Here, Canning urged Parliament to avoid creating Britain's own Prometheus.⁸

As when Canning scuppered Buxton's first proposals in 1823, many West Indians in London – and certainly those without 'property' in Trinidad – were ecstatic. Even in the unlikely scenario that the Order was implemented properly, it would apply to only 30,000 enslaved people on Trinidad out of a total of 700,000 in the Caribbean. Moreover, the Tory government had signalled that it would not encroach upon the chartered rights of the older colonies. Canning's speech became a pro-slavery charter, described as 'classical' by James

Colquhoun and reprinted for sale by John Murray. Even 'better', in the same day's debate in the House of Lords, the colonial secretary Lord Bathurst had 'dwelt on and adduced ... leading facts and statement ... brought forward' by James MacQueen in his *Blackwood's* articles. 'This,' gloated MacQueen, 'is the triumph of the Colonies.'[9]

As the West Indians celebrated, Buxton came close to a breakdown. He wrote to a friend that 'the degree of virulence against me is quite surprising', and other letters suggest a mind in turmoil and a man who was struggling to cope. 'The weight of business, and worse still of thought, which overhangs me at this time,' he wrote, 'is greater than I ever experienced before.' With such anxiety came exhaustion: 'I am fatigued,' he complained, 'I am distressed with fatigue.' Worse still was the torpor of the anti-slavery campaign. Despite the political boost of the John Smith saga, the government, having 'acted' in Trinidad, could now rest on its laurels. 'The Slavery question looks wretchedly,' wrote Buxton. 'I begin to think that, opposed as we are by the West Indians, deserted by the Government, and deemed enthusiasts by the public, we shall be able to do little or nothing.' The Quaker abolitionist William Allen was equally pessimistic: 'The present is a momentous crisis,' he wrote to Buxton. 'My wish is that we should not concede too much.'[10]

Some of Buxton's colleagues were more sanguine. Zachary Macaulay might have regretted that 'our progress in [the cause had fallen] far below our wishes', but he held up the Order as a cause for optimism, writing to the social reformer Hannah More that the West Indians, 'though angry and growling', had yielded 'their reluctant assent to plans of reform'. Wilberforce meanwhile praised Buxton for 'the progress which, through the goodness of Providence, we have already made, and the good hopes which we may justly indulge as to the future'. For Wilberforce, it was cause for gladness that Parliament was 'consulting about the interests and comforts of those [Africans], who, not long ago, were scarcely rated above the level of ourang-outangs'.[11]

Others assured Buxton that abolition was a long-term project and that setbacks were inevitable. His brother-in-law Joseph Gurney told him that slavery was 'a monster who must have a very long succession of hard knocks before he will expire'. So why, he asked, 'should we expect to get his extinction into full train in less than ten years?' It turned out that achieving emancipation within a decade would have exceeded Buxton's wildest expectations: 'He would be satisfied if Slavery could be abolished,' reported a Colonial Office aide, 'at the end of 70 years.' It was a startling admission that the end of slavery might not happen in Buxton's lifetime.[12]

Few 'rank-and-file' abolitionists were prepared to wait at all, let alone for seventy years. When they read reports of Canning's speech and details of the Trinidad Order, they knew they had suffered another setback. The *York Herald* decried the Order as 'far short of that which was expected by the friends of a gradual but CERTAIN emancipation', while a civic official at Chester expressed his sregret at the partiality of the proposed plan, and was of opinion that ministers, being alarmed, were backing out of their pledge'. There was even greater anger when Buxton appeared to bow to government pressure to leave the West India Question alone for the time being: 'We cannot make any public movement,' noted Thomas Clarkson, 'out of Delicacy to Ministers.'[13]

George Stephen, the thirty-year-old son of the abolitionist stalwart James, began to complain that the Anti-Slavery Society was drooping 'under an accumulation of political bias and aristocratic ascendancy and, worse than either, of tame monotony'. In time, Stephen's impatience would revolutionise the campaign against slavery, but in 1824 the chief malcontent was Elizabeth Heyrick. The Quaker daughter of a Leicestershire clothier, Heyrick had been a precocious child, possessed of a talent for painting that gave her father 'half a mind' to 'make an Angelica Kauffman of her'. She was kind and sensitive, her biography filled with anecdotes of charity and rescued kittens, but a zealous sense of Christian duty burned within Heyrick too. She campaigned for penal reform, the protection of animals, and the welfare of the poor, and she raged against slavery. In 1824, aged fifty-four and incandescently angry with the apparent timidity of the abolitionist leadership, Heyrick published a pamphlet, *Immediate, Not Gradual Emancipation*. It was a roaring success, speeding through multiple editions in England and then in Boston and Philadelphia, where American abolitionists used her clarion voice to rouse their own countrymen.[14]

Heyrick railed against Buxton's alleged weakness and Wilberforce's deference to the grandees of the slaveholding lobby. 'The interests and the prejudices of the West Indian planters,' she complained, 'have occupied much too prominent a place in the discussion of this great question. The abolitionists have shown a great deal too much politeness ... towards these gentlemen.' For Heyrick, emancipation was not a political issue, but a moral imperative. She knew that Buxton had proposed *gradual* emancipation because slavery was 'in direct opposition to ... the spirit and letter of the Christian religion'. But in doing so, Buxton had neglected his true Christian duty to eradicate slavery *now*. 'It [would have] been well for the poor oppressed African,' she observed, 'had the assertors of his rights entered the lists against his oppressors with more of the spirit of Christian combatants, and less of worldly politicians.' Heyrick demanded that the Anti-Slavery Society should dispense with timorous politicking and recast its campaign as a *'holy war* – an attack upon the strongholds, the deep intrenchments of the very powers of darkness, in which courage would be more availing than caution'. For many of the Dissenting Protestants, Quakers, and Evangelicals who were swelling the local chapters of the abolitionist movement, Heyrick gave expression to their fury: if Smith and Shrewsbury had fallen in a foreign field, they would not lose the same fight on the home front. As she asked her readers, if Christians thought that slavery was a sin, why should they tolerate its existence for a moment longer?[15]

The Anti-Slavery Society held its first annual general meeting in June 1824. In other circumstances, it could have been a time for celebration: within eighteen months of that first meeting in the King's Head, the House of Commons had passed resolutions in favour of amelioration and eventual emancipation; Thomas Clarkson's first tour of the kingdom had fostered anti-slavery activity throughout the provinces; and hundreds of petitions pleading for 'colonial reform' had been laid before Parliament. The government had even implemented amelioration by way of the Trinidad Orders. In reality, though, the government had obstructed the anti-slavery campaign at almost every turn, and the abolitionists were splitting into camps: one favouring caution, gradualism, and amelioration, the other demanding the immediate liberation of enslaved Africans.[16]

The AGM marked the debut of a new abolitionist leader. Thomas Babington Macaulay was twenty-three, the son of Zachary, and a curious young man. The younger Macaulay had been a shy Clapham schoolboy who hated cricket, marbles, and girls; indeed, one of his classmates described him as 'almost an alien from those who ought to have been his companions' and 'utterly destitute ... of all the fire of sentiment'. But Tom Macaulay also showed 'marks of uncommon genius'. By the age of nine he had written a twelve-book imitation of Virgil's *Aeneid* – in Latin, of course – and memorised the Authorised version of the Bible. This latter faculty proved most useful when the Macaulays' family maid, Sally, threw away the oyster shells that young Tom had laid out in their south London garden. In umbrage, he stormed into the drawing room and quoted Deuteronomy 27:17 to his mother: 'Cursed be Sally, for it is written, "Cursed is he that removeth his neighbour's landmark".' A stellar career at Cambridge ensued, as did a studentship at Lincoln's Inn, and by 1824 he commanded the attention of the assembled anti-slavery delegates. Although one of Macaulay's peers lampooned the speech for its pompous self-importance and stilted delivery, his father Zachary was overwhelmed 'to see the support of his son given to the cause for which he was sacrificing his life and fortune'. Walking home afterwards, the elder Macaulay expressed himself 'with unusual warmth' as 'the tears stood in his eyes'. Of course, there was always room for improvement. 'By the way, Tom,' the father remarked, 'you should be aware that when you speak in the presence of royalty, you should not fold your arms.'[17]

June 1824 also witnessed the start of Thomas Clarkson's second organising tour of Britain. Having abandoned his original mission in the wake of the Demerara Rebellion, Clarkson rode again into the places that the abolitionists had neglected. The first of these was Wales, and this was difficult terrain. To the west of Chester and Shrewsbury, low levels of literacy compounded a language barrier, with Clarkson complaining that 'few in the County can read or speak English'. Transport was not much easier. At each stop, Clarkson wasted days and even weeks seeking carriage for himself and his parcels. There was a further problem of critical mass because few Welsh settlements were sufficiently populous to make stopping worthwhile. At Ruthin, where the locals maintained 'sad prejudices' towards John Smith, only three people attended Clarkson's talk. Eventually, the London Society asked him to concentrate on larger towns alone.[18]

Even here new problems arose. Regretting the influence of pro-slavery publications 'every where', Clarkson obtained few recruits at

Carmarthen because his arrival clashed with the always-popular Quarter Sessions that entertained the locals with the trials of alleged thieves and killers. At Caernarfon, petty politics and class prejudice meant that 'the Gentlemen of the Town' would not support an anti-slavery committee composed of mere 'Tradesmen'; at Anglesey, Clarkson was confronted with 'great ignorance of the Subject, great Misconceptions of our Views, and the same Ultra Government feeling, which seems to have characterized North Wales'. That same sense of 'subordination and Ignorance' had spread to Cardigan in the south-west. There was *some* success. Clarkson rejoiced in the recruitment of John Elias, 'the great Preacher of the Methodists', who could command the following of 'many thousand People in any Good Cause'. There was even the hope, as Clarkson turned to the north-west of England, that William Wordsworth would help him to distribute anti-slavery tracts around the Lake District, but early enthusiasm from the poet faded into nothing. 'There is an Evident Indisposition,' concluded Clarkson, 'to meddle further in the Matter, and to wait to see what Government does.'[19]

It is possible that the abolitionist leadership had hamstrung Clarkson from the start. At the AGM in June, and in the published report that followed, the Anti-Slavery Society had articulated a new 'official' policy. Just as James Cropper had suggested in 1822, they would lobby the Board of Trade to 'equalize' the customs duties that were imposed on all sugar coming into Britain, regardless of its origin. In short, the abolitionists believed that if they could strip the West Indian colonies of economic protection and expose slave-grown sugar to competition from the East, the slave system itself would collapse. Perhaps the Interest feared this too, since their minute-books from London, Liverpool, and Glasgow are filled with panicked motions and fearful resolutions to shore up their standing with the relevant government ministers.[20]

Yet there were several major issues with the policy of 'equalization'. For one thing, Thomas Clarkson did not like it: he believed that the commercial 'Sugar Question' should not intrude upon the political and moral issue of slave emancipation, and he felt no enthusiasm for promoting the policy during his travels. For another, 'equalization' had a more popular rival: at the same time that James Cropper was advancing complicated theories of customs reform, Elizabeth Heyrick was inviting British consumers simply to abstain from purchasing West Indian sugar. In her pamphlet *No British Slavery*, she argued persuasively that, if the British market for slave-grown sugar collapsed, the planters would have no choice but to free their slaves or face ruin. By doing so, Heyrick and her devoted 'abstentionists' asked Britons to stand in their village shops and make a straightforward choice between 'slave' and 'free', a choice that did not require a sophisticated knowledge of fiscal mechanisms. Heyrick's impact was astounding. 'Everywhere People are asking me about *immediate abstention*,' Clarkson noted in his diary, 'and whether ... they should not leave off West India sugar & use the East only. There is certainly a Disposition to make a Sacrifice for the Cause.'[21]

Still, the anti-slavery leadership would not budge. In a misguided assessment of how most people felt about West Indian slaveholders, and indeed about the supposed economic benefits of slavery, James Cropper protested that 'the immediate disuse of slave produce' would lead to widespread unemployment and economic distress across Britain, especially in his native Liverpool. The decision was therefore taken that 'abstention' would be recommended *only* if 'the sugar question' failed in Parliament. In the months to come, a subcommittee of the London Society would even explore the formation of a 'Tropical Free Labour Company' with the ambition of extending the 'free-labour' cultivation of sugar in India. By placing such faith in the power of free labour, the abolitionist leaders had assumed that enslaved Africans, if freed, would willingly perform the same, back-breaking work of sugar cultivation that was currently forced upon them. In contemporary opinion, the recent histories of Haiti and Sierra Leone suggested there was no guarantee of that happening. More seriously, the West India Interest and the Colonial Office would go to extreme lengths to prove that 'free black labour' was impossible.[22]

As the leaders of the Anti-Slavery Society debated economic strategy, William Wilberforce was ailing. Now in his mid-sixties, he had fallen seriously ill while travelling to Buckinghamshire after the June 1824 AGM. Upon arriving at Iver Grove, the home of the retired admiral James Gambier, he collapsed. It was not until four o'clock the next morning that Wilberforce woke to find himself in bed, fully dressed. Resting for the next month, and then spending time at Bath, he toyed with writing a biography of Pitt the Younger, for public life was now beyond him. Warned by his doctors that the stress of further politicking would endanger his life, and pressured by his wife, Barbara, he committed to resigning as an MP. At the same time, Wilberforce dismissed the idea of a peerage, observing pointedly that 'the example of a man's retiring, when he feels his ... powers beginning to fail him, might probably be useful'. Not all commentators were convinced of Wilberforce's sainthood. The essayist William Hazlitt thought that he had too often sought public acclaim, balancing 'what he thinks right' with 'what will be thought [right] by other people'. And the West Indians, of course, despite their patrician kinship, bade farewell to a foe. But Thomas Fowell Buxton was in no doubt about Wilberforce's legacy, writing in his diary of an 'unaffected pain' that stemmed 'from a consciousness of my inability to be his successor'.[23]

Wilberforce understood the weight of the load that Buxton carried. He knew that Parliament was 'made up of West Indians, Government men, a few partisans, and [only] a few sturdy Abolitionists'. But he had no qualms about the competence of his heirs. 'I am not now much wanted in Parliament,' he wrote: 'our cause has powerful advocates, who have now taken their stations.' Indeed, despite recent months, Buxton still had the stomach for battle. Adopting 'the maxim ... of the navy in the last war, "Always fight"', it was now his 'firm and unalterable intention to devote all [his] life and [his] efforts to advocating the cause of the slaves'.[24]

Zachary Macaulay, the stern Scotsman, was the most reliable of Buxton's lieutenants, and the vile abuse he received from the West Indian lobby was proof of that. *John Bull* was a rabidly conservative Sunday magazine which had a front page adorned by a crown, a Bible, and the motto 'For God, King, and the People'. In many ways it was the ancestor of right-wing tabloids, and *John Bull* had chosen Macaulay as the target of its vitriol. For *John Bull*'s editor, Theodore Hooke, Macaulay was a hypocritical charlatan who was using religious zeal as 'a cloak and garb' for his ulterior, mercenary purpose of seizing 'all the good things the world can produce'. Macaulay was mocked as 'Saint Zachariah' and the cunning 'Professor of Zachmackery'. Colonial newspapers promptly commended *John Bull* for its 'admirable talent' and for 'lashing with all the severity of just satire [against] the meddling, troublesome, and visionary Reformers of the day'. Macaulay withstood the vilification until 1824, when he sued for libel and £10,000 in damages. He would lose, but not because he was wrong. Instead, at the request of *John Bull*, the Lord Chancellor, Lord Eldon, intervened to establish a 'factual' inquiry into the dispute; and when Macaulay appealed against this intervention to the House of Lords, Eldon was appointed to adjudicate on his own decision. Macaulay knew the game was up and dropped the case, but his honour was preserved: 'You stand much too high,' the Duke of Gloucester told him, 'to be affected by anything such a truly despicable paper can publish respecting you.'[25]

Macaulay soon added to his responsibilities when he became the editor and, as Hannah More put it, the 'sole and most prolific poet' of the *Anti-Slavery Monthly Reporter*. Now, thanks to Macaulay's diligence, and at the cost of four shillings per hundred copies, any interested party could order a monthly digest of slavery-related news from London. It was an astonishing success. Most editions would have a print run of more than 20,000 copies, none fewer than 12,000, and between 1825 and 1831 the *Reporter* sold more than 1.7 million copies overall. It was not a leisurely read. Macaulay filled some editions with forensic tables recording the number of births, deaths, and punishments on West Indian plantations; others were dedicated to 'dissecting and criticising the slave code of the colonies'. Yet for the reader who dug into the data – and Macaulay trusted his readers to do this – the *Reporter* provided precious insights into the reality of slavery. By publishing the laws that were in force in the colonies, Macaulay could show how little was being done by way of amelioration; and by tracing the steady downward trend in the slave population of the West Indies, he could illustrate that slavery was unsustainable. In short, Macaulay found a way to quantify the horror of slavery. In a controversy that was otherwise defined by abolitionist appeals to humanity, or by West Indian threats of blood and thunder, he was quietly building one of the first political campaigns that relied not just on feeling, but on fact.[26]

7.

Am I Not a Man and a Brother?

The cry which resounds from the West Indies is raised by men who are trembling less for their property than for the privileges of their caste ... These are the persons who love slavery for its own sake ... They may have no possessions, but they have white faces ... They will lose the power of oppressing, with impunity, every man who has a black skin.[1]

Edinburgh Review, January 1825

As Thomas Clarkson bustled down dead ends in Wales, and as Elizabeth Heyrick raged against the leadership of the Anti-Slavery Society, a new man arrived at the Colonial Office at numbers 12 and 13 Downing Street. Thomas Moody was forty-four and tanned from a lifetime in the West Indies. Having left his native Cumberland as a teenager, Moody had spent eight years teaching at Codrington College, the conservative Anglican school on Barbados where wealthy planters bought a typically English education for their sons. Then, at the height of total war against Napoleon, he accepted a commission in the Royal Engineers, administering military supplies on the Demeraran coast. Moody served with such distinction during the British invasion of Guadeloupe in 1810 that he received military honours *from France*.[2]

After the war, like many officers, Moody was put on half-pay. He worked as an attorney and an aide-de-camp before, in 1816, he was charged with supervising 'captured negroes' whom the Royal Navy had rescued from rogue slave ships. Ever since the abolition of the slave trade, the British fleet had been hunting down these ships, but dealing with their 'cargo' was an enduring problem. Given the terrors of the Middle Passage, the Africans would not be forced to make the return trip, nor was there much chance of the British delivering the Africans to their 'home' stretch of coastline. Such a policy would even increase the Africans' risk of re-enslavement, since Spanish and Portuguese slavers were still plying their trade in the Gulf of Guinea. As a last resort, the British government's solution was to remove these Africans to smaller West Indian colonies where they would live and work not as slaves, but as indentured apprentices.

The behaviour and development of these apprentices was the subject of intense scrutiny, because one of the great questions about slavery, even before 1823, had concerned the ability of Africans to live and work like free white men. At the behest of William Wilberforce, two royal commissioners were charged with investigating Africans on the Virgin Island of Tortola and with answering the question: 'Could free Africans work to support themselves?' Thomas Moody was an almost obvious choice as a commissioner: he had read widely on history, economics, and the social sciences, and he had precious experience of the 'tropical labour' performed both by the white men of the Royal Engineers and the 'captured negroes' of the Caribbean. He was joined by John Dougan, the son of a Demeraran planter and a former privateer who was, by coincidence, Moody's uncle-in-law. Ordered to explore the 'actual condition' of Tortola's Africans, Dougan and Moody conducted dozens of interviews, recording each apprentice's name in both 'African' and English, their age, their height, their 'state of bodily health', any 'distinguishing marks', and the 'trade, craft, or employment' in which they were engaged.[3]

As the historian Anita Rupprecht has related, Moody and Dougan fell out rapidly, ostensibly over procedure: Dougan wanted to preserve his interview notes, Moody wanted them destroyed; Dougan wished to interview the planter and apprentice together, Moody feared that inviting criticism of the master in person would sever the ties of authority. Each complained to Westminster about the other, and their secretary recorded that Dougan was 'miserably placed ... by the state of Irritation and Disunion of the Commission'. But more than method divided the two men. Dougan was a repentant slaveholder who regretted that he had ever 'possessed ... that unfortunate species of [human] property'. Converted to abolitionism by James Stephen, he now sought to atone for past sins by inquiring sincerely whether Africans could sustain themselves when freed. The work of the commission, he believed, was 'an arduous Duty of Humanity'. In contrast, Moody's decades in the West Indies had convinced him of the merits of slavery and, by the mid-1820s, he had acquired several plantations and hundreds of slaves on Barbados. Increasingly suspicious of his colleague's motives, Dougan believed that Moody was the agent 'not of His Majesty's government, but of the colonial assemblies' and that Moody's mission was 'not so much the protection of the liberated Africans, as the defence of colonial slavery'.[4]

Dougan's breaking point came with the interview of two young apprentices, Kitty and Amelia, who described their daily life in painful detail. Besides the routine torture of sugar-cropping, Kitty and Amelia were forced by their master, a man called Maclean, to clear brushland and lug heavy building materials over miles of rough land; all the while, they were flogged and fed little. However, Kitty and Amelia had arrived for the interview 'very well dressed and in a style beyond their condition; they both wore a white thin striped muslin lady's dress, with sleeves so long as to be tied up with ribands'. Dougan simply could not reconcile their testimony with their appearance until he asked Amelia to 'lift up her fine outer garment'. Underneath, he found 'a filthy and ragged petticoat' and, beneath that, bruised skin: it was a 'shocking contrast'. Kitty and Amelia were telling the truth, but Maclean had dressed them in pristine frocks to conceal his abuse.[5]

Dougan was livid, and his temper only worsened as Maclean confessed to whipping the women with 'tamarind switches'. And when Moody offered Maclean the chance to clear his name, Dougan gave up 'all hopes of conciliation'. He resigned his commission and sailed home, a departure which Moody explained to the Colonial Office as a pitiable consequence 'of [Dougan's] health, having for some time past obviously been affected by a termination of blood to his head'. Back in England, but no longer possessed of the authority and status of a Royal Commission, Dougan published his own report to little acclaim. He died soon afterwards, penniless.[6]

Moody seized the moment. Dougan's resignation allowed him to become the British government's leading expert on 'tropical labour' and, as the sole remaining commissioner, he crafted a report that reflected all his own prejudices. He wrote that Africans were uncivilised and savage, that nothing but the whip would compel them to work, and that free African labour was impossible. Moody also described

Africans as uniquely durable in tropical conditions. 'The African race of men,' he advised, 'are able to bear [the] effects of the sun, and to undergo the labour required in agriculture' and this was the distinguishing feature between black men and white men, who were 'unequal to the labours of agriculture in the torrid zone'. White Europeans, he believed, simply could not 'enter into competition with the African race, in occupations requiring much exposure to the sun, or in agricultural industry'. It followed, at least in Moody's perverse worldview, that Africans were ideally and perhaps exclusively suited to sugar-cropping. These were opinions that Moody would repeat for years to come in papers and pamphlets, on West Indian committees, and even within the Colonial Office. Indeed, when he returned to London in 1824, taking up rooms on Baker Street, Moody resumed his correspondence with an old friend, who just so happened to be the minister of state for the West Indies.[7]

Born into Derbyshire's landed gentry, Robert Wilmot-Horton was educated at Eton and Oxford before entering Parliament on the liberal wing of the Tory coalition. He was the cousin of Lord Byron, who wrote the lines 'She walks in Beauty, like the night' about Wilmot-Horton's wife, Anne: the poet's relationship with Anne is thought to have been more familiar than familial. A rising star among the Canningites, Wilmot-Horton had joined the Colonial Office in 1821, and when departmental reforms gave him responsibility for Britain's 'western colonies' from 1824, he moved to the very centre of the overlapping networks and interests that were fighting over slavery. It was an exhausting role, and he soon complained to Canning that he had lived 'for many months in a complete atmosphere of W. Indian speculations & politics'.[8]

Because of these ministerial responsibilities, Wilmot-Horton's papers in the Derbyshire Records Office are an incomparable source on the British government's attitude towards slavery in the 1820s, and they reveal that Wilmot-Horton rarely approached the issue with neutrality. Despite liberal attitudes towards trade and religion, and genuine concern for the plight of Britain's poor, Wilmot-Horton was convinced that slave emancipation was dangerous and impractical. There was little secrecy about his feelings, either, and he told the Tory MP Henry Drummond that, if ever forced to choose between 'the Ultra-Abolitionists' or 'the moderate West Indian', he would not hesitate 'to avow ... the latter'. By 1824 Wilmot-Horton had already written a pro-slavery article for the *Quarterly Review* with the West Indian chairman Charles Ellis and, when he appointed Thomas Moody as 'Home Secretary for Foreign Parliamentary Commissioners', he made the Colonial Office a bastion of pro-slavery ideology.[9]

Over the next four years, Wilmot-Horton and Moody discussed the African capacity for labour in the language of explicit racial difference. At one point, Wilmot-Horton wrote to Moody about 'the truth of one great first principle ... a law of the Almighty, that the black and white races of men have unequal powers to endure the toil and trouble of cultivating the soil in our West India colonies'. For the Under-Secretary of State, this was just as obvious as 'that black is not white'. Wilmot-Horton spread this toxic gospel in the Cabinet, too, corresponding with William Huskisson about 'the character of the African race', the 'constitutional indisposition' which characterised 'the negro race', and 'the nature of the African ... to be indolent'. So long as Wilmot-Horton and Moody held sway at the Colonial Office, the slaveholding Interest breathed easily. Even more insidiously, the 'official' stamp on Moody's opinions now legitimised the contagious discourse about race and civilisation that was underpinning the British defence of slavery.[10]

In the 1770s, when the Jamaican planter and historian Edward Long devised a vulgar and explicitly racist philosophy to justify slavery, he had argued that the African was 'almost completely indistinguishable from the animal ... his image completely overlapping with that of the orang-utan'. In promulgating this poisonous doctrine, Long subscribed to the idea of polygenism: that the different human races constituted separate species which originated in different 'creations'. By the 1820s, polygenism was out of fashion and leading 'racial' thinkers instead sponsored 'monogenism', which held that even if 'the Caucasian' was different from 'the Ethiopian' or 'the Malay', all such races were human. In Britain, the leading monogenist was the Bristolian doctor James Cowles Prichard, whose *Researches into the Physical History of Man* is one of the most important works of pre-Darwinian anthropology. Building on the ideas of European scholars such as the Comte de Buffon and J.F. Blumenbach, Prichard argued for the essential unity of mankind and the idea that all human races were 'degradations' from the divine original as described in the book of Genesis. The slaveholders disagreed politically with Prichard, who was an abolitionist 'from his earliest years', but they were bound to follow his intellectual lead, not least because contradicting Prichard would have undermined their reading of the Old Testament.[11]

Indeed, having relied so heavily on scriptural literalism to argue that slavery was not sinful, the West Indians could not represent Creation as an allegory. The Jamaican cleric George Wilson Bridges therefore ridiculed the notion that Eve had given birth in the Garden of Eden 'to the white tribes of the North and the distinct Negroes of Ethiopia', while the pro-slavery curate Benjamin Bailey agreed that 'We are all the workmanship of one Divine Artificer'. An anonymous pro-slavery polemicist even sought to 'silence the absurd idea of the negroes being an inferior species', with one magazine rejecting polygenist thinking entirely: 'The notion ... that there are distinct species among mankind,' it declared, 'is utterly contradicted by every appeal to physiology and zoology.' Africans might have been British 'property', but they were children of the same God.[12]

Supposedly endemic differences between Africans and Caucasians were another matter. The Liverpool slaveholder John Gladstone wrote about 'the natural dispositions of the Negro race', while the pro-planter hack James Franklin referred to 'vices of idolatry and heathenism so peculiar to the African race'. Complementing these abhorrent semantics, West Indians argued that Africans were physically distinct from Europeans. Thomas Moody asserted that 'the Englishman ... generally [differed] in form, colours, and features, from the ... African races of mankind', and that such 'extreme physical differences' were nature's inherent guarantee against miscegenation. At the same time, the planter H.P. Simmons opined that the African's physical 'organization ... when compared with every other variety of the human race, [was] extremely defective'. Here, Simmons deployed the popular pseudo-science of phrenology to suggest that Africans were 'remarkable for the narrowness of their intellect and the smallness of their forehead'.[13]

However, the West Indians were not alone in positing a racial hierarchy *within* the bounds of humanity. The abolitionists might have begged the famous question, 'Am I not a man and a brother?' They might also have believed in the unity of races, but they too were 'negrophobes' and they did not equate the campaign for African freedom with the pursuit of African equality. When William Wilberforce hosted a dinner for the African and Asiatic Society, for instance, his guests of colour ate their meal behind a screen. Wilberforce also believed that liberated Africans belonged to the lowest rungs of society: 'Taught by Christianity,' he declared, 'they will sustain with patience the sufferings of their actual lot ... [and] will soon be regarded as a grateful peasantry.' In a similar fashion, Zachary Macaulay deplored miscegenation and 'the degraded concubinage [that is] so generally prevalent between the whites and the free coloured women' in the colonies. George Stephen, the firebrand son of James, refused help to the relatives of a former slave because he claimed it was 'no part of [his] anti-slavery charity to maintain a family of half-castes'. The abolitionists hated slavery, but they never once considered Africans to be their equals; in the event of emancipation, the liberated Africans would merely form a 'free black peasantry'.[14]

Of course, the abolitionists and the Interest disagreed over the role of slavery in the piece. For Buxton and his allies, slavery was a brutalising system which inhibited the development of the African race; conversely, the West Indians believed that slavery was necessary to the *improvement* of the Africans. They arrived at this conclusion with the help of the Scottish Enlightenment concept of stadial progress, according to which all societies passed through four stages of civilisation. In the beginning, all people were hunter-gatherers who scrambled for food in tribes and packs. People reached the second stage of civilisation when they became pastoral farmers who tended to sheep, pigs, and cattle. After that, cultivating the land provided the clearest indication of development; accordingly, the penultimate stage of civilisation was occupied by arable farmers who grew crops. The apogee of 'civilisation' was attained only when people became commercial city-dwellers trading in goods and services. In the second half of the eighteenth century, philosophers such as David Hume and Adam Ferguson had placed this four-stage model at the core of developmental theory and 'conjectural history'. In the 1820s, the model held good: it was a matter of civilisational pride that Britain was 'a nation of shop-keepers'.[15]

Slaveholders and their collaborators subscribed almost universally to this four-stage theory and to the developmental power of agriculture.

For the bigoted cleric George Wilson Bridges, it was 'agriculture alone which leads mankind from the last degree of savage life to the first [degree] of civilized society'. James MacQueen agreed entirely, writing that 'the produce of the soil is proof of the industry of [a] country, and the industry thereof a proof of its progress in civilization'. It followed from these assumptions that West Indian slavery, where Africans learned to cultivate the land under the tutelage of a 'civilized' people, was a powerful engine of progress. In other words, slavery was not cruel and degrading but salutary and instructive, a 'positive good'.[16]

Yet for stadial theory to apply entirely to 'the West India Question', the Interest first needed to show that Africa was stuck in the lowest stage of civilisation. Notwithstanding their fierce criticism of 'telescopic philanthropy', they did so without meaningful experience of Africa itself: few West Indians visited the continent and even James MacQueen, who became an 'expert' on African geography, was an armchair explorer. Instead, the West Indians ransacked travelogues for evidence of the African 'savagery' that they wanted to find. One authority was Mungo Park, the Scottish surgeon whose *Travels in the Interior Districts of Africa* recounted his expedition along the Niger River. Prepared with the West Indian historian Bryan Edwards, Park's *Travels* was cited by slaveholders to show that Africans, or at least 'seven-eighths of [them]', lived naturally in conditions of 'hopeless and irredeemable slavery', thereby excusing British enslavement of them. Almost as popular was *Travels in the Timmanee* by another Niger-obsessed explorer, Alexander Gordon Laing, who was praised by one pro-slavery magazine for 'so well describ[ing] the ferocity and brutality of the African tribes'. The memoir of the English explorer Dixon Denham, who was cited by Jules Verne, confirmed that 'before the Africans were received by the Planters, they were savages ... of the lowest possible description'. Working from this 'canonical' set of travelogues, the Interest's scribes arrived at a monolithic definition of 'the African' that paid little heed to diverse cultures and ethnicities. 'The African hordes resemble each other in their barbarous lives,' concluded George Wilson Bridges: everything 'monstrous, vile, and contemptible' was found 'universally' among them, and the 'picture of one contains the outline of them all'.[17]

Within this literature, African society was defined by three key features. The first was cannibalism, with one pamphleteer asserting that West Indian slaves were 'neither more nor less than the ancient cannibals, the Anthropagi, "men who wore their heads beneath their shoulders"'. The Buckinghamshire magistrate Anthony Davis was adamant that Africans filed their teeth 'for eating human flesh, for such was their native habit'. For the pamphleteer Anthony Brough, Africa was 'a land of ... cannibalism' where the 'only permanent passion was revenge'.[18]

Second, there was a predilection for violence. One pro-planter magazine referred to African homelands as 'native lairs of ferocious anarchy and bloody paganism', and one of the more sophisticated pro-slavery ideologues wrote of 'dreadful enormities, and bloody sacrifices, which stain and mark the career of petty sovereignty on the [African] continent'. Who, then, was 'an African prince'? For *Blackwood's*, he was 'a creature who amuses himself ... with cutting off human heads'. When that prince prayed to 'the demon of his beastly worship', he watered African soil 'with blood poured out like water'. Africans were 'maimed – mutilated – murdered every day', all in alleged thrall to 'the hatchet ... of this crowned brute'.[19]

Third and most telling was stagnation. In Thomas Moody's opinion, some parts of Africa had once shown promise: there had been commerce and agriculture in ancient Egypt, Carthage had 'eclipsed all the nations of the World in Wealth and enterprize', and Abyssinia had its 'martyrs, its Bishops'. But their one-time majesty made no 'great impression on the black races of men' to the south of those regions, and so black Africans inhabited a civilisational backwater. *Blackwood's* agreed, claiming that African 'intellect has stood still for many thousand years and has, up to this moment, done absolutely NOTHING'. Africa was 'one dark realm of primitive barbarity, wherein the natives are alike incapable of ... making any progress in civilization or science'.[20]

In the West Indian imagination, however, slavery was 'improving' the African, lifting him up from barbarism and through the stages of civilisation. The Demeraran planter Henry Holmes claimed that Britons had 'shut their eyes' to this gradual but self-evident process because, for those West Indians in the know, the progress was remarkable. 'Will any man who looks at [the African's] case dispassionately,' asked the *Barbadian*, 'and calls to mind his origin, and the barbarous hordes whence he was subtracted, say that he is not an improved, a more moral, a better instructed, and a more rational animal in the West Indies, than he was in the fens of native Africa?' The idea that enslavement to the British was 'improving' the African informed one of Lord Liverpool's only known statements on slavery. Writing to Nicholas Vansittart, his former Chancellor of the Exchequer, the prime minister mooted a policy of forcibly emigrating 'a European half-military Peasantry on a large Scale' to the colonies. If the British founded 'two or three Villages or forty or fifty Families of Europeans' in Jamaica, in sight of 'the Cathedral and College' that Liverpool also planned to build, the increased white presence on the island would 'promote the success of the general Plan & ultimately the civilization of the servile Population'.[21]

The Interest even argued that enslaved Africans were improving *physically*. William Shand, the owner of 3,400 enslaved people, suggested that 'the Features of the Negroes are exceedingly altered' and now 'more expressive', and whereas native Africans had noses 'flat to the Cheek', this was 'very rare in the Creole Negro'. The pro-slavery novel *Marly* described a similar transformation, whereby black West Indians had become 'strong-built handsome-looking black people' who were 'greatly improved, both in features, in size, and in strength from the African race'. Indigenous African features of 'thick lips, and the broad nose [were] giving place to what Europeans consider beauty'. Soon, they would 'have a resemblance to their masters in every respect, except colour'. For some members of the Interest, this was why the policy of 'amelioration' was both intrusive *and* unnecessary: African 'improvement' apparently occurred anyway under conditions of slavery.[22]

Even so, civilisation was not a status, it was a process; and a reversible process at that. The West Indians therefore warned that, if Parliament were to emancipate the enslaved and remove the direct influence of the British planter, all this 'good work' would be undone. Here, in what historians have called 'the war of representation' over slavery, the abolitionists and West Indians fought over two battlegrounds: the free republic of Haiti, whose independence had been recognised by France for a price of 150 million francs; and the British colony of Sierra Leone.[23]

For the abolitionists, Haiti was a marvel. They celebrated its government, 'framed on the model of the United States', and they praised the achievements of the current regime, 'under which great improvements are stated to have taken place'. Samuel Roberts was the son of a Sheffield silver-plater who earned the soubriquet 'the Pauper's Advocate' for his campaign against the Old Poor Law, and he believed that Haitian history showed that 'free negroes will not only work, but [that] they are capable of governing, as well as of being governed'. Accordingly, the abolitionists lamented the 'impolitic tardiness' of the government in establishing commercial relations with Haiti, a policy they could explain only 'by the predominance of West-Indian prejudices'. On the contrary, the West Indians believed that Haiti was an ominous portent of the post-slavery world. They believed that, ever since the removal of white influence, Haiti had become 'a retreat for Savages with the vices of half civilized Society'. The African propensity for violence had resurfaced, too, with 'Britannicus' informing the *Edinburgh Review* that 'more monstrous crimes [had] never disgraced human nature – ingratitude, robbery, [and] murder' had created 'a scene of atrocity more horrible than any perpetrated in France under the terrific tyrant of Robespierre'.[24]

The abolitionists thought just as well of Sierra Leone, which they described as 'the instrument of imparting to thousands of Africans, raised from the lowest depths of misery and debasement, the blessings of British freedom, and of Christian light'. Taking an opposite view, the West Indians believed 'the Free Negroes [there were] poor, wretched, and miserable'. The *Barbadian* described the colony as 'Pandaemonium', while George Wilson Bridges damned it as a 'deadly experiment'. At the same time, James MacQueen 'reported' that Sierra Leone's free Africans had 'retrograde[d] in the woods into a state of nature and barbarism, or become vagrants about Freetown'. The extent of civilisation in Sierra Leone was also the subject of a long-running dispute between MacQueen and Kenneth Macaulay, a cousin of Zachary, who had governed the colony in the 1810s. Macaulay had failed in his work, asserted MacQueen: Sierra Leone was 'a heterogeneous mass of ignorance, barbarism, indolence, injustice, and oppression'.[25]

For the Interest, Sierra Leone and Haiti were the evidence that civilisational collapse would surely follow from emancipation; they were the supposedly empirical grounds for assuming that the 'earthly paradise' of the British West Indies would degenerate into a barbaric wilderness in the event of African freedom. Implicit in all of this was the spectre of slave retribution: if the rumours of rebellion had terrified the colonists of Demerara in 1823, the revenge of 'uncivilized' Africans upon their former masters was cause for continued alarm. The *Morning Chronicle* warned that emancipation meant 'turning loose a set of half savages, who will soon desolate the island, and leave the marks of blood and fire wherever they go', and William Cobbett predicted that emancipation would write 'a second chapter of the ... bloodshed of St Domingo'. One pro-slavery journalist even feared 'the entire of our slave colonies becoming one great holocaust'.[26]

Even so, the Interest buried a concession deep within this toxic rhetoric: if slavery was a civilising force, it meant that the enslaved would someday 'deserve' freedom. A few writers intimated a schedule. *The Voice of the West Indies* suggested that emancipation would be feasible upon the maturity of 'the *third* generation', while a 'Merchant' identified '1860 as the nearest period at which ... we could arrive at [emancipation] without injury to anyone'. More commonly, West Indians suggested that freedom should be delayed for as long as possible. The Bahamian authorities settled on the passage of 'some considerable distance of time ... before the completion of the metamorphosis', while James Colquhoun reminded Robert Wilmot-Horton that 'you cannot alter the Negro in the present State of Society, unless perhaps by very slow degrees'.[27]

Of course, the West Indians were holding Africans to an impossible standard of which all men, regardless of colour, fell short. 'If men are to wait for liberty till they become wise and good,' remarked Thomas Macaulay, 'they may indeed wait forever.' They were also ignoring a welter of evidence that free black people were already contributing markedly to British culture. There was the author and composer Ignatius Sancho who made friends of David Garrick and Laurence Sterne, had his portrait painted by Gainsborough, and became the first black person to have an obituary in the national press. There was George Bridgetower, a violinist who gave the inaugural performance of the *Kreutzer Sonata* alongside Beethoven. The West Indians had also forgotten Olaudah Equiano and Ottobah Cugoano, whose writings in the 1780s had struck such blows against the slave trade. Yet if the slaveholders wanted another 'good' reason for delaying emancipation, the events of the mid-1820s would give it to them.[28]

*

Lewis Celeste Lecesne was born in Jamaica, or maybe in Haiti – nobody is quite sure. But by the 1820s he was a respected merchant in Kingston, described as 'a man of great natural shrewdness, most accurate and trustworthy in his statements, and possessed of a manly frankness of character worthy of a British subject'. Lecesne was married to Hannah, the sister of the victualler John Escoffery, and the brothers-in-law were inseparable. They worked as liquor merchants; they joined the local militia, both rising to the rank of sergeant; and they owned houses, land, and people. Lecesne also performed his Christian duty by fostering and educating a cabin boy, Barnet Burns, whose travels in New Zealand made him a celebrity: despite initial fears of native 'cannibals', Burns became one of the first white men to immerse himself in Maori culture and later, as a showman, he thrilled European crowds with his tribal dress and facial tattoos.[29]

Yet while Lecesne and Escoffery built lives that were little different from those of other Jamaicans, one fact placed them at a series of political, economic, and civil disadvantages: they were black. Until 1813, Jamaica's 36,000 free persons of colour had been forbidden from bequeathing estates worth more than £2,000, or navigating vessels along the island's coastline, or giving evidence in court against whites. Even in the 1820s they could not serve on juries, vote, stand for public office, or work for profit on a white-owned plantation. All this despite paying the same taxes as the island's whites. This was why Lecesne and Escoffery had spent 1823 building a petition for the equality of all free Jamaicans, notwithstanding their colour, but with the abolitionist campaign heightening tensions in the colonies, this was a dangerous business.[30]

In light of their political activity, Lecesne and Escoffery were arrested as 'dangerous persons' under a warrant issued by the Jamaican governor, the Duke of Manchester. Now, the dispute over Lecesne's birthplace resurfaced: the authorities claimed that he was Haitian, so that he could be deported summarily. A last-minute injunction from the colony's Supreme Court stayed this fate, but offered little lasting relief: it only gave more time to the two men's enemies to fabricate charges. Accordingly, the slaveholder Hector Mitchel persuaded the Jamaican House of Assembly to form a secret Committee of Investigation, and while there is no record of the Committee's proceedings, its report concluded that Lecesne and Escoffery were Haitian spies who had been selling arms to discontented slaves. These findings rested on the evidence of a single witness, an enslaved person; another who refused to testify was imprisoned in solitary confinement; and testimony from thirty leading residents of Kingston as to Lecesne's and Escoffery's good characters was dismissed as 'unworthy of serious consideration'. Despite these travesties of justice, the colony's Attorney General, William Burge, approved the report and concurred 'in the firm conviction ... that Lecesne and Escoffery were aliens of a dangerous character'.[31]

The constables of Kingston promptly arrested Lecesne and Escoffery in their shop and charged them once more again with being 'aliens and dangerous persons'. There were no hearings, there was no trial. Forbidden from saying goodbye to their children, they were bundled onto a ship in the harbour and ferried to Haiti, where they were dumped on the wharves of the port of Jacmel. Despite the Jamaican belief that Haiti was their homeland, neither Lecesne nor Escoffery knew anybody there. They were soon reduced to vagrancy and, in a moment of the darkest irony, the Haitian authorities contemplated arresting them on suspicion of being British spies. Only a serendipitous meeting with three English merchants revived their fortunes. The merchants paid for passage to Britain, where Lecesne and Escoffery would plead their case before Parliament.

They were met in London by Stephen Lushington, an abolitionist lawyer and the Whig MP for Ilchester. Everything about Lushington conveyed the impression of a formidable man: he had a piercing stare, an aquiline nose, and a mane of thick, black hair. Although now in his forties, he retained the athletic frame which had allowed him to play first-class cricket for Surrey and the famed Marylebone Cricket Club. A true all-rounder, Lushington had also been a fellow of All Souls College, Oxford, until marriage compelled his resignation: dons of the day were obliged to be single. The son of a chairman of the East India Company, Lushington had been involved in the anti-slavery campaign since the first meeting in the King's Head in 1823, and Lecesne and Escoffery could not have wished for a better advocate.[32]

In May 1824, Lushington presented Lecesne's and Escoffery's petition to the House of Commons. He deplored the abuses that his clients had suffered. He insisted on the accountability of the Jamaican authorities. And he would not rest 'until he had rescued the character of the British nation from the foul disgrace of having participated in an act of such odious oppression'. Leading the government's reply, Robert Wilmot-Horton entrenched his reputation as a West Indian knave by suggesting that there was not 'conclusive evidence of the fact of [Lecesne and Escoffery] being British-born subjects'. He reposed his faith in the Jamaican authorities, who were 'empowered by law to remove [them] from the island'. Lushington was denied. Though he tried again in 1825, it was not until 1826 that he secured an inquiry; even then, the Tories obscured the truth, refusing to publish the eventual report which excoriated the Jamaican authorities. Another five years passed before the full compensation of £11,000 reached Lecesne and Escoffery.[33]

In the colonies, the reaction to Lushington's activism was apoplectic and when he published the 'Yellow Book', a record of his speeches and the evidence relating to the Lecesne affair, he briefly became the West Indians' most hated antagonist. The Jamaican assemblyman Richard Barrett ranted that Lushington was the herald of 'the English mob [and] ... all the desperadoes in the United Kingdom'. Employing a familiar vocabulary, Barrett claimed that the abolitionists were aiming 'to plunder and massacre one race of men [the Jamaican whites], for the chance of civilizing a different race'. Hector Mitchel, having jailed the enslaved person who refused to inculpate Lecesne, responded to Lushington by declaring that 'West Indians ... dislike the contact and the smell of a negro'. Mitchell claimed that white colonists 'loved the pure blood of our English countrymen better than the mixed stream that flows in the veins of ... the negro'. In Mitchel's view, black men like Lecesne and Escoffery could never be truly British.[34]

Ironically, these Jamaican tirades provided Lecesne and Escoffery with another means of redress. When George Wilson Bridges published the second volume of his *Annals*, he damned Lushington as a man who had 'blindly espoused ... the cause of murder and rebellion', and described Lecesne and Escoffery as 'two French prisoners who had ... attempt[ed] to revolutionize the island, and who were impatient to sheath their daggers in the breasts of its white inhabitants'. Accordingly, the three men sued Bridges' publisher, John Murray, for libel. Lushington enlisted Macaulay, Brougham, and the younger James Stephen in the fight; in his defence, Murray instructed

John Taylor Coleridge, who had written pro-slavery articles for Murray's *Quarterly Review*. In the end, the jury had little trouble in finding Murray guilty. Yet because he had already removed 671 copies of the *Annals* from London's bookstores, and because he had apologised for publishing 'matter inconsistent with the truth', the court was lenient. Murray was fined one shilling.[35]

Little is known of the rest of Escoffery's life, but Louis Lecesne settled in London, working once more as a victualler until his eventual bankruptcy. He returned to Jamaica only once, in 1830, when the colonial House of Assembly at last passed legislation for the civil equality of free people of colour, and he was 'hailed with the utmost joy by the free black and coloured inhabitants'. Lecesne also became a prominent member of the Anti-Slavery Society, christening his next son 'Stephen Lushington Macaulay', and he would feature prominently in Benjamin Haydon's painting of the global Anti-Slavery Convention in 1840. However, Lecesne's horrific experience at the hands of the Jamaican authorities appears not to have encouraged clemency on his own part. In 1834, when the fifteen-year-old Thomas Fielder was accused of stealing his handkerchief on Fenchurch Street, Lecesne brought charges before the Old Bailey. Fielder begged for mercy, but Lecesne upheld his case: the boy was sentenced to transportation for life.[36]

The summer of 1825 was the high point of the grass-roots campaign that Elizabeth Heyrick was leading against West Indian sugar. Although she considered abstention 'so small and insignificant that it seems almost burlesque to dignify it with the name' of a sacrifice, Heyrick believed that if British families committed to 'ABSTINENCE FROM THE USE OF WEST INDIAN PRODUCTION', it would 'give the death blow to West Indian slavery'. Indeed, she considered this economic warfare as an essential step on the path to Caribbean reform: 'When there is no longer a market for the productions of *slave labour*,' she explained, 'then, and not *till then*, will the slaves be emancipated.' This was an explicitly women-led campaign and Heyrick had raised the standard in the *Hummingbird*, her own periodical, where she wrote that the time was now past 'when the energies of the female sex were wasted upon laborious and everlasting tasks of needle-work, and their literature confined to cookery books'. The British women who controlled their families' purse-strings had rallied to Heyrick's banner. In Leicester, she and her allies distributed 'workbags' containing anthologies of anti-abolitionist literature. In Wiltshire, fuelled by 'free sugar', one West Indian sympathizer despaired that his neighbourhood was being overwhelmed by 'Anti Slavery Needle Parties, and Anti Slavery Tea-parties'. The Sheffield Female Anti-Slavery Society meanwhile took out advertisements informing shoppers that 'by six families using [free-grown] East India instead of West India Sugar, one Slave less is required'. Surely, the women of Sheffield reasoned, 'to release a fellow-creature from a state of cruel bondage and misery, by so small a sacrifice, is worthy the attention of all?'[37]

The Whig MP and abolitionist Henry Brougham was effusive in praising these endeavours, writing to the Countess of Jersey that such women were 'powerful and universally diffused allies', not to mention those who had 'most influence on society'. Some leading abolitionists, though, condemned female campaigning as unseemly. Zachary Macaulay despaired of this interference, and Wilberforce believed that 'for ladies to meet, to publish, to go from house to house stirring up petitions ... [was] unsuited to the female character as delineated in Scripture'. He explained to Macaulay that 'it is to the political character of the subject that my repugnance chiefly applies'. Still, patriarchal disapproval would not contain the insurgency. The chairwoman of one ladies' association riposted that, while 'men may propose only *gradually* to abolish the worst of crimes ... no Ladies Association will ever be found with such words attached to it'. Nor did the censure make the abstentionist campaign any less effective: of the households that she visited, Heyrick reckoned that nine-tenths joined the boycott. Further afield, she made such an impact that a national pro-slavery magazine took aim at 'the benevolent societies of Leicester'.[38]

By striking at the planters' domestic market, Heyrick and Britain's women were seeking to undermine one of the most common defences of slavery: that the slave system was essential to the prosperity of the British Empire. Abstentionism thereby multiplied the articles, pamphlets, and books which sought to attack or to justify slavery from an economic perspective. Although they had formed part of the slavery debate since 1823, the potential for 'free African labour', the benefits of protective tariffs, and transatlantic commerce now became staples of conversation. In 1825, these economic arguments were thrown into even sharper relief by two key events. First, the government admitted sugar from Mauritius to the British market on the same terms as West Indian sugar, thus creating a glut in the market and depressing prices. Second, and more pressingly, Britain would suffer the worst financial crisis since the South Sea Bubble.

8.

Wages or the Whip

The Country banks are breaking,
The London banks are shaking;
Suspicion is awaking,
E'en Quakers now are quaking;
Experience seems to settle,
That paper is not metal;
And promises of payment,
Are neither food nor raiment.[1]

'Pan in Town' (1825), Thomas Love Peacock

In 1825, Britain was booming. Unemployment was low, bread was cheap, industries were thriving, and engineers were developing plans for the first railways. The King's Speech of the previous year had suggested that 'at no former period has there prevailed throughout all classes in this island a more cheerful spirit of order, or a more just sense of the advantages which, under the blessing of Providence, they enjoy'. The post-war depression was a mere memory, and bankers were enjoying the profits and optimism that attend a bull market, one cause of which had been a loose monetary policy. Encouraging speculation that had lain dormant in the 1810s, the Liverpool ministry had reduced interest on government securities and extended the lifespan of low-value notes. At the same time, the Bank of England pumped excess cash into the economy, much of which was taken up by the smaller 'country banks' which offered often-risky credit to investors.[2]

Some part of this speculation was domestic, and 624 joint-stock companies were formed in 1824 alone. Permission for incorporation was granted almost automatically since William Huskisson and his

Board of Trade declined to perform much due diligence. 'To probe to the bottom the merits of the various speculations,' Huskisson averred, 'and to … decide which was likely to be a beneficial undertaking, and which a bubble' simply was not the job of government. A little discretion would have gone a long way, for some of the schemes in which pensioners, widowers, and ambitious middling sorts were allowed to invest their savings were truly speculative. The Metropolitan Bath Company undertook to pipe sea water from the coast to central London so that city-dwellers could enjoy the healthful benefits of salt-water bathing. For £25, an investor could buy a share in the London Cemetery Association for the Security of the Dead, which sought to prevent body-snatchers from disturbing the peace of the departed. The Resurrection Metal Company promised to harvest iron cannon-balls from the seabed beneath the sites of famous naval battles.[3]

The major part of British speculation concerned Latin America. Over the previous fifteen years the Spanish Empire had crumbled, and the republics which emerged – Gran Colombia, Peru, Mexico, and others – held out lucrative opportunities for British investors. These new nations were short of cash and, promising lavish returns on government bonds, they courted millions in British capital. As money followed money, some £17 million was raised in London for loans to Latin America, a figure accounting for half the European bond market in 1824. Similar amounts were invested in private enterprise, in the companies that would marshal European trade with the new republics. British investors, as if they were financial conquistadores, expected bountiful returns from a continent rich in gold, silver, tin, coffee, and sugar. It was for the security of such contracts and investments, as much as for geopolitics, that George Canning had effectively proposed the Monroe Doctrine to the American government, by which the United States had warned the French and Spanish against recolonising the New World.

On occasion, the enthusiasm for Latin America descended into mania, as with Gregor MacGregor's plans for the burgeoning new nation of Poyais. Informing potential investors that the King of the Mosquito Coast had made him chieftain of Poyais, MacGregor came to London in search of the capital and manpower that his new Eden needed. As a veteran of the Peninsular War and a hero of the Bolivarian Revolutions, MacGregor had little difficulty in drumming up support.

Joshua Bryant's depiction of the Battle of Bachelor's Adventure
during the Demerara Rebellion of August 1823.

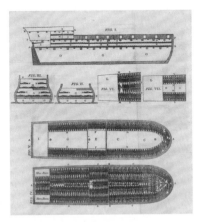

The notorious diagram of the *Brookes*
slave ship, first published by abolitionists
in Plymouth in 1788.

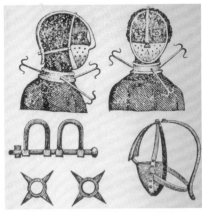

Iron masks, collars, leg shackles,
and spurs were used to restrict Africans
on slave ships.

Turner's *Slave Ship*, which was inspired by the *Zong* Massacre of 1781.

George Morland's 'Slave Trade' mezzotint (1814),
after John Raphael Smith's original watercolour (1788).

James Hakewill was an English architect who toured Jamaica in 1820 and 1821. These are his engravings of Kingston's Harbour Street (above) and the Montpelier Estate belonging to the Interest's chairman, Charles Rose Ellis (below).

CUTTING THE SUGAR-CANE.

The painter William Clark was invited to Antigua by the island's planters to depict life in the colonies. In 1823, he published *Ten Views of the Island of Antigua*, including these sanitised scenes of cutting sugar cane (above) and the work that went on inside the boiling houses (below).

INTERIOR OF A BOILING HOUSE.

The leading abolitionists in 1823:
Thomas Fowell Buxton (above left), Thomas Clarkson with his 'box' (above right),
Zachary Macaulay (below left), and William Wilberforce (below right).

Cruikshank's infamous *John Bull Taking a Clear View of the Negro Question* (1826),
which depicts the abolitionists as indulging in hysteria and telescopic philanthropy.

The grand West India Docks in east London, c. 1810.

The Interest in 1823: its chairman, Charles Rose Ellis (above left); the agent for Jamaica, George Hibbert (above right); the banker Alexander Baring (below left); and their political guardian, George Canning (below right). All four men had themselves painted by the leading portraitist of the time, Thomas Lawrence.

John SMITH

Appt. 1817 – Retd. – – Died. 1824
Register No. 175

British Guiana

IMMEDIATE;

NOT GRADUAL

ABOLITION;

OR

AN INQUIRY

INTO THE SHORTEST, SAFEST, AND MOST EFFECTUAL
MEANS OF GETTING RID OF

WEST INDIAN SLAVERY.

PHILADELPHIA:
PUBLISHED BY THE PHILADELPHIA LADIES' ANTI-SLAVERY SOCIETY.
PRINTED BY MERRIHEW AND GUNN,
No. 7 Carters' Alley.
1836.

The death in a Demeraran prison cell of the
Christian missionary John Smith was a major
catalyst for the anti-slavery movement.

Even years after its initial
publication, this pamphlet by
Elizabeth Heyrick of Leicester
was spurring abolitionist
activity around the world.

William Shrewsbury's chapel in Barbados,
as depicted by a Wesleyan mission newsletter.

Moreover, City bankers had already ploughed his furrow: if reputable financiers were pouring cash into other parts of the continent, then why not Poyais too? The bankers Perring & Co. provided MacGregor with a hefty loan; a bond issue in the Poyais government realised another £200,000; and hundreds of private investors, many of them from the Scottish town of Leith, stumped up small fortunes for passage to this paradise. MacGregor's brochures promised a capital city, St Joseph's, which rivalled Havana for the grandeur of its boulevards, banks, and cathedrals. Gold could be hewn from the mountains with a pickaxe; crops of sugar, coffee, and indigo could be raised at leisure. Heaven had been remade on Earth. But when these would-be colonists arrived in Central America, they found only swamp and jungle. Poyais did not exist.[4]

This farrago exemplified the lengths to which rabid investors, flush with cheap money, would scramble for profit. Observing keenly, the West India Interest had encouraged the craze: the more that Britain invested in Latin America, the more valuable the West Indies became as hubs of transatlantic trade. The merchants of Kingston were insistent that the colonies afforded 'the best means for successfully carrying on the trade between [Britain] and ... the South American states'. The slaveholding MP John Rock Grossett agreed that 'the Atlantic outworks of the empire' would connect domestic markets with 'the ancient country of Montezuma'. There would also be direct trade between Latin America and the West Indies, for in British depots the 'South Americans and Mexicans might find every description of British or foreign commodity, to be taken in exchange for bullion and tropical products'. Of course, there was a none-too-subtle subtext to this commercial analysis. If the West Indies were to become the vital link in a chain between the motherland and South America, policy-makers in London could ill afford to undermine the West Indian economy by emancipating its workforce.[5]

By late 1825, however, plans to make the West Indies the commercial gateway to Latin America were put on hold. The City, which had long ignored the swirling rumours, reckoned at last with the failure of Mexican agriculture and Argentinian mining, and with the poverty of the former Spanish Empire in general. The money stopped, and the confidence of the market was shaken. Entrepreneurs who had taken out risky loans found that optimism was no match for reality, and the bubble burst. Shares were sold, not bought; prices plummeted, and companies were exposed as shams. Pessimists began to withdraw their gold from British banks and, by October, there was a run on the smaller banks which had funded so much of the speculation. The government responded by raising interest rates, hoping to lure some money back indoors, but in mid-December the London bank of Pole, Thornton, & Co. – founded by the abolitionist Henry Thornton – collapsed, taking forty-three country banks with it. In some places, there was so little money that trade was reduced to barter. John Gladstone reported to William Huskisson that Gloucester's oldest bank – Turner, Turner, and Morris – had failed 'to secure a supply of bank-notes and sovereigns' and so dissolved. Gladstone observed that it was 'impossible to supply a currency in sufficient quantity for the general purposes of circulation ... and the want of it must therefore be productive of evils and inconvenience'. The future conservative MP Charles Knightley was even forced to delve into his daughter's piggy bank to finance a journey from Daventry to London; otherwise, he had 'not the means of getting a shilling'.[6]

By the weekend before Christmas, the Bank of England was down to its last hundred thousand sovereigns. With the next day's demands for money expected to exceed reserves by a factor of four, the suspension of cash payments was feared as probable. Harriet Arbuthnot, the wife of a government minister and a confidante of the Duke of Wellington, recorded the panic that was sweeping through Westminster. 'What will happen in the country,' she wrote, 'I do not know. The banks are breaking in every direction & ... there is now in fact no circulation, for gold cannot be supplied & every thing is at a stand ... In the manufacturing districts they do not know how to pay the wages & serious riots are expected.' She was not alone in fearing anarchy: the Home Secretary, Robert Peel, ordered battalions of soldiers to guard the Bank.[7]

This was the closest that the British financial system came to collapse between the South Sea Bubble of 1720 and the credit crisis of 2008, and its survival in December 1825 was apparently a matter of luck. In the telling of the pro-slavery financier Alexander Baring, who had studiously avoided investment in South America, the crisis abated only when £1 million in notes was discovered in the vaults of the Bank. Even so, the long-term solvency of the Bank depended on its reserves of gold, and things remained uncertain until Nathan Rothschild, the German émigré banker, rode to the rescue. As the Bank teetered on the brink, Rothschild's agents were dispatched to the major centres of European finance with instructions to buy gold at almost any price. On 16 December, they found £150,000 in gold sovereigns in Paris and bullion was flowing back into the country within days. Lord Liverpool, who had been chairing crisis meetings on an almost hourly basis, was sufficiently confident that he chose to spend Christmas at his country retreat.[8]

Although the Bank of England survived the Panic of 1825, other institutions did not. A total of eighty banks collapsed and, of the six hundred and twenty-four companies formed during the bull market of 1824–25, at least five hundred failed. Alexander Baring reflected that 'there had existed the wildest gambling and the most absurd and mad adventures, to be compared only to, and hardly exceeded by, the South Sea Bubble'. Many who had invested directly in Latin America were ruined; many others were collaterally damaged. The West Indian merchant William Manning believed that bankruptcy, for men of his generation, was synonymous with death, and plenty chose suicide over living with the former. Besides leaving a deep and human impact on the British economy, the Panic of 1825 intruded directly into the debate over slavery. Most relevantly, the pessimism and uncertainty caused by the Panic allowed the West Indians to ask a rather leading question of the government: if slavery was economically essential to the colonies, and the colonies were essential to the Empire, how could Britain – in light of the Panic – possibly afford the economic risk of emancipation?[9]

Economics was at the heart of the fight over slavery, but not always in the ways one might think. When evangelical abolitionists such as Buxton and Wilberforce approached slave emancipation from this perspective, they often had two ideas in mind. First, that economic freedom was just as important as personal freedom. In this view, true liberty was attained only by hearing the Gospel and then by exposing oneself to a free market in which the Holy Spirit moved the 'invisible hand' of Adam Smith's imagination; the economic fortunes of a man were therefore the manifestation of the divine will. Second, they believed that slavery was sinfully inefficient and that free labour, stimulated by the reward of wages, was more productive. Accordingly, abolitionists such as James Cropper had preached a creed of free labour to the public, to the government, and to the West Indians themselves. They insisted that a freed African workforce could sustain the planta- tions because 'the desire of bettering his condition [would] always induce the Black man in the West Indies to work'. Adhering to theo- ries of labour put forward by Smith, Ricardo, and others, they believed that a man working for himself would work harder than if compelled by a master: wages, not the whip, drove economic growth. These were ideas that the social theorist Harriet Martineau would depict perfectly in her 1832 *Illustrations of Political Economy*.[10]

The West India Interest conceded that 'free labour' was in theory more efficient, but they disagreed entirely that free labour could ever 'work' on the plantations. This was more than crude intransigence. After all, if the West Indians thought that they could make more money out of free labour, there would have been no logical reason for resisting slave emancipation. Instead, informed as they were by racist assumptions about African 'civilization', the planters clung dogmatically to the idea that only slave labour could deliver prosperity to the West Indies.

The most sophisticated pro-slavery economist was a twenty-seven- year-old Ulsterman. Alexander McDonnell was the Belfast-born son of a doctor, and he is often remembered as a chess player: an opening gambit is named after him, his matches against Louis de la Bourdonnais are seminal moments in the game's history, and he was eulogised as 'the best player in Great Britain'. Yet when McDonnell was drawn into colonial affairs through commercial dealings with James MacQueen, he became secretary of the West India Merchants and an articulate draughtsman for the Interest at large, writing 'almost all the Papers given in to Government on Colonial subjects'. His *Considerations on Negro Slavery* (1824) was almost the Interest's textbook, going through 'a very Large Edition' and nearly selling off a second. In later works McDonnell addressed the constitutions of the colonies, the practical details of manumission, and demography, but his most substantial 'contributions' were in political economy. In *Free Trade* (1826) and *Colonial Commerce* (1828), dense and lengthy works of histor- ically informed economics, McDonnell railed against the free-trade, free-labour ideas of classical economists such as Smith, Ricardo, and

J.R. McCulloch, ideas that McDonnell believed would ruin the Caribbean colonies if ever translated into British policy.[11]

McDonnell was not a typical member of the Interest. Politically he was 'a decided Whig', whereas 'the mass of practical West Indians [were] tories', and Thomas Moody occasionally intervened to prevent McDonnell leading 'unthinking, credulous ... listeners' astray. Still, the slaveholders knew that McDonnell was their most able advocate. The *Barbadian* marvelled that, 'with a clear head, a ready pen', he had 'a decided advantage over the ... theorists and enthusiastic advocates ... on the anti-colonial side', and Moody, who often invited McDonnell to Downing Street to discuss economics, thought him 'unquestionably clever', obtaining considerable influence by [his] cool and reasoning manner'. Even James Stephen respected McDonnell: the Ulsterman was 'an author ... of no small account' and 'one of the best accredited colonial champions'.[12]

In mounting the economic defence of slavery, McDonnell and his colleagues began from the premise that plantations could not function under a free-labour system because freed Africans, being 'uncivilized', would not possess 'artificial wants'. In contemporary terms these 'wants' meant the desires for luxurious, expensive goods that drove consumers to work longer hours for better wages. Ignoring the fact that a lifetime of brutalisation might have inhibited a man's desire for refined consumer goods, McDonnell wrote caustically of the 'trifling' wants of colonial slaves; it followed that, if 'the African' did not want to buy expensive goods, he had little incentive to work for better wages. Moreover, the basic wants that 'the African' *did* possess were limited by climatic factors. As the British consul to Haiti explained, 'the nature of the climate prevents clothing being ever much thought of by the working classes; and as there is no great inclemency of weather to guard against, lodging must be equally unimportant'. Furthermore, basic wants could be satisfied easily because of the fertility of Caribbean soils. According to one planter, Jamaica was 'a country so super-eminently bountiful of the gifts of nature ... [that] the most trifling and feeble attempts at agriculture repay the labourers far beyond what [a] European could conceive possible'. This fecundity was a serious problem. If even a small patch of land could allow a free African tenant farmer to grow what he needed to sustain himself, or to sell at the local market, then why would he seek out wage labour? 'Where great disparity exists between the lavish returns of labour and ordinary subsistence,' wrote McDonnell, 'great idleness will afflict the land.'[13]

Compounding this 'problem' was the fact that sugar-cropping was hellish work, eternally redolent of slavery. Of course, conceding that completely undermined the pro-slavery argument that the West Indies were a pastoral paradise, but underneath the hypocrisy the slaveholders knew that the cost of 'tropical labour' was greater than any possible reward. As Thomas Moody put it, the tropical climate – working under 'the vertical sun' – rendered 'steady and intensive labour' almost insufferable. Writing to Wilmot-Horton, he explained that 'in the History of mankind in hot Climates, when agricultural labour is more painful, ... mankind [has] never voluntarily encountered its toil, beyond that degree necessary to obtain subsistence.' There was a supposedly empirical basis to this thinking, too: in Haiti, it appeared that only the violent laws of the *Code Rurale* procured labour from former slaves. *The Times* believed that similar compulsion would be needed to 'yield the necessary quantity of sugar' in the British colonies.[14]

This was the crux of the whole pro-slavery thesis; this was why, from the moment that Buxton first proposed amelioration and gradual emancipation in 1823, the Interest had fought so viciously to resist the reform of slavery. The freed Africans would be 'uncivilized', so they would have few economic desires; the fertile Caribbean soil meant they could satisfy those desires rapidly; and the awful nature of sugar cultivation meant that higher wages would never persuade them to keep working on the plantations. As McDonnell explained to Moody and Wilmot-Horton at the Colonial Office, 'if ... Slaves, when made free, would be willing to work for reasonable wages', there would be 'no grounds for resisting emancipation'. As things stood, however, the slaveholders believed that emancipation would ruin the West Indies.[15]

The Interest coated its pro-slavery economics in a nebulous form of nationalism. 'The same blood flows in the veins of the colonist,' argued the planter Joseph Foster Barham, 'as in those of the people of England,' and so he and his colleagues were 'essentially British land-owners'. The journalist William Cobbett agreed that the planters 'ought to be scrupulously attended to, as if they were farmers in

Cornwall or in Yorkshire' and so 'entitled to the same protection in their persons and fortunes, as our brethren in Great Britain and Ireland'. At home, this protection took the form of the Corn Laws, which inflated the price of bread to cushion agricultural incomes, and the Interest expected similar protection from East Indian sugar *and* anti-slavery agitation. 'The Colonial Proprietor of sugar,' concurred Wilmot-Horton at the Colonial Office, 'has an inherent right of employing his capital in the most productive manner. Can he with justice be compelled to employ his capital less profitably?' Protection was the Interest's natural right.[16]

The slaveholders also argued that withholding protection and pursuing emancipation would constitute what the historian Seymour Drescher has called 'econocide', an act of economic self-sabotage. Eric Williams's thesis that abolition was dependent on the economic decline of the colonies is foundational to modern scholarship, but few in the 1820s would have accepted that as fact. It was common ground, for instance, that the colonies provided a secure supply of coffee, rum, and sugar, and also that the West Indies were one of Britain's most reliable export markets. Domestic manufacturers were told that 'every shop in the Colonies is stored with your goods', while the *Gentleman's Magazine* reported that 'almost everything which the West India Planter *eats, drinks, wears,* or *consumes* is imported from the Mother Country'. At all times, the West Indians beseeched their brethren: we buy from you; we sell to you; do not abandon us.[17]

The ruin caused by emancipation would also rebound upon Britain itself, especially on the western ports that were enmeshed in the Atlantic trade. 'What is your Bristol, your Liverpool, your Manchester, your Glasgow,' asked one pro-slavery lecturer, 'if you take from them the West India Colonies?' Desolation, was his answer: 'Nothing – worse than nothing – one universal scene of beggary and starvation.' The merchant George Saintsbury reinforced this point when he claimed that emancipation would ruin 'thousands of our fellow countrymen and neighbours, hospitable families or dependent widows and orphans, [who were] deriving their subsistence from the colonies, but residing in every county and almost every parish throughout England'.[18]

Colonial profit was presented as another potential casualty of emancipation. Reprising the nationalist dimension of their rhetoric, the West Indians claimed that 'emigrants to our … islands never lose sight of the intention to return to their native country'. They were British and, because of that, sugar money always came 'home'. Archibald Alison explained that 'the great bulk of West India proprietors reside in Great Britain, and their extensive colonial estates ... transmit their produce in the shape of sugar remittances to this country'. Was it not obvious that 'the profits of cultivation of every acre of land in the British West Indies [were] a source of wealth perennially flowing into the very heart of the parent state'? Given the Panic of 1825, where millions of pounds had disappeared in Latin America, this was a well-aimed and well-timed argument.[19]

For the Interest, it was impossible 'for human ingenuity to contrive, or even to wish for colonies more productive of benefit to the mother country' than the West Indies, but emancipation would sacrifice advantages that nowhere else could replicate. 'The inhabitants of the East Indies,' scoffed the slaveholders of Glasgow, 'are all foreigners.' It is an obvious, compelling sign that not all Britons had reached what historians call the 'imperial meridian'; not all British imperialists had yet abandoned the first, western empire in favour of a decided 'swing to the east'.[20]

Historians had long assumed that the 1820s and 1830s were the halcyon years of liberal economics, when reforming statesmen sought to translate free-trade theory into an expansionist economic policy. Everything, it was thought, led on to the repeal of the Corn Laws and the reform of sugar duties in 1846. Now, historians have acknowledged the existence of a competing, *conservative* ideology which promoted tariffs, duties, and the colonies. In journals such as *Blackwood's* and the *Quarterly*, slaveholders, politicians, and conservative economists argued for the merits of colonial commerce. Yet what historians have failed to realise is that such conservative economics were really pro-slavery economics, provoked not by intellectual contempt for free trade but by the need to respond practically to anti-slavery activism which had embraced the twin pillars of 'free trade' and 'free labour'. In the mid-1820s, it was West Indian slaveholders who constructed one of the earliest and most cogent British cases for protectionism.[21]

As ideologues debated economics, and as Britain recovered from the Panic of 1825, Thomas Fowell Buxton prepared for a renewed political assault on slavery. Chief among his targets were the colonial assemblies

which, almost three years after receiving the proposals for amelioration, had implemented few, if any, of the measures. Even the Duke
of Manchester, the pro-planter governor of Jamaica, complained that
'another year has been allowed to pass away without any effectual
measure ... for the improvement of the condition of the Slaves'.
Buxton therefore determined 'to bring two or three enormities' – that
is, recent atrocities – to the attention of Parliament 'as a prelude to
[a] Bill for compelling the assemblies'. There was even some hope
that the Liverpool ministry, after years of prevarication, was ready to
assist. 'I saw Canning yesterday,' wrote Buxton in February 1826. 'He
was very friendly; intimated that the Government meant *to do something.*' A plan was readied for March. On the first of the month, Buxton
presented an anti-slavery petition that had been signed by 72,000
Londoners, reportedly the largest ever laid before the House of
Commons. What was the government going to do now?[22]

Thomas Denman spoke next. An abolitionist MP from Nottingham
and a future Lord Chief Justice of England, he brought the attention
of the House to an alleged insurrection in Jamaica. In the coastal town
of Port Maria, a white butcher called Roberts had scolded his slave,
William Stirling, for failing to dress properly for business. In response,
Stirling had uttered the cryptic words, 'Massa, you will have [a] bad
Christmas'. Pressed on what he meant, Stirling chose not to apologise
for his unkempt appearance. Instead, he blamed his dishevelment on
a local commotion: enslaved Jamaicans, he said, were conspiring to
rebel. The lie soon spiralled. Stirling claimed that neither Kingston
nor Spanish Town would be safe, and that the rebels would over-run
the local fort. They would kill everyone. Within three days, the
Jamaican authorities had arrested eight ringleaders of the phantom
rebellion. In the trial that followed, the defendants were given no
chance to face their accuser and there was no cross-examination of
Stirling's evidence. All eight were convicted, and all eight were
executed, among them Stirling's father: for fear of reprisal, the butcher's boy had maintained the charade even at the cost of his father's
life. What corruption of society was required, asked Denman, and
what corruption had in fact occurred, to produce such a perversion
of justice and such a waste of life?[23]

By the following month, Canning had formalised the ministry's
position. He regretted that the colonial assemblies had not fully

implemented 'amelioration', but he assured the House that progress *was* being made. And while Canning professed that 'all parties were agreed in the desire of terminating such a system', he nevertheless declared the government's intention to give the colonies another year of grace. The Foreign Secretary begged Buxton's patience until then, and he offered two tokens of sincerity. First, the government would slash the 'bounty' subsidies that West Indian merchants received when importing sugar into Britain. Second, he vowed to send his 1823 resolutions to the House of Lords. While the slaveholders and their allies in the other place objected, as they always would, they passed the resolutions a few days later.[24]

None of it meant anything. The resolutions might have had the full backing of Parliament, but they had no legal force. Once again, Canning had promised the world but ensured the delivery of precisely nothing. Buxton fumed. 'Last night we had our debate,' he wrote. 'Canning was not satisfactory: he preferred to give the West Indians another year, and then to legislate. I am as tired as a person well can be.' Zachary Macaulay shared in the anger. 'Canning's speech on Wednesday did us much harm,' he vented. 'All his facts about Colonial improvements were falsehoods ... I [have] set to work and produced a paper pointing out [his] gross mis-statements.' One last hurrah saw Henry Brougham force the Commons to divide on a motion expressing 'deep regret' at colonial conduct, but when that was defeated by one hundred votes to thirty-eight, the abolitionists agreed to pause proceedings. Now, in June 1826, Parliament dissolved for the first general election in six years.[25]

With each constituency fixing a local timetable, the first poll opened in early June and the last closed in mid-July. The result was never in doubt. Despite nationalist gains in Ireland and lingering discontent over the banking crisis, the Tories romped to a landslide victory over the Whigs, who had campaigned on a platform of granting full political rights to Catholics. Lord Liverpool's majority in the Commons grew by more than one hundred seats. Because the Anti-Slavery Society had consented to Canning's year-long delay in dealing with the colonies, slavery was not the nationally explosive issue it might have been, but in certain places it trumped even the Catholic Question as a source of division. In Buxton's constituency of Weymouth, which returned as many as *four* MPs to Parliament, slavery defined the contest; indeed, pro-slavery Tories were determined to unseat the abolitionist leader. One of the insurgent Tory candidates was the retired colonel James Gordon, who owned six plantations and 1,300 slaves on Tobago and went to extraordinary lengths to secure his election. 'It is said that [he] spends 1500 pounds a day,' wrote Buxton, and 'his party confess to 1000 [more].' Votes were bought with more than money, too. 'He has nine public houses open,' Buxton complained, 'where anybody, male or female, from town or country, is very welcome to eat and get drunk; and the truth is the whole town is drunk.'

The Weymouth election also witnessed serious voter intimidation, with the Tories 'resort[ing] to main force to prevent the polling of Whig votes'. The only polling booth in Weymouth had been placed in the furthest corner of the town hall and, on the first day of polling, a raucous mob stationed itself between the door and the booth. This Tory barricade was so effective that only six votes were cast that day. 'No Whig voter reached the table without a violent struggle and very rough treatment.' On the second day of polling, the town hall now guarded by the local cavalry, the Tory hordes scaled the walls of nearby houses, clambering onto the roof of the building and lowering themselves into the hall through its windows. Special constables were sworn in and then garrisoned in the hall, but 'on two successive days the mob broke all their staves to pieces, and drove them out'. Buxton was horrified, regretting that 'the election is carried on with the utmost violence'. But even if Weymouth returned James Gordon *and* the pro-slavery Masterton Ure, the abolitionist leader prevailed: he finished top of the poll by sixty-nine votes.[26]

The Interest was not alone in making targets of candidates, for in the Staffordshire constituency of Newcastle under Lyme the Anti-Slavery Society launched an extensive campaign to defeat Robert Wilmot-Horton. In the eighteen months since he had assumed control of the Colonial Office's 'western' affairs, Wilmot-Horton had emerged as the government's leading spokesman on slavery. He found it a tedious business and described the debates on amelioration, when anti-slavery MPs spent hours recycling accusations of colonial cruelty, as a 'stultifying ordeal'. Soon his 'health and spirits were breaking down under the accumulated pressure' of directing '*all* the details' and doing '*all* the duty'. In the run-up to the 1826 election, Wilmot-Horton had led the government's truculent response to Henry

Brougham's motion on colonial conduct, and he had also published a pamphlet, *The West India Question Practically Considered*, in which he begged his readers not to demonise the slaveholders. But by rallying the Interest to his side, with James Colquhoun praising him for 'taking so statesmanlike a view' of the question, and with George Hibbert hoping the pamphlet would have 'a real & wholesome influence upon the Public mind', Wilmot-Horton had turned himself into an obvious villain for the abolitionists. At the hustings that June he discovered 'that a sudden hostility had been created against me' and that 'the cry of "no slavery" was to my astonishment raised against me'. He survived the election, but lasting enmities were formed. When they next spoke, Buxton assured Wilmot-Horton that he was not 'personally accessory to that opposition', but he still told the junior minister that, because he was 'a friend to Negro slavery', Wilmot-Horton could never have Buxton's support.[27]

When the new Parliament convened in November 1826, the Anti-Slavery Society was at a crossroads. Canning had neutered the campaign by giving the colonies another year to comply with London's policy of amelioration. The economic wounds inflicted by the previous year's Panic still festered, meaning that few politicians would entertain attacks on a labour system which appeared to underpin the imperial economy. Moreover, the *cause du jour* was the emancipation of Catholics, not slaves, and for the next two years the political narrative would be dominated by 'popery'. Caught in a bind, the abolitionists turned east, to Mauritius in the Indian Ocean.[28]

When the British seized Mauritius from the French in 1810, they had imposed the same prohibition on slave trading as on the rest of the Empire and, until 1825, Westminster had assumed the obedience of the Mauritian authorities. Yet when Zachary Macaulay's 'lynx eye' settled upon some disturbing reports, and when the abolitionists were visited by Edward Byam, the former Commissary General of Mauritius, they grew increasingly suspicious. Byam related that, on his last night in Mauritius, his wife had been 'awakened by a low voice calling to her from without'. She had risen from her bed, walked to the window, and found the courtyard below 'filled with negroes' who fell to their knees and implored her, because 'she was going to the country of

Almighty God, to tell Him of their sufferings and to entreat Him to send them relief'.[29]

Allowing for the creative licence of the narrator, there was probably some truth to the story. The suffering of enslaved people on Mauritius was certainly horrendous. They were being flogged, stoned, starved, and dismembered. Some of them had been roasted alive in blast furnaces. One enslaved man was forced to eat his own ear, while a boy of twelve was whipped so badly that he developed sloughing ulcers. Infanticide was the resort of parents who preferred their children to die than to live on Mauritius. Another indicator of depravity, at least for the abolitionists, was the frequency of interracial sexual relations: 'Cohabitation between the Whites and the Blacks,' complained Macaulay in the *Reporter*, 'is frightfully common among all classes in the Mauritius.' Yet so little was known of Mauritian events that the abolitionists had even elected Robert Farquhar, its long-serving governor, to a blue-riband vice-presidency of the African Institution.[30]

In terms of the laws governing the colony, however, the more offensive activity in Mauritius was the continued importation of slaves. 'In a British colony,' Buxton told Parliament, 'for the last fourteen years ... the slave trade in all its horrors has existed.' Far from the watchful eye of the Navy's patrol ships, the slave traders of the Indian Ocean had been preying on the coastal communities of East Africa and Madagascar and sending their victims to Mauritius under the most horrific conditions. One eyewitness claimed that 'the packing [of the slaves into the ships] goes on until ... they are wedged together in one mass of living corruption'. Suffocating for want of air, starving for want of food, and parched with thirst for want of water, many would perish before sight of land. Since 1810, ships had imported approximately 110,000 people into Mauritius and, given that the population of the colony had never exceeded 55,000, this meant that *the same number* of people had died in illegal captivity. Even George Canning could not ignore this flagrant violation of British law, and so Buxton gained a parliamentary committee to investigate the Mauritius scandal.[31]

That committee, however, had gone into purdah when Parliament was dissolved in the summer of 1826. It therefore fell to the younger James Stephen and Edward Byam to prove the charges. Given £1,000 by Samuel Gurney, a Quaker relative of Buxton's, Stephen and Byam spent the rest of the year traversing England, taking depositions from soldiers who had served in Mauritius. They conducted interviews in Hull, Norwich, and Liverpool, but not without difficulty: on at least one occasion, commanding officers forbade their soldiers from speaking to the investigators on neutral ground, insisting that interviews were held under military auspices.

In some ways, the Mauritius episode was a welcome distraction for the major parties to the West India Question. The Interest was delighted that, for a while at least, abolitionist ire was focused elsewhere. Although the Liverpool ministry had already deferred dealing with the West Indies, it was nonetheless relieved that Buxton had found another quarry. And while the abolitionists were frustrated by the continued prevarication of the government, they could now do something decisively in *some* part of the Empire. One abolitionist even suggested that 'the Antislavery public, in any true sense of the term, was created by the Mauritius case', and while this was an exaggeration, Mauritius was a useful lightning rod for anti-slavery sentiment in otherwise troubled times. Indeed, over the next few years, political upheaval, deaths, and serious illness would threaten the very existence of the abolitionist movement.[32]

9.

The Centre Cannot Hold

A good deal of this improvement in the State of the Colonies may perhaps be attributed to the executive Government at home becoming sensible of the danger and injustice of some of the proposed measures … The nation in general is beginning to see that it has been imposed upon by a set of designing men and feels now more inclined to judge of the matter divested of the malice and falsehood with which it was surrounded.[1]

The Glasgow West India Association, March 1827

At about ten o'clock on a Saturday morning in February 1827, the collapse of the British *ancien régime* began in a library in central London. Fife House, a rambling Whitehall mansion, was built in the 1760s for a Scottish nobleman who was so repugnant that his wife had tried to shoot him, and since 1809 it had been the London residence of Robert Jenkinson, Lord Liverpool. Like so many prime ministers before the twentieth century, Liverpool had chosen not to live and work in 10 Downing Street – which was, in William Pitt's phrase, a 'vast, awkward house' – but to conduct the affairs of state from the comforts of home. And so it was there, in Fife House, that Liverpool went through the morning's business with his secretaries before taking some papers to his library, where he planned to read while eating breakfast. As usual, Liverpool's meal was delivered to him by a servant. The prime minister did not acknowledge the servant's presence, but that was not unusual either. But when the servant returned twenty minutes later, he found Liverpool slumped on the floor, unmoving and unconscious, a letter crumpled in his hand. Liverpool's personal physician was close at hand and London's most eminent doctor, Henry Halford, was summoned too, but there was little they could do. The prime minister had suffered a stroke.[2]

The following Monday, *The Times* pronounced that Liverpool was 'politically, if not literally dead'. When fit to travel he retired to the family pile at Coombe to recuperate and, by March, despite losing all movement in his right-hand side, there were signs of improvement. Yet as the Tory diarist Mrs Arbuthnot noted, the return of 'a little more consciousness ... does not amount to a return of reason'. Incapable of moving freely or of speaking at length, Liverpool knew that his career was over. When his wife talked hopefully about a return to the political frontline, he could only stammer a reply: 'No, no, not I ... too weak'.[3]

Despite being prime minister for almost fifteen years, Liverpool is often regarded as a mediocrity, a cipher in a Cabinet that belonged to him in name only. There are grounds for that criticism, and good reason for his minor role in this story, notwithstanding Canning's suspicion that Liverpool's opinions on slavery 'tend[ed] the same way' as his own. Liverpool was not the most gifted orator or the sharpest wit in the government, for that was Canning. Nor was he the most competent administrator (probably Peel) or the greatest intellect (probably Huskisson). He did not even command the greatest loyalty in the House of Lords, where Wellington basked in the glory of Waterloo. Debilitating illness and diminished self-confidence were to define his later years, to boot: just two days before his stroke, it was recorded that the prime minister was 'beginning again his nonsense about going out of office ... He is frightened to death'.[4]

Despite these failings, Liverpool bequeathed an enviable legacy. His government had defeated Napoleon twice, dragged the economy out of post-war depression, prevented financial meltdown in 1825, and established Great Britain as the world's leading imperial power. He had delivered the kind of political stability that many had thought impossible in the post-Pitt era. In his last Cabinet, Liverpool had not only assembled the great men of the political nation, he had then controlled them. Under lesser leaders the ambitions and egos of Canning, Peel, and Wellington could have sundered a government, but Liverpool's gift for man-management and even his very presence calmed their passions: so long as Liverpool was at the helm, the pretenders could enjoy the consolation that nobody else had beaten them to the premiership.[5]

When news of Liverpool's illness made its way through Westminster, the favourites to succeed him brokered a truce. Wellington and Peel agreed 'that they must be quite quiet' for reasons of decorum, and they would not 'give any opinion or state their own intentions' until the King had decided upon a successor. There was even some gossip about a Whig premier, an appointment that would have rebuked the presumptuous Tories, but in truth the King had one choice only. He was the leader of the House of Commons, the MP with the greatest personal following, and a statesman who was revered across Europe; more to the point, no ministry could survive his opposition and he made it known that only the 'substantive power' of the premiership would do. Even though the King had serious misgivings over his liberal position on Catholic Emancipation, the only essential player on the stage was George Canning.[6]

The first casualties of Canning's ascent were Peel and Wellington. Peel knew that the older Canning was the likely and perhaps sensible choice, but he would not serve in the Cabinet of such 'a violent Catholic partizan'. Wellington's departure was more acrimonious. When Canning told the Duke that the King had asked him to form a government, Wellington responded by asking who would be prime minister; Canning's brusque reply – that the King would not have asked him if he were not the obvious leader – sent Wellington spinning into a tantrum, and he resigned. When the staunchly conservative Lord Eldon and dozens of other anti-Catholic Tories followed the Duke out of office, and as Liverpool's broad church disintegrated into tribal squabbling, it became clear that Canning would have to form a coalition with moderate Whigs.[7]

This was not much easier than dealing with the far-right wing of the Tories, for Canning's conduct at Westminster, barbed and scheming, had created a surfeit of enemies on the opposing benches. Indeed, it was said that he made a new adversary with every speech, and that he could not even take tea without first concocting a stratagem. More seriously, Canning was an avowed enemy of the Whigs' key objective, parliamentary reform. His proposed coalition was therefore attacked by the Whig leader, Earl Grey, who denounced the alliance of liberal Tories and moderate Whigs as 'disgraceful & unprincipled'. Grey also denounced Canning himself: the son of an actress, complained the Earl, was *de facto* unfit for the premiership of Great Britain.[8]

Even so, a few moderate Whigs acquiesced in Canning's plans. Lord Lansdowne came into the Cabinet without a portfolio, a young Lord Palmerston stayed on at the War Office, and by the end of April the new prime minister had a government. Of senior Tories, few remained. F.J. Robinson was created Viscount Goderich, instructed to lead the House of Lords, and moved from the Treasury to the Colonial Office; Huskisson kept control of the Board of Trade; and William Sturges Bourne took over at the Home Office as a favour to Canning, an old friend. Nobody pretended that anyone other than Canning would direct foreign policy, but he appointed a new Foreign Secretary. Ominously for the abolitionists, Canning chose a West Indian planter.

John Ward, the Earl of Dudley, owed much of his wealth to land and coal mines in the Midlands, but he was also the heir to three Jamaican plantations. Once, in 1807, he had swum with the tide by declaring that, if abolition did not lead to emancipation, it would be 'a compromise of conscience'. Now, however, with Buxton taking aim at slavery itself, he raged in Parliament about the 'rash experiment' of emancipation, denouncing the fantasy of 'free black labour', and presenting petitions on behalf of Antiguan colonists. Dudley also took great offence at a radical, doomed-to-fail proposal that any and all slaveholders should be expelled from Parliament. The new Foreign Secretary, who had even served on the Interest's Literary Committee, was an obvious target of abolitionist complaints, and Macaulay condemned him for taking 'so conspicuous a part as an advocate of colonial interests, and labour[ing] with so much zeal to discredit the efforts of the Anti-Slavery Society'.[9]

There were now five major groups in mainstream politics: the Canningites; other liberal Tories who consented to serve under Canning; the High Tories who damned Canning as a traitor; moderate Whigs who forgave Canning his opposition to Reform; and liberal Whigs who did not. If the structure of British politics in 1823 had been inchoate, by the spring of 1827 it was chaotic. 'We hear a great deal of Whig principles,' the Duke of Wellington complained, 'and Tory principles, and Mr Canning's principles; but I confess that I have never seen a definition of any of them, and cannot make to myself a clear idea of what any of them mean.' Wellington was not the only one befuddled. As the sister of Lord Melbourne and the future wife of Lord Palmerston, Emily Lamb was ideally placed to assess the shifting landscape, but she too despaired of its complexity. 'There is so much confusion,' she wrote, 'and splitting among families and parties that it is quite a ... danger to talk politics at all, and yet it is impossible to talk of anything else.' All was tentative, uncertain, and fragile. Lord Liverpool's illness had removed the plug in the dam and, over the next six years, the old order – that *ancien régime* – would be swept away.[10]

At other times, when a single issue could have united a fractured polity, this disorder might have created an opportunity for the abolitionists. In 1827, however, the issues of parliamentary reform and Catholic Emancipation were already dominant, and there was little time or space for anything else. Moreover, even if Canning had been minded to reform slavery – and *nothing* had suggested that he was – his ministry was so weak, defeated repeatedly in the summer, that it could not have passed major legislation. Worst of all was the sudden, unforeseen lack of leadership which crippled the anti-slavery movement: Thomas Fowell Buxton was on his deathbed.

As Canning assembled his Cabinet, the campaign against slavery had remained in abeyance. No matter how naively, Buxton was honouring his pledge to give the colonies another year to cooperate. Even the Mauritius arm of the campaign had ground to a halt: though Buxton lobbied for the renewal of the inquiry into Mauritian affairs, Canning declined to reconvene the investigative committee. When Robert Farquhar, the former governor of Mauritius, demanded that Buxton produce evidence to substantiate his charges, he could not oblige.

The early months of 1827 had also seen a resurgence of pro-slavery activity. In January, the Interest had launched the *West Indian Reporter*, a monthly magazine designed to provide 'an antidote to the mischief' of Macaulay's abolitionist *Reporter*. Funded by the Interest's Literary Committee, edited by a 'Mr Clarke', and published by the vaunted London house of Effingham Wilson – other clients included Tennyson, Hazlitt, Browning, and Coleridge – one hundred copies of the pro-slavery *Reporter* were available for eight shillings. In its first issue, the *Reporter* launched vitriolic attacks on abolitionists in Surrey, urged the protection of West Indian sugar, and predicted the degeneration of the British Caribbean into a new Haiti in the event of emancipation. There was nothing new here. Given the year's political developments, the *Reporter*'s choice of epigraph was apt: a warning from the new prime minister that the premature liberation of enslaved West Indians would 'at once kindle a flame only to be quenched in blood'.[11]

At such a time, the Anti-Slavery Society was in dire need of vigilance and leadership. Yet in the spring of 1827, Buxton had broken down entirely. In mid-May, a friend came to Buxton's London home for breakfast, but his host failed to make it down the stairs. When he eventually appeared, Buxton was 'much oppressed with headache, and very languid'. His doctor ordered 'leeches, quiet, and total abstinence from business', yet when Buxton insisted on working 'while a particle of strength still remained', he drove himself deeper into illness. Later that week, while examining evidence from James Stephen's researches into Mauritius, Buxton paced up and down the lawn of East London's Ham House in anguish, exclaiming: 'Oh, it's too bad! It's too bad! I can't bear it!' On the Saturday, Buxton described himself as 'for two or three hours … distressed beyond measure'. The next day, he was seized by 'a fit of apoplexy' and collapsed.[12]

Reports of Buxton's breakdown threw the leaders of the Anti-Slavery Society into despair. The elder James Stephen was disconsolate: 'What is to be said or done in our cause!' he cried to Macaulay. 'My hopes were never lower except in Divine interposition.' For ten days, Buxton drifted in and out of consciousness. His brothers and sisters gathered at his bedside, preparing for the worst; his children were summoned from school and university to say goodbye. His friends soon gave up hope, ceasing 'to inquire from hour to hour, and day to day, with breathless solicitude, about every little symptom that might have occurred'.[13]

Yet on the eleventh day, Buxton stirred. 'What a change has the mercy of God to us all produced!' rejoiced Macaulay. When he woke, Buxton recalled nothing of his illness and refused to believe he had slept so long: it was not until the presentation of that day's *Times* that he was convinced of the correct date. Now, having set himself 'on fire', Buxton agreed to cool down. He went on holiday to the family home at Cromer, amid the calm and quiet of the Norfolk Broads, and the remainder of 1827 was given to 'religious meditation'. It might have been essential to Buxton's health, but it was an inopportune time to rest. The abolitionists had already missed their chance to contradict pro-slavery testimony to the Privy Council on a manumission scheme in Demerara and now, as Buxton convalesced, inertia overwhelmed the anti-slavery movement. As Zachary Macaulay reflected, this was 'a season of almost complete inaction'.[14]

Prince Frederick was the second son of George III, the younger brother of George IV, and a long-serving commander-in-chief of the British armed forces, but he was far from a popular public figure. As the paramour of the socialite Mary Anne Clarke, he was accused of using the military patronage at his disposal to enrich Mrs Clarke and her friends. Critics also lambasted his leadership of the 1799 Anglo-Russian invasion of the Netherlands, a disaster that found Frederick immortalised in the caustic rhyme 'The Grand Old Duke of York'. But when, in the first week of 1827, Frederick died of dropsy in a mansion on Arlington Street, he was the occupant of an even more important station in British public life: he was heir to the throne.

The Duke of York was granted the honour of lying in state before being transferred for burial in St George's Chapel at Windsor. The funeral, when it took place in February, was a maudlin circus. Already scheduled for a cold winter's evening, proceedings were delayed for more than two hours as the pallbearers struggled to manoeuvre the Duke's oversized coffin into the chapel. The renowned diarist Charles Greville carped that 'nothing could be managed worse than it was'. The funeral was rendered even less comfortable for the mourners by the removal of all matting from the chapel, leaving the middle-aged and elderly royals, politicians, peers, and generals with nothing to stand on but cold, damp stone. 'I presume,' Canning joked, 'that … whoever filched the cloth or the matting from under our feet in the aisle, had bets or insurances against the lives of the Cabinet.' As it happened, quite a few of those bets would have come in: Wellington fell sick, as did the Duke of Montrose. The Bishop of Lincoln died.[15]

Canning would not escape the reach of that night at Windsor. A few days later, 'every variety of form of which cold and rheumatism are capable' waylaid him. Steam baths and quinine would not avail him and, for a while, his survival looked unlikely: that morning in the Fife House library, the letter found crumpled in Lord Liverpool's hand was 'a discouraging bulletin on Canning's fluctuating state of health'.

The effects of Canning's illness never left him. In June, he looked 'dreadfully ill'. In July, a guest at the Privy Council – who had never seen Canning before – was heard to ask, 'Who is that gentleman ... who is so near his end?' In August, Mrs Arbuthnot noted that 'Mr Canning is at the very point of death': the prime minister had been 'attacked with violent inflammation which has baffled all the skill of his physicians'.[16]

By this stage, Canning had taken up the Duke of Devonshire's offer of a holiday at Chiswick House, but matters did not improve. Another guest was shocked by Canning's decline, noting his 'ghastliness of feature and dejection of air'. Bedridden, he told his secretary Augustus Stapleton that one hundredth of the pain he was then suffering – in his lungs and his liver – was worse than everything else he had endured in life. At twelve minutes to four on the morning of 8 August, having whispered his last words to his wife, George Canning died.[17]

His death was no shock, but that did not diminish its impact. 'Europe lost in him its ablest statesman,' it was said, 'and the Commons in England the finest orator of his day.' *The Times* was not always kind to the departed, but it eulogised that 'the loss of such a man at such a time was well calculated to draw forth the strongest expressions of deep regret among all classes of his fellow-subjects'. Even a few of the abolitionist victims of Canning's cunning regretted the passing of a 'great man'. Thomas Macaulay was pained that Canning should have fallen 'at the very moment of reaching the very highest pinnacle of human ambition' and mourned that 'the noblest prize that industry, dexterity, wit, and eloquence ever obtained' had vanished 'into nothing in the very instant in which it had been grasped'. Macaulay's father was no less sympathetic, writing to Hannah More that 'our mighty men are falling like the thistle-down before the storm'.[18]

Henry Brougham was less charitable. 'I must fairly say,' he wrote to the elder Macaulay, 'that I regarded him as our very worst adversary on all that related to West Indian affairs. He was virulently prejudiced against us.' He begged Macaulay to remember Canning's statement in the Commons on John Smith's death in Demerara. 'I assure you,' raged Brougham, 'I could have felled him to the ground for that heathenly and planterly and almost slave-trading speech ... Nothing could show more bitter hostility to us and ours. He was quite prepared to laugh us off the field.' Most egregious, at least in Brougham's view, was the methodical nature of Canning's obstruction. He had not been a 'rash' enemy, but one who would 'affect to have the same object in view, and pretended to be waddling towards it, by another and more roundabout road, while he is in reality running in the very opposite course'. The resolutions of 1823, 'an insurmountable bar' which had hamstrung the anti-slavery campaign from the start, could not have been far from Brougham's mind.[19]

Conversely, the Interest knew it had lost its most influential ally. John Gladstone had once hailed Canning as 'the Minister to whom Parliament & the Country looked in connection with this subject'. James Colquhoun, the colonial agent for St Kitts, had attached 'unquestionable Authority [to] the Opinions given by ... Mr Canning as to the improved Conditions of the Negroes'. On occasion, as Thomas Moody observed, West Indian praise of Canning 'at the expense of other persons' had become a matter of jealousy among other government officials.[20]

Now, 119 days after he had last appointed a prime minister, George IV was forced to find another. This time he chose F.J. Robinson, now the Viscount Goderich. The current Colonial Secretary and a former Chancellor of the Exchequer, Goderich was renowned for his financial acumen and administrative competence: even if a 'wobble' during the Panic of 1825 had tainted his reputation, he remained synonymous with the economic growth of the early 1820s. 'Prosperity', indeed, was his nickname. Yet what most endeared Goderich to the King, and what guaranteed his elevation to the premiership, was the fact that he was neither Wellington nor Peel, both of whom were *non grata* for refusing to serve under Canning.[21]

Like his predecessor, Goderich found that forming a government was far from easy. Whereas the Canningites and liberal Tories gladly transferred their allegiance to the new premier, most Tory MPs stuck with Peel. At the same time, Wellington and the High Tories nurtured their hatred of anyone and anything that smacked of liberalism, and so they rejected Goderich *and* his policies. Only with great pains were the bones of a Cabinet thrown together. To placate the Whigs, Lansdowne was given the Home Office, while the conservative financier J.C. Herries – who believed that the national balance sheet should distinguish profitable slave colonies from 'less productive possessions' such as Ceylon – became Chancellor.[22]

Yet for all of the Whigs' and Goderich's relative liberalism, the Interest was quite content with the new ministry. The slaveholder Lord Dudley remained as Foreign Secretary and, more importantly, Huskisson was moved from the Board of Trade to the Colonial Office so that he might, as Goderich explained, 'confer the greatest benefits upon ... the Empire'. Huskisson himself was hesitant about the move and he would have preferred to be Chancellor, complaining to Wilmot-Horton that 'these Slave Questions ... will drive me mad', but the West Indian chairman Charles Ellis assured him that 'the Colonial Office is preferable [to the Treasury], not only as higher in Political Rank, but as the one in which you can render the greater service to the Country'. Huskisson would disappoint the Interest by annulling the Jamaican Assembly's negligent attempts to implement ameliora- tion, but they flattered him all the same. As John Gladstone told Huskisson, who was still MP for Liverpool, the 'West Indians naturally rejoice in your appointment to the charge of the Colonies, knowing that we shall now have justice done [to] us'.[23]

Despite its turbulence, 1827 was a good year for the Interest, and Charles Ellis was so relaxed about the standing of the slaveholders that, when he received word in France of Canning's death, he resumed his holiday instead of going to London. In contrast, the anti-slavery movement lay in torpor, and one memoir would describe 1827 as the abolitionist 'year of anxiety'. Buxton, their stalwart leader, had almost died before spending six months in recuperation; amelioration was a dead letter; and the Mauritius inquiry had stalled. 'What,' asked the *Anti-Slavery Reporter*, 'is the result of all the hope and promises held out to us?' The answer was 'bitter disappointment' and the 'contuma- cious rejection on the part of the slave-colonies of every overture of mercy'. The abolitionists could not do much about it, either. 'The grave question,' regretted Macaulay, 'must be reserved for another occasion.' Worse again, as 1827 drew to a close, the campaign against slavery was dealt another fearsome blow, this time by the English courts.[24]

Not all enslaved people worked in the fields; a minority were in domestic service. Some were cooks, some were butlers, others were cleaners, and others still would be taught to read and write so they could administer plantation business. For an enslaved person, these could be the better jobs in which life might just be tolerable. If a planter was married, there would also be a lady's maid: she would wait upon her mistress, wash and mend her linens, help her bathe, apply her make-up, and fan her in the heat. On one Antiguan estate, Grace James was such a lady's maid to Mrs Ann Allan.[25]

In 1822, when Mrs Allan sailed to Britain, she had taken Grace with her. And as her mistress called on family and browsed the shops of London, Grace breathed in freedom: in accordance with the *Somerset* judgment, she was treated as a free woman. Later in the year, when she had finished her business, Mrs Allan persuaded Grace to return to Antigua not as an enslaved woman, but as a hired servant; once free for an hour, Grace was told, she was free for ever. Sailing from London on the *Killingbeck*, they arrived in the West Indies in January 1823 and, for a short while more, Grace worked freely for Mrs Allan. But when she and her mistress fell out over 'a trifling matter' on the Allan estate, Grace was 'publicly flogged ... and told she was still a slave'.

Grace was not daunted. Seeking a sympathetic ear among Antigua's authorities, she initiated legal proceedings against Mrs Allan to have her 'right of freedom judicially declared and solemnly determined'. Logically, her case was sound: if Grace had been a free woman in England, and if she was now enslaved in Antigua, had she not been imported illegally? What was known as the case of *The Slave, Grace* went before the Antiguan courts, which held – unsurprisingly – that Grace had been properly returned to slavery. Still fearless, Grace appealed to the High Court of the Admiralty, the London court which settled the Empire's maritime disputes. Fully conscious of the legal and political value of her case, Stephen Lushington became Grace's champion.

The case 'respecting the slavery of the mongrel woman, Grace' was heard in 1827 by Lord Stowell, an aged giant of the bench. The son of a Newcastle coal merchant, Stowell had been a prominent historian of the Classics before turning to the law; now in his eighties, *The Slave, Grace* would be his last case. Stowell had given two previous decisions on slavery. The first gave Grace and Lushington hope: when HMS *Crocodile* had seized a Portuguese slave ship, Stowell upheld a lower court's decision to condemn the vessel and to liberate the Africans on board. The second case was more concerning: Stowell had ruled that the Navy's seizure of the French slave ship *Le Louis* off

Liberia was unlawful because it was illegal to stop and search a foreign ship in international waters. The *Louis* – and the Africans it carried – were restored to their 'owners'. Stowell might have described himself as a 'rather stern abolitionist', but his political and moral sympathies were constricted by his principled interpretation of the law.[26]

The question before Stowell in 1827 was this: did a former slave, who had been 'free' in England, revert to being enslaved when she returned to the West Indies? For the abolitionists to succeed, they needed to convince Stowell that Lord Mansfield's judgment in *Somerset* was just as applicable in the colonies as it was in England. They did not succeed: Stowell found that British policy supported 'the rights of proprietors over the persons committed to their authority, in the character of slaves.' More damningly, Stowell held that Grace could derive 'no character of freedom that could entitle her to maintain a suit like this ... merely by having been in England'. Once a slave in the West Indies, Grace James was *always* a slave in the West Indies.[27]

When Stowell's judgment was published, the Interest was jubilant. 'The decision is so highly important to the West India Proprietors,' crowed the pro-slavery *Reporter*, 'and so beneficial to them, on account of the additional security which it affords them to property.' One pro-slavery publication from Glasgow hailed Stowell as 'one of the greatest Judges of whom England could ever boast, [who] distinctly asserted the validity of Slave property'. The Interest's Literary Committee meanwhile paid for the widespread distribution of Stowell's judgment. In the colonies, the *Antigua Free Press* trumpeted that 'Reason and equity have triumphed over cant and hypocrisy', while Jamaica's *Royal Gazette* exulted that the English courts had finally decided that slaves were property 'under the special guarantees of the laws of England'. The abolitionists were less enamoured of the court's judgment. 'The sentiments of Lord Stowell,' complained the pseudonymous 'Briton', had 'created much of painful and dissatisfied feeling.' His remarks, it was feared, had stamped 'Slavery with the impress of a spurious sanctity'.[28]

As Lord Stowell sat in judgment, Viscount Goderich floundered. He might well have formed a Cabinet, but commanding a majority in the Commons was beyond him. Attacked in the press from the left by Earl Grey's Whigs, and from the right by a rump of High Tories,

Goderich's situation was aggravated by personal strife. His wife, Sarah, had long been known as a hypochondriac, but after the deaths of two children and severe depression, not to mention her husband's difficulties, her health was truly fragile. In December, Goderich told the King that neither he nor his wife's health would suffer high politics much longer, for this was a crisis – or a 'blow-up', as a colleague put it – that could not be saved. William Huskisson took pity, describing the prime minister as 'quite unnerved, and in a most pitiful state'. And though some of Goderich's distress was attributed to his weakness as a leader, most was blamed on 'the constant worry in which he has been kept by his all but crazy wife'. The poet Emily Eden looked mournfully on the scene at Downing Street: 'Sarah is worse than ever,' she wrote. 'It is a shame to let anybody see the abject slavery in which she and Mr Robinson live. It is quite a Fowell Buxton case.'[29]

As Goderich's troubles rumbled into the New Year, he accepted the collapse of his ministry. Uniquely in British history, it had never once seen Parliament meet. On 8 January 1828, humbled and broken, he spoke to the King. He did not offer his resignation, but it was not needed: in a final act of humiliation, George simply told his prime minister to find a replacement. In a sadly fitting coda to the least memorable premiership in British history, Goderich broke down and began to cry. The King, bewildered but not unkind, proffered the royal handkerchief. 'At last this most disreputable Government has come to an end,' celebrated the arch-Tory diarist Mrs Arbuthnot. 'They have not dared to face Parliament with all their disputes & maladministration & [they] have fairly run away.' Goderich had never been hostile to the abolitionists, but in January 1828, when he chose the man to succeed him, he delivered one more blow to the ailing campaign for emancipation. There was only one man who could have replaced Goderich, but he was also the most pro-slavery frontline politician of the day. Described by Henry Brougham as a 'spirit of darkness and intolerance whom [Canning's] crowning had chased away to [his] native shades', he was the Duke of Wellington.[30]

IO.

Before the Deluge

The truth is there never has been, and never will be, in the grammar of slave-holders, any present tense for the oppressions of slavery.[1]

Anti-Slavery Monthly Reporter, September 1828

Although all is apparently quiet in the political atmosphere ... I am assured that things are not to be – that is the calm before the storm which is about to originate a total change in our Councils and in our policy.[2]

James MacQueen to William Blackwood, March 1829

In January 1828, Arthur Wellesley, the Duke of Wellington, was fifty-eight years old. Although greyer, thinner, and increasingly deaf, Wellington had retained the patrician bearing and haughty self-confidence with which he once bestrode the battlefields of Europe. He had first joined the Cabinet in 1818 as Master-General of the Ordnance, a role with responsibility for Britain's artillery, fortifications, and military supplies, and the Duke had since emerged as an elder statesman of British politics. He was an effective envoy to diplomatic conferences, a respected advisor on military and imperial affairs, and the dominant figure in the House of Lords. He was also the figurehead of the High Tories, the conservatives whose hostility to reform – whether parliamentary, religious, or colonial – was implacable. This military rigour and unyielding conservatism should have unsuited Wellington for the premiership, which in this era of factions and alliances required empathy and flexibility, but he was now the only serious candidate for the office. The day after Goderich resigned in tears, Wellington was summoned to Windsor Castle by the King.

Wellington's most trusted lieutenant would be his Home Secretary, Robert Peel. Though he has been quiet so far in this story, nobody could question Peel's importance to national politics in the early nineteenth century. He had survived six bad years in Ireland as Chief Secretary and, during his first spell at the Home Office under Liverpool, instigated sweeping reforms of the penal system. Under Wellington he would establish the Metropolitan Police Service; and then, in 1834, he effectively founded the modern Conservative Party by promulgating the Tamworth Manifesto that laid out the governing principles of British conservatism. He also became the first prime minister from an industrial background, and a feted champion of free trade who sacrificed his own career to the national interest by forcing through the repeal of the Corn Laws in 1846.

The West Indians could not have wished for a more capable guardian. Although Peel cared nothing for the protection of West Indian sugar, a series of parliamentary speeches confirmed his contempt for slave emancipation. In one, he stated that 'moral improvement ... alone' could prepare Africans for freedom. In another, he warned MPs that, after emancipation, 'the Colonies would present a scene of civil war and a succession of barbarous conflicts'. That speech enthralled the West Indians, who quoted it as an epigraph in their monthly *Reporter*, and the young William Gladstone was 'much pleased' with it. Yet this was far from Peel's most notorious speech. At other times, he drew Parliament's attention to the great problem of amalgamating 'two distinct and separate races' in a free society and he repeated Canning's comparison of the African to Frankenstein's creature: Peel begged Parliament not to free 'the monster'. On cue, the Interest lauded Peel as a hero. During his brief exile from the Home Office in 1827–28 one assemblyman from St Vincent had regretted Peel's 'absence from HM's councils'; he then received the dedication of one of John Gladstone's pro-slavery pamphlets; and even into the 1830s the West Indians would seek Peel's advice on 'the present state of our colonial interests'.[3]

Joining Peel on the front bench was Henry Goulburn, the new Chancellor of the Exchequer. Physically, Goulburn was striking: his nurse had sat upon him as a child, an accident which caused permanent indentation to his skull and partial blindness in his right eye. Intellectually, he was a contradiction: brilliant but lazy, and a spendthrift who advocated fiscal retrenchment. When it came to slavery, Goulburn was more curious still, the personification of the overlapping and conflicting priorities that were endemic within the debate over slavery. He was the heir to his family's plantations in Jamaica and a racist who believed that it was 'only by making the negroes comprehend the truths of religion that permanent restraint can be imposed on the licentiousness of their manners'. Yet Goulburn also resented the moral burden of slavery and privately admitted the need for emancipation. Understandably, the abolitionists did not quite know what to make of him. Despite knowing that Goulburn was 'anxious to do what might be done for his slaves', Zachary Macaulay kept up an inveterate 'personal hostility' towards the Chancellor.[4]

William Huskisson was kept at the Colonial Office, but the arrangement did not last long. In May, when the Cabinet came out against reforming rotten boroughs – that is, parliamentary constituencies with minuscule electorates – Huskisson resigned in a fit of pique, but only in the expectation that Wellington would woo him back 'indoors'. When the prime minister accepted the resignation without a quarrel, Huskisson was mortified. Panicking wildly, he tried to recant his 'mistake', yet Wellington would have none of it. 'The Duke said very coldly,' wrote Mrs Arbuthnot, 'that it was no mistake.' Huskisson was out. The resignation stemmed from a pitiable clash of egos, and the diarist Thomas Creevey believed that Huskisson had 'acted like a knave throughout'. Even so, it was a significant moment: Huskisson's fellow Canningites followed him out of office and, by summer, the High Tories controlled the government. 'The Huskisson party,' rejoiced Mrs Arbuthnot, 'will soon be quite forgotten or only remembered to be laughed at.'[5]

Robert Wilmot-Horton was already 'out of office'. He had signalled his intention some months earlier to resign and seek the governorship of Canada, but when this request was 'refused *graciously*' by the King he found himself without a position. The St Vincent assemblyman John Dalzell paid tribute to his 'very great and very lasting service to the West India Colonies', and though James Colquhoun regretted that Wilmot-Horton was 'no longer [the West Indians'] defender', he congratulated him upon his 'Emancipation from Slavery'.[6]

Wilmot-Horton's pro-slavery muse Thomas Moody had followed his patron into exile, but the Interest need not have worried about having weakened influence at the Colonial Office. Huskisson's replacement was George Murray, a former governor of Canada and of Sandhurst College and, until 1828, the commander of British forces in Ireland. Tall, thin, and with 'manners devoid of affectation', Murray was described by James MacQueen as a 'plain honest straightforward British Soldier'. Another observer commended him as 'very clever, an excellent man of business, a very good speaker, & ... in every respect well qualified'. Besides, Murray was a potential friend to the Interest. In July, he thanked MacQueen for a copy of his latest article in *Blackwood's*, a lengthy screed on the importance of slavery to the Empire. Murray will 'do well', MacQueen told William Blackwood, 'providing he only gets [the] right information'.[7]

Historians have rarely disagreed about the sympathies of the Wellington ministry. They have concluded that it 'stood four-square with the planting interest', that on Wellington's watch the 'West Indians knew they were safe from censure', and that 'Wellington and his party in the Lords were prepared to safeguard the planters in their objections to black freedom'. There are obvious, explicit proofs of this. In June 1828, the Duke presented a glowing but misleading report to Parliament on the progress of amelioration. 'It was more wonderful to behold,' he declared, 'the progress already made, than to express any strong censure for what remained to be done.' Here, the prime minister conveyed a clear message: no matter how obstructive the colonial assemblies had been, he would not discipline them; no matter how many instructions the government might send, Wellington and Murray accepted that they would be 'entirely disregarded'.[8]

The absentee West Indians praised the Duke's 'sagacity' and James MacQueen entertained the hope that Wellington would 'put an end to [the] dangerous proceedings' of the Anti-Slavery Society altogether. The prime minister was listening to the pro-slavery lobby, too. He retrieved Thomas Moody from the political wilderness 'to speak on the subject of West India Affairs, and the effect of Emancipation on their future defence', and his personal copies of MacQueen's articles were 'after perusal ... all pencil marks'. Following an audience with Wellington, MacQueen reported that the Duke was 'determined to protect <u>all</u> our Colonies'. He had even asked MacQueen, rhetorically,

'Do you and others think that I am going to govern this Country according to the dictations and principles of the [anti-slavery] *Edinburgh Review*?' With confidence, the *West Indian Reporter* assured its readers that the Tories were 'equally bound to provide for the security of their white fellow subjects, as for the benefit of the blacks'. Not without reason, either, would the American abolitionist William Lloyd Garrison reflect that, if they were British, 'American slaveholders ... [would] belong to [the Tory] party, and hate liberty and equality for *all* the people, as sincerely as ... the Duke of Wellington, or Sir Robert Peel'. For Garrison, who was touring the British Isles as the slavery debate intensified, 'the Tory party in England were against the abolition of the foreign slave trade, and the emancipation of the slaves in the British dependencies. They have always been, and always will be, *as Tories*, in favour of white and black slavery'.[9]

The period between Lord Liverpool's resignation in 1827 and the summer of 1828 had been remarkably unstable. In fourteen months, there had been four prime ministers, four Colonial Secretaries, three Foreign Secretaries, three presidents of the Board of Trade, and five Chancellors of the Exchequer. All the while, the Anti-Slavery Society and the campaign for emancipation had been thwarted not only by political instability, but also by Buxton's illness, lesser ailments suffered by Brougham, and Lushington's noble obsession with the plight of free people of colour. Even the tireless Zachary Macaulay had been ineffective, busied by the collapse of his family's business and then laid low by an illness of his own. 'My dear father,' wrote his daughter, Selina, 'continues [to be] a great invalid. It is affecting to see a person of his activity and energy incapable of the smallest exertion of mind or body.' By 1828 the abolitionist campaign was in such a lull that when Robert Wilmot-Horton – that 'auxiliary of the West Indians' – brought the subject of slave manumission before the Commons, only *one* abolitionist MP was in attendance. Five years after the foundation of the Anti-Slavery Society, and five years after Canning's resolutions had theoretically committed Parliament to reforming slavery, nothing much had been done, and nothing much achieved. Now, under Wellington, the chances of progress grew dimmer.[10]

The Duke of Wellington's private papers reveal that he was working doggedly to frustrate the abolitionists. In a speech to the House of

Lords in July 1828, the prime minister appeared to deny the right of Parliament to pass laws for the colonies. 'We have no more the power of governing those Colonies by force,' he declared, 'than we have the power of governing this country by force. We can only govern them, as this country is governed, by means of laws which are enacted by the sanction of the [colonial] Houses of Legislature.' Thomas Macaulay thought the speech 'as bad as possible'. The junior James Stephen, who was growing in stature at the Colonial Office, promptly wrote to the prime minister in the hope that he had been misquoted. Wellington's reply to Stephen was a tour de force of aggressive indignation. First, the Duke made clear that 'the [Colonial] Secretary of State had no right to give orders to the Colonial Assemblies'. Second, Wellington 'deprecated the measure of forcing upon the colonies the provisions of law recommended for their adoption'. Third, and most chillingly, Wellington addressed the Anti-Slavery Society's tendency to appeal 'to the people at large' and to invoke 'the popular voice'. The Duke believed that such tactics amounted to the attempted intimidation of the government, and he asked Stephen to pause and 'peruse the Histories of the Revolution in Santo Domingo', which had been caused by a similar 'clamour'. In the wider context of the slavery debate, Wellington's letter is stunning. Here was the prime minister, writing directly to a senior civil servant at the Colonial Office, repeating one of the slaveholding Interest's fundamental talking-points.[11]

The new prime minister did not confine his pro-slavery sentiments to that speech and that letter. In August 1828, as he and Murray debated whether to send further instructions to the colonial assemblies, Wellington reminded the Colonial Secretary that they had 'now got th[is] question into our hands'. In other words, so long as the reform of slavery was entrusted to the ministry, real progress could be delayed, perhaps indefinitely. Murray quite agreed. 'It is very important,' he replied, 'that government should be allowed to manage this question in its own way.' But Murray also knew the political value of *appearing* to ameliorate slavery. 'We should endeavour to impress upon the West Indian body,' he wrote to Wellington, 'the necessity of doing some-thing; but ... we should not prescribe ... the measures which they are to adopt.'[12]

Beyond these messages, there was obvious reluctance in the ministry's discussion of experimental measures in the Crown colonies, which Robert Peel likened to testing new surgical methods on the unfortunate patients of country hospitals. 'Compulsory manumission' was the policy of allowing enslaved people to buy their freedom for a given price, and the Colonial Office spent the late 1820s debating its implementation in Demerara. The prime minister took the view that, if an African ever saved enough to buy his freedom, he should need to prove that 'he has conducted himself honestly and faithfully' while acquiring that money. Even Murray was taken aback by Wellington's proposal. 'I do not think it would be just,' he suggested, 'to require a man to bring proof of his honesty when there is no charge of his dishonesty against him.'[13]

The Duke's hostility to slave freedom infected his views of other colonial policies. He noted in 1829 that 'no slave, whether male or female, ought to be permitted to marry without the consent of the owner', though his worst was reserved for the reform of colonial justice. Under Wellington's scheme, a planter who was found guilty of cruelty towards an enslaved person would *not* forfeit ownership of that person; but if that enslaved person could not prove an allegation of cruelty against his owner, the 'false' nature of such a complaint would be taken as proof that the complainant deserved punishment. The prime minister's logic was flawed, circular, and vicious. He also insisted that the slaveholders' property, 'which they have enjoyed under the repeated sanction of the Legislature for nearly two centuries', should remain inviolate. 'We must not plunder the proprietors in the West Indies,' he told Murray, 'in order to acquire for ourselves a little popularity in England.'[14]

At a time when the abolitionists were struggling to engage the wider population, the advent of the Wellington ministry was a crushing blow. Even if the Tories refrained from making an explicit, public declaration in favour of slavery, and even if their equivocal language could be framed as 'moderation', the behaviour of the government was legitimising vehement resistance among the slaveholders of Britain and the colonies. 'If apology were possible for ... palpable deviation from the plainest roles of moral conduct,' mused Macaulay, 'the planters ... might find it in those subtle reasonings with which certain persons of high colonial authority have perplexed themselves and the public on this question.' Things were so bad that the *Anti-Slavery Monthly Reporter* had a lower circulation – 15,000 – than at any time since its foundation, and Thomas Fowell Buxton, still weakened by his collapse in 1827, was contemplating retirement. 'Ought [I] to hazard the "inevitable death" with which [my doctor] last year threatened me,' he asked Macaulay, 'or [should I] desert a cause which now more than ever wants the aid of all its friends?'[15]

Safe in the knowledge that slave emancipation would never happen on the watch of the High Tories, the West Indians went on the offensive, expanding their literary campaign. The slaveholders had learned from experience that 'to get a publication read, or even seen, in London, by any particular individual' was 'by no means easy to accomplish'. When they had commissioned pro-slavery books and pamphlets and then left them at the homes of eminent men, those works had been 'appropriated by the servants to their own use as waste paper, or ... altogether rejected'. It was a rare admission of weakness, but now the West Indians would focus on distributing material 'to [Britain's] Institutions, Clubs, Subscription Reading Rooms, [and] Libraries'.[16]

They would also concentrate on recruiting new publications to the pro-slavery cause, one of which was the conservative magazine, the *Spectator*. Its founder and editor Robert Rintoul was an abolitionist who protested that slavery was 'an unmanly and detestable vice of society', but he knew his readership: the *Spectator* lent unqualified support to the Interest. In November 1828, the reviewer of a West Indian travelogue claimed that agricultural labourers in Norfolk and Bedfordshire endured a far worse life than Caribbean slaves. The next month, the *Spectator* chose to put its faith in the accounts of slavery that were given by the planters, not by James Stephen. This pro-slavery position was maintained throughout 1829. In March, the magazine lambasted 'the misdirected zeal of Abolitionists'; in April, it regretted that 'a great deal of maudlin sentimentalism has long prevailed ... on the subject of West Indian slavery'; and in July it parroted the standard pro-slavery line that 'nothing will ever induce the Negro to labour freely'. It was not difficult for the leaders of the West India Interest to identify the *Spectator* as a friendly publication, and their *Reporter* would praise the magazine's readership as 'the unprejudiced public'.[17]

The *Spectator* was soon joined in the pro-slavery ranks by *Fraser's Magazine*, an arch-conservative monthly co-founded by the prolific

Irish journalist William Maginn. While working at *Blackwood's* in the mid-1820s, Maginn had execrated the young Thomas Macaulay, describing his *Edinburgh Review* essays on African 'capacity' as 'egregious and wilful misrepresentation from beginning to end'. He now steered another major publication into the Interest's hands: *Fraser's* was so enthusiastic about slavery that it sought an arrangement with the Interest's Literary Committee to supply and distribute material, and the Committee agreed to purchase 200 copies of each issue of *Fraser's* for resale in Britain's western ports. Some pro-slavery articles in *Fraser's* were written by Stephen Isaacson, an historian who had preached in Demerara before marrying a West Indian heiress. From 'experience', Isaacson claimed that he had 'never witnessed a case of cruelty [or] had a complaint breathed in my ear by a single negro'. He also lured the *Christian Remembrancer* to the Interest's embrace. Later, when Isaacson attacked the abolitionists in a sermon, the *Remembrancer* duly opined that 'we have never read ... a more manly defence of the West India Proprietors, and a more clear refutation of the hear-say argument of the Anti-Slavery gentlemen'.[18]

Even more important to *Fraser's Magazine* and to pro-slavery campaigning was John Galt. Known to posterity as a novelist and proponent of colonial emigration, Galt's favoured arguments were typical West Indian fare: planters treated their slaves well; slavery was essential to economic prosperity; and property in people was entirely lawful. The cause of Galt's sustained involvement in slavery could well have been financial, since in 1829 he was imprisoned on account of an £80 debt, but as early as 1825 Galt had written pro-slavery articles for *Blackwood's* and confided in Robert Wilmot-Horton that his attachment 'to what is called the Government party has of late ... been strengthened by circumstances which require only to be alluded to'. Galt's fiction provides a further suggestion of a sincere pro-slavery conviction. In *Bogle Corbet*, a tedious and patently autobiographical adventure about a Scottish orphan who becomes a West Indian merchant, the title character announces to the world that 'the moment that [any] property is recognised, in the same instant the claim of man over man is [also] acknowledged'.[19]

With *Fraser's* and the *Spectator* joining *Blackwood's*, the *Quarterly*, and *John Bull* in the pro-slavery ranks, the slaveholders held an even greater advantage in the periodical press. This was reflected in the daily newspapers, too, with the slaveholders now listing the *Morning Herald* and the *Morning Journal* as 'useful publications'. They placed equal faith in the British paper of record, *The Times*, and the increasingly unruly James MacQueen was rebuked for questioning 'the dignified and impartial conduct which the editor of the <u>Times</u> ha[d] pursued ever since 1823, with regard to the West India controversy'. The West Indians could even float the slanderous rumour, without fear of contradiction, that the Anti-Slavery Society had siphoned off £4,000 of funds from the educational Mico Foundation to make up for falling subscriptions. Surveying the state of the literary battlefield, the abolitionist George Stephen found only cause for concern: 'For reasons best known to themselves,' he reflected, 'all the press was against us, except the honest *Morning Chronicle*, and the constant, unflinching *Edinburgh Review*.' Emboldened by this safety net, the West Indians spent the late 1820s devising traps for the abolitionists.[20]

One such trap was laid in the summer of 1828, when three members of the Interest's Standing Committee – the Irish merchant Colin Macrae, John Kingston, and Robert Alexander – applied for tickets to an anti-slavery meeting at the Freemasons' Hall. They approached the abolitionists in a conciliatory spirit and the West Indian trio was even allowed to sit on the meeting's platform. Thomas Pringle, the secretary of the Anti-Slavery Society, then agreed that the West Indians could address the meeting, 'so long as they kept within the bounds of good order and decorum'. As the meeting went on, Alexander passed a note to Thomas Fowell Buxton, intimating his wish to speak. The abolitionists, however, had fixed their agenda and would not deviate from it: Alexander was not allowed to speak, and this delighted him. The trio reported back to the West India Committee that they had been silenced, and Alexander then wrote about his 'ordeal' to the editor of the *New Times*, another pro-slavery newspaper. 'Mr Macaulay,' he complained, 'did not choose to extend either his good breeding or his courtesy beyond his own circle, and my intentions ... were consequently defeated.' Another West Indian, likely Macrae, complained to the same paper: 'Whether intended or not,' he wrote in mock fury, the conduct of the abolitionists 'had the effect of preventing any person, except the *initiated*, from addressing the meeting on that day.' It was a brilliant publicity stunt: the Interest fabricated the pretence of building bridges and, when they were not allowed to speak, they depicted their abolitionist foes as high-handed, contemptuous fanatics who would not engage in reasoned debate.[21]

Nevertheless, it would be a mistake to characterise these years under Wellington as plain sailing for the Interest. There was rumbling discontent with the leadership of Charles Ellis, who was created Baron Seaford in 1826. The honour had been conferred at the suggestion of Canning, for whom Ellis was the 'person who after my own family is the nearest to me in the world', but it was not a popular decision: Zachary Macaulay complained that 'the elevation of his rank' was 'the fruit of [his slaves'] bondage'. More critically, Ellis's personal and diplomatic approach to politics was resented by resident colonists and rank-and-file absentees, who preferred hysterical threats of resistance. The *Barbadian* also deplored 'embarrassing ... abuses' within the Interest, where an oligarchy of grandees was excluding the ordinary slaveholder 'from the secret consultation' that shaped pro-slavery policy. Though the slaveholders maintained good standing with the Liverpool ministry, James MacQueen, who was never embraced by the absentee planters in London, grumbled about 'the utter disunion among [them], their indolence, and ignorance'.[22]

The storm against Seaford broke in April 1829. At the London Tavern in Bishopsgate, the Interest assembled to discuss the advertised business of 'revising and enlarging the powers of the Standing Committee'. As debate commenced, Robert Gordon – a Jamaican slaveholder and MP whom Henry Brougham mocked as 'Bombastes Furioso' – raised his hand. What he proposed did not revise the powers of the Standing Committee; it emasculated them. He moved to create a new committee, an 'Acting' Committee that would 'attend to, and consider all matters which may appear to them of importance'. While this Acting Committee would operate 'under special authority' from the Standing Committee and 'report' to it, nobody pretended that it would not be in charge. Moreover, in what amounted to a personal attack on Seaford, the chairman of the new committee would be elected annually, not for life. Put to a vote, Gordon's motion sailed through, almost without challenge. Recognising this 'organizational coup', Seaford and his deputy Charles Pallmer resigned immediately. Seaford had already lost 'all interest in Politics' after Canning's death, and now he entered semi-retirement. Pallmer, the former 'hail fellow' of Lord Liverpool, was soon declared bankrupt: owing almost £11 million in today's money, he fled to Paris, surrendered to his creditors in absentia, and bolted to Jamaica.[23]

The new Acting Committee was instructed to capitalise on the Interest's political security and to mount a more combative defence of slavery; and with the pro-slavery *Reporter* writing euphemistically of 'a vacancy having occurred', the leadership of the Interest was now conferred on Richard Temple, the Marquess of Chandos, who was thought to have 'an anxious desire to bring these important national interests [of slavery and the planters' rights] under the honest consideration of the country'. Although George Hibbert was asked to approach Chandos on behalf of the Interest, responsibility for choosing him had lain with William Burge, the former Attorney General of Jamaica who had prosecuted Lecesne and Escoffery and since become the colony's new agent in London. Burge would boast that Chandos had been *his* choice: 'I first asked Lord C. to become the Chairman,' he wrote. 'I attended the Deputation who made the formal application.' But Burge's choice was curious. Chandos was the son of the Duke of Buckingham, an obese, blackmailing 'blubberhead' who was 'odious and unpopular to the last degree'. The apple had not fallen far from the tree and Chandos, a 'dissolute charmer', was following his father's examples of 'of infidelity and indebtedness'. His fecklessness would eventually lead to bankruptcy and the sale of the family estate at Stowe, at which point *The Times* deplored him for reducing 'his honours to the tinsel of a pauper and the bauble of a fool'. The folly of choosing Chandos would become obvious in time, but in 1829 the West Indians – at the apparent zenith of their strength – were confronted by an unexpected and catastrophic problem. For six years, the Interest had been shielded from the abolitionist campaign by their Tory guardians in government. That spring, however, the disintegration of the conservative consensus began to quicken. Now, the Tories were plunging into a bloody internal battle, and the Duke of Wellington had fired the first shot.[24]

In the 1660s, as Restoration England recovered from the Civil War, the Cavalier Parliament sought to narrow the religious divisions that had propelled the nation into twenty years of carnage. Yet rather than pursuing policies of religious toleration, Charles II's ministers enacted a series of laws which discriminated against Dissenters and Catholics by concentrating political power in the hands of Anglicans. The 1661 Corporation Act reserved public office for communicants of the Church of England. The Conventicle and Five Mile Acts made it difficult and dangerous for Dissenters to worship together. The Test Act of 1673 then required all public officials to renounce the Catholic doctrine of transubstantiation and, five years later, in the wake of the Popish Plot, all members of Parliament were obliged to disavow Catholicism before taking their seats. Nor were the ancient universities spared: Catholics could not study at Oxford, or graduate from Cambridge. Over time, policies of indemnity and toleration whittled down the effect of these laws on Dissenters, so much so that the 1828 Sacramental Test Act, which formally relieved non-Anglican Protestants of their civil disabilities, passed through Parliament with relative ease.

The 'Catholic Question' was more difficult to answer. For historically minded Britons, Catholicism symbolised subterfuge, treason, and war with Spain and France. The logic ran that Catholics could never be loyal subjects of the Crown since they also owed fidelity to the Church at Rome, which was the embodiment of earthly tyranny and spiritual corruption. To those ends, Catholics had been excluded from the royal line of succession, and the British coronation oath included a vow to defend the established Protestant religion. This fear of 'popery' and the desire to keep traitorous papists away from the levers of power was especially acute in Ireland, where more than eighty per cent of the population was Catholic. Yet by denying the majority of Irishmen the right to self-governance and advancement, the British had only made the 'problem' worse. Some statesmen recognised this danger and, after the United Irish rebellion in 1798, Pitt the Younger had tried to force Catholic Emancipation through Parliament. On that occasion, George III refused to repudiate his coronation oath and, when he withheld the royal assent, Pitt resigned in protest. It would take one of the most brilliant Irishman of all time to solve the Catholic question.[25]

Born on the remote western coast of Ireland, Daniel O'Connell was a tall, strong man in his forties with red cheeks and blue eyes, described by a novelist as 'he that walks so firm and stout'. One of the most accomplished barristers in the British Isles, but denied silk because of his faith, O'Connell was the foremost champion of Irish nationhood and Catholic equality. There was no better man to lead a campaign of such importance, for even in a golden age of oratory few could match O'Connell's prowess. 'He lends an eloquent voice,' remarked the diplomat Thomas Vyse, 'to the sentiments, the passions, and even to the prejudices of six million men ... He is a glass in which Ireland may see herself completely reflected.' O'Connell dressed like an Irishman too, with one observer marvelling at his frequent appearance 'in the full dress of a verdant liberator – green in all that may or may not be expressed, even to a green cravat, green watch-ribbon, and a slashing shining green hat-band'. Allying with English Catholics and liberal Whigs, this Irish titan became *the* political celebrity of the 1820s – or, in some views, the leading troublemaker.[26]

In 1823, O'Connell had founded the Catholic Association as a vehicle for pursuing Catholic Emancipation. Membership of the Association was open to the Irish population at large and it was priced at 1d. per year, a 'Catholic rent' that gave O'Connell a precious war chest. Mammoth meetings, the cooperation of the Catholic Church, and O'Connell's mastery of both oratory and polite society chipped away at the Anglican supremacy. In 1825, a private member's bill for Catholic relief was carried though the Commons and, though the bill was defeated in the Lords, the government took O'Connell seriously. The election of 1826 saw O'Connell throw his weight behind pro-Catholic candidates across the British Isles, but the turning point came in 1828 when Wellington appointed William Vesey-FitzGerald, an Anglo-Irish Tory, to the Board of Trade. Under the rules of the day, FitzGerald was forced to give up his seat for the Irish constituency of Clare and stand again in a 'ministerial by-election'. When he did, O'Connell ran against him. As a Catholic, O'Connell could not take a seat in Parliament, but there was nothing to stop him standing for election, and when O'Connell beat FitzGerald in a landslide, Wellington's government found itself in the horns of a dilemma. Until now, Catholic Emancipation had been anathema to conservative Tories; it was only the year before, after all, that they had refused to serve under the pro-Catholic Canning. But now, if they refused to let O'Connell take his seat, they ran the risk of an Irish revolution: as Home Secretary, Peel was advised that the island was 'on the eve of Rebellion, or civil war'. Despite deep-seated contempt for Catholicism, Peel began to wonder if there was 'less evil' in conceding Catholic rights than in maintaining aged constitutional principles. Wellington, too, began to acquiesce in the idea of Catholic Relief, with Mrs Arbuthnot fretting that her great hero was not taking 'a sufficiently Protestant view' of the situation.[27]

When the conservative Anglicans who formed the Tories' base got wind of these deliberations, they mounted a manic resistance that served 'to divert public attention from the Colonial Question'. Sixty thousand protestors gathered at Penenden Heath to denounce the betrayal of the Church by the government. Militantly Protestant associations known as 'Brunswick Clubs' thundered about the impending demise of the Church and the constitution; unsurprisingly, the Marquis of Chandos was the occasional chairman of the London club. Other 'violent Orangeists' assailed Wellington in the press, on the streets, and in Parliament. Peel even lost his seat for Oxford University in a by-election, with one newspaper mocking his plight with the lines, 'Oh! Member for Oxford! you shuffle and wheel! You have altered your name from R. Peel to Repeal!' Despite Wellington's hatred of 'popery', his military pragmatism was the decisive factor. He understood the horrors of war, and did not want to fight in Ireland. He therefore agreed with Peel that, while emancipation posed 'great danger' to the constitution, civil strife was a 'greater danger' still.[28]

The objections of George IV were yet to be overcome, but when Wellington told the King that refusal of the royal assent would trigger the resignation of the government, the last hurdle was overcome. The King wrote to his prime minister that 'as I find the country would be left without an administration, I have decided to yield my opinion to *that* which is considered by the Cabinet to be for the immediate interest of the Country. God knows,' the King remarked, 'what pain it costs me to write these words.' The Catholic Relief Act was passed in April 1829. Although O'Connell's election for Clare was voided on a technicality, he ran again – unopposed – and finally took his seat in the Commons. In his maiden speech, he chided the government for its neglect of Dublin's poor, for its voracious taxation of Ireland, and for the cruelty inflicted on Irishmen in the courts. 'The people,' he warned the House, had 'sent him there to do their business.'[29]

Catholic Emancipation could and should have been the triumph of Wellington's ministry, but just as repealing the Corn Laws would destroy Peel and the Conservative Party in the 1840s, the Catholic Question now tore apart the Tories from the inside. The measure had carried the Commons with the support of liberal Tories, Whigs, and radicals, but most of the 142 MPs who voted *against* the government were conservative Tories who now became the Ultra-Tories, the incorrigible enemies of Wellington and Peel. These Ultras languished in 'metaphysical despair', complaining that 'the whole nation is convulsed'. They damned the new liberalism as 'a system of letting loose all ties and bonds whatever, but that of selfish interest'.[30]

For some anti-slavery campaigners, Catholic Emancipation had been a wanton, wasteful distraction from the plight of the enslaved people of the Caribbean. 'In what sense,' spluttered the Sheffield abolitionist Samuel Roberts, 'are the rights of Roman Catholics stronger than those of British-born Negroes? What degree of comparison is there between the outrages inflicted on the former, and those inflicted on the latter?' Roberts could not have known it, but Catholic Emancipation was a turning point in the history of slavery: even if Wellington had prevented revolution in Ireland, he was propelling British conservatives into a revolution of their own.[31]

II.

The Fall of the House of Liverpool

A year ago, we were far from sanguine in our expectations of an early extinction of Slavery. On the contrary, our hopes were low. They have risen since that time ... The change is not in us, but in the circumstances in which we stand ... Better times, we trust, are approaching.[1]

Anti-Slavery Monthly Reporter, October 1829

When he was editing the memoirs of his father, Charles Buxton described the late 1820s as years of 'comparative repose' for the anti-slavery campaigners. For the more impatient among their ranks, these were the times that tried the soul. James Cropper lamented that he could see 'no feeling in the country ... to make me think ... emancipation could be carried'. George Stephen, the younger brother of Colonial Office lawyer, James, estimated that 'not one in ten thousand of the whole population had any but the most vague and general idea of the nature of the state of slavery itself'. There was little more optimism at Westminster. Eighty or so 'Ultras' might have refused to forgive Wellington for Catholic Emancipation and Buxton's colleagues might have been 'in the highest glee about ... the vexation of the Tories', but there was no opening for the abolitionists. The prime minister had lost the right wing of his party, but he retained the confidence of the King; in turn, the Wellington ministry was standing squarely behind the slaveholders. When a deputation from the Anti-Slavery Society met with the Colonial Office in 1830, they were horrified to find that 'whatever may be Sir George Murray's personal feelings and opinions on the subject, the determination of the Ministry at present is to do nothing; and if it is left to Government ... West India Slavery may exist, with little mitigation, for ages yet to come'.[2]

Nor was there much good news from the colonies. Ever since they had launched their campaign, Buxton and the anti-slavery elders had followed a policy of unrequited respect towards the government, and this was proving to be a serious strategic error. For fear of offending authority, they had placed limited pressure on the Colonial Office, which had gone on to issue dead-letter instructions to the West Indian colonies. And so, by early 1830, when the abolitionists compiled digests of ameliorative reforms, it was obvious that almost nothing had been done. In the four Crown colonies, where slave 'protectors' were empowered to supervise the punishment of enslaved people, the authorities had inflicted 1.3 million lashes of the whip in the previous two years alone. At the same time, Buxton was enduring continued frustration on Mauritius, writing to his wife that he was 'heartily grieved' that George Murray was 'not prepared to act as I wish'.[3]

The anti-slavery campaign was so moribund that the West Indians were concerned less by the prospect of emancipation and more by diminishing profits. In recent years, a handful of factors had plunged the planters into commercial difficulties. First, West Indian sugar was facing increased competition: East Indian cultivation was expanding rapidly, slave-grown sugar from Mauritius had been admitted to the British market, and cheap produce from Brazil and Cuba was under-cutting British merchants in the European markets that normally soaked up the West Indian surplus. Accordingly, since 1815 the price of muscovado sugar had fallen by half.[4]

Costs were escalating too. Since the abolition of the slave trade, British planters had been forbidden from importing 'fresh' labour and, even though most colonies had resisted amelioration, it still cost more to maintain than to replace a workforce. There was a further crisis of credit. Cultivating sugar was a capital-expensive enterprise and the costs of land, buildings, machinery, and freight were such that most planters were highly leveraged. And while merchant banks had gladly issued loans to eighteenth-century sugar barons, the sagging market meant it was now 'almost impossible to obtain a Loan upon Colonial Security'. Although the abolitionists were sceptical of the slaveholders' claims – after all, the Interest had been pleading poverty for forty years – this really *was* a crisis. For John Gladstone, 'the Interests of the Planters never were in so ruinous and depressed a state as they are at present'. The Glasgow Interest started laying off representatives;

the *West Indian Reporter* desperately promoted sugar's value to the wider British economy, exulting in its role in 'the composition & preparation of many taxable commodities'; and the Interest busied itself with procuring government aid. Deputations sallied forth to the Treasury and the Board of Trade; petitions went up to Parliament for the reduction of duties; and a select committee of the House of Commons began to explore the causes of 'colonial distress'. In these moments of West Indian distraction, anti-slavery hopes were revived. The late 1820s might have been the nadir of the abolitionist campaign, but this was a darkness before dawn. 'A complete revolution in the system of antislavery tactics' was about to occur.[5]

Henry Pownall was an unlikely revolutionary. An Anglo-Catholic lawyer and the chairman of the Middlesex Quarter Sessions, he was described by *The Times* as 'a staunch supporter of conservative principles'. Pownall delighted in local history and botany, playing a leading role in the Royal Horticultural Society, and his portrait now hangs in the Supreme Court on Parliament Square. An obituary would pay tribute to the ruthless approach he took with the Fenians accused of bombing Clerkenwell prison. Yet on 15 May 1830, as the Anti-Slavery Society gathered for its annual meeting at the Freemasons' Hall near Covent Garden, Henry Pownall was restless.[6]

The meeting was packed. Tickets had been sold from bookshops and publishers dotted around central London and, on that Saturday afternoon, 'the hall was completely filled in every part, so that even the passage to the platform was choked up'. The *Monthly Reporter* suggested that 'probably 1,000 or 1,500 went away, without being able to obtain permission'. As the meeting dawdled forward, Buxton moved the same kind of earnest, timid resolutions which had defined the campaign so far. 'No proper or practicable means,' he proposed, 'should be left unattempted for effecting at the earliest period the entire abolition of slavery.' For many in the Freemasons' Hall, the phrase 'at the earliest period' was offensively ambiguous, and a sop to the government. Whatever sound and fury there once had been, it signified nothing. This was when Pownall begged leave to speak. He launched into an impassioned speech on the evils of slavery, the abolition of which could brook no delay. He was begged to yield the floor, but he would not: 'Neither distance, nor weather, nor domestic inconvenience,' it was observed, 'ever availed for one moment to impede him.' At last, Pownall demanded that Buxton's resolution should be amended to read that 'from and after January 1, 1830, every slave born within the king's dominions shall be free'.[7]

The hall erupted. 'The shouts, the tumult of applause were such as I never heard before, and never shall hear again,' recalled George Stephen, the younger brother of James. 'Cheers innumerable thundered from every bench, hats and handkerchiefs were waved in every hand.' The old guard was flummoxed and appalled by this breach of decorum, but Stephen and his allies – 'a little knot of some half-dozen' – wove their way through the crowd, steeling their colleagues 'to resist all attempts at suppression'. They allowed no silence, shouting down appeals for calm and quiet. 'At the first subsidence of the tempest,' wrote Stephen, 'we began again, reserving our lungs till others were tired. We soon became the fuglemen of the mighty host, nor did we rest, till Wilberforce rose to put the amendment [to a vote], which was carried with a burst of exulting triumph that would have made the Falls of Niagara inaudible.'[8]

Riding the momentum that Pownall generated, Stephen and his friends pushed for more 'energetic measures'. The first step was changing the name of the Anti-Slavery Society, the words 'mitigation and gradual' being dropped to reflect this new urgency. The correspondence committee that had overseen the network built by Thomas Clarkson was reinvigorated and instructed to bring the provincial anti-slavery associations 'as far as possible into entire concert and co-operation with this Society'. Stephen called the band of brothers who engineered this project the 'young England abolitionists', and their elders were far from impressed. Although Macaulay knew the campaign had to move forward decisively or risk division, he was appalled by the wanton conduct of his 'impetuous and unscrupulous allies' and, for once, the fears of offending political opinion were well-founded: Pownall's motion was too much for the Whig leader, Earl Grey, who refused the vice-presidency of the Morpeth Anti-Slavery Society in his native Northumberland.[9]

Despite the revulsion of the patrician class, the anti-slavery nation was waking. The Baptist minister Benjamin Godwin spent the spring delivering lectures on slavery in Yorkshire mill-towns, and his speeches were fashioned into 'a text book richly fraught with materials for those who may wish to emulate ... this able and estimable minister of Christ'. The senior James Stephen published the second volume of his mammoth 'delineation' of West Indian slavery, which Macaulay commended as 'a mighty book, which marks the hand of a giant'. The Quakers were re-engaging with the slavery question, too. At their yearly meeting, wealthy Birmingham merchant Joseph Sturge demanded that 'the interests of a few planters in this country should not, for one moment, be put in competition with all that is dear to 800,000 negroes, merely because the Atlantic rolls between us and them, or on account of the colour of their skin or the woolliness of their hair'. However much the Interest might 'bribe the ministers of the Crown [with] another splendid dinner at the Albion with all its costly viands and dulcet strains of soothing speeches', Sturge implored his fellow Quakers to hold steady, to ensure that 'the doom of slavery is settled'.[10]

The Colonial Secretary, George Murray, then delivered an unexpected bonus. Having spent two years in wilful denial, he now conceded to Buxton 'that slave trading to a vast extent had prevailed at the Mauritius, and that all our statements had been well founded'. The abolitionists were even allowed to select the official tasked with eradicating the Mauritian slave trade. They settled on John Jeremie, who as Chief Justice of St Lucia had exposed the cruelty done to enslaved people in that colony. At first, Jeremie protested that nothing would ever induce him 'to go to a slave colony again', but Buxton wore him down: 'It signifies very little whether you are killed or not, but [it matters] very much whether the right man goes to the Mauritius'. Jeremie departed, but he would not enjoy his time in the Indian Ocean: suffering dreadful abuse at the hands of the Mauritian planters, he sought sanctuary on an anchored man-of-war before the colony's governor ordered him back to Britain for his own safety. It was only when Jeremie returned to the colony with a military force that anything close to progress occurred in Mauritius.[11]

By 1830, George IV was sixty-seven and he had been on the throne for a decade. His reign began with the Queen Caroline Affair, a tawdry spectacle which saw the King put his wife on trial for adultery, an act of stunning hypocrisy. There followed a decadent coronation and George quickly became the first British monarch that satirists felt comfortable mocking openly. There was a weight of material to work with, but the King's waistline was the softest target: not even a wardrobe of craftily designed jackets could disguise the corpulence bequeathed by His Majesty's diet. According to the Duke of Wellington, who often resented serving such a man, one royal breakfast comprised 'a pigeon and beef steak pie, of which he ate two pigeons and three beef-steaks, three parts of a bottle of Mozelle, a glass of champagne, two glasses of port and a glass of brandy!' The effects of this gluttony were exacerbated by laudanum, the bitter tincture of opium that the King took daily. By June 1830, George was not long for the world. 'The King gets gradually worse', wrote Mrs Arbuthnot, observing that his doctors had been 'obliged to puncture his legs again, & all prospect of his recovery is entirely at an end'. That end came within weeks, and the King spent his last night at Windsor Castle. 'A blood vessel in his stomach burst. He put his hand up to his breast, exclaimed "Good God, what do I feel? This must be death!" & died in a few minutes.'[12]

Few people have had a more profound influence on British culture. George IV had commissioned the renovation of Buckingham Palace and the construction of Marble Arch and the Brighton Pavilion; he was instrumental in establishing the National Gallery; he bought works by Rembrandt and Rubens for the nation; he patronised Gainsborough, Reynolds, Constable, and Stubbs; and he supported the work of Robert Southey and Jane Austen. Despite this astounding legacy, George IV would not be missed. 'There never was an individual less regretted by his fellow-creatures', read the notice in *The Times*, which condemned George's 'reckless, unceasing and unbounded prodigality' and his 'indifference to the feelings of others'. Even stout Tories struggled to speak warmly of the dead. For Mrs Arbuthnot, the King had been 'made up of opposite qualities', but 'the bad preponderated & consequently he had few real friends'.[13]

In the absence of any legitimate heirs, the throne now passed to George's brother William, the Duke of Clarence and the Lord High Admiral of the Navy. For the abolitionists, this development was far from auspicious. In his very first speech in the House of Lords in 1792, Clarence had proclaimed himself 'an attentive observer of the state of the negroes' and declared that 'their state was far from miserable; on the contrary ... they were comparatively in a state of humble happiness'. Naval service in the Caribbean, where Clarence was flattered with 'parades, banquets, and multi-gun salutes', made him 'an eye witness to what was called slavery' and he believed that 'the moment this trade was lopped off from this country' other European empires would swoop upon the British slave colonies. The next year, Clarence deemed it 'impolitic and unjust to abolish the slave trade', an enterprise which employed 'immense capital' and was 'highly beneficial to this country'. Clarence damned the abolitionist James Ramsay as 'a tyrant to order and good government' and abolitionists generally as 'either fanatics or hypocrites, and in one of those classes he ranked Mr Wilberforce'. In 1799, Clarence was again 'extremely warm' against abolition, shocking Macaulay that 'so young a man, under no bias of interest, should be so earnest for the continuance of the Slave Trade, and especially now its horrors are confessed by all'.[14]

Clarence's broadsides earned him celebrity in the colonies, and the Jamaican planter Simon Taylor was hugely impressed by this noble defence of slavery. 'The Duke of Clarence,' he wrote to George Hibbert, 'has been very indefatigable in collecting information on the Subject and knows it better than most Men in the upper House.' Clarence maintained this pro-slavery position even after 1807, complaining that the abolition of the slave trade had weakened 'the Maritime Strength of the Country', which he thought was now at greater risk of invasion by France.[15]

The accession of William IV nonetheless presented an opportunity to the abolitionists, since tradition dictated that the death of a monarch should trigger a general election. As Britons voted in the summer of 1830, hustings were dominated by parliamentary reform. There was further dispute over taxation and the Corn Laws but slavery, at last, was starting to define electoral contests. Most notably, Henry Brougham's candidacy for Yorkshire was propelled by Protestant Dissenters and the anti-slavery association at Leeds, while electors in Scarborough and Whitby were implored to choose Brougham 'on anti-slavery grounds'. Despite the intervention of Robert Wilmot-Horton, who wrote two open letters to Yorkshire's voters in support of the Interest – letters that put Wilmot-Horton on a par with 'such men as Macqueen and Moody' – Brougham swept into office. Lord Morpeth, who was elected alongside Brougham, believed that 'the foremost topic among us all may now be ... negro slavery', while the retired Wilberforce hoped that this stunning election of an explicitly anti-slavery candidate would 'have a powerful effect'.[16]

Slavery was equally important at the other end of the country. In Bristol, where each voter could cast two ballots, it was almost certain that one of the city's two MPs would be a pro-slavery Tory, but in the summer of 1830 a schism erupted between Bristol's Whigs, some of whom hoped to replace the retiring West Indian merchant Henry Bright with an abolitionist. The anti-slavery Whigs attached themselves to Edward Protheroe, a radical who had recently supported an abolitionist motion in Parliament. Protheroe knew that taking a decided stand against slavery would cost him 'the support of many friends', and that he would be threatened 'with the united wealth and forces of the [slaveholders] in Bristol, [and] with the active co-operation in their behalf of the same interest in London'. Undeterred, he set up headquarters at the Bush Tavern.[17]

The favoured candidate of Bristol's pro-slavery Whigs was James Evan Baillie, a Scottish merchant and banker whose family owned the Dochfour estate outside Inverness and whose sprawling business holdings included 2,500 slaves across five Caribbean colonies. Baillie arrived in Bristol at the head of a 'very imposing' procession of West Indian supporters, a public entrance which stunned the city's abolitionists. 'I stood in silence,' wrote one of them to the *Bristol Mirror*, 'contemplating the procession, and whilst viewing it as it passed, I thought how many human backs had been lacerated – sighs heaved – groans uttered – and sales of human beings effected to have produced the ostentatious display. I turned away ... from the guilty pageantry.'[18]

The ensuing contest among Bristol's Whigs was effectively 'a trial of strength between the West India interest and the abolitionists', and it sparked a series of violent confrontations. On the evening of Baillie's procession through Bristol, Protheroe's headquarters were stormed by pro-slavery goons, '60 to 100 sailors and ... carpenters [who were] in a dreadful state of ... intoxication and armed with common bludgeons'. Smashing through the Bush Tavern's windows and occupying its ground floor, the pro-slavery mob was driven out only by a rival gang, who then retaliated against Baillie's own base. Twenty-seven people were hospitalised and a local newspaper reported that 'for some time the whole town was in a state of ... violent disorder and agitation'. A deployment of constables briefly pacified affairs but the campaign continued to boil over, with the mobs targeting the candidates directly: once, when Protheroe spoke from the windows of his tavern, he was felled by a wooden missile that drew torrents of blood. After weeks of fighting, the pro-slavery mob won out. With West Indian merchants threatening tradesmen with a loss of custom if they cast a ballot for Protheroe, and with money 'pouring forth like water in the purchase of votes', the slaveholder Baillie was returned. Protheroe's concession speech was a poignant affair. 'Perhaps it was too much to expect,' he said, 'that the first struggle of the friends of humanity in this ancient seat of West India commerce could be suffered to succeed.'[19]

When the new Parliament met in November 1830, the splintered nature of politics meant it was unclear who had actually 'won' the election. A minster at the Treasury thought that Wellington might have gained twenty seats; Henry Brougham thought the prime minister had lost fifteen. Whatever the precise numbers, historians agree that tension over Reform, taxation, and perhaps even slavery meant that Wellington had barely scraped a majority in the Commons. Parliament also met in a wider context of political unrest. In France, Charles X had tried to censor the free press and limit the political rights of the *bourgeoisie*, but this power grab provoked 'Three Glorious Days' of fighting in Paris before the July Revolution installed Louis Philippe at the head of a new, constitutional monarchy. In August, inspired by their French neighbours, the southern provinces of the Netherlands seceded over religious and economic grievances: the independent Kingdom of Belgium was proclaimed in October. Elsewhere, officers at the Polish military academy stoked an uprising against Russian rule that spread rapidly through eastern Europe; in Switzerland, ten thousand men marched to Zimiker Hill to demand a new constitution for the canton of Zurich. All of this, thought Henry Brougham, was 'most advantageous to our cause, because it denounces wrath and destruction on those who would by force withstand the popular opinion'.[20]

Britain was not immune from this upheaval. In the wake of falling wages and bad harvests, the Swing Riots had engulfed the south-east of England. Named after 'Captain Swing', a fictitious farmer whose descent from hard-working prosperity into destitution symbolised the common plight, the rioters burned hayricks, maimed cattle, and vandalised farm machinery. Imperilled landowners received threatening letters from 'Swing' himself: 'Revenge for thee is on the Wing,' read one, 'From thy determined Capt Swing.' The Tory minister Charles Arbuthnot's estate was 'threatened with having a mob coming to break our machine', forcing him to hurry home with 'two servants, four soldiers & arms & ammunition in abundance'. His wife had *some* sympathy for 'the peasantry, who in many parts do really suffer under great privations', but she blamed most of the turbulence on 'incendiaries & agitators'.[21]

A different kind of tension was enveloping the capital. 'Troops and artillery have been brought to London,' it was recorded, 'the guards doubled, the police on the alert.' This particular state of panic was coloured by the growing demand for parliamentary reform, though Mrs Arbuthnot was not convinced. 'It is quite preposterous,' she spluttered, 'that the idle vagabonds who compose the mob of London care a pin about Parliamentary Reform. What they want is plunder; those who have nothing want the property of those who have something.' She blamed the radicals Henry Hunt and William Cobbett for spewing provocative filth from the Rotunda meeting house at Blackfriars. There, Hunt and Cobbett would 'assemble & harangue crowds of the lower orders in the most seditious manner, and from that place [they would] issue in large bodies & come & alarm the peaceable people in the West End of the town'. Wellington agreed with her, or perhaps she with him. 'The Duke is greatly affected by all this state of affairs,' she noted: 'He feels that beginning reform is beginning revolution.'[22]

It was in this context, in the autumn of 1830, that Earl Grey intreated Wellington to contemplate Reform. In response, the prime minister denounced the very *idea* of it. 'The representation of the people at present,' he told the House of Lords, 'contained a large body of the property of the country, and in which the landed interests had a preponderating influence.' Under such happy circumstances, Wellington would not even consider change. 'He was not only not prepared to bring forward any measure of this nature, but he would at once declare that, as far as he was concerned, as long as he held any station in the government of the country, he should always feel it his duty to resist such measures when proposed by others.' For a premier with a slim majority in the Commons, and for a government vulnerable to attack from left and right, it was politically suicidal. Many newly elected Whigs and some liberal Tories had made Reform their priority for the session, and Wellington had just declared himself their enemy. Charles Greville opined that there had never been 'an act of more egregious folly, or one so universally condemned by friends and foes'.[23]

The Wellington ministry staggered on for another fortnight but its predicament was clear. In mid-November, when the government sought to reduce the Civil List that maintained the royal family, the Whig economist Henry Parnell proposed to subject the List to the scrutiny of a Commons select committee. The proposal was innocuous in itself, yet in the debate that followed the two extreme wings of the Tories – the Canningites and the Ultras – joined forces with the Whigs. When the House divided on Parnell's motion, the government lost. 'The ultra-Tories united with the Whigs,' it was observed, '& we were beat by 29' votes.[24]

Although the political establishment recognised Wellington's missteps, it was taken aback that the government lost when it did. 'Everyone was so intent on … Reform,' reflected Greville, 'that the Civil List was not thought of, and consequently the defeat of the Government last night was unexpected.' Indeed, the loss was so surprising that Wellington was nowhere near Parliament when it happened: he was dining with Mrs Arbuthnot when a knock at the door heralded Peel and Goulburn with the bad tidings. Given that the Commons was due to debate Reform the next day, and given that the government was now likely to lose any vote, Wellington saw the writing on the wall. He had consented to Catholic Relief to prevent a war in Ireland, but he would not tolerate any further desecration of the constitution. He resigned 'at an hour's notice'.[25]

The Tories were now incapable of forming a government, so the King was forced to turn to the Whigs. On 16 November, he invited Earl Grey to form the first truly Whig government since 1783. A slight, balding man with a sharp face and red cheeks, Grey was a capable leader and a beguiling, persuasive speaker: 'There is nothing approaching this damned fellow in the kingdom,' remarked one of his listeners, 'when he mounts his best horse.' Other aspects of his character were less wholesome: Grey was a serial adulterer who was described by Lady Holland as 'a fractious and exigent lover'. More notoriously, he pestered Georgiana, the Duchess of Devonshire, until she 'gave in' to his advances, and their bastard child was raised as if she were Grey's own and much younger sister.[26]

In spite of his appetite for Reform, Grey was *not* a liberal. He was a pillar of the landed elite whose family had owned Howick in Northumberland since the early fourteenth century. He was an Old Etonian and a product of Cambridge, and he had ridiculed George Canning for being the son of an actress. Upon assuming power, moreover, he had committed himself to defeating 'democracy and Jacobinism' and then assured Dorothea, the Russian Princess Lieven, that he would 'select the aristocrat [for his Cabinet], for that class is a guarantee for the safety of the state and of the throne'. His word held true: Grey's first government included a duke, a marquess, two earls, and four viscounts, and the new prime minister boasted that 'the acreage possessed by his Cabinet surpassed any previous record'. The Grey ministry was also a family affair, and Mrs Arbuthnot raged that he had 'given good places to his son, his three sons-in-law, three brothers-in-law, besides nephews'. The Whigs might have been more amenable to slave emancipation than the Tories – and Grey's son, Viscount Howick, was one of them – but these men were not radicals or *arrivistes*; they were patricians who regarded themselves as Britain's natural ruling class.[27]

Even so, whilst the slaveholding Interest had long relied on friends and allies in government, it was now left without support. Peel was in opposition, Wellington was marooned in the Lords, and Henry Goulburn had been dismissed; when Wilmot-Horton left the Colonial Office in 1828, Thomas Moody had gone with him. William Huskisson was absent, too. He had flounced out of Wellington's Cabinet in 1828, but his departure from the King's councils was rendered permanent by a shocking event of September 1830.

Over the last decade, the merchants and businessmen of north-west England had been arranging for a railway to connect Liverpool with the booming industrial city of Manchester. By 1826, the engineer George Stephenson had been commissioned to design the route, thirty-five miles of track that lay across Merseyside and southern Lancashire. As an MP for Liverpool and an advocate of faster, freer trade, Huskisson had been integral to securing support for the scheme. On 15 September, as trains driven by Stephenson's engines made the journey from Liverpool to Manchester, he was an honoured guest of the railway.[28]

Wellington was there too, and he shared a train – but not a carriage – with Huskisson. When their engine stopped near St Helen's to take on water, Huskisson sought out the Duke to bury the hatchet and, while the travelling dignitaries milled about on the railway's southern track, the two men ended their feud. Then a shout went up from further down the line: 'An engine is approaching! Take care, gentlemen!' The *Rocket*, one of Stephenson's other engines, was nearing on the parallel track. Some passengers climbed calmly into their carriage; others stood well out of the way. Huskisson did neither. As Simon Garfield has described, Huskisson had been a clumsy, accident-prone child who had 'drifted into the arena of the unwell' shortly after birth. He once fractured his arm while getting out of bed and, when he tried to jump over the shallow moat at Blair Castle in Perthshire, he tore ankle ligaments so badly that he sustained a limp for life.[29]

That day in September 1830, this comedic clumsiness took on a tragic hue. As the *Rocket* drew closer, Huskisson panicked. Standing on the tracks, he clambered up the steps to his carriage and grabbed hold of the door, only to find it had not been bolted shut. Now, at the worst possible moment, the unlocked door swung outwards, dangling the hysterical Huskisson over the track. The engineer of the *Rocket* tried to throw the engine into reverse, but he could not slow down in time. Huskisson was caught, dragged down onto the tracks, and the wheels of the *Rocket* 'passed over his leg & thigh, crushing it in a most frightful way'. The injuries were horrific. The surgeon Joseph Brandreth was travelling in one of the *Rocket*'s carriages and, when he rushed forward to assist, he found that Huskisson's leg had 'a frightful appearance... Half way between the knee and ankle [it] was almost entirely severed, except a small portion on the outside ... Half-way but rather higher up between the knee and body, the whole flesh was torn off above the bones broken'. Huskisson wailed in agony. 'It's all over with me,' he cried. 'Bring me my wife & let me die!' Taken to Eccles, where a team of doctors from Manchester worked on him for hours, he deteriorated rapidly: 'countenance pale and ghastly', recorded the chief surgeon. At nine o'clock that night, Huskisson succumbed to his injuries. He became the world's first railway passenger fatality.[30]

*

As the Tories imploded and the Whigs prepared for power, four years of dormancy were coming to an end for the Anti-Slavery Society. Churches high and low were now engrossed by the campaign and 'the religious public ha[d], at last, taken the field'. And as reports of further cruelty made their way across the Atlantic, it was increasingly clear that the colonists could not be trusted to put their house in order. 'They have of late flogged slaves in Jamaica for praying, and imprisoned the missionaries,' reported Buxton, 'and they have given the nation to understand that preaching and praying are offences not to be tolerated in a slave colony.' For the slaveholders, these were spectacular own goals. 'The West Indians have done us good service,' Buxton wrote. 'Our slavery concerns go well.' More importantly, there was now a pervasive belief among the abolitionists that *immediate* and not gradual emancipation should be their goal, just as Henry Pownall had demanded. In Edinburgh, the evangelical theologian Andrew Thomson rallied Scottish campaigners to this new standard of 'immediatism'. In a rousing speech, the effects of which rippled across the British Isles, Thomson commanded abolitionists to 'tell the legislature, plainly and strongly, that no man has a right to property in man, that there are 800,000 individuals sighing in bondage, under the intolerable evils of West Indian slavery, who have as good a right to be free as we ourselves, that they ought to be free, and that they *must* be made free!' In the days after Thomson's speech, two petitions for emancipation circulated in Edinburgh: one for gradual emancipation, one for immediate emancipation. The latter was twenty-two times more popular; the ground was shifting. Four thousand miles to the west, in the British Caribbean, the slaveholders knew it too.[31]

12.

Reform, That You May Preserve

We have got the cholera at Sunderland. I think it a far inferior evil to the Reform Bill.[1]

Mrs Arbuthnot, 6 December 1831

On the first Thursday of 1831, a gaggle of planters gathered in the courthouse at St George, the capital of Grenada. It was a curious date for such a meeting. In ordinary times, the planters would have been on their estates, supervising the harvesting, threshing, and boiling of sugar on which their livelihoods depended. But these were not ordinary times. And so, from across the island, from the parishes of St Patrick in the north and St David in the south-east, the Grenadians had ridden the coastal roads and traipsed the mountain tracks to this summit. They took as the formal subject of their discussion the commercial crisis that falling sugar prices had inflicted upon the West Indies, but it was not long before the talk turned to slavery. The Grenadians agreed that a united colonial voice was needed to confront the danger posed by a new Whig government that was expected to look more favour- ably on slave emancipation than the Tories had done. They promptly dispatched invitations to the furthest reaches of the Caribbean. Two months later, stalking in the shadows of Washington, Adams, and Jefferson, seventeen delegates from across the British West Indies assembled at Bridgetown, Barbados, for the first Colonial Congress.[2]

As the Congress conducted its business over the last few days of winter, the delegates discussed trade and tariffs and focused 'with the most serious apprehension [on] the effect which the [abolitionists'] reiterated clamours' were having 'on the deliberations of Parliament and the measures of Government, with reference to the question of colonial slavery'. The secretary of the Congress was the Grenadian journalist Alexander McCombie and he implored the delegates not only to seek the protection of the King from the designs of 'evil ministers', but also to cooperate with the Interest in London. Of particular concern was the potential for a new Order in Council enforcing ameliorative measures in the Crown colonies, a prospect that Bristol's slaveholders denounced as 'unnecessary, illegal, unconstitutional, vexatious, and unjust'. If the government followed this path towards emancipation, the delegates predicted only ruin for the Caribbean: in their opinion, 'property', prosperity, and African progress all depended upon slavery. After seven days of debate, the Congress closed with a 'Grand Entertainment' at the municipal mansion of the King's House. Four hours of extravagant dining were capped with four more hours of libations that were responsible for 'the evident delight that beamed on the features of all around'.[3]

In those moonlit hours of drunken clarity, the Colonial Congressmen might well have understood that slavery was not *yet* in peril, not least because Grey's Whigs had formed a minority government that was powerless to bring about real change. 'I have no notion the present Govt can last,' opined Mrs Arbuthnot: 'They have scarcely any supporters, they <u>cannot</u> redeem any of their pledges, [and] they create great violence amongst themselves.' Moreover, even if the Whigs *could* have abolished slavery, there was little indication that they *wanted* to do so: as Viscount Althorp, the Whigs' leader in the Commons, remarked to Macaulay, their 'object was to avoid pledging the Government to anything more than the measures for the amelioration of the slave population'. Stephen Lushington struck another note of pessimism when he expressed 'little confidence in the merely voluntary good-will of the new government' on matters of slavery.[4]

Indeed, while the appointment of friendlier ministers such as Viscount Howick meant that anti-slavery campaigners could track 'documents of great value [going] into the Colonial Office, and then by the reiterated motions of Mr Buxton usually succeed in bringing them to light', the political ascent of the Whigs generated false hope. It was certainly easier to foresee slave emancipation under a Whig than a Tory government, but the priority of the new Grey ministry was not the reform of the colonies; it was the reform of Parliament.[5]

There was no question that Reform was badly needed. The electoral franchise had not been extended generally since the mid-fifteenth century when, under Henry VI, voting in the counties had been opened to freeholders with annual rental incomes of more than forty shillings. At the same time, the distribution of parliamentary seats was hideously imbalanced, with the monied and landed classes controlling dozens of rotten and pocket boroughs. Old Sarum, a byword for electoral corruption, was the Wiltshire constituency where the city of Salisbury had first been founded and, despite the abandonment of its castle and cathedral in the fourteenth century, its eleven non-resident electors still returned two MPs to Parliament. Gatton in east Surrey was even worse: there were but seven voters there. There was a marked concentration of these boroughs in Cornwall. Though neither St Germans nor Mitchel had more than seven voters, both constituencies returned two MPs, as did the sixty-seven buildings of Bossiney on the county's northern coast. Such boroughs were easy pickings for West Indians: one of Bossiney's two MPs was Edward Rose Tunno, a Tory whose father-in-law owned 841 enslaved people in Jamaica.

Perhaps more pressingly, the electoral system had taken no account of urbanisation and industrialisation, two powerful forces that had been transforming Britain since the early eighteenth century. Where the provincial hubs of the nation had once been Bristol and the wool-market of Norwich, the advent of steel, coal, and cotton had revolutionised the demographic map. Parliament simply had not kept pace, and so many of the country's biggest towns and cities were deprived of political representation: the industrial centres of Manchester, Birmingham, Leeds, Bradford, and Sheffield had a combined population of three-quarters of a million, but they sent a total of zero MPs to Westminster. This, not slavery, was the focus of liberal energies.

Even so, the spring of 1831 was not without its abolitionist moments. On 15 April, Buxton addressed the House of Commons on the diminishing slave population of the Caribbean. Upon the acquisition of Demerara and Berbice in 1814 there had been roughly 775,000 enslaved people in the British colonies but the population had since fallen by roughly 14 per cent to 665,000. In Demerara, the population was down by 12,000; in Trinidad, 'where the slaves die off like rotten sheep', by 6,000. Yet over the same period the *free* black population of Demerara had doubled, while the Haitian population had boomed since independence. In the era of Thomas Malthus, this was instructive. Malthus was an English clergyman whose 1798 *Essay on the Principle of Population* beguiled the politicians and economists of the early nineteenth century. Therein, Malthus propounded his famous 'trap': the idea that population rose and fell in accordance with the availability of resources. Malthus had also argued that population could be 'repressed' by 'moral restraint, vice, and misery'. For the abolitionists, Malthusian theory confirmed that slavery – the most repugnant of moral restraints – was responsible for the falling population of the West Indies. Buxton advised his fellow MPs that populations were rising in Africa despite war, among Jamaica's free Maroons despite 'savage life', and in Haiti 'despite vice and misery'. In Buxton's analysis, only enslavement could explain why the black population of the British colonies was falling. Slavery was literally costing lives.[6]

At the end of his speech, almost eight years since he had first proposed *gradual* emancipation, Buxton declared that he would no longer tolerate delay on the part of either the government or the colonial assemblies. Driven forward by the 'immediatist' movement spearheaded by Henry Pownall and Andrew Thomson, he called at last for the unqualified, immediate emancipation of British colonial slaves. He demanded that Parliament should immediately 'consider of and adopt the best means of effecting [the] abolition [of slavery] throughout the British dominions'.[7]

Buxton did not know, however, that the West Indians had beaten him to the punch. The next day's *Times* reported that, merely hours before Buxton made his speech, 'numerous ... noblemen and gentlemen connected with the West India Interest ... had [held] a long conference with Earl Grey and Viscount Goderich', who had returned to the front bench as Colonial Secretary. This conference probably explains the government's response to Buxton: instead of endorsing an abolitionist agenda that dovetailed neatly with the Whigs' own 'liberal concerns', Althorp offered only to impose higher tariffs on the colonies which did not 'ameliorate'. It was a desultory proposal that everyone knew Buxton would reject; it was a salutary reminder that dealing with the Whigs would not always be easier than dealing with the Tories; and it was proof that nothing – not even slavery – would take legislative precedence over Reform.[8]

*

By the spring of 1831 the Grey ministry had already squeezed its first
Reform Bill, drafted by the 'Committee of Four', through a second
reading in the Commons. However, passing legislation was – and
remains – a complicated affair. The first 'reading' of a bill in the
Commons is a purely formal stage of legislation, but the second
reading is followed by a substantive debate and then a 'division',
meaning a vote. If a bill passes that division, it is subjected to the
painstaking consideration of a committee of MPs, who may table
amendments that the Commons then debates in the 'report' stage of
the process. After this decisive 'third reading' takes place, a similar
process is followed in the House of Lords.

When the first Reform Bill went into committee in April 1831, it was
wrecked by Isaac Gascoyne, the Liverpool MP who not coincidentally
had spent thirty-five years defending slavery. When it was clear that
Gascoyne had gutted Reform, the government requested and received
the dissolution of Parliament: if the Whigs could not shepherd Reform
through *this* House of Commons, where they did not command a
majority, they would try again with another. In May and June, therefore, Britain's voters went to the polls in an effective referendum on
Reform. Upon returning to Weymouth, Buxton found that his constituents were 'eager for Reform beyond conception' and the election
resulted in a landslide victory for the Whigs, who now commanded a
majority of more than 130 and a clear mandate for Reform.

The abolitionists knew what this meant for their immediate prospects. In Staffordshire, local activists concluded that 'men's minds
[were] so taken up with the great question of Parliamentary Reform'
that it was wiser to let the moment pass without 'wearying our friends
in useless endeavours'. Still, there was hope, principally because the
prospect of Reform struck terror into the West Indians. As Parliament
was constituted, the slaveholders could guarantee the return of maybe
sixty pro-slavery MPs. 'The wealth of these men,' it was explained,
'enabled them to send many members to the House when rotten
boroughs were as plentiful as blackberries'; that is, the slaveholders
could buy as many seats as they could afford. There was the occasional
sign that voters' habits were changing. In the 1831 election at Lancaster,
for instance, the election of the West Indian merchant Patrick Maxwell
Stewart had been contingent on disingenuous statements in favour of
emancipation – which he promptly repudiated once he got to

Westminster – but the abolitionists knew that 'an unreformed Parliament was not to be coerced' into abolishing slavery. A *reformed* Parliament, however, was infinitely more likely to tackle the colonies directly. Tellingly, the Duke of Wellington feared that 'a reformed House of Commons [would] immediately attack ... the West Indies, that all property [would] become insecure'.[9]

For a while, then, the abolitionist leaders were content to support the Whigs in their pursuit of Reform, hoping that the achievement of one great goal would lead in time to the achievement of another. In the meantime, they strove to maintain friendly terms with the Whig leaders whose help they would eventually need. In June, Buxton invited several ministers to dinner at the Truman's brewery in Spitalfields. Naturally, Henry Brougham was in attendance, 'in high glee ... in a shabby black coat, and very old hat'. Lord Grey came too, 'grave and thoughtful as he seemed'. The dinner itself was 'not political' and the men feasted on beef steaks cooked in the brewery's furnaces. It was only after port that Buxton went off for an audience with Grey. They discussed a recent speech by Viscount Howick, Grey's son and the junior minister at the Colonial Office, and the prime minister's reactions were wonderfully reflective of the ambiguity that the abolitionists faced: he was delighted when Buxton praised the speech for its 'honesty and feeling, as well as for its talent', but Grey worried that 'his son had been carried by his zeal rather too far'.[10]

As he sought to keep the Whigs on-side, Buxton appeared to row back from his springtime demand for immediate emancipation. In his private papers he disavowed the desire to liberate 700,000 enslaved people at once, and he retreated to the politically safer ground of 'gradualism'. Buxton now professed a more conservative ambition 'to strike a blow at the root [of slavery]; to ensure, in the first place, that no new victims shall enter this dreadful state; to declare, in short, that from a given period all children shall be born free ... I wish first to prevent any more waters flowing in to the lake, before I begin to empty it'. Reproaching the wild and enthusiastic 'immediatism' that Pownall and Thomson had helped to create, Buxton returned to a measured, doleful pace. It was one that many senior abolitionists preferred to match.[11]

George Stephen was not among them. Forthright, outspoken, possessed 'of a hot temper', and prone 'to see the worst in people', the thirty-six-year-old Stephen believed that the renewed timidity of his elders was jeopardising the survival of the abolitionist movement. He blamed them for the fact that the 'Antislavery societies in the country were languid, and almost inanimate', and he mourned that copies of the *Anti-Slavery Monthly Reporter* 'were not read ... [but were] reduced to waste paper, and sold as such in barrowfuls'. In the summer of 1831, at the Society's general meeting, Stephen lost his patience. Forcing his way onto the meeting's platform, he advocated the formation of a separate anti-slavery corps that he would populate with his 'young England abolitionists'. Freed from the burden of political decorum, this new 'Agency Committee' could take 'energetic measures' without endangering the respectability of the parent body. It was a bold, daring, and necessary move, but Stephen's proposal was rejected entirely. It was not even put to a vote. The younger man was patronised by his elders as 'well-meaning but impractical' and his plan was criticised roundly for being too radical, too likely to alienate supporters in Parliament.[12]

Stephen was disconsolate, but he had struck a chord with some who were in the hall. As the delegates streamed out of the meeting, Stephen was approached by James Cropper, the merchant whose 1822 campaign to equalise sugar duties had sparked the wider movement against slavery. 'Friend Stephen,' said Cropper, 'thou must dine with me at my hotel to-morrow, and bring thy papers with thee. I have some friends who wish to hear thy explanations.' The next day, Stephen ate with Cropper, the Birmingham grain merchant Joseph Sturge, and two dozen other Quakers who had taken a keen interest in the West India Question. The younger man relished 'the refreshment that [he] obtained by an excellent dinner, and two or three glasses of good wine' and, as the men ate, nothing was said of slavery. Yet before the first glass of port was passed, his hosts asked Stephen to talk seriously: if he had the means, what would he do? 'I should go on to the end,' he answered, 'and do my best to carry it through, if I can raise £1,000.'

'All right', came the reply from the Quakers.

Cropper immediately pledged £500 to fund Stephen's mission. Joseph Sturge, described by his biographer as 'a thorough man of the people ... [without] aristocratic fastidiousness', put up £250 more. With smaller contributions from the other guests, Stephen's own father, and William Wilberforce, the remaining £250 was subscribed.

Now, Stephen had his money. Within a fortnight, the Quakers and Zachary Macaulay had persuaded the Anti-Slavery Society to permit the formation of an 'Agency Sub-Committee'.[13]

In order 'to prevent the idea getting abroad that there was division in the camp', the Agency Committee took the offices next door to the parent Society at 18 Aldermanbury. Precautions were taken nonetheless: lest the enthusiasm of Stephen and his acolytes led to indiscretion, the Agency men would use different doors to the same building. Stephen's committee now embarked on a crusade to apply 'pressure from without'. It started at once to build a new network of enthusiastic 'immediatists' and, by dispatching 'letters of instruction' to trusted contacts in the provinces, it performed crucial groundwork for an expected 'general expression of the public feeling'. Stephen designed the Agency Committee for efficiency. Meeting daily at three o'clock, the first person to arrive would serve as chairman and, 'to secure work and not tattling', the quorum was set at three. If Stephen and his allies were present, they could start at three, finish at four, and have everything their own way. It might have been conceived as a means of divesting the anti-slavery 'aristocracy' of its control over the movement, but the Agency Committee was no democracy.[14]

By the summer of 1831, the Grenadian journalist Alexander McCombie was consumed by melancholy. The Colonial Congress had given him hope 'that a system of [West Indian] union would be permanently established', but 'how miserably were those hopes disappointed'. Instead of taking bold measures to unite the slaveholders of the Caribbean, the colonies had 'contented themselves with drawing up Petitions to the King and Parliament, which they left to reach the pigeon-holes of Downing-Street office, by the usual route; and which have consequently been ... thrown aside to rot among other waste Colonial paper'. It followed that the whites of most British colonies were content with limited action, but not in Jamaica.[15]

Perhaps curiously, given its size and stature, Jamaica had not been invited to the Colonial Congress. Yet as McCombie reasoned, the island was 'detached from the Windward Islands' and 'of sufficient weight and importance' to look after itself. True enough, the Jamaicans had been making their own plans for resistance and, by the end of the Tories' time in power, the Colonial Office was seriously concerned by Jamaican rhetoric. When George Murray expressed a wish that the colony's House of Assembly should not 'persist in the course they have taken', Jamaica's parochial magistrates declared their 'deep indignation' at the government's alleged 'attempt to destroy that constitutional authority with which we have been solemnly invested'. By 1831, as news of Buxton's apparent conversion to 'immediatism' reached the Caribbean, the white Jamaicans took further aim at the London Interest, which they accused of neglecting and betraying the resident colonists. Augustus Hardin Beaumont, a New York-born adventurer who had fought in the Belgian Revolution before settling in Jamaica, chastised the 'extreme apathy' of 'the haughty aristocrats' of the London Interest who appeared to be losing ground.[16]

White Jamaicans therefore began to wonder, as they had done in 1823, whether they should strike out on their own. The pseudonymous 'Creole' wrote in the Jamaican papers about a 'spirit of patriotism' that was afoot in the parishes and, once again, the colonial gaze fixed upon the United States. The *Cornwall Chronicle* considered the Jamaican plight 'a close analogy to the Americans in remonstrating on the Stamp and Tea Acts'. The correspondent 'Socius' asked his fellow islanders, who were the 'Neighbours and Brothers of America', whether they would 'sit forever and submit to insult, oppression, and disgrace?' The House of Assembly even told William Burge, the colony's agent in London, that the islanders 'shall possess and shall maintain the right of governing ourselves in such matters' as slavery, and that any attempt to enforce amelioration in Jamaica would provoke the colonists to 'look to other sources for [their] preservation'.[17]

Britons returning from Jamaica told similar stories of discontent. The missionary Peter Duncan described the threat of secession as being invoked repeatedly: 'It is often a common subject of conversation', he said, 'that they wish the island was under the American flag'. The admiral Charles Elphinstone Fleeming likewise attested that 'the conduct of the Government would make the star-spangled banner be hailed with delight in Jamaica'. The sailor and West Indian heir Frederick Marryat meanwhile used his novel *Newton Forster*, written during 1831, to suggest that the slaveholders would 'not flinch and the islands of the Caribbean will be inrolled [*sic*] *as* another star, and add another stripe to the independent flag, which is their natural protector'.

Rumours abounded that colonial 'emissaries ... have more than once visited America'.[18]

Few observers in the United States took this talk literally. The Jamaican rhetoric about 'internal affairs' and 'foreign interference' aligned neatly with the polemics of South Carolinians who were contemplating secession from the Union over federally imposed tariffs, but Robert Munroe Harrison, the American consul in Jamaica, doubted whether the colonists would ever make good on their promise of revolution. He wrote in dispatches that Jamaican belligerence was 'the language of mere passion; of persons driven to desperation, who speak without reflection'. Edward Jordon, a black Jamaican journalist who had founded the *Watchman* newspaper to expose the misdeeds of the plantocracy, was equally doubtful of the colonists' intentions to rebel. He believed that, if they 'dared to unfurl the flag of rebellion, every man of them would be hanged in twenty-four hours, without reference to judge or jury ... so that the puny threat of a seditious Assembly, excites only a return of ridicule and contempt'.[19]

All the same, these threats were taken seriously at Westminster. Viscount Goderich wrote fearfully from the Colonial Office about the Jamaicans declaring 'their allegiance to be no longer due to the government ... [and] seek[ing] protection from some other nation'. He even sent a 'Despatch marked "secret"' to Spanish Town which expressed a concern that 'overtures had been made by some persons put forth as <u>feelers</u> from the Jamaica Planters to the Government of America U.S. as to taking that Island under its Care'. Was there 'any reason to believe,' Goderich asked, 'that any of the planters have placed themselves directly or indirectly in communication with the Government of the United States on subjects connected with their Allegiance?'[20]

The governor of Jamaica at the time was Somerset Lowry-Corry, the Earl of Belmore, who was the lord of the neoclassical Castle Coole outside Enniskillen. Having dabbled in parliamentary politics, Belmore had spent several years evading his creditors by sailing the eastern Mediterranean in a schooner with his family, his vicar, his doctor, and his lapdog Rosa. In Egypt, Belmore carved out a reputation – quite literally – as a graffiti artist. Journeying up the Nile, he stopped at Giza to chisel 'BELMORE' into a stone near the summit of the Great Pyramid, an act of vandalism that he repeated at the Ramesseum at

Luxor; across the river, his brother scrawled 'AL CORRY' onto a pillar at the temple of Medinet Habu. In 1828, when the Wellington ministry offered Belmore the post in Jamaica, he spied a chance to clear his debts, and developing lucrative relations with wealthy Jamaicans became his priority. Before sailing west, Belmore was only too glad to accept an invitation from George Hibbert, still then the agent for the colony, to dine with 'Gentlemen interested in Jamaica' in 'the Colonial Library' at the West India Club House.[21]

This was probably why, as the rhetoric sharpened in the summer of 1831, Belmore declined to assert his authority. When the Jamaicans made plans to elect an independent governing council, Belmore assured them that he would not deem their conduct 'unconstitutional' so long as they did not plot sedition. The governor also wrote to the parochial authorities, promising them that London would not interfere 'with the spirit of the resolutions' that Canning had conjured in 1823. Neither move assuaged the planters' fears. A meeting at the Montego Bay courthouse decried the 'despotic measures' of the new Whig government, with the parishioners of St James declaring they were ready to 'absolve themselves of their allegiance' to Britain and to 'seek the protection of some other power that was able and willing to secure to them the enjoyment of their rights'. In the parish of Manchester, the colonists deplored any government that might sacrifice the West Indies 'to the mad projects of a band of zealots and fanatics'. The next month, the *Courant* newspaper declaimed against 'the tyrannical and unnatural conduct of the Mother-Country'.[22]

The cheerleader of this dissent was George Wilson Bridges, the obnoxious Anglican cleric who had libelled Lecesne and Escoffery. Since then, Bridges had fallen further into ignominy. After breakfast one Friday in May 1829, the enslaved woman Kitty Hylton had gone to Bridges in his library to seek instructions for dinner that evening. Bridges mentioned turkey; accordingly, Kitty slaughtered a bird from the yard. By mid-afternoon, however, it appears that Bridges had changed his mind: when the good reverend saw the dead turkey in the pantry, he flew into a rage. He pinned Kitty to a dresser and kicked her for an hour, shouting at the terrified girl that he 'wished he could see her a corpse, as he hated her so'. Exhausted by the kicking, Bridges called on another enslaved person that he owned, Charles, to pick a bundle of bamboo switches. Kitty was taken into the cow-pen, thrown onto the grass, and Charles was ordered 'to cut all the flesh off her'. When Bridges' bidding was done, Kitty was sent down to the plantation's rockpool, 'blood running down to her heels', to wash up. This was not the end of the ordeal. As Kitty walked back to the house, Bridges stalked her along the path, 'pelting her ... with stones' before chasing her about the farmyard, swiping at her with a stick. When Bridges caught her, Kitty was thrown into the wash-house, where she was made to burn the incriminating evidence of her bloodied frock. When the poor girl then came down with a fever, Bridges tied Kitty's hands behind her back and locked her in the plantation's guardhouse. All this, because Bridges had changed his mind about eating turkey for dinner.[23]

Kitty eventually escaped from Bridges' clutches and reported her beatings to the local Council of Protection. The physical evidence against Bridges was damning. One of Kitty's examiners had never seen 'a woman so ill-treated'. Her eyes were black, her body was 'terribly lacerated', and there were signs of 'switching from the nape of the neck to her posterior'. However, none of Bridges' other slaves would testify against their master, not even Charles. By a margin of fourteen to four, the white slaveholders and personal friends of Bridges who sat on the local Council of Protection declined to bring charges against their esteemed minister. This left Bridges free to stoke unrest among Jamaica's colonists. Adopting the nom de plume of 'Dorcas' – a philanthropic disciple in the book of Acts – Bridges urged the formation of a separate, secessionist government for the island. 'Send your members to St Jago not as legislators,' he wrote, 'but as delegates; let them take possession of the House of Assembly, and form themselves into a Colonial Union. The storm is approaching. From my mountain watch-tower I perceive it ... If you would not have your blazing canefields to be your watch-fires, the shrieks of your wives and children your alarm-bell, and your burning houses for your beacons, attend to [my] warning voice!'[24]

When the Anti-Slavery Society got hold of documents relating to the Hylton affair, and when Goderich insisted on a renewed inquiry into Bridges' conduct, white Jamaicans rallied to Bridges' banner: his 'persecution' was taken as 'fresh proof of having numerous spies among us' and it served to inflame the 'resistance', which was 'becoming every day more united, compact, and formidable'. The *Courant*, by far the most bellicose Jamaican newspaper, declared that it was 'time the voice of the public was raised in one simultaneous shout, which, vibrating through every part of the island, will serve to defend, in the person of the persecuted Rector of St Ann, the rights and privileges of all'. The abolitionists in London could tell a rather different story, but the white Jamaicans now believed that the Whig government was charging towards a bill for slave emancipation, an event that would provoke the colonists into widespread rebellion.[25]

In the second half of 1831, two storms broke in the Caribbean. The first was the hurricane, 'the awful convulsion of the elements, which ... desolated the fair island of Barbados, and precipitated thousands of its population into eternity'. On the morning of 10 August, 'the sun arose without a cloud, and shone resplendently through an atmosphere of the most translucent brightness'. Colonial life went on as usual: the merchants sold their goods, the planters drove their slaves, and the slaves tilled the soil. It was not until five o'clock that the Barbadians noticed 'the clouds gathering very densely from the N[orth]'. Stiffening breezes and a rain shower brought a 'dismal blackness [to] the horizon all around' and, within minutes, there was 'an impenetrable body of cloud extend[ing] upwards towards the zenith, leaving there an obscure circle of imperfect light'. By half-past ten, squalls of wind and rain were blowing in from the north; by midnight, the wind had become a gale and 'the continual flashing of lightning' lent an awful grandeur to the scene. Shortly after two o'clock, 'the astounding roar of the hurricane which ... cannot by language be described' announced the doom of the island. Bridgetown was enveloped by darkness, a pitch and starless black that was lit only by 'fiery meteors ... falling from the heavens'. Pockets of calm and silence offered hope, but the hurricane 'burst from the western points with violence prodigious beyond conception, hurling before it thousands of missiles – the fragments of every unsheltered structure of human art'. Until barking dogs were heard at daybreak, there was only the noise of clattering tiles, crumbling walls and roofs, and 'the combination of a thousand other sounds'. With winds reaching 130 miles per hour, the damage done was catastrophic, the cost approaching some $7 million. The human losses were awful. 'Many unfortunate beings who were shockingly mangled during the storm,' recorded one survivor, 'but not entirely deprived of existence, will long remain as monuments of its fury. Their crippled bodies and mutilated limbs, will, throughout the residue of their days, present sad memorials of the grievous affliction with which the Almighty Disposer of events has permitted this little spot to be visited.'[26]

The second storm of 1831, just as the white Jamaicans predicted, was a terrible revolution against tyrannical overlords. But this would not involve colonial defiance of an overbearing Parliament and the 'evil ministers' of the Crown. Instead, in the fortnight after Christmas, Jamaica would witness the greatest and bloodiest rebellion against enslavement in the history of the British Empire.

13.

A Most Extensive Conspiracy

This question would never be carried until some black O'Connell, or some swarthy Bolivar was found to take it up.[1]

Henry Drummond, 1830

Do not imagine that the tale of the Jamaica servile war shall remain untold. Justice shall be done to all parties. It shall be written to convince the liberal, not to adulate the inhuman ... It shall describe events as they were, and not ... flatter the vanity of militia-officers.[2]

Augustus Beaumont, 1832

On the morning of Tuesday, 27 December 1831, John Henry Morris received an alarming letter. Morris was a sugar planter, the owner of 149 enslaved people, and the proprietor of the Kensington estate in the St James parish of north-western Jamaica, a mountainous region of limestone, wild hogs, and great rivers. The letter came from his friend and neighbour Benjamin Haughton Tharp, who informed Morris 'that [his] house was to be burnt, and [his] family destroyed as of that evening'. Morris hurried to his stables, clambered onto his horse, and rode the six miles of dirt track that lay between Kensington and Maroon Town, the military outpost where Major John Pennefather, a brusque Irishman, commanded the Army's 22nd Regiment of Foot. Morris pleaded for help, begging the soldiers to protect his home and his kin, but Pennefather – who later won laurels in Sindh and the Crimea – was unconcerned. He told the terrified planter that 'we were a parcel of alarmists; that he was satisfied nothing would take place'. Morris pleaded again, reminding the Major that the wife of one of his troops had given birth only two days ago and that both mother and child were on his property. The soldier's reply spoke nothing of gallantry: 'He did not care a damn if she was burnt, [for then] there would be one woman less in the garrison'.[3]

Morris returned to Kensington in a state of shock. As the sun fell in the sky, he bundled his wife, the new mother, and the two-day-old child into his carriage and this desperate party set off for the coastal sanctuary of Montego Bay. Their escape was none too soon. Ten minutes later, a posse of rebels 'attacked and plundered the estate'. By seven o'clock, reportedly 'infuriated by liquor', they had set fire to the plantation house, the homes of the enslaved, and the trash-houses in which planters kept that perfect tinder, dried sugar cane. The assault on the Morris property was not an isolated burst of violence. Kensington had in fact been chosen as the wellspring of a wider rebellion, 'numbered one' because it sat high on a ridge over the rest of the parish. As the flames licked the sky, Kensington became a beacon to thousands of other rebels: now was the time to rise. Aall across north-western Jamaica, those rebels signalled back with fires of their own. The message had been received, and 'a most extensive conspiracy' was now afoot.[4]

From their taverns, bedrooms, and verandas, the colonists of north-western Jamaica saw the fire in the heavens. At the post office in Montego Bay, the customs collector observed 'a serious fire raging … apparently about eight or ten miles distant'. An officer in the local militia reported that 'since sun-set, six fires, apparently of estates, have been seen from the court-house'. With the flames 'extending to the northward', he feared that 'the whole of the east of the parish [would] be destroyed before day-light'. The custos of the neighbouring parish of Trelawny confirmed that 'the whole country was in a blaze'. The twenty-two-year-old Wesleyan missionary Henry Bleby was a recent arrival in Jamaica and, from his home to the west at Lucea, he shuddered at how 'the heavens were lighted up by the burning … the horizon for miles [illuminated] with a strong lurid glare'. Few would sleep that night. Fear and rumour raced along the streets of Montego Bay, and the colonists trembled before the 'many fearful proofs' of rebellion that were 'multiplying with every hour'. There was alarm 'in every breast; anxiety sat upon all faces … and many began to look for a renewal of those terrible scenes of cruelty and massacre which had taken place in St Domingo'. The militiamen said goodbye to their families, who were rushed onto four ships in the harbour. In scenes remarkably similar to those in Demerara in 1823, the outbreak of rebellion plunged the white colonists into panic. But it should not have surprised them.[5]

Indeed, all through 1831, even as the Colonial Office was fretting over a 'patriotic' revolution of Jamaican whites, there had been signs of growing unrest among the colony's enslaved population. There were newspaper reports of deliberate fires in the west of the island, 'the work of an incendiary'. In the parish of St Ann, the rectory belonging to George Wilson Bridges was 'broken open, and entered in the most daring manner, by a most daring villain, a negro', a Methodist congregant called William Jones. That summer, Jamaica baked in 'a most unprecedented continuance of dry weather' and 'the general aspect of the country was that of a burnt savannah'. As the planters sweltered in this heat, it was common knowledge that trouble was brewing.[6]

The issue was that Buxton's motion for immediate emancipation had been misinterpreted as the *delivery* of immediate emancipation, or at least as a promise that freedom would arrive by Christmas. The rumour circulated among enslaved Jamaicans – who were already grating at a decision of the House of Assembly to curtail their Christmas holidays – that William IV had heard their cries, that Parliament had done its duty, but that the planters were blocking their freedom. The Baptist missionary William Knibb, now in his eighth year in Jamaica, observed that his congregation was 'anxiously waiting till King William sends them their free paper' – that is, the emancipation decree. The Colonial Office was fully aware of this misapprehension. Although Viscount Goderich was sympathetic to abolition, he believed that the enslaved had 'many strange and exaggerated conceptions of facts', and so he had furnished the colonial governors with a royal proclamation that urged the enslaved 'to render entire submission to the laws as well as dutiful obedience to their masters'. At the same time, Goderich instructed the governors to 'deny the existence of any purpose to disturb ... the present relations of society in the colonies'. In Jamaica, however, the Earl of Belmore did none of this; he stayed quiet.[7]

And so, as the blazing heat of the Jamaican summer dipped into the heavy weather of autumn, enslaved Jamaicans were impatient for freedom. One militiaman reflected that he had 'never known so strong an excitement [among the slaves], particularly from the month of August to the month of December'. In the account of the missionary Henry Bleby, reports 'began very extensively to prevail, that serious disturbances would take place at the approaching holidays, and that a combined effort would be made by the blacks to earn their freedom'. It was not until 22 December, only five days before the burning of Kensington, that Belmore finally issued Goderich's proclamation and ordered 'a prompt employment of the militia forces'. It was much too little, and much too late. By now, that 'most extensive conspiracy' was ready to unfold.[8]

The leader of this rebellion was a Baptist deacon named Samuel Sharpe. Nobody quite knows when Sharpe was born: various accounts have placed him, at Christmas 1831, between the ages of twenty-six and fifty-one, but Henry Bleby was certain that Sharpe was 'the most intelligent and remarkable slave' he ever met. The young preacher was drawn to Sharpe's magnetic physical presence. 'His fine sinewy frame,' wrote Bleby, 'was handsomely moulded, and his skin as perfect a jet as can well be imagined ... He had teeth whose regularity and whiteness a court-beauty might have envied, and an eye whose brilliancy was almost dazzling.' He understood how Sharpe had persuaded so many to rebel. 'I was amazed both at the power and freedom with which he spoke ... and at the effect which was produced upon his auditory.' When Sharpe spoke 'on the subject of slavery', his audience would be 'wrought up almost to a state of madness'.[9]

There was no doubt that Sharpe had forged his plan in the crucible of religion, or that he conceived of his rebellion in millenarian terms. In contrast to the slaveholders' interpretation of biblical texts, Sharpe drew inspiration from the Israelites' captivity in Babylon; and from the New Testament, he learned of a Messiah who came not in peace, but with a sword. Above all else, Sharpe was convinced of Matthew 6:24: 'No man can serve two masters'. It was no coincidence that Sharpe recruited followers at the prayer meetings that he, as a deacon, could organise and lead. As the rebel Edward Hylton related, these meetings began without a hint of conspiracy. Sharpe would preach a sermon and his congregation would sing their psalms; but when most trickled out of the halls and huts in which they met, a few were asked

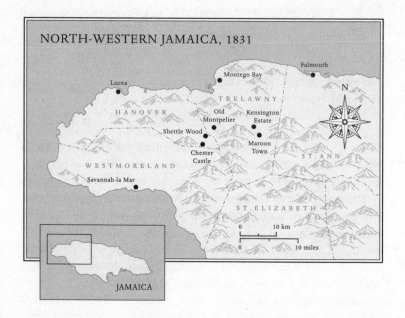

NORTH-WESTERN JAMAICA, 1831

to stay behind. At this stage, they were joined by Sharpe's most devout disciples, who had sneaked across the countryside 'stealthily and with extreme caution', and Sharpe addressed the potential recruits once more. 'In a low, soft tone, [so] that his voice might not be heard beyond the walls of the building', Sharpe denounced the evils of slavery. With all his fearsome powers of eloquence and persuasion, he 'kept all his hearers fascinated and spell-bound from the beginning to the end of his speech'.[10]

Sharpe told the huddled masses about the news from England. He told them that 'the King and the English people wished the negroes to be emancipated, and expressed his belief that the "free paper" had already been sent out ...' and that the only obstacles they had to overcome, in order to secure their freedom, were the obstinacy and selfishness of the planters'. Sharpe was equally clear that they could not wait any longer: worse than withholding freedom, the colonial whites were now 'making a studiation to kill all the black men, and save all the women and children, and keep them in slavery'. This was untrue, but it was an effective tactic: 'If the black men did not stand up for themselves and take their freedom,' Sharpe told them, 'the whites would put them at the muzzles of their guns, and shoot them like pigeons.' What Sharpe said, enslaved Jamaicans believed. They knew that he was intelligent, literate, and the head teacher at the Baptist church. In their own words Sharpe was the 'daddy' among them and so, when he delivered this paean to freedom, they 'kissed the Book' and swore an oath on the Bible to join him.[11]

In some accounts, Sharpe's plans for the rebellion were quite limited. He later claimed to have advocated only 'passive resistance' whereby his rebels would 'sit down' and refuse to work after the Christmas holidays until they were paid wages. In that sense, the timing of the rebellion makes sense: in Jamaica, the harvest usually began between Christmas and New Year, because leaving it any later risked spoiling the crop and the loss of millions of pounds to the planters. Perhaps reasonably, Sharpe believed that if the planters were forced to choose between killing the rebels and losing their crop, or granting freedom and then paying the freed Africans to harvest the cane, they would choose the latter option. It was a considered, thoughtful plan of economic resistance, of civil disobedience. But Sharpe also understood the likelihood of violence, so there was an explicitly military aspect to his planning. The rebels were divided into companies, each with responsibility for seizing then defending an estate. A crack force of 150 troops known as 'The Black Regiment' would wear a uniform of 'blue jackets and black cross-belts'. Some of Sharpe's key men took the title of 'captain', others of 'colonel'. Sharpe, of course, was the 'general'.[12]

On Christmas morning, Sharpe summoned his commanders to a breakfast conference. 'The thing is now determined upon,' he told them. 'No time is to be lost. The King of England and the Parliament have given Jamaica freedom, and it is held back by the whites ... Rise at once and take it!' A short while later, those commanders regrouped at the home of George Guthrie, one of Sharpe's most trusted lieutenants. 'In a few days may we get our rights,' he told his comrades, 'and may Little-Breeches and the other gentlemen who oppose us lay at our feet!' Little Breeches was Guthrie's nickname for his master, William Grignon, a middle-aged lawyer who administered a dozen plantations. Having come to Jamaica at just fourteen, Grignon had stewed in the worst of colonial life. He was racist and callous, and an 'act of wanton oppression' towards a young girl on the Salt Spring estate had earned him the hatred of many black Jamaicans. Guthrie looked forward to revenge over Grignon with particular relish: 'I'll be the first to do his business,' he vowed. 'I'll give him a [bullet] as I follow him.' Snapping his fingers, Guthrie turned to his guests. 'Well, gentlemen, I am glad to see you. I have spirits and wine: what will you drink?' Choosing wine, they toasted their imminent liberation and went home to await the day of reckoning.[13]

By now, all but the most ignorant colonists knew that something was a foot. Two white clerks professed they had 'every reason to believe that a general insurrection of the slaves ... on Tuesday evening, will take place, with the intention of burning the properties and murdering the free inhabitants'. Many of Jamaica's missionaries knew too, and they made a last-ditch attempt to deter the enslaved from action. On Boxing Day at the Ramble estate, preachers prayed for calm and reason. At the opening of the new Baptist chapel at Salter's Hill, William Knibb again urged deference. 'I learn that some wicked persons have persuaded you,' he said, 'that the King has made you free. Hear me,' he pleaded. 'What you have been told is false ... I entreat you not to believe it, but go to your work as usual.' Those who heard Knibb were 'perfectly furious and would not listen to ... dissuasions from engaging in such a perilous enterprise'. In fact, they accused Knibb 'of deserting them, and threatened to take revenge' upon him. Other missionaries were less perceptive. Though Henry Bleby heard the rumours, he detected nothing amiss as he rode from Montego Bay to Lucea: 'There was not ... the slightest indication of the storm which was about to burst over our heads with such appalling and desolating violence'. Going from congregation to congregation, Bleby 'had no apprehension that the torch of the incendiary, and the weapon of the destroyer, would in a few short hours spread desolation and misery over the beautiful paradise' of north-western Jamaica.[14]

In Montego Bay, every able man had been called to arms. These men were not soldiers; they were planters, merchants, bookkeepers, and shopkeepers. Few of them expected to survive and the lawyer James MacDonald feared that, if the rebels took their fight to the towns, only pitiful resistance would be offered. 'Our militia is very weak,' he fretted, 'and we have little to expect from the regulars, unless positive orders are sent to them to act.' Sensing this weakness, the colonel of the local militia 'deemed it proper to withdraw [his regiments from] the out-posts'. He dared not expose his amateur soldiers to the fury of the rebels. This was a contest, he regretted, to 'which I do not consider them equal'. The only regiment that stayed inland was led by William Grignon, the bigoted lawyer on whom George Guthrie wished to wreak vengeance. When the rebellion broke, Grignon and 250 men of the Western Interior Regiment – almost all of them white planters – were in occupation of the Belvedere estate and the Shettle Wood barracks some ten miles south of Montego Bay. Yet for 'very unsatisfactory reasons' Grignon abandoned the barracks for Old Montpelier, a sugar plantation to his north-east that belonged to the former West Indian chairman, Charles Ellis. From Old Montpelier, in relative safety, Grignon awaited relief by the black men of the parish's Seventh Company. By five o'clock, Grignon had his reinforcements; by seven, he was under siege from the rebels' Black Regiment.[15]

In his report of the Battle of Old Montpelier, Grignon painted a picture of disciplined rebel soldiers who marched upon the field of battle in four smart columns while keeping up 'a considerable firing of muskets' on his men. The rebels enjoyed the advantage of darkness: with night falling fast, Grignon could see nothing but the flashes of their muskets. It was not until one rebel lost his cool and set fire to a trash-house that Grignon 'discover[ed] more clearly the position of their assailants'. Like any great commander, he seized the moment. The battlefield now illuminated by burning cane, Grignon reported that he ordered his men into the mill-yard where they dispersed the rebels with a flurry of musket-shots, wounding one and killing two of the Black Regiment's 'colonels'. Now, he delivered the *coup de grâce*. According to his own account, he ordered his men to hold fire, and drew the rebels back to within range of his muskets. A twenty-minute battery of fire was then enough to seal a signal triumph. In his own words, Grignon 'had been attacked by ten thousand men' and, having survived the peril of the darkness, 'a few well-directed volleys [had] sufficed to put the undisciplined slaves to flight'. It was only fate that prevented Grignon from savouring victory in the field. In the belief that 'an overwhelming body of negroes was collecting in every quarter around us' and 'being in want of both ammunition and provisions', Grignon led his men away, along the narrow road to the north and to Montego Bay.[16]

Of course, not much of that was true.

Another, more realistic account of the Battle of Old Montpelier has the rebels swarming rag-tag upon the estate, 'raising a loud discordant noise with shells, horns &c'. Moreover, it was not Grignon but the black men of the Seventh Company who defended Lord Seaford's property. Throughout it all, Grignon and his men were paralysed by fear, 'wholly incapacitating them for making any effectual resistance'. They froze, they drew themselves up into a defensive square, and they left the fight to the men of colour. When the Seventh Company forced the Black Regiment back beyond the stone wall that marked the plantation border, Grignon fluffed his lines. Emerging from his refuge and retaking command after a victory earned by others, he was faced with a simple choice. As the rebels fell back, running every which way, their spirit had appeared to break: at least two of their colonels were dead and, when four hundred foot soldiers regrouped at a nearby sheep pen, only fifty of them had guns. If Grignon had pursued the scattered rebels into the countryside and suffered the risk of an ambush, he could have snuffed out the rebellion in that part of the island. Instead, he beat the retreat with 'ignoble haste', leaving his fallen comrades unburied, and ran to shelter among the women and children of Montego Bay.[17]

Even worse, Grignon's cowardice had left the rebels 'in unmolested occupation of the country'. For eight days after the battle, 'scarcely a white man was to be seen from Montego Bay to Savanna-la-Mar, and from Black River to Lucea'. When the rebels eventually returned to Old Montpelier, they burned down the house and tossed the corpse of a colonist into its smouldering carcass. The Black Regiment took the fight into the hills, invading plantations still at peace, recruiting new rebels to their cause, and leaving a trail of fire and blood behind them. On the Hazelnymph estate, Robert Gardiner was 'sent a great number of [rebel soldiers] ... to command' and he was ordered 'to urge the others in the neighbourhood to join'. When he failed to rouse his neighbours, Samuel Sharpe performed the task himself. 'I heard General Sharpe's army coming,' Gardiner recalled. 'They were wild, blowing shells, and making a great shouting.' The cries echoed through the valleys, 'War! War!' If Sharpe was sincere about confining his rebellion to economic resistance, that moment had passed.[18]

Yet not all was marked with violence. The rebels told William Annand, the overseer of the Ginger Hill estate, that if he gave up his muskets and gunpowder he could 'remain undisturbed on the property as long as [he] chose'. Another white overseer was given the choice between his life and his authority on his estate, and he readily sacrificed the latter. Another elderly rebel was content to gallop around the fields in his former master's hat; one woman simply dumped her washing-load onto the ground before tossing it into the fires kindled by her comrades. Other rebels' most violent conduct was to kill and cook the farm animals that they had been forced to tend for years. From estate to estate, the rebels' behaviour varied widely, likely in correlation with the brutality they had suffered. Whatever the degree of violence, though, one thing was clear: in Britain's largest and most precious slave colony, thousands had cast off their shackles. With the provincial militiamen stuck in Montego Bay, the whites of Jamaica were no longer in control.[19]

At the seat of colonial government in Spanish Town, rumours of a 'strong spirit of insubordination' had been swirling for some time. Such rumours, after all, had informed Lord Belmore's instructions to call out the northern militia, which had seen Grignon stationed at the Shettle Wood barracks. Nonetheless, the governor had failed to act decisively or to meet his challenge. It now fell to Sir Willoughby Cotton, the commanding officer of the British forces in Jamaica and a veteran of Wellington's campaigns in Spain and Belgium, to put down the rebellion that Belmore had failed to prevent. On 30 December, he took two companies of the 84th Regiment onto HMS *Sparrowhawk*. He was followed the next day by HMS *Blanche*, 'conveying 300 men from the 33rd and 84th regiments, 16 artillery soldiers, two 8-gun field pieces, rockets &c'. It was an arsenal readied for war.

When Cotton arrived in northern Jamaica, as many as 60,000 rebels were in the field. Making his headquarters at Montego Bay, he found the town in a 'most wretched' state, 'in the greatest confusion and panic'. With bands of rebels lining the roads to the south of the town, Cotton understood 'the utter impossibility of affording parties of [the] military to every estate'; instead, he focused first on propaganda. Issuing a proclamation to the rebels 'in the name of the King', he announced that 'all who are found with the rebels will be put to death without mercy. You cannot resist the King's troops'. Yet Cotton also promised that 'all who yield themselves up, provided they are not principals and chiefs in the burnings that have been committed, will receive His Majesty's gracious pardon'. One hundred black prisoners were released from British jails to carry this message deep into rebel territory.[20]

In some cases, Cotton's proclamation had a profound effect. As early as two o'clock on 2 January, he reported to the Earl of Belmore that some rebels were returning to their labour and that the army's 'prisoners are increasing so rapidly that ... it will be necessary to have them lodged on board one of HM's ships'. The next day, Belmore was confident enough to place a bounty on the heads of the rebellion's leaders: he would award £300 – more than enough for an enslaved person to buy his or her freedom and substantial land – for information as to the whereabouts of the rebel colonels Gardner, Dove, and Johnson, and Samuel Sharpe himself, whom Cotton described as the 'director of the whole, and styled also Preacher to the Rebels'.[21]

Still, many rebels fought on and Cotton was forced to engage them. One of his early manoeuvres involved amphibious landings of troops into rebel-held areas around Montego Bay. Every day, one hundred and fifty marines were sent ashore from the *Blanche* and the *Sparrowhawk* to act as lookouts on the roads leading into the town. Other marines patrolled the bay in rowing boats and HMS *Blossom*, anchored at Savannah-la-Mar, made further landings on the southern beaches. Yard by yard, mile by mile, the British edged inland.

In other places Cotton reorganised the militia, impressing every able man into the ranks. When the militiamen of Lucea were dispatched to guard the Round Hill estate, it fell to the remaining few to defend the town. Among the conscripts was Henry Bleby, who as a missionary was normally exempted from active duty. 'I was far from yielding a cordial consent,' he complained, 'to this demand upon my services.' For a stranger to physical labour, let alone warfare, Bleby's forays into the interior were gruelling. He moaned that he was 'harassed by journeys, day after day, amongst the woods and mountains, often riding for eight or ten hours in succession beneath a scorching sun, and sleeping, without pillow, sheet, or mat ... on the boarded or earthen floor of the house where we might happen to stop for that night'.[22]

Cotton was slowly reasserting British control over the northern parishes. Just as in Demerara in 1823, the rebels were outgunned, and Cotton's men marched forth with the full might of the British military. Besides their muskets and bayonets, the redcoats had Congreve rockets, massive sheet-iron missiles, based on an Indian design, that had a range of more than a mile. In the British account, this 'formidable ... materiel of modern warfare' was 'very useful, not only in destroying the enemy, but in inducing many to surrender'. For their part, the rebels went about with lances, cutlasses, a few muskets, and in some cases only stones: their belief that Thomas Burchell, a former Baptist preacher at Montego Bay, would supply arms from London was rooted in fantasy.[23]

Sharpe's men were hamstrung by several other factors. While they developed intricate systems of signalling from hilltops to alert each other to the approach of their enemies, their only effective tactic remained the ambush. Here, 'they would wait until the soldiers came within range, and then fire upon them from their hiding-place with the few muskets or fowling-pieces which they had amongst them, while others would pour down a shower of stones'. But more often than not, 'no execution was done beyond a few bruises and contusions', whereas trained British muskets would kill or scatter the guerrillas. Bleby recounted one time that a band of rebels 'had posted themselves on the side of a hill commanding the narrow mountain road'. It was a formidable defensive position and, 'when the [British] soldiers came in sight, they discharged upon them a volley of musketry and stones'. Had the rebels maintained this position, on higher ground and sheltered by the tropical canopy, they might have held off the redcoats. Instead, they 'ran and attempted to gain the brow of the hill' and so 'exposed themselves fully to the unerring aim of the military'. When Bleby passed the battlefield, he saw 'sixteen bodies dragged into the road ... putrefying in the sun'. As he trotted past the carnage, struggling not to vomit, 'hundreds of carrion-crows [fed] on [the corpses] and scarcely lifted their drawing wings while our horses stepped over the miserable remnants of mortality'. The stench was 'perceptible at the distance of a quarter of a mile'; five years later, the bones of the dead rebels were still lying along the roadside.[24]

Failures in recruitment would also haunt Sharpe and his allies. The planter Anthony Whitelock reported that, on the morning of 29 December, the enslaved at Argyle not only came to work but even told Whitelock that 'they had been protecting their master's property the night previous from the rebels who had burnt [the] Chester Castle trash-houses'. Other black Jamaicans, perhaps fearful of colonial retribution, had even rallied *to the soldiers*. When Cotton wished to march a certain route, he deployed black 'loyalists' to cut down roadside canes that would otherwise give cover to rebel snipers. Augustus Beaumont meanwhile led the Cornwall Rangers and fifty Africans 'of the greatest use' in removing the logs and abbatis – sharp wooden obstacles pointing towards the enemy – 'which the insurgents had thrown across the road leading to Catadupa'. Beaumont and his men 'moved about with a celerity which shamed the slow movements of the regular militia' and he reported that 1,500 rebels had been re-homed without violence: when freedom looked impossible, these rebels had accepted defeat. 'We killed no old men, no old women', he crowed. 'We murdered no children.'[25]

At five o'clock on the afternoon of 4 January, Cotton made a note of his progress. 'The measures adopted, together with the proclamation issued,' he reported to Belmore, 'have had the most extraordinary effect.' The rebels were forsaking their guerrilla campaign, the mountain road to Maroon Town had been reopened, and attacks by his troops were striking panic into even the most committed insurgents. Now, Cotton directed a sloop of war to the mouth of the Great River, where more British marines were landed with the mission of recovering the station at Round Hill. From the decks of the *Blanche*, moored in Montego Bay, sailors and refugees rejoiced on the morning of the 5th that 'the face of affairs has been very much changed for the better'. By 6 January, Cotton declared that 'the neck of this widely spread and organized insurrection was broken'. In Montego Bay, as the colonists began to breathe more easily, 'the ladies and other women who had embarked on board the ships in the harbour were landing and resuming their domestic avocations'.[26]

However, in the deepest woods of Cockpit Country, hundreds of rebels remained at large and, where they had been especially violent, they would not surrender for fear of the punishments that awaited them. Such rebels had fled into the 'inaccessible forests and fastnesses' of the island's interior, where it would be impossible for the British to follow them 'without very great loss'. The *Courant* newspaper called for hounds to be imported from Cuba and for the authorities to 'let the dogs loose, until every slave who confines [himself] in the woods ... is brought to his senses'. Instead, the British employed the Maroons, the free black people who had long lived in central Jamaica, as trackers. One account suggests that the Maroons were paid for every pair of severed black ears they could present to the British soldiers, who had thus placed a 'premium upon murder'. More likely, they were paid to find rebels and report their whereabouts to the redcoats: for instance, upon 'pursuing those [rebels] who absconded to the woods in the neighbourhood of Marchioneal', the Maroons found '21 houses ... completely ready for occupation, and these placed in such deep recesses of the wood as might probably have long escaped attention'.[27]

The rebels who 'went home' voluntarily faced double jeopardy. Although pardoned by the soldiers in line with Cotton's proclamation, they often suffered violent reprisals at the hands of the local militiamen. Some of these men had seen their estates laid waste; others had witnessed their families flee in terror; and many more had suffered the acute humiliation of waiting for the professional soldiers of the imperial army to relieve them. And so, as they stomped back into the charred and blackened ruins of the countryside, the militiamen were 'bent on vengeance and among them were individuals whose political rancour approached insanity'. On one estate, they exacted revenge by turning their guns on the huts where the rebels lived, 'which soon fell beneath the effects of such a fire'. At Great Valley, one rebel begged for and received the pardon of the redcoat Captain Oates only to be shot in the back minutes later by a disgruntled militiaman. William Grignon added to his deplorable crimes when, having mistaken the sound of burning bamboo for musket-fire, he ordered his men to shoot the peaceful Africans at Chester Castle. The most notorious incident involved Lieutenant John Gunn, who shot dead 'on the spot' a rebel whom General Cotton himself had pardoned only an hour before. When Gunn defended his conduct by citing his belief in 'a continuance of those measures which appeared to him essentially necessary for the welfare of the island', his court martial had 'much pleasure' in acquitting him and returning his sword.[28]

As the historian Christer Petley has shown, Cotton could do little to prevent the expression of this colonial rage. Hamilton Brown was a planter, a local grandee, and an officer in the militia who relished the part that he played in the retaliation. He reminisced about how he took up 'in[to] the woods &c ab[ou]t 40 Incendiaries & Rebels – several of whom were Drivers & other Head men ... 10 were hanged & 13 sentenced to 300 lashes of the Cat, & the different Work Houses for Life'. The local dignitary James Hilton was no less severe in his recriminations. 'Immediately on his arrival', he 'made known in the neighbourhood, and particularly on those properties the slaves of which were disaffected, that he would annihilate the first party that chose to perform the smallest act of rebellion'. Even Lord Belmore was disconcerted by the violence, issuing an order that no executions should take place without his permission. 'In the rage for making examples,' one missionary observed, 'the colony lost many able hands it could ill spare.' More than 200 rebels had been killed in battle, but the exact number who were butchered in the aftermath remains unknown: when Belmore's government demanded an answer from each parish, the letters were tossed aside or answered with blank paper.[29]

By the time that Belmore repealed martial law in Jamaica, on 8 February, the rebellion was thought to have caused £1.15 million in damage and another £160,000 in funding Cotton's military response – well over £130 million in today's money. The greater cost, however, would be human because the Jamaican courts now embarked on months of show trials and public executions. At Lucea, the colonists made elaborate ceremonies of the killings. Condemned for treason and conspiracy, the convicted rebels were dressed in white caps and tossed into an ox-cart, their arms tied together and a rope placed around their necks. Surrounded by a guard of the most merciless planters, the colonists paraded their captives for miles around the parish and then 'into the midst of the burned properties'. At the conclusion of this 'mournful cavalcade', each rebel was taken 'home' and executed quite deliberately on the grounds of the plantation to which they once belonged.[30]

The most brutal 'justice' was served at Montego Bay. One rebel was executed for cooking a pig, one for crippling a cow. Another named George Spence was convicted of 'rebellious conspiracy' for simply watching his plantation burn. A further travesty of justice saw the name of one defendant not given to the court, which then forgot to pass sentence. When the nameless rebel had the temerity to enquire, 'What are you going to do with me?', he was taken to the gallows, watching, and shot to pieces. One white colonist then spied an enslaved man looking on, and he dragged him over to the corpse, forcing his hand into the wounds in the dead man's skull. 'You want freedom, do you?' he asked. 'This is the sort of freedom we'll give you, every devil of you!'[31]

There was often no more than half an hour between conviction and execution, a procession that Henry Bleby bemoaned for its 'indecent and inhuman haste'; he noted that 'the gibbet erected in the public square [was] seldom without occupants'. For weeks on end, three or four rebels would be hanged together, their bodies left to sway in the breeze, and it was not until the next batch of convicted men arrived that the executioner would sever the ropes. When the bodies fell to the dirt, they were left there in a mounting pile that was cleared only when black paupers from the nearby workhouse came to ferry the dead to the mass graves dug outside the town. Many of the 'guilty' men were the picture of dignity as they faced down their fate. 'The eye was undimmed,' it was recorded. 'Not a limb trembled; no muscle of the face could be seen to quiver; but, with the dignified bearing of men untroubled with misgivings as to the justice of their cause, they yielded themselves to their doom.' The rebel Patrick Ellis was quite ready to meet death. 'Give me your volley,' he demanded of the firing squad. 'Fire! For I will never again be a slave.'[32]

In total, 626 rebels were tried for treason and 312 were sentenced to death. Hundreds of white Jamaicans had crowded round the gallows for the first executions, but by the time the last few took place the colonists were buying and selling their wares, undistracted, in the nearby markets. For the execution of Samuel Sharpe, however, Montego Bay paid attention. After his capture in the dying days of the rebellion, Sharpe had talked at length in his jail cell to Henry Bleby, who became a comfort and a confidant. In Bleby's record,

Sharpe regretted that he did not control his rebellion, but he would not apologise for starting it. 'I would rather die upon yonder gallows,' he said, 'than live in slavery ... If I have done wrong in that, I trust I shall be forgiven.' When the moment came, in May 1832, Sharpe marched to the gallows in a new white suit tailored specially for the day. Standing on the scaffold, he declared: 'I depend for salvation upon the Redeemer, who shed his blood upon Calvary for sinners.' There could have been no more obvious martyr to freedom and, though Sharpe was 'immolated at the polluted shrine of slavery', his deeds would echo through the ages. In 1975, Sharpe was anointed as a National Hero of Jamaica, for even if his rebellion had failed on its own terms, it would help to bring down slavery nonetheless.[33]

14.

Mere Anarchy

The fruits of reform are to be gathered ...
The shackles of the slave are to be broken.[1]

Leeds Mercury, May 1832

The British winter of 1831–32 was shot through with a nervous tension. In October and November, a handful of towns and cities had flirted with revolution when the House of Lords threw out the second draft of the Reform Bill. In Derby, church bells had pealed to celebrate the bill's defeat and, in the riots that ensued, three protestors were shot dead after a jailbreak. Elsewhere, the Duke of Newcastle's home at Nottingham Castle was burned down by a mob. Nearby Colwick Hall was 'stripped of everything & afterwards set fire to', and Nottingham itself was 'in a shocking state': 'the mobs were outrageous & impelled by the worst spirit'.[2]

There was worse violence in Bristol, much of it provoked when the city's senior judge, Sir Charles Wetherell, informed Parliament that Bristolians were decidedly against Reform, despite 17,000 of them having just signed a petition in its favour. When Wetherell returned from London to open Bristol's new courts, the mob was waiting for him. Five hundred angry young men chased the aged jurist through the streets of the city into Mansion House on Queen Square, and only the intervention of the Dragoons allowed Wetherell, disguised as a woman, to escape. The rioters contented themselves by looting Mansion House's wine cellar and they spent the next two days in a drunken orgy of violence, breaking convicts out of prison and razing grand buildings. At dawn on the third day, as they were demolishing the southern wall of Queen Square, a second dragoon charge put an end to the chaos. Forty-three rioters were imprisoned, seven were transported, and five were hanged in front of the city's New Gaol. The last victim of the Bristol Riots was Thomas Brereton, the dragoon commander who was accused of negligence for not firing on the unarmed protestors. Before his court martial could conclude, Brereton shot himself through the heart.

During these winter months 'the whole country [was] in a horrid & fearful state'. Some Tories believed the trouble was the sole and exclusive fault of the Reform-minded Whigs. 'The Ministers did everything they could,' blustered Mrs Arbuthnot, 'to excite riots all over the country upon the rejection of the Bill.' Then again, she thought little more of the bill than of the rioters. 'There never was a more atrocious proceeding on the part of a Govt,' she wrote, 'than the proposal of this Reform which ... is a complete and entire change of our whole Constitution.'[3]

It was in this febrile context that news of the Christmas Rebellion arrived from Jamaica, the first report reaching Westminster during a Cabinet meeting on 19 February. 'Great loss of life, severe executions, and the destruction of 52 estates,' noted Lord Holland, who was both the Chancellor of the Duchy of Lancaster and a Jamaican slaveholder. 'I would not be surprised any time to hear that Jamaica is in possession of the Negroes,' wrote Viscount Howick in his diary. The abolitionists, mindful of the political backlash they had suffered after the Demerara Rebellion in 1823, were concerned. Buxton wrote that 'the gun is cocked, and on the shoulder', while the Anti-Slavery Society predicted fearfully that 'the mutual hostility now existing, between the slave and the slave-holder, will lead to such a termination of the system as will involve the oppressor and the oppressed in one common calamity'. The King, who was kept abreast of developments by Viscount Goderich, was nonetheless satisfied with 'the vigour and activity in the Measures taken ... for the Suppression of the Insurrection and the Prevention of further Outrage'.[4]

The London Interest held up the rebellion as proof that Africans were savages who could not be trusted to live and work as free men, and the slaveholders duly circulated spurious anecdotes as 'evidence' that freedmen would always wreak horrible vengeance on their former masters. One Jamaican planter had supposedly been tied to a tree and forced to watch 'a set of brutes perpetrate horrors upon [his wife] at which the heart must revolt. His two daughters were afterwards served in the same manner; and then the father was cut in pieces and a portion of his bowels absolutely thrust into the mouths of his daughters'. Despite the absence of evidence, many of these tales were taken as fact and the West Indians soon found themselves in receipt of public sympathy. Writing to a fellow Jamaican planter, George Hibbert observed that 'public opinion, as expressed through the journals, has ... of late taken a turn in our favour'.[5]

The Interest seized the moment. For much of the previous year, the slaveholders had pursued the appointment of a House of Lords select committee to inquire into the 'true' nature of colonial slavery. As Nicholas Draper has discussed, these inquiries were major set-pieces in the battle over slavery, discursive arenas where adversaries competed for intellectual authority in the public sphere. But with some sixty members of the House of Lords implicated in West Indian affairs, the Interest had good reason to think that any such inquiry would recommend the preservation of slavery. Several of the more perceptive West Indians realised that deferring to the House of Lords would undermine the argument that Parliament had no right to interfere in the colonies, but now – in early 1832, with Jamaica on fire – the Interest renewed its applications to the government. A few members of the Cabinet resisted fiercely. Henry Brougham, the abolitionist Lord Chancellor, was 'greatly against' the committee and he complained that 'the West Indians would have it all their own way and it would be all "deception"'. Yet when the slaveholder Lord Holland assured his fellow ministers that West Indians 'could not outdo the saints in ... the propensity to lie', and when Goderich suggested that it would be 'wrong and hazardous' to postpone the creation of a committee, the West Indians got their wish. The House of Lords would now examine 'the several West India Colonies in relation to the Slave Population'.[6]

The Interest could not have wished for a more favourable panel of investigators. Among the twenty-five peers to be appointed were the Earl of Harewood, the Marquess of Sligo, Viscount St Vincent, Lord Holland himself, Viscount Combermere, and the Earl of Selkirk, all of them slaveholders. Even more perversely, the Marquis of Chandos and Lord Seaford, the current and former chairmen of the West India Interest, would sit on the committee too. The only avowedly abolitionist appointee was Edward Harbord, the Earl of Suffield, and when seven 'neutral' peers declined to take part in the hearings, the slave-holders found themselves in a majority. They would abuse this power flagrantly, even calling upon Seaford to give evidence about his own slaves to his own inquiry. George Hibbert assured colleagues in Jamaica 'that the Results of the Committee's enquiries will tend to check the endless agitation of this Question by irresponsible persons'.[7]

The abolitionists were anguished. Buxton had asked Suffield plaintively 'whether the Anti-slavery party, that is <u>yourself</u>, will have any authority or control in the Committee', but he knew the answer. He also knew that the slaveholders would use the committee as 'a pretext for delay, and nothing else', and he reported to the Anti-Slavery Society that the inquiry was 'a calamity for our cause'. Zachary Macaulay was no more optimistic, complaining in the *Anti-Slavery Reporter* that the committee had been 'obtained [only] by the importunity of the Colonial Interest', whose ambitions were clear: 'to show that the recent Order in Council is injurious in its tendency', to sustain 'the awful national guilt of longer upholding the system of colonial slavery', and 'to enable the West India planters to persist in their insane career'.[8]

Of course, the abolitionists kept fighting. First, they protested against the committee by collecting 135,346 signatures on 'a roll of parchment extending upwards of a mile in length'. More effectively, when the committee began its hearings, their best men worked with Lord Suffield to analyse and refute the pro-slavery 'evidence'. Before each hearing, George Stephen gave Suffield 'a short statement of ... all the antecedents of every witness called by the West Indian peers ... and a list of questions to be put to the witness, the questions branching out into others, according as the answer might be expected'. And as the pro-slavery peers lobbed leading, incurious questions towards their witnesses, Suffield 'made copious notes', which enabled Stephen 'to prepare the cross-examination for the following day'. All the while, Zachary Macaulay worked through the night to furnish Suffield with the facts he needed to challenge pro-slavery assertions. Macaulay's daughter, Selina, worried about the strain this placed on her father, who now seemed not to sleep, being 'extremely busy from 3am till 12pm about this West Indian Committee'.[9]

In time, this work bore fruit. One of the few anti-slavery witnesses called by the Lords was William Knibb, the Baptist missionary who had been ministering in Jamaica since 1823. On his first day of testimony, Knibb had given painful, powerful descriptions of the cruelty and depravity which defined plantation life. When he arrived at Parliament the next day, Knibb was escorted without explanation to a side-room off the lobby. There, standing alone, was the Earl of Harewood, the leading slaveholder in Barbados and the peer whose motion had secured the very inquiry in which both men were now involved. Was this attempted intimidation? If so, Knibb had spent nine years under threat of violence and even death in Jamaica, so one can scarcely imagine that he would have been daunted. But Harewood issued no threats. Rather, he confessed to Knibb that the previous day's evidence had given him a sleepless night. Now, he had to know: 'Is that the state of things on my estate?' he asked. 'If you say it is, I will by the next mail direct the removal of my manager.' Harewood had been converted. Slowly, but surely, the weight of evidence had begun to affect even the most ardent champions of slavery. Yet for Knibb's fellow missionaries who remained in Jamaica, the conflict over slavery was about to take a new and more sinister turn.[10]

Within days of quelling the rebellion, Jamaica's House of Assembly began an inquiry into its causes. In a report that circulated widely on the island, the legislature identified three main factors. The first was the 'evil excitement created in the minds of our slaves' by the discussion of slavery at Westminster, something that had been aggravated by 'the false and wicked reports of the Anti-Slavery Society'. The second factor, consequent to the first, was the 'delusive expectation' of the enslaved that they were due to be freed and that, if emancipation did not occur, 'they must be prepared to fight for it'. Third, and most decisive, was the 'mischievous abuse' perpetrated by the missionaries who had been ministering to Jamaica's enslaved population. In other words, nonconformist and especially Baptist missionaries had been preaching a radical, subversive strain of Christianity, the misguided lessons of which had transformed 'content' slaves into the soldiers of the Christmas Rebellion, which now, in light of this, was being referred to as 'The Baptist War'.[11]

There is considerable evidence to suggest that the Jamaican inquiry was founded with the exclusive ambition of blaming the missionaries. Even before the inquiry began, 'almost every man that composed it

had [already and] publicly branded the missionaries as the authors of
the rebellion'. The interrogators consequently urged witness after
witness to lay the fault at the feet of the preachers. Some statements
referred to 'the general belief of all classes, that the Baptist missionaries had by their preaching and doctrines stirred up the rebellion',
others that the preacher Thomas Burchell was going to sail back from
Britain on a liberating mission. Augustus Beaumont, who had worked
with loyalist Africans to restore the lines of communication, accused
the House of Assembly of 'garbling the evidence' to manufacture the
desired conclusion.[12]

The inquiry's findings reflected the frenzied religious prejudice that
had been convulsing Jamaican politics for some time. As early as
December 1828, the House of Assembly had accused nonconformist
preachers of trying 'to extort money from their congregations by
every possible pretext'. Two years later, George Wilson Bridges had
invited Lord Belmore to crack down on 'the calumnies and dark
insinuations of the Sectarians'. Now, in the aftermath of the rebellion,
this bigotry was given a fuller and more violent expression. A popular
conspiracy theory held that a Methodist preacher had been cruising
along the northern coast of Jamaica in a schooner, staying out at sea
by day but sneaking ashore by moonlight to make 'active communication with the rebels'. The colonial legislature even tried to pass a
law making the preaching of 'seditious' religion punishable by transportation for life or twelve months of hard labour.[13]

There were calls for a more intimate revenge upon the missionaries.
The *Courant* pronounced that 'shooting is ... too honourable a death
for men whose conduct has occasioned so much bloodshed, and the
loss of so much property'. The newspaper therefore prescribed a dose
of lynching to cure the body politic: 'There are fine hanging woods
in St James,' it advised, 'and we do sincerely hope that the bodies of
all the Methodist preachers who may be convicted of sedition may
diversify the scene.' Such vigilante justice would be meted out by a
pro-slavery terrorist group whose mastermind was none other than
George Wilson Bridges. In the autumn of 1831, as white Jamaicans
were mulling revolution against the tyranny of the Whig ministry,
Bridges had encouraged the formation of 'A COLONIAL CHURCH
UNION SOCIETY'. Writing in the *Courant*, he argued that such a
society would protect Jamaica from the designs of the Whigs *and* the

abolitionists. Inspired by conservative Anglicanism, this union would also offer 'an antidote to the destructive poison of the Sectarian [missionaries] ... those base agents of our enemies'.[14]

In late January 1832, lusting for revenge against the alleged authors of the late rebellion, the Jamaican colonists founded the Colonial Church Union in the parish of St Ann. Electing James Hilton and Henry Cox as joint presidents, the CCU embraced two main principles: the 'purest loyalty for the King', and 'attachment to the doctrines and tenets of the established Churches of England and Scotland'. According to its manifesto, the CCU would seek to 'collect within the [Union] the whole strength of the island' and 'to preserve the remnant of property left to us, and to prevent this island becoming a second St Domingo'. Membership came at the annual cost of twenty shillings, and this membership was formidable, involving 'nearly all the white men of the island who were interested in the maintenance of slavery'. Recruitment was especially prolific in the northern parishes where the colonists were 'eye-witnesses to the ruin and destruction' of the rebellion, and the American consul to Jamaica described these volunteers as a 'brave and well disciplined body of men'. The CCU now commenced a vigilante campaign of terror against the missionaries accused of fomenting rebellion and, in this putrid brew of religious bigotry, overt racism, and violence, it is not difficult to discern antecedents of the Ku Klux Klan.[15]

The CCU had some practice in these dark arts. Six years before at Christmas, a militia regiment known as 'The White Company' was guarding plantations against disquiet. Seeing fit to minister to the Company, Bridges delivered a sermon 'couched in the most inflammatory language, censuring the establishment of missionaries in that island, and exciting a body of men, with arms in their hands, to acts of outrage and blood-shed'. At midnight on Christmas Day, the White Company marched on the house of the local Wesleyan missionary, Mr Ratcliffe. They attacked with 'muskets and horse-pistols', firing fourteen shots into the house where Ratcliffe, his wife, and his children slept. These shots were not fired at once; they were stretched out over hours, a deliberate drip-feed of fear. The next Sunday, Bridges re-preached exactly the same sermon and, as he did so, he alluded 'with triumph and satisfaction to the preceding outrage'.[16]

The Ratcliffe incident was a rehearsal for early 1832, when the CCU went earnestly to business. In the first week of February, a Navy officer on half-pay and a slaveholding militiaman burned down the Baptist chapel at Salter's Hill that William Knibb had opened at Christmas. A few days later, a mob of twenty-two militiamen, ten magistrates, and the chief constable of St James tore down the chapel at Montego Bay. The complicity of the Jamaican authorities was already obvious: they had known about the attack in advance, but chose to do nothing. All men of God were now in danger. Despite the Moravian Church's ambivalence towards slavery, the German missionary Heinrich Pfeiffer was torn from his bed by forty men of the CCU and whisked off to jail in a distant parish. Detained without charge for nine days, Pfeiffer was woken every thirty minutes to deprive him of sleep, and starved of food: before he could eat his meagre rations, his jailer threw them onto the dirt floor of the cell. Pfeiffer was eventually charged with sedition, but his trial collapsed when the only witness for the prosecution, an enslaved woman, let slip that she had been bribed to bear false witness with the promise of freedom, a patch of land, and a gold doubloon.

CCU hoodlums now roamed the northern valleys of Jamaica in pursuit of their prey. Of particular interest was Thomas Burchell, the pastor who had allegedly promised guns and freedom to Samuel Sharpe and his brethren. When Burchell returned to Jamaica in 1832 – without said weaponry, of course – he was seized by the CCU and brought before a bloody assize. The case against Burchell was paper thin: he had neither encouraged the rebels, nor planned to furnish them with materiel. The CCU therefore browbeat Burchell's congregation into perjury. At Montego Bay, one militiaman held his sword over a slave's head, pointed to a nearby gallows, and demanded: 'If you do not tell me something about the Baptist parsons, you shall *be hung up there.*' At Lucea, another interrogator clapped the muzzle of his pistol to a slave's head, screaming: 'Tell me that Mr B. *did tell* you to do so, or I'll BLOW YOUR BRAINS OUT!' On the strength of such evidence, and despite one witness recanting his statement, Burchell was jailed. When a prick of conscience compelled the judiciary to dismiss the charges, Burchell found liberty no safer than captivity: only the personal intervention of the island's Chief Justice saved him from assassination.[17]

Other activities of the CCU were more calculating. Since 1829, the *Watchman* newspaper in Kingston had been exposing the cruelties of slavery to the wider world. It was a daring enterprise, rendered all the more obnoxious to white planters by the black skin of its editor, Edward Jordon, who once was sacked as a merchant's clerk for campaigning too vigorously for the rights of Jamaica's free people of colour. The plantocracy naturally held the *Watchman* in contempt, believing that its 'types and presses [had sown] sedition amongst the coloured classes'. In the spring of 1832, the CCU spied a chance for vengeance when Kingston's bookstores were furnished with an abolitionist pamphlet that declared: 'We shall be happy ... to give a long pull, a strong pull, and a pull all together, until we bring the system down ... and let the oppressed go free.' The ink had scarcely dried on the page when Jordon was arrested and charged with sedition. Lord Belmore was ready and willing to sign a warrant for his execution – for endeavouring 'to excite or stir up any free person or slave to commit any act of insurrection or rebellion' – but the case collapsed when the prosecution could not prove Jordon's authorship. When he was released, both Jordon and his barrister, Price Watkins, were placed under surveillance by the CCU.[18]

Despite these excursions into the courts, the CCU's enthusiasm for wanton violence was undimmed. In St Ann on Good Friday, a prayer group for black Jamaicans was interrupted when a troop of the CCU charged through the lath-and-plaster walls of the hut in which they were meeting. Dragging away the worshippers, the Union men stripped them down, laid them out, and lashed them while warning that further prayer would not be tolerated. The white gentlemen of the neighbourhood found further amusement by shooting through the walls of a house belonging to two Wesleyan missionaries. When the CCU men had spent their ammunition, they drew swords and stormed the premises. Along the coast at Falmouth, they used axes, ropes, and breezeblocks, supplied from the cargo ships in the harbour, to bring down the Baptist chapel.

Only a few good men put up resistance against these depredations and, as Henry Bleby recorded, it was often 'the coloured friends of the missionaries' who rose to the occasion, who were 'determined to protect [church buildings] from violence'. At a chapel outside Kingston, for instance, the free blacks of the city armed themselves and stared

down a mob of horsemen and 'vile myrmidons'. Bleby himself became
a bête noire of the CCU, with George Wilson Bridges vowing to 'shoot
that d—d fellow Bleby by accident'. Likewise, the editor of the *Courant*,
William Bruce, remarked that, 'If a mad dog was passing my way, I
would have no hesitation in shooting him'. Accordingly, the CCU
sequestered Bleby's chapel as a guardroom, ransacked his office, and
menaced his wife when she would not serve liquor to the vandals.
The preacher, his wife, and their infant son soon took flight from
Lucea to Falmouth, some thirty-five miles to the east, but they would
find no peace. With no space to spare at the Baptist mission, Bleby
rented a house in the town and, on his family's first night in Falmouth,
the local cell of the CCU paid a visit.[19]

It began with a brick, a letter signed 'Mob', and the promise of tar
and feathers. Bleby took heed of the warning and, when the white
magistrates of Falmouth refused to help, he sought out 'a few stout,
active, coloured friends' to stand guard over his house. The next
evening, while sitting down to dinner, Bleby heard 'the trampling of
many feet and the sound of many voices approaching'. From his front
door, he saw 'by the light of the moon, a large body of men at the
gate, probably from eighty to a hundred'. He turned back inside,
bolted the door, and ushered his family upstairs. In the next few
moments, the garden gate was torn from its hinges, the windows
smashed through, and the front door kicked down off its frame.
Having detained Bleby's 'stout' guardians in the garden, the Union
men announced themselves as constables who had come to take tea
with the new arrivals. The welcome was less than polite. The CCU
men grabbed Bleby, threw him to the floor, and beat him about the
head with a weighty stick. The ringleaders barked orders to the foot
soldiers below, and a huge keg of tar was hauled in from the street.
Rolling up their sleeves, the Union men covered Bleby's head with
the thick, sticky liquid, pushing it into his eyes.

The leader of the vigilantes, 'a fellow named Dobson', picked up
a burning candle. He was on the verge of setting light to the
missionary when Mrs Bleby knocked the candle from his hand; he
rewarded her intervention with a kicking. Dobson tried once more,
now with the last lit candle, but again Mrs Bleby saved her husband.
This second interruption saw her locked up in a nearby cupboard,
but even this could not contain her: when the rage of the CCU was

turned upon her five-month-old son, who had begun crying from the bedroom, and when Dobson ordered his henchmen to 'throw that cursed brat through the window', she broke out of the cupboard, fought past the mobsters, and ran from the house with the child in her arms.

Bleby, though, was still lying prone in the upstairs room, badly beaten and dripping in tar. The CCU was on the brink of a murderous triumph until, at the last moment, Bleby's black allies mounted a rescue mission. Freeing themselves from their captors, and making weapons of firewood, they fought through the hoodlums and hauled Bleby to his feet. Grabbing two pistols from his bedroom, he stumbled down the stairs before his friends hoisted him over the garden fence to safety. When a detachment of imperial soldiers arrived belatedly to police the house, they found a battleground strewn with shattered glass, broken doors, and tar. There was also an unconscious CCU man whom his brethren had mistaken for Bleby in the darkness: they had beaten him viciously, fracturing his skull, and the man was 'subject ever after to periodical fits of insanity'. Bleby was safe for now, spending the night at the soldiers' barracks, but he would not find justice. The next day, a vindictive magistrate sought to bind over Bleby for breaching the peace and, when the missionary prepared an affidavit on the night's events, none of the magistrates would prosecute the case. Even when Bleby found a willing judge in Montego Bay, not one of the local constables would arrest Dobson or his goons. In the spring of 1832, as both enslaved Jamaicans and missionaries fought for survival, all on the island was anarchy.[20]

While the CCU rampaged across Jamaica, the Whigs in London were trying to pass the Reform Bill. Although the bill had romped through the Commons, the measure met with intractable resistance in the Lords, where the Tories jettisoned the disfranchising clauses that would have eliminated dozens of rotten boroughs. With William IV declaring subsequently that he would not create the new peers that the Whigs needed to overcome the Tory majority in the Lords, an exhausted Earl Grey and his ministers resigned. From 9 May 1832, Britain was without a government and, over several days of rudderless bedlam, the Court scrambled to find a new premier. There was none to find: the Whigs would not yield on Reform, but Reform could not pass the

Lords; the leading Tory MP was Robert Peel, but his betrayal over Catholic Relief still rankled with the rest of his party; and though the Duke of Wellington had emerged as the most likely candidate to lead a makeshift government, none of his likely ministers would tolerate even moderate Reform.

As crisis gripped Westminster in May 1832, worse was unfolding on Britain's streets, for the latest defeat of Reform had incensed the nation. In the West Midlands, a crowd of 200,000 listened to Thomas Attwood, the radical leader of the Birmingham Political Union, who promised armed revolt in support of the ousted Whigs; an exiled Polish general volunteered to lead the insurrection. Calls to abolish the House of Lords and the monarchy made Adelaide, the Queen Consort to William IV, fearful of regicide. The clergyman Sydney Smith wrote of a 'hand-shaking, bowel-disturbing passion of fear', and Wellington's nickname of 'the Iron Duke' gained traction when he installed defensive shutters 'sufficient to resist a musket ball' on his London home. Economic violence was threatened, too, with protestors encouraging a run on the Bank of England with the slogan, 'If you want to stop the Duke, go for gold'. In these Days of May, Britain was 'within an ace of revolution'. Disaster was averted only when Wellington accepted that he could not form a government, leaving the King with no choice but to recall the Whigs. Wellington then wrote to the Tory peers, urging them to abstain from any further votes on Reform: as with Catholic Relief in 1829, Wellington was the enemy of change; but now, as then, he suborned his own beliefs to the greater good. By early June, the Great Reform Act had received the royal assent.[21]

Debate about how far Reform *really* changed British politics has raged among historians, but in 1832 astute observers on both sides of the Atlantic knew what it meant for slavery. Besides abolishing the rotten boroughs that West Indians had manipulated for decades, Reform created dozens of constituencies in the industrial heartlands of the Midlands and the North, as well as giving the vote to everyone – well, every *man* – who held at least £10 in property. All this meant that the next Parliament would be elected by the same middling classes who were swelling the ranks of the Anti-Slavery Society. Demerara's *Royal Gazette* reported a 'prevailing fashion ... to look upon the passing of the Reform Bill as the precursor of future evil to the Colonies'. The arch-conservative Richard Vyvyan, a reliable supporter of the Interest in the House of Commons, complained that 'the West India Colonies … were to be governed and controlled by the delegates of the inhabitants of the shops and the factories, and even of the watering-places of the United Kingdom'. The slave-holders simply could not maintain their influence in a House of Commons where MPs were elected by ordinary people, not chosen by Old Corruption.[22]

In the wake of Reform, Buxton moved quickly. Only days after Grey and the Whigs were restored to power, he gave notice that, on 24 May, he would move in the Commons for a select committee inquiry into *immediate* slave emancipation. This was far from a simple counterpunch to the pro-slavery committee in the Lords. Indeed, given that most significant legislation was scrutinised by such a committee, the division of the House over its very creation would effectively constitute a vote on slavery itself. Still wary of abolition, the govern-ment pleaded with Buxton to cancel his plans, but he rebuffed their overtures. Buxton denied wanting to cause difficulty for the govern-ment simply for the sake of being difficult, but he told Viscount Althorp that he could not 'either postpone [his motion], or substitute for it, anything short of Abolition'.[23]

On the morning of 24 May, Buxton went riding with his daughter, Priscilla, in St James's Park. As Miss Buxton records, her father held no great hopes for the evening ahead and he was resigned to having even friends 'driven to vote against him'. As they trotted around the park, rider after rider came up to Buxton, asking the same question: 'Are you persisting?'

'Yes,' Buxton would reply.

'Positively?'

'Positively,' he confirmed.

More often than not, Buxton drew looks of amazement from his inquisitors, who would turn the heads of their horses and take their leave. On some occasions, he elicited a measure of support: Thomas Spring Rice, the Secretary to the Treasury and a vice-president of the Anti-Slavery Society, told Buxton that he would, of course, vote for the motion. In contrast, the unwaveringly conservative Adolphus Dalrymple told Buxton, 'Frankly, I mean to make an attack on you.'[24]

Having survived this interrogation on horseback, Buxton and his daughter went home for an early dinner. By four o'clock Priscilla, her brothers, and the family friend Catherine Hoare had taken their seats in 'the ventilator' of the House of Commons, an attic chasm of bare wooden benches and rough floorboards that served as an exhaust shaft for the grand chandelier of the chamber but also as a gallery for visitors and women, who had been banished from the House in 1778. Looking down from their smoke-filled eyrie, they saw that Buxton had not yet arrived. He had, in fact, been summoned to the Colonial Office for last-minute negotiations. In the meantime, a hefty West Indian petition was presented by the Marquis of Chandos with a prayer for the 'protection and relief' of Britain's slaveholders, while Adolphus Dalrymple made good his morning threat by seconding Chandos and defending the honour of the West India Interest.

It was not until six o'clock that Buxton arrived and, as a prelude to his motion, he presented two petitions, one from the Archbishop of Tuam and another the Dissenters of London, a symbolic alliance of Irish Anglicans and English nonconformists. Then he turned to the matter at hand. He railed against ongoing cruelty in Demerara. He condemned the contumacy of the colonial assemblies. And he deplored the rise of the Colonial Church Union and its undertaking 'to drive all the Missionaries from the colonies, and to destroy all the chapels'. At last, Buxton demanded that colonial slavery should be exposed to the keener eye of a reformed Parliament, and he begged to move that a select committee should 'consider and report upon the best means of abolishing the state of slavery throughout the British dominions'.[25]

Yet the motion was not put. Having failed to convince Buxton behind closed doors, the Whigs' leader in the House, Viscount Althorp, now pleaded in public for a caveat: that emancipation should be contemplated only 'in conformity to [George Canning's] resolutions of 1823', a timeless condition that would allow the government to resist doing anything 'immediately'. Buxton declared himself 'determined to oppose' any such amendment, and so MPs were faced with a choice: supporting Buxton now meant opposing the government. As a fiery debate involving Peel, Baring, Burge, Macaulay, Lushington, and O'Connell enthralled the chamber, envoys from the benches went to Buxton, all pleading with him not to force the vote. 'You'll only alienate the government' was a common warning. And with 'merely a nominal difference' between the motions, 'why should he split hairs?'

In Buxton's estimation, he was approached by more than one hundred MPs, one of them clambering up the benches of the chamber on four separate occasions before dispatching a final written question: 'Immovable as ever?'

As the ambassadors of moderation plied their trade, the gallery began taking bets. 'Oh, he won't stand!' exclaimed one spectator. 'Oh, he'll yield! I'd give a hundred pounds, I'd give a thousand pounds, to have him divide!' The entreaties lasted all night, but Buxton was resolute. As his future son-in-law, the Whig MP Andrew Johnston, recalled, 'I sat by him through the whole of that anxious evening, and was astonished at the firmness he displayed'. Even George Stephen, who had long chastised Buxton for his conservatism, stood in awe of him. 'I verily believe,' he recollected to the American abolitionist Harriet Beecher Stowe, that 'Mr Buxton was the only man in England who could have withstood it all.' Buxton himself compared the ordeal to 'a continual tooth drawing' but, not for the first time, the stubborn dray horse of Wilberforce's choosing won through. He stood his ground and, when Althorp's amendment was put, MPs were forced to choose between prevarication on the lines once drawn by Canning on the one hand, and Buxton's urgent terms on the other. There was no hiding place here but, as the abolitionists knew, a vote for *either* side meant a vote for an inquiry into slave emancipation of *some* description.[26]

MPs vote by walking through one of two lobbies in the Palace of Westminster: those in favour of legislation walk through the 'Aye' corridor and those in opposition through the 'No', where the MPs are counted by non-voting colleagues known as 'tellers'. Late that night, as the members of the House of Commons made their way along their chosen paths, Priscilla Buxton's 'heart beat higher at every number ... from fifty [votes] upwards'. For a short while, the abolitionists thought they had won an inquiry into *immediate* emancipation. Yet when the division completed at two o'clock in the morning, Althorp's motion had won by one hundred and thirty-six votes to ninety-one. Buxton was crushed. Over the next few days, Stephen Lushington tried in vain to convince his friend that 'the minority was [in fact] a great victory', but Buxton would not buy it. He was convinced of his own failure and distraught by the desertion of some MPs 'who ought to have swelled [his] numbers'.[27]

Other abolitionists were more hopeful. The minority of MPs in favour of immediate emancipation was 'far beyond ... expectation' and Zachary Macaulay regarded the very vote as 'a great step' for the cause. More to the point, although Buxton had been unable to dictate the terms of the inquiry, the Commons had still voted to investigate the extinction of slavery, a result which he quickly realised was 'a seven-league stride'. There was now an effective means of neutralising whatever pro-slavery conclusions the House of Lords might reach. Even William IV, who was unremarkable for his political acumen, recognised this dichotomy: the committee in the Lords belonged to 'Proprietors of the West India Estates, ... while the Committee in the House of Commons originates [with] those who are Clamorous for the Abolition of Slavery'.[28]

At the same time, detailed reports of the CCU's violence were arriving in Britain and Buxton's son, Charles, reflected that 'the planters, by their obstinacy [were chilling] the sympathy with which many had been inclined to regard them' after the rebellion. In particular, the CCU's persecution of missionaries was firing up rank-and-file abolitionists who attended Methodist and Baptist chapels. Following an unusually rowdy meeting in central London, Zachary Macaulay wrote to Henry Brougham that it was 'absolutely in vain to attempt to control ... this sort of excitement in the cause'. The persecution in Jamaica had roused 'the immense body of Methodists and Dissenters ... They have not only caught fire themselves since that time, but have succeeded in igniting the whole country'. In Staffordshire, it was thought that 'the riotous destruction of chapels ... prove[s] that the white inhabitants of Jamaica ... are totally unfit to be trusted with making or carrying into execution such ameliorating laws as the government desires'.[29]

Over the past nine years, Jamaican resistance had been informed partly by fears that the Colonial Office was in cahoots with the Anti-Slavery Society, a fear that was groundless when the Tories were in power. Of course, James Stephen Jr had always been their enemy and, in 1831, he had written a memo claiming that amelioration was not working, that the evils of slavery were 'beyond the reach of legisla-tion', and that they could 'be remedied only by laws directly abolishing the relationship of master and slave'. Now, however, in early 1832, the Jamaicans had real cause for concern: not only was Stephen working alongside the abolitionist poet Henry Taylor, he was also working for two sympathetic ministers, Goderich and Howick.[30]

Henry Grey, Viscount Howick, was only twenty-seven years of age when his father, Earl Grey, made him the junior minister at the Colonial Office. Howick was already an abolitionist at the time, but the events of the Jamaican winter had convinced him that slave emancipation could no longer be delayed. 'It is quite clear that the present state of things cannot go on much longer,' he wrote to Belmore, 'and that every hour that it does so is full of the most appalling danger ... My own conviction is that emancipation alone will effectively avert the danger, and that the reformed parliament will very speedily come to that measure.' It was a significant turn of events: whereas the Demerara Rebellion of 1823 had convinced Tory ministers that abolitionist agitation was a *threat* to colonial security, the Jamaica Rebellion of 1831 and its aftermath now persuaded Whig ministers that slavery itself was the root cause of the violence.[31]

On his own part, Goderich, the failed prime minister whose appointment to the Colonial Office had resurrected his political career, refused to believe that Christian missionaries had incited rebellion for personal gain, or simply to watch Jamaica burn. These were men, he told Belmore, who 'devote[d] themselves to an obscure, and arduous, and ill-requited service ... There is nothing obtained [other] than the consciousness of having contributed to the diffusion of Christianity throughout the world'. For the increasingly abolitionist Goderich, it was the grace of Christianity and not conspiracy that had caused insurrection among the enslaved of the Caribbean. Conversion and religious instruction had inculcated 'new feeling respecting their servile condition' so that, in the colonies, 'an indigenous race of men ha[d] grown up, speaking our own language, and instructed in our religion'. The 'blind submission' of such men had come to an end.[32]

15.

The Condition of England

It struck me that if Mrs Jellyby had discharged her own natural duties and obligations, before she swept the horizon with a telescope in search of others, she would have taken the best precautions against becoming absurd.[1]

Charles Dickens, *Bleak House*

In the wake of the Great Reform Act, Thomas Fowell Buxton was not the only abolitionist who seized the moment. Over the previous year, George Stephen had been directing the anti-slavery Agency Committee, energising abolitionist associations across Britain, and distributing propaganda in the provinces. Now, in the summer of 1832, and well aware that the next general election could return the first anti-slavery Parliament in British history, Stephen and his allies declared independence: the Agency Committee became the Agency Society. This new organisation did not abjure its parent movement, nor would it abandon the offices at Aldermanbury, but the divorce allowed Stephen and the Young Englanders to pursue more daring tactics. They now engaged West Indian slaveholders in a brazen battle for the votes of Britain's new electors.

Anticipating the danger that Reform would pose to them, the Interest had already renewed their own propaganda campaign and so gave its Literary Committee 'a sum of money ... to be managed at their discretion'. Winding up the *West Indian Reporter* and cancelling its contract with Effingham Wilson, the Interest chose to concentrate on sponsoring shorter, pithier pro-slavery pamphlets. In the first six months of 1832, the British public was treated to invectives on the economic value of slavery, the health of the Empire, and the recent

Jamaican rebellion. The Literary Committee also resolved to invent 'some more effective system … by which the West Indian interest may be kept alive, and fairly represented to the public'. In the summer, they struck upon their new medium, the placard, and they quickly defaced the walls and buildings of the capital with pro-slavery graffiti that appeared to mesmerise Londoners. When George Stephen saw these placards and the 'groups [that were] … collected round them, spelling them out', he realised that such a medium could reach beyond traditional readerships to 'a class that probably never opened a book once a year'. Galled that the West Indians had beaten him to such an 'aid to agitation', Stephen went straight to the printers Bagster & Sons. Writing out three placards on the spot, he ordered them to be 'posted … over every West Indian placard that was visible'.[2]

Henceforth, Stephen maintained 'a regular supply' of placards and, without telling Buxton or Macaulay, he recruited a 'little army of bill-stickers' to follow the West Indians around the streets of London, keeping their distance behind street corners and market stalls. When the West Indians had put up their posters and left with their paper and glue, Stephen's army sprang into action, 'veiling over [the West Indian] bills before morning'. In Stephen's own telling, the pro-slavery slogan of 'Ships, colonies, and commerce' was scrubbed away; in its place, 'every wall was covered with huge placards avowing Antislavery faith', while images of cartwhips, chains, and the enslaved themselves were 'stereotyped on every board'. Of course, the West Indians fought back. From London, James Colquhoun assured the slaveholders in Bristol that the Literary Committee had 'printed placards pasted over the Anti-Slavery ones' throughout the capital.[3]

This placarding war was not well received in government. Shortly after the first run of Stephen's posters, an agent from Downing Street visited the premises of Bagster & Sons. It seemed that the prime minister was furious at such a breach of decorum and at the apparent betrayal of Buxton's promise not to excite public opinion. Earl Grey's agent demanded to know the author of the placards, but the printers offered only defiant silence. 'They would have got nothing from a single man in the office,' marvelled Stephen, 'had they put them all to the torture.' The fury of the ministry was then expressed to Buxton, who at the next meeting of the Anti-Slavery Society denounced the placards as 'disgraceful weapons'. He vowed never to 'stoop to arm

[him]self from the armoury of the incendiary' and, in full knowledge that Stephen was the mastermind, Buxton invited him to speak next. Yet if Buxton had expected contrition, Stephen gave him sarcasm. 'I denounce not only the placards,' he began, 'but the author too. I wish I could discover him. I would hold him up to your abhorrence; but he dare not intrude here ... He dare not face the withering indignation,' he said, turning to Buxton, 'of my honourable friend.' As sniggers broke out around the room, even Buxton laughed. 'You have fairly done me,' he conceded.[4]

The levity was short-lived. For one thing, Stephen's placarding campaign had cost more than £500 and when the bill from Bagster's arrived at Aldermanbury, nobody wanted to pay it. 'Friend Stephen,' asked a secretary, showing him the invoice, 'what am I to do with this?'

'Pay it, to be sure,' Stephen replied.

'I will show it to the committee, but they will not pay it.'

'Well,' protested Stephen, 'I won't [pay it] at any event.'

'I tell thee, friend Stephen,' said the secretary, 'that they will not mix themselves up with such violence and wrong.'

'Neither will I,' said Stephen. 'I will have nothing to do with it.'

'But the man must be paid?' asked the secretary.

'To be sure he must,' Stephen insisted, 'and you must pay it.' As all and sundry disclaimed responsibility, the Quakers stepped in: a few days later, Stephen received a cheque in the post for £500. The money came with a note that it should not pay for the placards – 'We want no account of it' – but Stephen's benefactors invited him, cryptically, to use the money 'as thou wilt'.[5]

There was another, more serious cost to the placarding campaign. Buxton might have taken Stephen's mockery in good grace, but it was clear that a schism now lay between the moderate parent body – who still preached deference to governmental policy – and Stephen's radical allies, who would use whatever means they could to achieve immediate emancipation. Even Stephen's ailing father believed that he was 'going too fast'. Three days after Stephen mocked Buxton, the AGM of the main Society voted to condemn the intemperance of Stephen's agents, resolving that 'no person employed by the Committee be allowed to issue any documents from their office that have not been sanctioned by the Committee'. The immediatists could not tolerate this censorship. As the campaign against slavery intensified in 1832, they even contemplated ousting Buxton, declaring their readiness to 'set another king over Israel'.[6]

Four thousand miles to the west, the CCU was rampant. As pro-slavery vigilantes hunted down missionaries, burned chapels, and terrorised the free black population of Jamaica, even Earl Belmore – the obsequious friend of the slaveholders – was induced to issue warrants for their arrest. This earned Belmore fierce condemnation by the *Courant* and the *Cornwall Courier*, whose editors urged white Jamaicans to 'tar and feather [missionaries] whenever you meet them and drive them off the island', excepting those – in a none-too-subtle reference to lynching – 'who may merit a greater elevation'. The ordinary white Jamaican paid more heed to these violent clarions than to Belmore, and parish constables simply ignored the arrest warrants. None too soon, Belmore was recalled to London for want of 'the wisdom or the firmness requisite for presiding over a country like Jamaica', but this was not in fact the result of Belmore's handling of the rebellion or the CCU: as Lord Holland explained, the time-lag in transatlantic communications meant that the governor was actually sacked 'hours before the account of the insurrection arrived in London'. Belmore's reply to Viscount Goderich seethed with self-righteous umbrage and a sense of victimhood. 'It has long been apparent', he wrote, 'that … a disposition pervades your correspondence to place an unfavourable construction on all my efforts'. True to form, Belmore's valedictory speech in Jamaica deplored 'any sudden measures [that could] produce consequences equally disastrous to the master and the Slave, to the United Kingdom and her Colonies'.[7]

Belmore's tenure had been disastrous and he deserved to be recalled. Even so, his departure created a void of governmental authority that only worsened when Willoughby Cotton, who was furious at being overlooked for the acting governorship, sailed for the Honduran coast for reasons of 'health'. The weeks and months that followed, when leadership of Jamaica devolved upon the local lawyer George Cuthbert, were the salad days of the CCU. When a Wesleyan preacher attempted to spy on a pro-slavery meeting at the Falmouth courthouse, he was seized, tossed through the courthouse window, and kicked down a flight of steps onto the street; the local magistrates saw everything and did nothing. At a meeting in the same town, the Union vowed to end missionary work for good, all the while 'maintaining the purest loyalty to his majesty' and 'veneration for the established religion'. There were further reports that 'a mob of white men ... armed with swords, muskets, bayonets, and pistols' had waylaid the Baptist missionary Edward Baylis, 'hawing, as they approached [his] house, like a company of savages'. When a free black Jamaican defended Baylis, the CCU 'cut him very severely with their swords ... and stabbed him with a bayonet in the side'. Commitment to the CCU was now expressed formally, too: every parish henceforth maintained a register of Union members, each of whom signed their name beneath the CCU's resolutions as a 'most solemn pledge ... to preserve them inviolate'. Every white man who did *not* sign up was proscribed as an enemy of Jamaica.[8]

As Jamaica descended into something close to civil war, the Whig ministry in London charged a new man with ending the colonial conflict. This was Constantine Phipps, the Earl of Mulgrave, a handsome man in his mid-thirties whom Victor Hugo described as 'tall, fair, with an extremely English appearance ... elegant, graceful, highbred, good-natured and dandyish'. Mulgrave certainly behaved like a dandy, spending much of his time in Tuscany, writing romantic novels in his villa, and patronising the opera houses and theatres of Florence. He had also proposed marriage to an Irish actress before a paternal threat of disinheritance undermined the engagement, but Mulgrave incurred the greater wrath of his family when he abandoned its conservative Toryism to join the Whigs in support of Catholic Relief and Reform.[9]

Mulgrave had been primed for the governorship in February 1832, weeks before Belmore received word of his dismissal. Talking at length to the Cabinet and a few respected West Indians, he settled on a plan of conciliation: 'operations of all sort – orders in council, vindictive or rewarding duties, and what not,' advised Lord Holland, 'should be suspended till the new governor should try to negociate some arrangement with the Planters.' And so, when Mulgrave arrived in Jamaica in late July, he set off on a tour of the island, interviewing whomever he could to secure a deeper understanding of the political situation. One of his first actions was to order that the heads of executed rebels – still 'exhibited on poles' – should be taken down and buried, and he quickly despaired of the men who held senior office in the colony. The Attorney General Fitzherbert Batty and the Chief Justice Joshua Rowe were 'popularity hunters', neither of them 'people to whom [he] could talk confidentially'. Willoughby Cotton meanwhile continued to sulk, 'excessively annoyed', and Mulgrave reported that he was 'a Tory of the highest grade and I fancy sometimes talks after dinner in a way that would be much better that no one holding a responsible appointment under your Government should do in a Colony such as this'.[10]

Mulgrave did not initially know what to make of the CCU and he told Goderich that it was 'impossible ... to gain an opinion as to whether [they] will assume a more formidable aspect', but ambassadors of the CCU soon presented themselves to the new governor. They might well have expected a friendly audience. After all, bending Belmore to their will had been child's play and even now, even in disgrace, the former governor was drafting articles for the *Quarterly Review* which claimed that Africans would never work for wages as free men. Mulgrave, however, was blessed with a firmer resolve, and he would not appease them. Enraged by this rejection, the CCU resolved 'at the hazard of [their] lives, not to suffer any Baptist or other sectarian preacher'. Sixty Union men enacted that policy when they stormed the Savannah-la-Mar house of Aaron de Leon, a black slaveholder who was hosting the Baptist missionary John Kingden. The CCU might have lost the gunfight that followed, but when the Union thugs escaped justice, they issued threats of blood and doom to all who would oppose them. They pulled white colonists from their horses and tarred them for not sharing in their enterprise. One recalcitrant overseer was abducted and taken to Coromantee Bridge, where he was blindfolded, stabbed, and tossed into the river.[11]

Eventually, two of Kingden's sixty assailants were apprehended, jailed at Savannah-la-Mar, and denied release on bail. Yet when Mulgrave heard rumours of a jailbreak, he marched the sixty miles from Spanish Town at the head of a redcoat regiment. Arriving at the jailhouse, he found the rioters 'in triumph', coming and going from their cells as they pleased, and visited freely by their friends and pro-slavery comrades. It transpired that the jailer was a member of the CCU, and so he had 'suffered the Union Party banners to fly on the walls of the prison'. Mulgrave dismissed him summarily and, when he could not find a reliable replacement, he stood guard over the prisoners himself. The governor had seen enough. 'It is high time,' he informed London, 'to put an end to the state of alarm ... to [the] state of things in which no man's house is his castle.'[12]

In London, George Stephen and the Agency Society were embarking on a new adventure. Earlier that year, 'friends from the Country' and the *Christian Advocate* had urged anti-slavery leaders 'to employ Agents to deliver Lectures explanatory of the nature and effects of Colonial Slavery in all the principal towns throughout the United Kingdom'. Such lectures were not an entirely novel means of campaigning, since Thomas Clarkson and a few others had lectured effectively in the past, but in 1832 the Agency Society would revolutionise the nature of political lecturing by devising a formal, systematic plan for disseminating anti-slavery arguments.[13]

Under their scheme, the Agency Society divided the cities, towns, and villages of Great Britain into six main circuits, each of which became the domain of an Agency-appointed lecturer. When they swore to the Agency creed that 'the system of Colonial Slavery is a crime in the sight of God and ought to be immediately and for ever abolished', and when they agreed to the definition of immediate emancipation as 'the establishment of a system of equality with the slave-born subject in the enjoyment of civil rights', these lecturers were employed on a contract worth £200. Each was given ideas and subjects for his lectures. Informed by lectures that Benjamin Godwin gave in Yorkshire the previous spring, James Stephen's encyclopaedic 'delineations' of colonial slavery, and the monthly *Reporter* – which now enjoyed a circulation of close to 70,000 copies – the lecturers focused on facts, statistics, and relatable anecdotes. Precise routes for each agent were shared with provincial associates who would book out meeting rooms, cultivate favour among local grandees, and stir up enthusiasm in advance of the lecturer's arrival. It was an efficient machine which operated with military precision: the lecturer assigned to the Potteries region in Staffordshire found that public halls and posting bills were waiting for him, and that the editor of the local *Mercury* newspaper was primed to print whatever he wished.[14]

George Stephen's opinions of the six main lecturers varied considerably. The Dubliner William Hume was 'a long-time Anti-Slavery

The miniaturist Richard Cosway and his wife, Maria, with Ottobah Cugoano, the author of a sensational anti-slavery polemic.

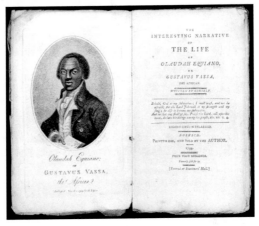

The frontispiece and title page of Olaudah Equiano's ground-breaking *Interesting Narrative*.

The wild schemes and speculation of the mid-1820s, such as the Poyais debacle (left), led to the collapse of dozens of banks during the Panic of 1825 (above).

The High Tories whose rebellion against George Canning caused successive governments to founder, including Goulburn, Wellington, Bathurst, and Peel.

The Tories split even further after Daniel O'Connell triumphed by forcing Catholic emancipation through Parliament in 1829.

As the abolitionists pressed for 'immediate' emancipation, and as the Whigs pressed for the reform of Parliament, Britain rioted: first in the 'Swing Riots' of 1830 (above), then in Bristol in late 1831 in protest at the Tories' intransigence (below).

The leader of the 'immediatist' wing of
the anti-slavery movement George Stephen,
photographed here in the 1860s.

The Agency Society's leading lecturer,
George Thompson.

The Birmingham merchant and Quaker
Joseph Sturge led the campaign against
apprenticeship after 1834.

The son of Zachary and, later, the great
historian Thomas Babington Macaulay.

The destruction of the Roehampton sugar plantation
during the Christmas Rebellion of 1831-32.

The boats of HMS *Blanche* engage the rebels at the Boyne Estate
on the Jamaican coast.

During the Days of May of 1832, more than 100,000 people gathered at Newhall Hill in Birmingham to protest the defeat of the Reform Bill.

This pro-slavery cartoon of 1832 depicts a standard West Indian talking point: that "free" British labourers suffered far worse than slaves in the Caribbean.

The destruction of the Roehampton sugar plantation
during the Christmas Rebellion of 1831-32.

The boats of HMS *Blanche* engage the rebels at the Boyne Estate
on the Jamaican coast.

During the Days of May of 1832, more than 100,000 people gathered at Newhall Hill in Birmingham to protest the defeat of the Reform Bill.

This pro-slavery cartoon of 1832 depicts a standard West Indian talking point: that "free" British labourers suffered far worse than slaves in the Caribbean.

The radical journalist William Cobbett, who was a vicious critic of the abolitionists.

As Colonial Secretary, Edward Stanley – later prime minister as the Earl of Derby – at last proposed measures for slave emancipation and carried them through Parliament.

The House of Commons in 1833, as depicted by Sir George Hayter.

An engraving of a treadmill in Jamaica, which was bound
into copies of James Williams's *Narrative of Events*.

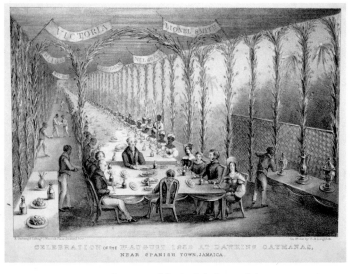

A contemporary depiction of the final abolition of slavery in 1838.
As the names of British governors, abolitionists, and Queen Victoria are flown
on the banners, the newly freed black Jamaicans sit at a separate table.

man, bold and plain-spoken, [and] with more of English frankness than Irish vivacity'. Edward Baldwin was 'from circumstances almost romantic a self-educated man' and 'a lecturer in the proper sense of the term: he properly understood his subject'. John Scoble was 'more industrious than persuasive', 'too opinionated to be as docile as discipline requires in active service in the field', and lacking in 'that practical good sense which alone can justify self-reliance'. They were joined by the Reverend Edmond Dewdney, on whose competence Stephen was silent, and the retired army officer George Pilkington, 'who wanted power and resigned the duty in about six months' to campaign for the Peace Society instead.[15]

The champion among the agents was the twenty-eight-year-old George Thompson, who was described by a Mancunian journalist as 'slender, yet firm – a little Roman about the nose – [with] a deep, dark, keen eye – [and] ruddy, though not the delicate hue of the rose'. A grocer's assistant from Islington, Thompson had no formal training in oratory since, as the patrician Stephen remarked, such a man was 'of course not likely to have received a liberal education'; indeed, Stephen mocked his learning as 'somewhat less than that which is ... found in a tradesman's shop'. Even so, Thompson was 'a frequent and effective speaker in [his] parish vestry' and, when commissioned by the Agency Society, he subjected himself to rigorous elocution lessons and 'undertook to master [the subject of slavery] in a fortnight'. Perhaps more importantly, Thomson excelled because he had an 'intuitive perception of the feelings of [a] popular audience'. Henry Brougham thought he was worth travelling fifty miles to hear.[16]

Spending several nights in each destination, Thompson and his colleagues began to foster a new, nationwide contempt for slavery. The first lecture in virgin territory might have attracted 'only five or six old women and children', but the second was 'sure to be attended'. By the time of the third, 'it became absolutely necessary to charge a price for admission, and the tickets were sometimes sold at a premium'. Edward Baldwin found that interest was notably stronger in 'agricultural counties' that were unfamiliar with 'matters not directly and palpably affecting [their] own interests'. In such places there was 'great eagerness ... manifested to obtain information on the system [of slavery], and a decided hostility to its endurance'. In one Lincolnshire village of eight hundred people, as many as one in five attended the lecture. Building on the work done by Clarkson in 1823–4, each of these lecturers bequeathed a substantial legacy of anti-slavery organisation. Local publishers were converted to the cause; churches of all faiths began to preach the gospel of emancipation; and the abolitionist network grew denser and wider. By the end of 1832, only eighteen months after Stephen formed the Agency Committee, the number of anti-slavery associations in Britain had boomed from approximately two hundred to more than twelve hundred.[17]

An even greater index of success was imitation. Terrified by the headway that the Agency Society was making, the Interest now gave the Literary Committee a slush fund to finance deeper investigations into anti-slavery practices. Some of this cash was used to pay 'an able short-hand writer' who infiltrated Agency lectures and reported back to the Committee, which quickly recognised the need 'to counteract the system resorted to by the A.S. Society of employing itinerant lecturers'. By late June, the West Indians had drawn up a shortlist of candidates for their own lectureships, '5 or 6 gentlemen' who had 'a local acquittance with the Colonies, and [were] accustomed to public speaking'. By July, they had settled on two ambassadors: James Franklin, the self-proclaimed expert on Haiti whose pleas for paid work had been a constant vexation of the Committee, and Peter Borthwick, a twenty-eight-year-old Scotsman with 'an olive complexion and a profusion of black hair' who had 'adventured unsuccessfully in various retail pursuits ... as a grocer and a stationer' before turning to the defence of slavery.[18]

The Interest instructed Borthwick and Franklin 'to proceed to the country, to such places as may be pointed out by th[e Literary] Committee, where an Anti-Slavery Lecture is likely to be given, [and] refute the statements there made'. They would be paid a daily rate of one-and-a-half guineas, but they would not enjoy much latitude: the West Indian merchant George Saintsbury, a future superintendent of Southampton docks, travelled with them 'as the organ of the views and wishes of this Committee'. Saintsbury received separate, secret orders to attend 'two or three of the first discussions [and to make] a ... report thereof'.[19]

In the second half of 1832, Borthwick and Franklin began chasing George Stephen's agents across the length and breadth of Britain, trying where possible to balance each anti-slavery lecture with a pro-slavery rebuttal. In October, Borthwick 'lectured twice in Warrington, twice in Bolton, and once in Bury' before racing to Cheltenham at the request of Christopher Codrington, the scion of the slaveholding dynasty who had founded the eponymous college in Barbados. Codrington had already intervened rather clumsily in the West India Question by claiming falsely that Buxton owed his personal wealth to slavery, and he now needed Borthwick to tackle the Baptist preacher William Knibb, who was sharing his experiences of Jamaica with anti-slavery audiences. Yet if the Interest had hoped to win back voters who might have been swayed by Knibb or Thompson, they were disappointed. In the first place, the West Indians were deftly outmanoeuvred. Anti-slavery scouts were tracing Borthwick from place to place, ensuring that in each town he found 'a forewarned audience, and a predisposed press'. The anti-slavery agents also appeared to have more stomach for the fight since, whenever one of them stayed behind to duel with Borthwick, they often found that the pro-slavery lecturer had 'fled, as if followed by fiends'. Most decisively of all, the ordinary Briton was simply more receptive to the arguments in favour of emancipation: George Stephen reckoned that, by bringing the merits and morality of slavery into 'an open arena ... in the broad light of heaven', the West Indians had played squarely into abolitionist hands.[20]

In December 1832, Parliament dissolved for the election of Britain's first reformed Parliament, and a keen sense of optimism propelled the abolitionists into even greater industry. There had been false dawns before but, at last, it seemed as if the prospect of emancipation was genuine. That summer, Thomas Fowell Buxton's select committee in the House of Commons had exposed the countless lies, deceptions, and half-truths that were peddled by the Interest. William Knibb was among the witnesses who testified powerfully to the iniquity of the colonial system, and Zachary Macaulay delighted in the fact that Sir James Graham, the First Lord of the Admiralty and the chairman of the select committee, had become 'a perfect Aldermanbury man' despite 'never troubl[ing] himself about [slavery] till this Session'. Even in the House of Lords, that bastion of the West Indian cause, anti-slavery sentiment was growing, with at least three slaveholders declaring 'themselves decidedly for emancipation as necessary to the

safety of their own property'. There was movement, too, in the political press. Several publications – including *The Times*, the *Spectator*, and
the *Quarterly Review* – appeared to abandon the West Indians.[21]

All this would count for nothing, though, if there was not a friendly
majority in the House of Commons. As the Dissenters of London
reminded the abolitionists, the importance of the impending election
could not be overstated. 'If this opportunity be lost,' they warned,
'years may elapse before another occurs, and the present awakened
feeling of the country will, in the meanwhile, be in great danger of
subsiding.' In the last weeks of 1832, the vast political machinery built
by Clarkson and Stephen clicked into gear. Petitions for immediate
emancipation flooded the Commons, as many as 2,600 in November
and December alone, and the petition from Morpeth exemplified the
new-found unity of British churches: it had been signed 'on the
Sunday ... at the Catholic chapel in the morning, the Methodist chapel
in the afternoon, and the Independent chapel in the evening'. The first
general election after the Great Reform Act, which ran from November
1832 to January 1833, was quickly defined by colonial slavery.[22]

On one level, the Agency Society appealed directly to the better
angels of the electorate's nature, persuading first-time voters to press
for emancipation as the most 'noble exercise of their newly acquired
privileges'. On another, and perhaps more significant level, the abolitionists focused their energies not on voters but on candidates. The
practice of obtaining pledges from candidates was frowned upon by
the elder abolitionists, who believed that parliamentary business ought
to be deliberative and that MPs should be 'unbiased and unfettered'
in their approach to policy, even policy on slavery. The younger abolitionists disagreed entirely and sought to bind candidates 'hand and
foot' to a promise that, 'in the event of their becoming members of
the ensuing Parliament, they will strenuously promote and vote for
the immediate and total abolition of British colonial slavery'. The
preachers of Hull urged their flocks 'to Refuse their Votes to any
Candidate, however plausible his Professions, who has not yet un-
equivocally pledged himself to use his utmost endeavours to procure
... IMMEDIATE EMANCIPATION'.[23]

The effect of the pledge campaign was remarkable. At Nottingham,
the local anti-slavery association called on the candidates, 'as men, as
Britons, and as Christians, to prove it to the world, that your hands

are clean from a crime so base and iniquitous'. The Lincolnshire MP William Ingleby reported that 'all the way through [canvassing], instead of the Corn Laws or anything else, slavery was the cry'. He told Buxton what one new voter – with a somewhat limited understanding of the parliamentary system – had said to him: 'I care not whether you be for Lords or Commons, but you shall have no vote of mine unless you promise me yours to set the negro free'. In Carmarthen, when the incumbent MP refused to take the pledge, the resulting outrage forced him into retirement. Elsewhere, truculent candidates caved in when they realised that the local anti-slavery association could and would swing its weight behind their rivals. 'There was scarcely a contested election throughout the country,' recalled George Stephen, 'in which the result did not virtually turn on the proslavery or anti-slavery promises of the candidate.'[24]

All the same, the primacy of slavery did not make this an easy campaign to win and, as the West Indians began to understand their peril, pro-slavery mobs sought to force the abolitionists from the field. When the Agency Society organised lectures in Borough Market and Whitechapel in London, the slaveholders rented mobs of sugar-bakers and dockers whose livelihood depended on the colonies to surround the venues, storm the doors, and shout down the speakers. In the nearby neighbourhoods of Hoxton, Poplar, Mile End, and Islington, 'many broken heads occurred'. The same tactics were used at Bristol, where an abolitionist meeting was 'broken up by the preconcerted violence of the West Indian party, and the gentlemen on the platform were compelled to quit to escape personal injury'. George Stephen himself was assaulted three times, and received by post a thirteen-inch dagger engraved with the message 'Death to the Abolitionist!!!' All this might have indicated that the slaveholders were growing desperate, but in these later months of 1832 the abolitionists found they had another foe to contend with, one of the most energetic and provocative groups in national politics: the Radicals.[25]

Abolitionists and Radicals should have been bedfellows. Both wanted to reform cruel and degrading hierarchies; both wanted to improve the lot of oppressed peoples; and both were developing novel, effective means of public persuasion. Yet ever since Buxton had first proposed gradual emancipation, the anti-slavery movement had drawn fire from Radical activists. The satirical journal the *Black Dwarf*, with a circulation of 12,000 copies, was a Radical mouthpiece and Wilberforce was a common target in its pages: 'The torture of children in our manufactories [and] the daily murders by famine in Ireland ... move not his patriot eloquence to any exertion,' raged its editor, for such affairs were 'beneath the notice of one who is eager to emancipate the negro from the LASH.' The free-speech advocate Richard Carlile excoriated self-righteous abolitionism as much as the brutality he had witnessed from the speakers' platform at Peterloo, and there was occasionally good reason for this criticism. When the Sheffield abolitionist Samuel Roberts drew his readers' attention to the children who swept British chimneys, Wilberforce admonished him in the strongest terms: 'I am a little scandalized,' he wrote, 'at your calling their case an evil not less grievous ... than that of Negro slaves.' It was this kind of selective, hypocritical philanthropy which appeared to convert Robert Wedderburn – a fiery Radical, the son of an enslaved woman, and the half-brother of the West Indian merchant Andrew Colville – from a 'committedly radical abolitionist' to a vicious critic of the anti-slavery movement.[26]

None of the Radicals was more vehement in his reproof of Buxton than the journalist William Cobbett. A long-standing enemy of Wilberforce, whom he identified with 'a morose and debilitating Puritanism', Cobbett was a well-documented 'negrophobe'. In *Rural Rides*, his paean to the pastoral idyll of pre-industrial England, Cobbett suggested that a dog he saw near Salisbury 'had a great deal more [sense] than many a Negro' and he believed that [East] Indians were less deserving of enslavement than Africans because they had 'hair upon their heads instead of wool; had human faces, and the smell of other men'. Cobbett was an accordingly strident critic of emancipation, denouncing anti-slavery campaigning as 'the bawlings of ... Methodistical bandits' and ranting that it was 'enough to fill us with indignation to hear [abolitionists] whine over the sorrows of a fat and greasy negro in Jamaica'. On occasion, Cobbett allied himself explicitly with the West Indians, who vowed to reprint any articles that he wrote about slavery and in 1830 covered his costs in publishing his *Exposure of the Practices of the Pretended Friends of the Blacks*.[27]

There was no natural affinity between domestic Radicals and West Indian slaveholders, but this common hatred of the abolitionists united them. It was therefore no surprise that many pro-slavery arguments aligned precisely with Radical critiques of anti-slavery philanthropy. Together, they contrasted plantations with British mines and collieries, with one overseer declaring that 'the hardest Labour performed by the Slave' was 'by no means so laborious as Coal-heaving' in Wales or north-east England. The merchant Colin Macrae confirmed 'there is not a Negro in Demerara who labours half so hard as a ... miner in England'. Factory work, especially by children, received equal scrutiny, with the artist George Cruikshank providing twelve illustrations for a pro-slavery book that contrasted the West Indian slave with 'the infant slave in our English factories'. One planter decried how children spent 'sixteen hours a day, stifled and choked with cotton fuz' in British mills; at the same time, a Radical poet lamented that abolitionists 'Proclaim'd the Negro's griefs' while ignoring the fact that Britain was sending its 'youth by thousands to the tomb'.[28]

Radicals also contrasted the supposedly varied and plentiful diet of enslaved people with Britain's 'famished miserables' who did not know 'where they shall get a breakfast', while one slaveholder from Bedford noted that millions of Britons dragged out a pitiful existence on 'a precarious crop of oats or potatoes'. As with food, so with clothing: one Grenadian politician grieved that British peasants were dressed 'in rags' and, during one discussion of slavery, Richard Carlile invoked 'the half-clothed ... brethren in Ireland'. In terms of shelter, the slaves again fared better: whereas they enjoyed the Caribbean weather, there was nothing 'well calculated to defend [the British worker] from the vicissitudes of season in Europe' or 'the inclemencies of a severe climate'. Not every British reader, it seems, took Mary Prince at her word.[29]

The penal system was a further British horror. Slaveholders complained that the abolitionists were 'astounded with the clank of the negro's chains' but never reflected that 'hundreds of their fellow-countrymen are doomed to bear heavier loads of the same bonds in our prisons and on board our hulks'. Notwithstanding his horrific treatment of Kitty Hylton, George Wilson Bridges believed that British 'justice', especially the 'conduct of parish officers towards paupers', was crueller than anything to be seen in Jamaica. Worst of all was the workhouse. One pamphleteer suggested that anyone who looked inside them would find 'instances of wretchedness so numerous and so peculiarly affecting' that he would only exclaim, 'Oh, England!'[30]

Who, then, deserved reproach? The planter? Or the British indus-
trialist who worked women and children to the bone before leaving
them to the poorhouse? For the West Indians *and* the Radicals, there
was no comparison between Caribbean slaves and the British poor.
The naval commander Charles Rowley declared that, if given the
choice, he would prefer 'the certainty of the black labourer' to the
difficulties faced by British workers. *The Times* agreed: 'The West
Indian Slave is, at the present moment, an enviable being compared
with myriads of British Labourers and Mechanics.' On this point,
Thomas de Quincey, the Romantic author of *Confessions of an Opium
Eater*, made an unexpected intervention in the slavery debate. While
de Quincey hailed the 'original generation' of abolitionists as good
men, he disputed the need for emancipation and claimed that 'not a
groan ascends to heaven from any child of Africa under authority of
British law'. One radical even imagined reversing the direction of
transatlantic philanthropy, with 'Negro Slaves ... sending their subscriptions and pity for the distressed free labourers of England'.[31]

Anticipating mid-Victorian criticisms of what Dickens called 'telescopic philanthropy', as well as present-day arguments against foreign
aid, Richard Carlile raged that abolitionists were 'wrought up into
fervours of ... sympathy for the salvation of the blubber-lip and
copper-coloured souls of the Chimpanzees and ourang-outangs', but
were unconcerned about the plight of 'ten thousand unemployed
industrious men' in Blackburn. 'Is not the saving of a white soul at
home,' he asked, 'as good as that of a black soul abroad? ... Who is
to say to what grade of animals the soul extends? Or where the human
species ends and that of the monkey begins?'[32]

These arguments are shocking to the modern ear but in the 1820s
and 1830s they found a receptive audience. Indeed, in many places,
the argument that Parliament should defer slave emancipation until
it addressed domestic poverty was the slaveholders' most effective
weapon. As the historian Seymour Drescher has noted, 'a slave child's
chance of survival to adulthood was more than twice as good on
the plantations of Demerara as in the textile factory towns of
Yorkshire and Lancashire', and one can well imagine a bereaved
parent questioning the wisdom of ameliorating Caribbean conditions
before those in the Manchester slums. Following a sixteen-hour shift

in a coal mine, Britons might well have wondered whether 'liberty' was worth it. In the 1830s, as the acceleration of the abolitionist campaign coincided with growing Radical concerns about suffrage, child labour, mortality, and the standard of living – in short, what Carlyle called 'The Condition of England Question' – these arguments gained traction.[33]

Richard Oastler, for example, was the Yorkshire champion of 'factory reform' and a 'Tory radical' who was instrumental in reducing the working day for women and children to ten hours. Despite hating 'slavery in every shape', Oastler was ambivalent about 'black' as opposed to 'white' emancipation and so he was 'charged over and over again with being a great enemy to the emancipation of the blacks'. Oastler maintained that his real 'battle was for the emancipation of British children' and that he would not exhaust his 'sympathies [on] the slaves in the West Indies, believing as [he did] that we have a still more horrid system of slavery at home'. There was even a rumour that the slaveholding Earl of Harewood, one of Yorkshire's largest landowners, had bribed Oastler 'to divert the attention of Englishmen from Black to White slavery'.[34]

The 1832 contest for the new constituency of Leeds was the microcosm of this antagonism between Radicals and abolitionists. The Radical candidate in one of the industrial swamps that the slaveholders decried was Michael Thomas Sadler, another champion of factory reform who had been apathetic at best about slavery. Indeed, one pamphleteer questioned 'whether till of late, and with reference to the prospect of the Leeds election, Mr Sadler has ... ever showed the least sympathy with Negro oppression, ever taken a single step to promote Negro freedom'. Conversely, the Interest feted Sadler, with one West Indian publication claiming that only Sadler's 'unprecedented exertions' had prevented the scandal of 'factory children' from 'being hushed up'. Sadler's Whig opponent at Leeds was none other than Thomas Babington Macaulay, and this month-long campaign was bedevilled by bad-tempered slander and mud-slinging. Neither the ordinarily effete Macaulay nor his Whig managers refrained from accusing Sadler of an addiction to profanity, of attending scandalous Sunday parties hosted by a former mistress of George IV, and of being 'the Hyaena who, when it wishes to decoy the unwary into its den,

has a singular knack of imitating the cries of little children'. The dirty
tricks worked: when the polls closed in January 1833, Macaulay had
beaten Sadler soundly.[35]

The general election of 1832 was one of the most crushing landslides
in British political history. The Tories, those natural allies of the West
Indians, were vanquished; the Whigs, the only party who would
entertain slave emancipation, now enjoyed a Commons majority of
more than 250 seats. Moreover, this was an avowedly anti-slavery
Parliament: of the 217 candidates who had taken the pledge in favour
of emancipation, only *five* had been defeated at the polls. Even better,
the West India Interest had been routed. Pro-slavery luminaries such
as the former chief whip William Holmes and John Atkins, the former
lord mayor of London, lost their seats, but the most notable casualty
was William Burge, the colonial agent for Jamaica. With his pocket
borough of Eye in Suffolk being disfranchised by the Reform Act,
Burge stood again for the new constituency of Oldham, where he
broke out into 'a violent pro-slavery philippic' on the hustings. But
when the Agency Society sent George Stephen to stand against Burge
as a spoiling candidate, and when William Cobbett performed a
remarkable volte face and campaigned for Oldham *as an abolitionist*,
Burge was beaten into fourth place in the polls. Jamaica's leading
representative in London was banished from Parliament. Nor was
there any room at Westminster for Frederick Marryat, the Grenadian
slaveholder who had used children's literature to evangelise for the
pro-slavery Interest. He stood for the London seat of Tower Hamlets,
declaring on the hustings that he would rather 'protect the British
seaman before he thrust his philanthropy upon the African negro',
and he was beaten handsomely by the abolitionist grandee Stephen
Lushington.[36]

Still, pro-slavery candidates were not defeated universally and the
new House of Commons contained as many as twenty leading West
Indians. In Glasgow, the city's West India Association threw its weight
behind its chairman, James Ewing of Strathleven, who became one
of the city's first two MPs. At Newark in Nottinghamshire, the voters
backed a straight Tory ticket of William Farnworth Handley and the
scion of a major slaveholding dynasty, William Gladstone. The young
Gladstone was targeted by his Whig opponent as an avatar of the

slaveholding class, and this was fair comment: Gladstone had written recently that 'in what it really consists [of], slavery [is] not necessarily an evil'. It made little difference to the result. When he topped the poll, the future prime minister used his victory speech to embrace his West Indian connections and to defend 'the abstract lawfulness of slavery': immediate emancipation, declared Gladstone, would 'exchange the evils now affecting the negro for others which are weightier, for a relapse into deeper debasement, if not for bloodshed and internal war'. It was a theme to which Gladstone returned during his maiden parliamentary speech, when he praised the unrivalled humanity of Demeraran slaveholders. Gladstone's first days in politics show that slave emancipation was not yet a fait accompli, and that the West India Interest retained *some* sway in British politics. The tide, however, had turned, and in 1832–3 the abolitionists were right to marvel at 'the sudden increase of velocity with which anti-slavery principles spread through the nation'.[37]

16.

False Dawns

Knowledge is power in Jamaica as well as in England, and that Mr Burge and his constituents will know ere long.[1]

Anti-Slavery Monthly Reporter (1833)

By the turn of 1833, the West India Interest was in disarray. Although an internal list of 'friends' gave the names of hundreds of influential supporters, dozens of West Indian MPs had been unseated and its allies in the press were wavering. The Standing Committee in London dispatched an urgent memo to the West Indian associations in Liverpool, Glasgow, and Bristol, begging for help to meet outstanding debts of more than £250,000 in today's money. Even the Marquis of Chandos, the Interest's chairman, had abandoned the slaveholders. Having failed to turn up to several key meetings, Chandos now confessed to 'a difference of opinion ... between myself and many of the West India Planters'. Incredibly, that difference was 'on the question of slavery' and, in early 1833, slavery's political figurehead declared himself an abolitionist.[2]

The pro-slavery lecturer Peter Borthwick had gone rogue. Although the citizens of Bath had 'contributed liberally to his support', and though Bristolians hailed him as 'the lion of the day', there were other 'inconveniences and difficulties' and, upon the receipt of troubling reports from Cheltenham, the Interest ordered him to 'repair to London immediately'. London's slaveholders issued fulsome apologies to the grandees of Gloucestershire and determined 'to prevent any future embarrassments', but when the chastised Borthwick was sent back to the front line, now with another minder, the pressure proved too much. It appears that he suffered something of a breakdown, with the Literary Committee expressing 'deep regret that his health ha[d] been in the least degree injured by [his] exertions in delivering recent lectures'. They granted Borthwick a fortnight of sick leave but, when he disobeyed his orders to move on from Edinburgh, complaints flooded into the London committee rooms once more. At this point, with Borthwick defying his masters in London, the paper trail fades into nothing.[3]

James MacQueen was in trouble, too. The autobiographical *History of Mary Prince* had appeared in print in 1831, exposing West Indian slavery as a system of intolerable cruelty; in response, MacQueen penned two articles for *Blackwood's* that damned Prince as a 'despicable tool' of the abolitionists. Yet when MacQueen fumed at the public's obsession with 'black filth' and suggested that the abolitionist Thomas Pringle had cavorted with Prince in his 'closet', he opened himself up to charges of libel. Pringle could not sue MacQueen directly because the articles' Scottish origin put them outside the jurisdiction of the Court of Common Pleas, so instead he brought an action against Thomas Cadell, the London publisher of *Blackwood's*.[4]

The February 1833 hearing of *Pringle v. Cadell* was not quite the spectacle that some had hoped. For one thing, MacQueen was absent: rather than defend himself, he went to the Caribbean to stoke the dying embers of the pro-slavery resistance. (This was actually a relief to Cadell's barrister, who did not want to call such an erratic witness, and even MacQueen's close friend Thomas Moody regarded him as 'a most unmanageable person'.) For another, the trial in fact exonerated Cadell, who disavowed the pro-slavery lobby and renounced MacQueen for assailing such honourable men as Macaulay. Cadell was even awarded damages in respect of Pringle's wrongful attacks on 'respectable [colonial] persons'. For MacQueen, however, the trial was a disaster. William Blackwood was furious at his name being dragged through the mud and he told MacQueen tersely that, as far as legal fees were concerned, 'the affair [was his] own'. This did not bother MacQueen at first, and he wrote cheerily to Blackwood that 'the Gentlemen of Antigua ... will pay all expenses and damages if it goes against us'. Yet when MacQueen was presented with a bill for more than £80,000 in today's money, and when the promised Antiguan cash did not materialise, the Glaswegian was embarrassed: he would never clear more than half the debt. Worse still, Blackwood now refused to publish anything by MacQueen that was not vetted intensely. After ten years of bile and biting invective, the Interest's most rabid attack dog was muzzled.[5]

The result of the House of Lords inquiry into slavery only added to the slaveholders' woes. The Interest had hoped for absolution, but the committee 'postpone[d] the Consideration of any detailed Report' and simply published 1,400 pages of 'Evidence collected before the House'. Some of it was 'of the most contradictory Description' and, by early 1833, Zachary Macaulay was exposing the lies of pro-slavery witnesses in the *Reporter*. It emerged that William Burge had 'marshalled the array of the pro-slavery host for the late conflict' and, in Macaulay's view, had 'not shown himself [to be] an able tactician'. The Interest's star witness had been the Duke of Manchester, the former governor of Jamaica, and Macaulay struggled 'to conceive anything more meagre and unsatisfactory than the testimony given by this nobleman': he had even described George Wilson Bridges as 'a person with whom any one would be glad to be acquainted, as a gentleman'. Burge's own testimony 'resemble[d] the *ex parte* pleading of an advocate [more] than the testimony of a sworn witness deposing to the facts of a case'.[6]

Even in Jamaica, the fortunes of the slaveholding class were in freefall. In December 1832, as a belated response to the reports of violence, a royal proclamation had outlawed the Colonial Church Union, ordaining that anyone found within its ranks would be stripped of public office and military rank. A circular message signed by the King then warned against the persecution of Christian missionaries. Emboldened by this explicit support from Westminster, the governor of Jamaica, Lord Mulgrave, spent late 1832 and early 1833 dismantling the CCU. First, he cut the head off the snake by dismissing the Union's co-president James Hilton from the judiciary, writing to London that he 'could not find a more fitting subject' for official censure. Hilton's co-president Henry Cox promptly resigned his own commission in protest, and the parishioners of St Ann pushed along an effigy of Mulgrave in a wheelbarrow before burning it during an orgy of pro-slavery defiance. 'No one connected with the Government could shew himself in that part of the Country' without provoking 'the violent Unionists' and, when the 77th Regiment left Kingston to suppress the discontent, colonial officials expected 'to hear of blood being spilt'.[7]

A middle-aged Irish planter named Hamilton Brown now assumed leadership of the CCU. After insulting Mulgrave as a man who 'Knows more of Books than of mankind & the World', Brown told anyone who would listen that he had 'a good old rusty sword' that he would use 'whenever my country requires' it. Mulgrave gave him the chance to demonstrate that courage when he ordered Brown's militia – almost all of whom were in the CCU – to muster for inspection. They met at Huntley Pastures: Mulgrave with a handful of soldiers, Brown and his men with 'an assemblage of their supporters in plain clothes, who were very violent in their language'. At twelve noon, Mulgrave took the salute and ordered Brown to form his men into three sides of a square. From the middle of this formation, imperious on his horse, the governor spoke. He despaired that 'certain persons whose professions should be held sacred, whilst exercising their calling according to the laws, should [have] been subjected to an illegal combination, threatening, if not perpetrating violence'. By persecuting Jamaica's missionaries, the CCU had disgraced themselves, their colony, and Christianity itself. Then Mulgrave turned to Brown, whom he condemned for the 'grossest possible breach of military discipline'. He was sacked in front of his men and, when he sought to reply, Mulgrave cut him off: 'I must not be replied to upon parade'. Without their leader, the rest of the CCU fell into line. Mulgrave reported that 'the non-commissioned officers and privates of the regiment ... behaved well'. For the *Watchman*, the violence of the CCU had been the swansong of a peculiar colonial bigotry, and this was its whimpering end.[8]

After ten years of fighting almost without hope, the abolitionists were on the edge of their glory. A younger generation led by George Stephen had convinced their elders that *immediate* emancipation was the only conscionable goal. The Jamaican rebellion had meanwhile convinced many Britons – including Whig ministers – that the endurance of slavery risked repeated scenes of bloodshed. The passage of Reform and the election of 1832 had then given the abolitionists a solid parliamentary platform. In January 1833, Buxton wrote excitedly of the forthcoming triumph. 'Parliament meets on Tuesday and I have reason to hope that the King's Speech will declare that Government has resolved to effect the total and immediate emancipation of the slaves.'[9]

The government had already spoken to the abolitionists about emancipation. When James Graham met with Buxton as a 'delegate of the cabinet' in November 1832, he stated plainly that 'the Government feel that some effectual step for extinguishing slavery must be taken this session'. Even more auspiciously, the Cabinet wanted guidance from the abolitionists on what this 'effectual step' should be. 'They admit that it is now within our power to dictate terms,' reported Zachary Macaulay, 'but it is their real wish to ... concur with us, and they therefore desire us to state our plan. If [the plan] is safe and practicable, they will adopt it as their own.' At that meeting with Graham, Buxton had outlined his vision of emancipation. At first, the enslaved would 'remain as they are', but working shorter hours and only five days a week. They would be 'delivered wholly from the arbitrary power of the master and from the whip', discipline being entrusted to a 'paid magistracy and a strong police [force]'. After a year or two, the freedman would be 'freed from the necessity of working for his former master, except by his own choice and by mutual contract'. He would then be paid with wages, 'bound to work in some way and for someone [only] ... to maintain himself and family by industry'. Ominously, Buxton also prescribed a legal code for dealing with 'idleness and vagrancy, which are to be met chiefly by [fines], and labour on the tread-mill'.[10]

All through the second half of 1832, Viscount Howick, James Stephen, and Henry Taylor – the Colonial Office's trinity of abolitionists – had been working the government's own scheme of emancipation. In January 1833, they duly presented three recommendations to Cabinet: that emancipation should occur by 1 January 1835; that the planters should receive financial relief by way of grants and protective tariffs; and that 'the vagrancy and idleness of the Slaves [was] to be prevented by a very heavy tax on their provision grounds'. No matter which vision of emancipation was turned into policy, and notwithstanding a rumour in *The Times* that the government would refrain from proposing *immediate* emancipation, Buxton expected the King's Speech, which of course was written by Grey's government, to contain *some* plan for slave freedom.[11]

On 5 February, William IV went in state to Westminster. Flanked by Henry Brougham and Earl Grey, the King took the speaker's seat in the House of Lords and Black Rod summoned the Commons.

Huddling in the space below the Bar, the MPs listened to the government's plans for 1833. When the King began with the warning that 'never, at any time, did subjects of greater interest and magnitude call for your attention', the abolitionists could not have agreed more. Adverting to the Portuguese Civil War, the Belgian Revolution, the expiring charters of the Bank of England and East India Company, and the dereliction of the Anglican clergy, the King came to the crux of his speech. He spoke of an island to the west where 'a spirit of insubordination and violence has risen to the most fearful height, rendering life and property insecure, defying the authority of the law, and threatening the most fatal consequences if not promptly and effectually repressed'. The scenario was dire, but the King trusted in the 'loyalty and patriotism' of his ministers. All would be rescued. But William IV was talking not of Jamaica: he was talking of Ireland. In fact, he had passed over slavery entirely. 'The King's Speech is decidedly Conservative,' observed Edward Law, Baron Ellenborough, 'It says nothing of the West Indies.'[12]

One can but imagine the crushing disappointment that the abolitionists felt. Buxton was certainly crestfallen, writing to his brother-in-law that he was 'affronted and vexed'. And after speaking to Lord Granville, the British ambassador to France, he was sure that the 'Government had given up all idea of emancipating the slaves'. In truth, Buxton's fears were exaggerated: the Whigs had intended to announce their plans until the last week in January, when two specific factors persuaded the prime minister to drop Howick's – that is, his own son's – scheme.[13]

First, there was the problem of the King, whose antipathy towards slave emancipation had only festered since the Christmas Rebellion. In the summer of 1832, he had written to Goderich that 'Slavery cannot be abolished in the West Indian Colonies without entailing thereby the loss of all those Colonies'. Calling upon the 'local Observation' that he undertook while serving in the Navy, and 'from matured Consideration of the Question', the King declared that emancipation 'would reduce [the slaves] from a state of comparative ease & Comfort to one of misery & Starvation, & would ruin the Proprietors'. In his opinion, the planters were much 'better acquainted with the Merits of the general question' than the abolitionists, who did not possess either 'knowledge or experience' and whose zeal was really informed 'by a desire to gain popularity'. The King's private secretary Herbert Taylor had hurried an embarrassed apology to Goderich, insisting that 'all [the King] said on the subject was [said] with proper good humour', but the challenge for the Grey ministry was clear. Only a year after the Reform crisis, when the King's refusal to create new Whig peers had provoked the Days of May, the government was simply unconvinced that William IV would give the royal assent to any measure of slave emancipation.[14]

Second, there was another crisis in Jamaica. When the colony's House of Assembly met for its new session in October 1832, Lord Mulgrave had asked the assemblymen to pass ameliorative measures along the lines of the 1831 Order in Council. Already at war with the governor over his prosecution of the CCU, the colonists were in no mood to cooperate. Indeed, they elected to make a show of their independence and, on 6 November, they denied the right of Parliament to legislate for them altogether. Mulgrave expressed his 'extreme surprise and disappointment' and relations worsened quickly, with mounting arrests of CCU vigilantes and Mulgrave's protection of missionaries acting as catalysts for further conflict. The final straw was rather innocuous: when Mulgrave and the assemblymen reached an impasse over the right of the legislature to examine witnesses under oath, the governor simply dissolved the House. 'They have shewn such a reckless determination to defy the British Parliament,' wrote Mulgrave to London, 'that it is impossible the King's authority can be upheld if some check is not at once put to the usurpations of the House of Assembly.' With Mulgrave being assaulted on the streets of Spanish Town, the Whig ministry feared that interference over slavery would escalate a constitutional crisis in Jamaica into a full-blown revolution. 'Mulgrave's precipitate dissolution of the House of Assembly may have embarrassed them,' reflected Lord Ellenborough. 'They may have been alarmed at the prospect ... of insurrection.' The scheme for emancipation was shelved.[15]

The abolitionists knew none of this. Curiously, even though Goderich told the slaveholding MP Alexander Grant that 'nothing [would] be said in the King's Speech', he kept the abolitionists in the dark, and this state of ignorance was allowed to persist. At first dejected, Buxton now rediscovered the vigour that had sustained him for a decade, and his new plan of action was simple: unless the government brought forward a plan for slave freedom by 19 March, he would move in the Commons for the immediate emancipation of colonial slaves. It was not an empty threat, and the government knew it. More to the point, given the number of MPs who had signed pledges in favour of immediate emancipation, they knew that Buxton might pull it off.[16]

The days and weeks ticked by and ministers engaged Buxton in a continual, 'anxious negotiation', begging him to refrain from 'active measures'. Yet by 16 March, with the government advancing nothing on its initial silence, Buxton explained his intentions in a letter to Viscount Althorp. Determined that his missive would not be 'misplaced' by ministerial messengers, Buxton walked the letter to Downing Street personally. Demanding to see Althorp, he was told by a porter that 'a council was sitting' and they would not take the letter. Standing on the cobbles outside, Buxton prepared for a lonely vigil, but there was a stroke of luck: the Duke of Richmond, the Postmaster General, was running late for Cabinet and, as he passed by Buxton, he offered to take the letter inside. Yet there would be no response: not from Althorp, or the prime minister, or even the Colonial Office. Two days later, Buxton announced to the House of Commons that he would move for immediate emancipation on the following evening.[17]

Buxton's duels with Canning proved ideal training for what followed. In a classic political manoeuvre, the government adjourned that day's debate, thereby bumping Buxton's motion off the schedule for the next. When he learned of the trick, Buxton sought out Althorp and sat down behind him. 'So, I hear these are your tactics?' he asked.

'We really are obliged to do so,' protested Althorp. 'We are in such a strait.'

Buxton would have none of it. Gently reminding Althorp that he had not come so far only to lose to his supposed allies, Buxton wore him down. 'Well,' sighed Althorp, 'if you will not yield, we must.' The adjournment was rescinded and, over the next few minutes, Buxton and Althorp hashed out a new timetable. They agreed that, on 23 April, the government would present its full and detailed plans for the extinction of slavery. Buxton was patently relieved. 'The Government have to-night taken the slave question into their own hands,' he wrote in his journal, 'promising to settle it in a "safe and satisfactory manner.'" His daughter wrote that her father was now 'able to sleep at night, and began to resume his cheerfulness'.[18]

Yet as time passed, and as the silence from Downing Street endured, Buxton feared that he had been misled again. He was 'full of chagrin and disappointment', seeking consolation from Lushington, and 'looking as if some heavy misfortune had befallen him'. Then came the news: the Colonial Office had postponed the announcement once more. Buxton had seen this before, first with Canning, then with Wellington, and now with the Whigs. It was a pattern of delay which, if allowed to repeat, could postpone emancipation indefinitely. Even the West Indians began to think that emancipation was 'dead': as William Gladstone wrote to his father, 'The rumour is now very prevalent, that the Government will bring forward no West India measure at all this Session.'[19]

Nobody knew it, but the government's silence was really the product of a crisis in Cabinet. At the age of thirty-four, Edward Smith-Stanley was a rising star of British politics. When the Whigs came to power in 1830 he had been appointed Chief Secretary for Ireland, in which office he had armed the Protestant yeomanry, demanded the payment of tithes in arrears, empowered the Lord Lieutenant to declare martial law where he saw fit, and prescribed the immigration of the English gentry as a cure for Irish ills. Almost inevitably, he made a serious enemy of Daniel O'Connell. Yet by early 1833, Stanley's star had waned so far that he needed two things: to relinquish the Irish office, and then to restore his 'standing as a sincere reformer, refuting the charges raised by his draconian measures in Ireland'. Grey also needed to keep Stanley in the government: as probably the most conservative of his ministers – indeed, as the Earl of Derby he would be a Conservative premier – Stanley was vital to retaining the support of moderate Whigs and liberal Tories.[20]

Given Stanley's personal abhorrence of slavery, the Colonial Office appeared to be the solution to all these issues, and so a minor reshuffle was on the cards. The only problem was that Stanley's arrival at the Colonial Office would require Goderich to move elsewhere, and he did not want to go. Moreover, Stanley was set on bringing in his own plan for emancipation and his own under-secretary, meaning that both Howick and his scheme – meticulously crafted over long months with James Stephen – would be laid aside. This presented

Earl Grey with a painful choice. He could either sack Goderich and Howick, his own son, or he could risk Stanley leaving the Cabinet and with that the stability of the whole government. In the first week of April, the prime minister chose the lesser of the two evils, politically speaking. Stanley went to the Colonial Office, Goderich was fobbed off with an earldom, and Howick resigned from the government in disgust with his father. Having 'slaved his life out for the last two years on the question of the niggers', as his brother put it, Howick even took a seat on the opposition benches, a move that 'wounded' the prime minister. Nonetheless, the ministry was saved. As Edward Littleton, Stanley's successor in Ireland, recorded in his diary, 'All these changes are generally approved by *all* Parties. Stanley's, because he is hated by the Irish, Goderich's because he is hated by the planters ... and Howick's because he has been arrogant and waspish'. But Stanley's arrival at the Colonial Office did not hasten emancipation. In fact, by early April, the strain and fatigue of Stanley's time in Ireland had caught up with him. Laid low by influenza, which in turn triggered his first acute attack of gout, Stanley needed to rest before he could even consider drafting a bill for emancipation.[21]

Again, the abolitionists knew none of this. Looking on from a distance, they had seen the friendly Goderich and their ally Howick bounced from office to make way for Stanley, a minister who had a reputation for brutality. And when the government announced *yet another* postponement of their plans – from 23 April to 14 May – they presumed, quite reasonably, that emancipation had been abandoned. What the Anti-Slavery Society needed, and what Buxton and George Stephen debated over breakfast on a clear, dry day, was a political stunt to shock the government into action. As the two men pored over mounds of papers in search of inspiration, a knock at the door announced the arrival of Thomas Pringle, the secretary of the Society. He brought with him a guest, a young bookkeeper by the name of Henry Whiteley who had returned from a spell in Jamaica. Whiteley spoke earnestly about what he had seen, but this was 'a tale of cruelty and suffering such as Mr. Buxton had heard a hundred times before'. Sensing that his hosts were preoccupied, and not wishing to overstay his welcome, Whiteley said goodbye. Yet no sooner did the door shut than Buxton had an idea. For years, both the government and the public had been listening to the same abolitionist voices, the same rhetoric, and the same anecdotes of cruelty. What they needed now, to remind everyone that electing abolitionist MPs was not the same as enacting abolition, was 'a fresh picture from the spot'. In other words, Buxton needed Henry Whiteley's story. Running after the young man with such enthusiasm that he forgot to put on his hat, Buxton caught Whiteley just as he was turning the corner into Portland Place. Taking him back indoors and enquiring after 'certificates as to [Whiteley's] character', Buxton asked him to 'put down this story in writing'.[22]

Working with Thomas Pringle and Samuel Bagster, who had printed George Stephen's impish placards, it took mere days to produce a twenty-four-page pamphlet, *Three Months in Jamaica*, which detailed how the sugar plantation had robbed Whiteley of his naivety about the colonies. In its pages, Whiteley confessed that he had gone to Jamaica with 'no clear conception of the nature of Colonial Slavery' and that he had once blamed Buxton, Lushington, and their colleagues 'for making so much ado in Parliament about Colonial Slavery, and neglecting ... the slavery of the poor factory children at home'. In Jamaica, however, Whiteley's eyes had been opened. The effect of his pamphlet, which brought home 'the terrors of the lash' to the reading public, was incendiary. In the space of a fortnight, 200,000 copies were printed and sold across Britain. Buxton marvelled that 'Whiteley, nothing but Whiteley is the order of the day; the sensation it creates is immense; the printers can scarcely supply the demand.'[23]

The Interest replied in kind with *Tom Cringle's Log*, a compendium of pro-slavery yarns first published in *Blackwood's*. Written by Michael Scott, a Glaswegian with decades of experience in the West Indies, *Tom Cringle* proved that slavery still had some literary cachet. The *Quarterly Review* lavished praise on the book; a young Anthony Trollope was charmed by it; and Samuel Taylor Coleridge, addled by opiates and confined to his refuge in Highgate, described Scott's work as closer to Smollett than anything he could remember. Despite *Tom Cringle*'s supposed merits, Whiteley won this paper war by a distance: most who were reading about slavery were reading Whiteley, and those who were reading Whiteley were demanding emancipation.[24]

At the same time, the Agency Society called for a more forceful exhibition of abolitionist anger. When George Stephen mooted a national convention of anti-slavery delegates, Buxton feared a damp squib: 'Will they come when you do call for them?' he asked. Stephen assured him that the provincial associations 'would have sent up men in armour, had a plausible reason been assigned'. This emergency convention took place on 19 April at Exeter Hall, an 'immense edifice' that, until its demolition, stood on the site now occupied by the Strand Palace Hotel. Passing through a grand doorway between two Corinthian pillars, the anti-slavery delegates climbed up curved marble stairways to the Hall's great chamber. With sunken galleries 'like the side-boxes of a theatre', a 'splendid range of raised seats', and a raised platform 'finished in front by a handsome iron rail', Exeter Hall was a spectacular venue. The chair itself was 'of handsomely carved mahogany, with massy open elbows ... [and] cushioned in the seat and back with purple leather'. That day in April, the 'merchants, squires, bankers, magistrates, clergymen, and dissenting ministers' who were filling the hall pledged themselves by solemn oath: 'We will never relax from our efforts, nor swerve from our purpose to exert that influence which we may collectively or individually possess, to effect by all legitimate means its immediate and entire abolition'. What followed was a stunning, poignant display of 'that influence'.[25]

Filing out of Exeter Hall, the delegates assembled on the Strand. Many of them dressed in black, in clerical garb, they began a slow and stately procession. Heading west along the Strand, they came to the public square that would soon be named after Trafalgar. To their right was the building site of the National Gallery, ahead of them the Mall leading down to Buckingham Palace. This march of the godly 'attracted the attention of all the street passengers and especial care was taken to announce that they were all anti-slavery delegates'. Veering left, they walked down Whitehall and, a few hundred yards later, they turned right into Downing Street. As they reached the door of Number 10, Althorp and Stanley stepped out to meet them. Buxton stepped forward. Locking eyes with the government's ministers, he pointed in turn to the men who had answered the summons and marched with him through London. They came from Cork and Belfast; from Edinburgh, Dundee, and Aberdeen; from Carmarthen, Bristol, and Liverpool; from Birmingham, Manchester, and Sheffield. The message was clear. These men were from everywhere; they represented everyone. And now, on Downing Street, they demanded the end of slavery.

'It cannot be doubted,' wrote the editor of Buxton's memoirs, 'that this manifestation had a great effect on the Government; it was the first occasion on which public feeling so emphatically expressed itself, and it was felt to be called forth by no ordinary earnestness of purpose.' George Stephen agreed. Writing some years later to Harriet Beecher Stowe, he avowed that, 'as an exhibition of the moral strength of the [abolitionist] party, its important influence with the government can scarcely be over-stated'. It seems that nobody was more affected than Edward Stanley, who upon reflection described this abolitionist demonstration as 'the more absolute and irresistible, because it is founded in that deep religious feeling ... which admits of no palliative or compromise'. At the time, he simply promised that he would brook no further delay. On 14 May, he would tell the House of Commons how slave emancipation would occur.[26]

17.

The Price of Liberty

For ten long years we have been fighting the arduous battle of the
Anti-slavery cause. You never offered us that assistance which we should
have so thankfully received – you never touched that heavy burden
with one of your fingers … What title you may have to demand an
explanation of my conduct … remains a mystery to me.[1]

Thomas Fowell Buxton, to a critic, 17 June 1833

With almost four weeks to wait until the revelation of Stanley's plans,
Buxton took refuge from Westminster at a fisherman's cottage near
Dagenham. Although a flurry of hostile pro-slavery letters caused
some distress, Buxton tried to relax in the warm spring sunshine. With
ships passing by on the Thames, and taking daily walks among the
flowers and long grasses of the riverbanks, Buxton gathered himself
for the last battle. Not all campaigners enjoyed such repose. Indeed,
in just ten days that spring, Anne Knight and Maria Tothill of the
Anti-Slavery Ladies' Committee orchestrated the most intensive,
expansive petitioning campaign in the history of British politics. They
collected 187,000 signatures for presentation to both the Commons
and the Lords and, with hundreds of rolls of vellum arriving in London
on horseback, stitching them into a single petition was a task of the
utmost difficulty. One member of the Ladies' Committee recalled that
they were 'hard at work at it from ten in the morning till past nine
at night' until the petitions 'became enormous, much heavier than
we could move, or even roll over'. The ladies sought a favour from
their male colleagues, who sent over some able hands and 'tureens of
paste'. The vellum eventually came together as 'two great feather
beds' and, when one fell apart, the ladies 'had to begin it all again'.

It was only by 'bracing them with broad tape [that] at last they were sewn up, each in a great sacking, and sent off', one to Lord Suffield for the House of Lords, the other to Buxton for the Commons. Quite how Buxton was going to present the petition was another matter.[2]

At the same time, Stanley and the Colonial Office were conducting intense negotiations with the slaveholding Interest over the terms of emancipation. Deputations rushed back and forth between the West India Club House near Piccadilly and the Colonial Office, while a diplomatic back-channel saw Howick meet privately with the Tobagonian slaveholder Patrick Maxwell Stewart and John Moss, a banker with ties to Guiana. The West Indians were even consulted on the first draft of Stanley's plan, with a delegation from the Interest attending the Colonial Office for a summit that did *not* go well. Denis le Marchant was Henry Brougham's secretary and he noted that 'Nothing could exceed the disappointment and mortification that pervaded ... The West Indians came out [of the meeting] saying that they were wholly and entirely ruined ... They termed the plan one of the grossest acts of spoliation that any Government had ever brought forward'. Only days before the scheduled announcement in the Commons, the Cabinet worried that all would fall apart: 'The ministry could not be indifferent spectators of these movements,' wrote Le Marchant. 'The Government was in great danger. Lord Althorp said that he had always foreseen that this question would break it up.' On the Saturday morning, an emergency meeting 'of the friends of the Government' convened at Whitehall and, while 'Stanley made an excellent speech' to calm the nerves of his fellow ministers, Westminster was now 'pregnant with rumours'.[3]

The abolitionists were angry, too, not least because Stanley was ignoring James Stephen and Henry Taylor during the drafting process. Stanley thought that Stephen's and Howick's plan was 'impracticable' and he had scrapped it almost at once, preferring to prepare his own. Taylor was incandescent at this insult and gave a scathing account of Stanley's behaviour to Isabella Fenwick, a confidante of William Wordsworth: 'Stanley leaps into his seat, gets the gout, gets the grippe, goes down into his county to be re-elected, and gives his spare time to the invention of a scheme for settling the W. India question without holding a word of communication with Howick, Stephen or myself!' It followed that, when the abolitionists read the first draft of Stanley's plan in *The Times*, they 'were almost as much dissatisfied as the West Indians'. Buxton, the elder Macaulay, and Lushington 'were all furious', while Thomas Macaulay tendered his resignation from the Board of Control in protest. At this crucial moment, only seventy-two hours before the scheduled announcement on the Tuesday, Stanley needed help, and so he brought the younger James Stephen back into the fold. Working on the Sabbath for the first time in his life, and toiling almost without sleep, Stephen reshaped the twenty-six pages of Stanley's proposal into something more palatable. It was *this* new measure of emancipation that would be presented to the Commons.[4]

On that Tuesday night, on 14 May, the chamber was full. There was no room on the benches. First, Buxton sought 'the assistance of some other members' to present the Ladies' Petition. It took some effort and it was only thanks to 'the united exertions' of four MPs, amid the laughter of the House, that the great mass of vellum, paste, tape, and ink was hauled onto the table. As the mirth died down, Stanley stood. Asking for 'the kindness and indulgence' of the MPs crowding the Commons, he announced that, on 1 August 1834, slavery would be abolished in the British colonies: the title of property in man would no longer be recognised in British law. However, there were two major caveats to the measure. First, the slaveholders and *not* the enslaved would receive compensation. By estimating the annual profit of the West Indian colonies at £1.5 million, and multiplying that figure by a decade, Stanley arrived at the £15 million that would be loaned to the planters in recognition of the confiscation of their 'property'. Second, most enslaved people would become 'free' in name only, for there would be a system of 'apprenticeship'. Whereas all children under the age of six would be liberated at once, adults would remain 'in place' as 'apprentices' for up to *twelve years*. Most of their work would be done 'free' for their masters, and they would be obliged to save whatever additional wages they earned to buy their own freedom.[5]

The government printed thousands of copies of Stanley's plan and circulated them around the country as a means of engaging the whole political nation in the resolution of the West India Question. The reaction was mixed at best. Thomas Raikes, the son of a West Indian merchant, complained that Stanley's Bill was 'so complex in its machinery that none think it practicable: and as it is not sufficiently decisive for the Abolitionists, and much too severe on the West India interest, it gives equal dissatisfaction to both parties'. In truth, Stanley's proposal *was* a bad bill since it was internally inconsistent and unpopular with practically everyone, but it was never meant as more 'than an opening shot' in a lengthy process of negotiation. The government had publicised the plan precisely so that objections could be ventilated, and solutions agreed.[6]

On the West Indian side, Glasgow's slaveholders predicted that Stanley's plan 'will be ruinous to the Colonies'. The young Elizabeth Barrett Browning, whose family owned the Cinnamon Hill plantation in Jamaica, whined that 'the West Indies are irreparably ruined if the bill passes'. Sir Richard Vyvyan, the Ultra-Tory MP whose bluster was beloved of American slaveholders, thundered that 'no ordinance of a conqueror in a country newly acquired by force of arms could be more tyrannical than the decree of those who framed the Reform Bill with respect to the colonies'. Indeed, the West Indians attempted to throw out the bill entirely: on 27 May, 1,500 leading City merchants staged a mass protest against Stanley's plans.[7]

The government quickly ceded ground. On 29 May, the Cabinet met in the drawing room at Holland House, where Althorp and Stanley were told to convert the loan of £15 million into a grant. Lord Melbourne and Charles Grant were so content with the measure that they fell asleep on their couches, at which point Earl Grey 'jokingly' urged his ministers to 'blow out the candles and leave them' in the dark. One week later there was another Cabinet dinner, this time at Lord Melbourne's, where Stanley was empowered to increase that grant to £20 million, 'provided he thought that by such concession he could secure the cooperation of a large portion of [the Interest] and possibly of the [colonial] legislatures themselves'. On 11 June, he received that assurance when Dudley Ryder, Viscount Sandon and an MP for Liverpool, declared that the Interest 'would not object to the measure of compensation proposed'. The £20 million grant was subsequently 'carried by a large majority' in the Commons, but not without the curious sight of the Marquis of Chandos, the former chairman of Interest, 'voting against so large a sum of money'.[8]

As the West Indians won concessions, abolitionist tempers simmered. Compensation had long been a talking point and it was the *sine qua non* of West Indian consent to emancipation, but the idea of rewarding the slaveholders was anathema to all but the most pragmatic abolitionists: the payment of that money, by recognising the confiscation of 'property', meant conceding that slavery was legal. For George Stephen, compensation was a corrupt bargain, and the 'purchase of negro liberty' amounted to the 'abandonment of principle'. And so, while Buxton told Parliament that he would 'oppose the payment of a single farthing by the Negro' for his own freedom, his acquiescence in *any* compensation threatened his moral leadership of the abolitionist movement. He was condemned by the Agency Society, upbraided by a constituent in Weymouth, and criticised by a regional anti-slavery committee. For some, he was now the embodiment of conspiracy and collusion with the Interest, and one open letter damned him as a traitor. 'I would rather see you ... take a retaining fee from the planters,' he was told, 'than that you should ... bring forward a motion in accordance with [those] sentiments.' From Bath, the ailing Wilberforce wept at the vitriol being unleashed in Buxton's direction: 'I feel more indignant than I can well express, at the unworthy treatment dear honest Buxton has experienced.'[9]

The apprenticeship was an even greater obstacle to agreement. Stanley had already reduced the apprenticeship from twelve years to seven as a counterweight to increasing the amount of compensation but, in a crisis meeting at Whitehall, thirty-three abolitionists implored him to reduce the term further. 'It is impossible,' claimed Stanley, who feared that curtailing the apprenticeship would scupper West Indian cooperation. 'Not to five years?' enquired the abolitionists. 'I cannot reduce it by a single year,' the Colonial Secretary explained, 'not by a day. I am pledged to the West Indians, [and they] regard it as the best part of the bill ... I cannot abate an hour of the apprenticeship.' When the abolitionists threatened another appeal to the people, Stanley confessed that he was 'well aware of your power ... You have caused us much annoyance, and you may cause us more'. But still he would not budge. 'There is no help for it,' he pleaded: 'the apprenticeship must stand, or the bill must go with it.' The abolitionists now expressed their demands in a more dramatic fashion. All along, George Stephen had assumed that Stanley would not yield, and so he had put the Agency Society to work: day and night, his clerks were printing circulars and making emergency arrangements. Stephen had even posted watchmen outside the Colonial Office, waiting for a signal to dispatch riders to the provinces. Days before the second reading of the bill in the Commons, sixty-six leading 'immediatists' piled onto the platform of the Freemasons' Hall. The venue was 'crowded to suffocate' and, with one voice, they demanded the curtailment of apprenticeship. In these moments, Joseph Sturge worried about 'the discord of our Anti-slavery camp'.[10]

Indeed, in July 1833 several influential abolitionists – including George Stephen and Daniel O'Connell – began to sound out colleagues about voting *against* the bill in order to protest the apprenticeship. Buxton begged them to reconsider, advising that 'moderate men of all parties would tremble at the idea of throwing the bill out' and that 'the good of the Negroes ought to be our sole guide'. He reasoned that, if elements of Stanley's Bill were objectionable, the abolitionists should deal with them in the discursive 'committee' stage of legislation. Buxton's pragmatism won through. On 22 July, the bill passed its second reading by unanimous consent.[11]

At the committee stage, though, all of the abolitionists' anxieties were let loose. Some colleagues implored Buxton 'to fight the money battle, and to defeat Mr Stanley, if possible'. When he voted in committee for the £20 million grant, even his sister questioned him: 'Surely you acted hastily last night in voting for compensation?' she asked. 'No', came Buxton's reply, as he roused himself from the sofa. 'No! I would do the same again. I did it to save bloodshed; that was my motive, and I am glad I did it.' On the apprenticeship, however, Buxton bowed to his radical brethren: on 24 July, he forced the committee to vote on limiting the apprenticeship to 'the shortest period which may be necessary to establish ... the system of free labour'. Buxton lost the motion, but the margin – only seven votes – was close enough to convince 'the Ministers ... that if they persisted, they would be infallibly beaten'. Reluctantly, Stanley reduced the apprenticeship from seven years to six for field-workers, and four for those who worked indoors. 'I for one have learned a new lesson of the nature of a reformed Parliament,' scorned William Gladstone, 'and of the disreputable necessity which it enforces even upon a man like Mr Stanley.' Buoyed by this success, Buxton even tried for another reduction, but Macaulay begged him not to 'press the thing further' lest Stanley should resign in protest, an event that would lead to 'no Bill at all, but instead of it a Tory Ministry'.[12]

Tempers were fraying more seriously among the West Indians. Although the central Interest now wished for the 'safe and satisfactory termination' of proceedings, and though its Acting Committee agreed to persuade the colonial assemblies of the wisdom of Stanley's deal, there was an obvious division between the absentee planters in London and the resident colonists of the Caribbean. William Burge complained that the London Interest was 'so intent on securing the 20 Millions that they ... never thought of nor cared for the colonial legislatures, [and] were evidently unwilling to say or do anything on their behalf'. Burge claimed that he was exposed to 'all sorts of attacks' from British-based members of the Interest, and Richard Barrett and Abraham Hodgson – dispatched from Jamaica to turn back the tide – were so incensed by Stanley, whom they vilified as 'always the enemy of Jamaica', that they revived the tired old threat of white Jamaicans violently resisting 'the anarchy which the measures of the Government would bring upon them'.[13]

Tension was equally evident along the lines of the individual colonies. Under Stanley's scheme, the compensation would not be handed out on a *per capita* basis: a planter with one hundred slaves would not necessarily receive twice as much as a planter with fifty. Rather, each colony would be given a lump sum calculated according to the number of enslaved people in that colony and the average market price of those people, a formula that was effectively a shorthand for each colony's profitability. That sum would then be apportioned among the colony's slaveholders depending on the skills and age of each enslaved person. Both across and within the colonies, the distribution of compensation was a zero-sum game: whatever one colony received, another could not. As George Hibbert predicted, 'It is probable difficulties will arise as to the Principle of Partition of the Twenty Millions, so as to give each Colony its equitable share of the Compensation'.[14]

The rivalry between Jamaica and Demerara (or, as it was now, Guiana) was especially pronounced, and it was the key theme of that summer's correspondence between William Gladstone and his father. In June, the younger Gladstone reported that Burge had been making snide remarks at dinner about half of the £20 million going to Jamaica, something he took to be a shot across Demerara's bows: 'I do not understand the part that Burge is playing,' he wrote. The next month, at 'a meeting of Jamaica people', the MP Robert Gordon 'got up &

began to abuse Demerara' and complained bitterly that 'Jamaica suffered ... for the interests of Demerara'.[15]

The Demerarans fought fire with fire. On 12 July, Gladstone reported that they would not take part in any further discussions, since they were perfectly content with the present arrangements. This was followed by boisterous meetings of 'Gentlemen interested in British Guiana' and by Demeraran claims 'for a Sum [of compensation] proportionate to the actual value of Slave property there'. To that end, Alexander McDonnell calculated a 'rate of compensation per head for each slave, according to the true principles of distribution, Capitations, compound ratio, & the slavery Bill for all colonies'. At every turn, they asserted the primacy of Demerara, and the West Indians descended further into internecine strife. On 19 July, Bristolians, Antiguans, Jamaicans, and other Demerarans came forward with new plans for allocating compensation money, all designed to enlarge their own share, and Gladstone wrote to his father that 'Clouds are arising from every quarter'. In time, the West Indians did reach an agreement over the relative value of their 'property'. Each enslaved African was worth about £20 in Jamaica and Barbados, while the average price was £50 in the newer colonies of Guiana and Trinidad. It is one of the most disturbing aspects of the whole history of colonial slavery that, in this way, the life of an African was valued at between £2,300 and £5,800 in today's money.[16]

The very occurrence of such debates was proof that the slaveholders had accepted emancipation as inevitable. From this point forward, any West Indian who continued to defend slavery did so without the backing of the Interest. Still, Buxton came close to wrecking the whole thing when on 31 July, just as the bill was going through its last rites, he proposed withholding half of the £20 million from the slaveholders until the expiry of the apprenticeship. In his reasoning, the first £10 million would be 'the largest deposit perhaps ever offered for the performance of a contract'; the second £10 million, 'founded in the caution and prudence which men of the world displayed in the bargains made by them in ordinary transactions', would be security for the delivery of 'the commodity'. It was a staggeringly misguided gambit and, in the debate that followed, Stanley's exasperation was plain to see. After ten painful weeks of negotiations, it appeared that Buxton was trying to undermine the very premise on which the West Indians had consented to emancipation. As the last man to speak before the Commons voted, Stanley sounded a warning: 'If the House ... adopted [Buxton's amendment], they would certainly endanger the Bill, unless the hon. member for Weymouth [that is, Buxton] was prepared to take it out of the Minister's hand'. It was a stark warning that any further meddling would induce the government to drop the bill altogether. Under threat of calamity, Buxton lost the vote comfortably.[17]

One week later, on 7 August, the Slavery Abolition Bill came before the House for its third reading. At half past six that evening, William Gladstone dropped a note to his father without the least embarrassment over their own roles in defending slavery: 'The Slavery Abolition Bill is just passed,' wrote the young Gladstone, 'God prosper it'.[18]

Of course, the bill was not yet law, and attention now turned to the House of Lords, where it seemed as if Lord Suffield was struggling to find the necessary votes. 'The Tories had collected their strength,' wrote Buxton to Macaulay, 'and were determined to throw out the bill.' Suffield, though, was 'watching over [the bill], as over a pet child, and for days sustained a running fire on every clause' until the Duke of Wellington accepted the futility of resistance. 'I see what influence you are working under,' he told Earl Grey, referring to Buxton: 'And if that individual is to have more power than [the] Lords and Commons both, we may as well give up the bill.' Still haunted by the events of the previous spring, when their intransigence over Reform had caused widespread rioting, the Tory peers relented. On 20 August, Viscount Goderich, now the Earl of Ripon, moved the third reading of the bill. There was only one more obstacle to overcome: the King.[19]

William IV's opposition to emancipation had been expressed forcefully the previous summer. Even as late as June 1833, there were troubling accounts of royal disapproval, all of which invoked the unwelcome prospect of the King withholding the royal assent. 'The King is no Abolitionist,' noted Henry Brougham's secretary: 'He was much in the West Indies when in the navy; [and] being a careless, superficial observer, he came home under the impression that the slaves were the happiest people in the world.' In the end, William's reservations were overcome by the efforts of two men. First, Stanley, who 'persuaded [the King] that part of the plan originated with himself'; second, Edward Ellice, a major slaveholder and the Secretary at War, who somehow managed to convince the King that he should not worry about assenting to the *same* plan because it was bound to fail. 'Ellice and he often talk the matter over,' it was reported, 'and the King is only quieted by Ellice's assurance that the [emancipation] scheme can't work, for the slaves themselves are not sufficiently apt instruments to put it into motion.' Bizarrely, the King's approval was contingent upon the expected failure of emancipation but at last, on 28 August 1833, he assented. On 1 August 1834, slavery in the British colonies would be abolished.[20]

From the space between the high Doric pillars of Australia House and Wren's church of St Clement Danes, where Aldwych meets the Strand, a street runs south to the Embankment. This is Arundel Street. It is now home to a luxury development that was promoted as an 'iconic landmark ... closely linked to the richest aspects of London living', but John Gay once wrote of a 'narrow street which steep descends / whose buildings to the slimy shore extends'. Once, there was a tavern here called the Crown & Anchor. Johnson and Boswell had supped and eaten by its fires. When the French Revolution impelled the London Corresponding Society to pursue radical reform, they took the tavern as their home. It was the setting of Gillray cartoons; Coleridge and Hazlitt lectured in its rooms; and it hosted two thousand revellers for the birthday party of Charles James Fox in 1798. At the Crown & Anchor, in August 1833, the abolitionists celebrated.[21]

There were absent friends that night. The health of the elder James Stephen had failed in the early 1830s and, though the spas of Bath did not save him, he saw enough to think that emancipation was secure. The Leicester firebrand Elizabeth Heyrick had died, too. It is doubtful whether any women were invited, but Heyrick – the champion of the boycott, the enemy of compromise – deserved a place at the table. None was missed more sorely, though, than William Wilberforce. A bout of influenza had caused him 'much ... pain and languor' in the early months of 1833 and time was short when the Abolition Bill passed the Commons. 'Oh, that I should have lived,' he said, 'to witness a day in which England is willing to give twenty millions for the abolition of slavery.' He would not see slave freedom made law. After a series of fainting fits, Wilberforce died in Belgravia in late July. Buxton's daughter lamented that, but for a few days more, her father 'might have taken back to him, fulfilled, the task he gave him ten years ago'.[22]

The celebrants at the Crown & Anchor had planned for an 'orderly, sober' dinner that would 'offend nobody', not least the Quakers. After all, they had been 'the very first persons ... who promulgated the doctrine that the buying, selling, or holding of slaves was contrary to the Christian religion', but the Friends' disdain for unruly festivities meant their attendance of the Crown & Anchor was predicated on the promise that nobody would raise a toast. The organising party acceded, with Daniel O'Connell confirming the sobriety of the occasion by insisting that music should not interrupt the speeches. Even George Stephen appeared to consent, removing himself to the extremity of the dining room 'to be out of the way of remonstrance'.[23]

But Stephen was never that sincere. Because he 'infinitely preferred music to speechifying' and because he was 'partial to ... toasting all things worth toasting', he and some colleagues who were 'ripe for any mischief' had hatched a plan to puncture the solemnity of the occasion. First, he sent a note to Buxton on the high table, suggesting that in such a radical tavern it would be impolitic not to toast the King, who had just assented to the end of slavery. Stephen laughed as Buxton squirmed, torn between his devotion to propriety and the promise made to the Quakers; as Buxton chose to toast, and as glasses went up around the room, he could only apologise to the men sitting sternly about him. There was greater mischief planned for O'Connell. When he rose 'all ready for an oration', Stephen gave a signal to the brass band that he had smuggled into a side room. As they emerged and struck up 'God Save the King', Stephen sent further notes to Buxton. How could they now neglect the health of the Queen, or the Tories, or the very Africans who would soon be free? Buxton was 'the picture of distress'; the Quakers were 'utterly discomfited'; and when Stephen 'congratulated two or three of them the next day, on the tender care [that] the police had taken ... in conveying them safely home without fall or injury', he received 'many an awful reproach'. He probably deserved it.[24]

In British mythology, 28 August 1833 – the day that the abolitionists were celebrating at the Crown & Anchor – is a milestone in the history of humanitarian progress. It was the first time, or so the story goes, that any country or empire had defied its self-interest and served the greater good by emancipating enslaved people within its territory. Nothing could be further from the truth, not least because it is a simple matter of record that Britain was *not* the first nation to do so. In fact, Britain was playing catch-up with much of the western hemisphere. In the United States, the process of abolishing slavery either gradually or entirely had begun with Pennsylvania in 1780. Within four years, Massachusetts, New Hampshire, Connecticut, and Rhode Island had followed suit. The Northwest Ordinance of 1787 then forbade the extension of slavery into what became Ohio, Michigan, Indiana, Illinois, Wisconsin, and Minnesota. Gradual abolition began in New York in 1799 and in New Jersey in 1804. Slavery would not be outlawed federally before the Civil War and the passage of the Thirteenth Amendment, but by that point the 'free states' had been free for decades. Because Napoleon attempted to *restore* slavery in the 1800s, the French story is slightly more complicated, but slavery had been abolished in Saint Domingue in 1793 and throughout the whole French Empire by Robespierre's Convention in 1794. Similarly, much of the former Spanish Empire had beaten Britain to abolition. In Chile, La Plata (Argentina), Uruguay; the Bolivarian states of Gran Colombia, Bolivia, and Peru; the Republic of Central America, and in New Spain and then Mexico, slavery had been gradually abolished either from birth or *in toto* long before George Stephen and the Agency Society had converted British abolitionists to 'immediatism'.

Moreover, the Abolition Act was neither the inevitable bequest of sweeping anti-slavery sentiment and the triumphant march of British 'justice', nor was it a simple coda to the better-known campaign against the slave trade. In reality, the passage of the Act had relied upon several factors: the political collapse of the Tories which led to Reform and the return of a sympathetic House of Commons; the persistent pressure applied by the Anti-Slavery and Agency societies; and the violent slave resistance that finally convinced the British public of the immoral, unsustainable nature of slavery. Until those factors combined in the early 1830s, defending slavery was a tenable, popular position for British conservatives, imperialists, economists, and more besides. Until 1833, slavery had been an essential part of British national life, as much as the Church of England, the monarchy, or the liberties granted by the

Glorious Revolution. When we remember it otherwise, we promulgate a self-serving and misleading version of British history.

Further still, slavery was abolished only because Parliament had recognised the legal right of 'property in man' and consequently agreed to compensate the slaveholders for the confiscation of that property. This cost the British government £20 million. In 1833, that was 40 per cent of the government's annual expenditure, and until the banking rescue package of 2008 it remained the largest specific payout in British history. More strikingly, as a proportion of government spending in 2020, (recognising, of course, the growth of the public sector) it was equivalent to approximately £340 billion and, to put *that* figure into perspective, the IMF estimates that the combined GDPs of all of Britain's former West Indian colonies amounted in 2018 to just £69 billion. In other words, British slaveholders received a windfall that was five times greater than the current wealth of the whole of the formerly 'British' Caribbean. But in the later months of 1833, what did this financial settlement mean? What were its consequences for the abolitionists, for the slaveholders, and – most of all – for the enslaved?

18.

The Cat and the Mill

Of course, the late bill has ruined the West Indians. That is settled.
The consternation here is very great.[1]

Elizabeth Barrett Browning to a friend, late 1833

At the turn of 1834, Thomas Fowell Buxton was looking forward to
'the leisure which lay before him'. He planned on resting, reading the
scripture, and prayer. Buxton could also reflect with a degree of relief
upon how, in the later months of 1833, the West Indian colonists had
accepted the Slavery Abolition Act with surprisingly good grace. This
could have been a torturous process, since the Act could not be
enforced directly in colonies with their own legislatures: Jamaica,
Barbados, and the like were obliged to transpose the Act into local
law. There had been *some* difficulties, not least because certain colonists
regarded the London Interest's consent to emancipation as the basest
form of treachery. Indeed, when Richard Barrett and Abraham
Hodgson returned to Jamaica from London, they denounced the
Abolition Act as a fraud that would sacrifice colonial rights on the
altar of misguided philanthropy, and the House of Assembly toyed
with rejecting the Act altogether. Yet when Lord Mulgrave made it
clear that compensation would not be paid until emancipation was
enacted, the planters fell into line. In early December, the Assembly
voted unanimously to incorporate the Abolition Act into Jamaican law.[2]

Now, as Wilberforce had been in 1807, Buxton was the toast of
London. Stanley whispered his congratulations in the Commons;
another MP told Buxton that his cause was 'worth living for, and
dying for'. Elevated into a position of moral authority, he became the
chaplain of a cross-party prayer group. 'It is curious,' he noted, 'how

many compliments we ... fanatics have had on the success of our measure.' Yet as Buxton's former enemies celebrated the fruits of his labour, the imminent delivery of slave freedom was provoking fresh rancour among Britain's most ardent conservatives.[3]

Richard Hurrell Froude was a young clergyman whose contempt for reform had won him friends in fellow theologians John Keble and John Henry Newman. Together, they had founded the Oxford Movement, the High-Church group which extolled the sacramental traditions of the pre-Reformation Church and which, as Simon Skinner has shown, became the most important politico-religious group in Victorian Britain. In November 1833, suffering from tuberculosis and hoping that warmer climes could ease his pain, Froude had left England for Barbados. Upon arrival he quickly concluded that slave freedom would be the herald of ruin. He wrote to Newman that the West Indies would 'become what they call "brown" islands, and relapse into a semi-savage state by the gradual withdrawal' of Britons who knew how to promote so-called 'civilized values'. Even without bloodshed, this would 'destroy the commercial value of the islands'. Froude hated the abolitionists. He lambasted 'Buxton's cant', he decried the machinations of 'the Utopians', and he was explicitly racist, writing to Keble that 'the negro features are so horridly ugly [that] ... one can distinctly trace the differences of caste in all shades from man to monkey'. The next month, Froude wrote to his brother that Africans were remarkable for 'excessive immodesty' and 'a forward, stupid familiarity'. For Froude, 'the niggers ... spoil[ed] the scenery altogether'.[4]

There was an equal sense of revulsion in American southerners. The slaveholder Charles Drayton II wrote from London that 'the great Slave question has started', and he understood that if emancipation was successful, it would 'transfer a great bearing on the United States', with 'the whole evil [falling] on the Southern section'. The only question concerned the extent of that evil. The *Richmond Enquirer*, once Thomas Jefferson's favourite newspaper, raged against British emancipation. 'The scheme appears to us to be woefully harsh,' it complained, 'and ruinous in its consequences ... Even our own shores' ,it fretted, 'may not altogether escape the hurricane.' More generally, emancipation was explained as the work of nefarious conspirators. 'The position of the various parties gave a fatal facility to combinations in Parliament,' the *Enquirer* told concerned southern readers: 'The fanatics, the whigs, the liberals all found it in their interest to unite against the West Indian proprietors; the latter could only count on the Tories.'[5]

Robert Monroe Harrison, the American consul in Jamaica, shared this deep-seated resentment towards British emancipation. The son of a Patriot soldier, Harrison had been seized and imprisoned on Royal Navy ships not once but twice, the first ordeal lasting more than seven years, and by the time he arrived in Spanish Town, where he deplored the prominence of 'Negroes, Mulattoes and Jews', he had already cultivated a virulent strain of Anglophobia. From the moment that Parliament passed the Abolition Act, Harrison inveighed relentlessly against the impending freedom of enslaved Jamaicans. In December 1833, he warned his superiors in Washington that 'Every man in the Island considers he is standing on a Volcano and knows not when it will explode'. In another report, Harrison predicted that free black Jamaicans would reprise the supposed horrors of the 1831 Rebellion, that their victims would be 'friends and relations of those murdered husbands who had their secret parts cut off and placed in the mouths of their wives and Daughters'. This was sordid fantasy, but astonishingly it was the language of American diplomatic cables. By June 1834, Harrison had made *eight* requests for American warships to save white Americans from the violence that he believed would soon engulf the British West Indies.[6]

Still, as 1834 wore on, even the abolitionists were anxious about how emancipation and the apprenticeship would actually 'work'. There had never been much clarity on this point and, in a much-quoted letter to Thomas Clarkson, Buxton had described the abolitionist project as 'a mighty experiment at best'. But now there were rumours of revolution, of the revenge of the enslaved, and the Marquess of Sligo – the new, slaveholding governor of Jamaica – was reporting fears 'of a general massacre of the whites'. In a similar vein, the governor of Barbados denounced the 'unbending spirit' of the planters and 'the tenacity with which they cling on to their arbitrary power over the Negroes'. There were 'forebodings of disaster lower[ing] over Antigua', too: at the colonial capital of St John's, 'some timorous families did not go to bed' on the night of 31 July 1834. 'Fear drove sleep from their eyes, and they awaited with fluttering pulse the hour of midnight, fearing lest the same bell which sounded the jubilee of the slaves, should toll the death knell of the masters.' Foreign merchants who traded with the colony thought better of tempting fate. Urging friends to join them, they weighed anchor and 'made their escape, through actual fear that the island would be destroyed'. There was reason yet to worry.[7]

Some of the most vivid accounts of Emancipation Day, 1 August 1834, were compiled by American abolitionists. Three years after the fact, and eager to glean what they could about the practicalities of emancipation, the American Anti-Slavery Society sent James Thome, the Kentuckian son of a slaveholder, and Joseph Kimball, a newspaper editor from New Hampshire, on a six-month tour of the West Indies. The report was published to widespread acclaim in New England, and here Kimball and Thome related how Wesleyan missionaries at St John's, Antigua, kept 'watch-night' on 31 July. The chapels and meeting houses swelled with the 'candidates for liberty', and 'all was animation and eagerness'. A 'mighty chorus of voices' filled the night air with songs of hope until the clock struck twelve. At that moment, the whole congregation fell to its knees and waited upon deliverance. 'All was silence, save the quivering half-stifled breath of the struggling spirit. The slow notes of the clock fell upon the multitude; peal on peal, peal on peal, rolling over the prostrate throng in the tones of angels' voices.' With a degree of creative licence, Kimball and Thome wrote that, on the twelfth note, 'the lightning flashed vividly around, and a loud peal of thunder roared along the sky'. This was 'God's pillar of fire, his trumpet of jubilee'. After a moment of profound silence, the new apprentices broke forth in prayer, shouting 'Glory!' and 'Alleluia!' The rest of the night was spent in prayer and the missionaries described the next three days, all given as holidays, as a trinity of Sabbaths.[8]

Back in London, the abolitionist leaders had gathered at the Freemasons' Tavern on Great Queen Street for a dinner chaired by the Earl of Mulgrave, the former governor of Jamaica. Anxious as they were, the abolitionists rejoiced when reports came back to Britain – weeks later, of course – of the peaceable transition from slavery to apprenticeship. 'Everything has passed off to admiration,' wrote Buxton. 'Mark the seal, "safe and satisfactory."' Across the Caribbean, long-standing fears of rebellion and carnage faded into nothing, dispelling the fears of the most paranoid planter. 'We have now accounts from the West Indies,' Buxton wrote to the Bishop of Calcutta, 'of the way in which the 1st of August was passed, and highly satisfactory they are.'[9]

Yet as the historian William Green has shown, such accounts of Emancipation Day are crude and facile. In reality, thousands of former slaves from across the West Indies refused at first to submit to apprenticeship. There was disorder in the Essequibo region of Guiana, and the militiamen were called to muster in Montserrat; hundreds of freedmen descended on Port of Spain, Trinidad, causing 'pandemonium' as they protested against the apprenticeship; and the governor of St Kitts was forced to declare martial law, ordering the island's militia to sweep the highlands, driving hundreds of runaways back to the plantations. Even so, these protests did not end in blood: the apprentices were unwilling to jeopardise their ultimate emancipation and, as they returned reluctantly to the plantations, the colonists began to celebrate their own benevolence.[10]

Even on the estates where slavery had been defended on its own merits, emancipation was praised as a 'stupendous change' and 'one of the sublimest spectacles ever witnessed'. Once it would have been 'certain disgrace for any planter to have avowed the least sympathy with anti-slavery sentiments', but after 1834 anti-slavery became 'the popular doctrine among all classes'. Now, the white colonist who opposed 'the principles of liberty' was damned as 'an enemy to his country'. The enthusiasm of these late converts was disingenuous, but their public shows of piety were remarkable. The Americans reported from Antigua that 'an agent of the English Anti-Slavery Society now resides in St John's, and keeps a book-store well stocked with the anti-slavery books'. There was even a bust of the anti-slavery lecturer George Thompson standing 'conspicuously upon the counter, looking forth upon the public street'.[11]

That much is credible, for in the years immediately after emancipation it was Thompson – not Buxton, Clarkson, or Macaulay – who was the best-known abolitionist. This was because Thompson, while debating against Peter Borthwick in Scotland, had met William Lloyd Garrison, the American compaigner who had come to Britain to learn something about anti-slavery agitation. 'Garrison in England will do the cause more good in 3 months,' advised the Rhode Island abolitionist Arnold Buffum, 'than 12 in America, in the reception he will there meet, and by his communications.' Touring Britain with Thompson, taking notes and publishing detailed reports of the debates, Garrison was awed by the British movement. They 'waste no ammunition', he reported to Connecticut: 'Every shot tells – *they write in earnest* – they call, as did old John Knox, a fig a fig, and a spade a spade. When I see what they are doing, and read what they write, I blush to think of my own past apathy, and mourn in view of my poverty of thought and language.' Garrison fell in with the wider British network and, at dinner one night, Buxton asked him, 'In what way, Mr Garrison, can we best assist your cause?' The American's answer was automatic: 'By giving us George Thompson.' Funded by a coterie of Scottish ladies' associations, Thompson travelled to New England in 1834. It was in equal parts a tour of triumph and disaster.[12]

Thompson's American hosts were delighted by his performances, by his soaring oratory, and by the sincerity of his conviction to emancipate enslaved people the world over. Yet even in slavery-free New England, in the Bostonian cradle of American liberty, Thompson suffered vicious personal abuse from other Americans whose liveli-hood depended on trading with the slaveholding South. He was damned by newspapers as a 'mouthing and noisy driveller' and 'a fugitive from justice' who was preaching 'treason to the Constitution'. He was also accused of cowardice for refusing to campaign in the slave states themselves. More sinister was President Andrew Jackson's pointed condemnation of 'emissaries from foreign parts' – that is, Thompson – who had been circulating anti-slavery material. Some Americans preached open violence against Thompson, with some New Englanders offering a bounty of $100 for 'the individual who shall first lay hands ... on Thompson, so that he may be brought to the tar kettle before dark'.[13]

Others practised this violence. In March 1835, Thompson was lecturing on Haiti in a Boston theatre when 'there was a simultaneous rush from the galleries towards the centre of the house'. Some in the audience cried 'Fire!', others that a pro-slavery mob had come. One gentleman panicked and 'went through the window – sash & all was followed by a[nother] man and a woman'. With 'everything in confu-sion' members of Thompson's audience began to faint; 'others were drunk with fear'. The Connecticut abolitionist Henry Benson reflected that, 'had [they] all rushed towards the door, they must inevitably have fallen & those below [been] crushed to death'. There were further attempts to assail Thompson and, in November 1835, he was forced to flee the United States 'to escape the assassin's knife'. At an hour's notice, and without his tearful wife, Thompson was spirited from his lodgings 'down to [Boston] wharf in a carriage'. His abolitionist allies stood guard until he was 'safely on board the packet, and the vessel down the harbour'.[14]

Despite Thompson's tribulations, British abolitionism endured as a beacon for the American anti-slavery movement. Garrison continued to deploy the tradecraft he had learned in England; the New England literary giant Ralph Waldo Emerson hailed British abolition as 'an event singular in the history of civilization'; and, upon his death in 1846, Thomas Clarkson was eulogised in New York as 'The Man! The Hero! The Christian!' The anniversary of British emancipation, the 'First of August', was celebrated fervently in both white abolitionist and free black circles, but never further south than Cincinnati. Of course, the British example cut both ways: in the decades before the American Civil War, there was very little that Southern ideologues wrote in defence of slavery that British West Indians had not written first.[15]

The price of freedom was £20 million; yet £20 million was equivalent to 40 per cent of the British government's annual budget, and extraordinary spending required extraordinary revenue. This compensation fund would not be raised by imposing fresh taxes; instead, the Treasury would issue new government bonds. In July 1835, the new Whig ministry led by Lord Melbourne – who had once described emancipation as a 'great folly' – sat down with syndicates of leading bankers who would compete for the right to raise the loan. The battle was fierce; after all, this was 'the largest single financial operation undertaken by the British state to [that] date'. First to fold was the slave-owning Barings syndicate, dropping out on 30 July with a paranoid complaint against 'some secret coalition or private arrangement with the other competitors'. Amid further rumours of conspiracy, another syndicate led by the MP and economist David Ricardo also withdrew. The last men standing were Nathaniel Rothschild and Moses Montefiore, who therefore set about raising £20 million.[16]

The task of deciding *who* would receive this compensation fell to a new governmental body, the Slave Compensation Commission.

Assisted by functionaries in the colonies but operating chiefly out of a Westminster office, the Commission was chaired first by the future Lord Chancellor Charles Pepys and then by John Bonham Carter, the Whig MP for Portsmouth. They marshalled a staff of six, three of them salaried and three volunteers, and the work of the Commission was, in the words of Nicholas Draper, an 'orderly bureaucratic process with published rules and formal procedures'. British slaveholders were invited to submit their claims by post, identifying which Africans they owned, and then to provide documentary proof of ownership.[17]

The Commissioners were diligent, seeking to respond to every letter by the close of the following day, but the volume of work overwhelmed them. From the summer of 1835, British slaveholders submitted more than 45,000 claims for compensation and, at one point, the Commissioners issued a public apology for delays, citing 'the extreme business in the office'. Their glacial pace infuriated some observers. The Times complained of the Commission's 'dilatory mode of doing business' and maligned its very process: 'As to the plan of doling out these adjudications by 100 or 200 in weekly appointments,' the paper complained, 'it does not meet the views or reasonable expectations of any one above the intellect of a child.' There were also the familiar trappings of bureaucracy. One clergyman from Bath had his claims rejected and returned in the post for 'not having been drawn up in the form prescribed by the Rules'; another claimant from Sussex was told that 'a more formal document than that [which he had sent] will be required'. The former MP James Wildman was infuriated at making 'two useless journeys to London' from his castle in Kent without securing an appointment on either occasion.[18]

The Commissioners' failure to communicate undermined their work even further. Mary Sutherland of London was entirely ignorant of how to apply for compensation, and so she feared that she had 'no other prospect than positive starvation'. Maria Flockton of Bermondsey was equally uninformed and she worried that, 'although the period is fast approaching for the Emancipation of the Negroes, I am totally ignorant of the means to be used in obtaining the compensation'. Their cases are a useful reminder that slaveholding infected British society from the grandest to the humblest homes, yet even 'elite' slaveholders remained unaware of the plans put in place by the Commissioners. Charles Marsham, the Earl of Romney, might have owned more than 400 enslaved people on St Kitts, but it was not until December 1835 that he told the commissioners he would 'be obliged … if you would inform me, where your office is'.[19]

Other problems were not of the Commissioners' making, not least the nearly 4,000 cases where title to the same enslaved person was claimed by more than one applicant. The Commissioners urged settlement before arbitration, but as many as 199 cases made their way into the colonial courts and another 156 to the Chancery Division of London's High Court. These disputes often arose when a slaveholder had died without making a will; at other times, duplicate claims were vexatious. Augustus Beaumont, one of the few Jamaicans to emerge from the Christmas Rebellion with a degree of credit, now turned predator. Although he desired 'not to appear litigious', Beaumont filed dozens of counter-claims for slaves in Jamaica. Cunningly, even despicably, he had combed the island's slave registry to identify incomplete claims that he could 'finish' as well as poor slaveholders whom he knew would rather settle out of court than pursue costly litigation.[20]

If a claim were approved, the money was paid out at the National Debt Office at the Bank of England, with the recipients of the compensation – or their agents – signing the registers kept behind the counter. From these registers, which have been studied extensively by the remarkable Legacies of British Slave-ownership project at UCL, a clear picture of British slaveholding emerges. While only three thousand slaveholders were resident in the United Kingdom in 1834, they held vastly disproportionate wealth and influence. Compensation was awarded to three dukes, one marquess, sixteen earls, two viscounts, fifteen barons, and seventy-five baronets; to more than one hundred past, present, or future MPs; and to twenty-three of Britain's one hundred and seventy-eight wealthiest landowners. This is not to say that all slaveholders were political or commercial titans, or that slave money bequeathed a life of riches. Anna Fraser, a young woman from Inverness, inherited one enslaved person in Berbice and this, she cried, was 'all the property I possess in the world'; indeed, she would die an impoverished spinster while lodging in a small chalet bungalow. The typical slaveholder was more likely to be conservative and Tory than liberal and Whig: as *The Times* reported of a West Indian meeting in 1833, there were few present who were 'not generally staunch Tories, or who would not resolutely oppose the existing [Whig] Administration on any other given question'. That same slaveholder was more likely to be Anglican than a Dissenter: although many prominent abolitionists were evangelical members of the Church, Anglican slaveholders had been the backbone of the pro-slavery Society for the Conversion and Religious Instruction and Education of Negro Slaves, and more than 150 clergymen were slaveholders themselves. For good reason, one historian has written about the 'strong evidence of Anglicanism [which] runs through the compensation recipients'.[21]

One such Anglican was the bigoted ringleader of the Colonial Church Union, George Wilson Bridges, whose post-slavery years were defined by ignominy. When his wife abandoned him, and when the governor of Jamaica gave him six months' leave that he might pursue her to England, Bridges was ostracised by his extended family, who even declined to tell him of his father's terminal illness. In 1837, tragedy struck when a shipwreck 'swallowed up' all four of Bridges' daughters and, 'driven wild' by the loss, he sold up in Jamaica and fled to the backwoods of Canada. Four years in the wilderness were followed by flight to Italy, and then to Gloucestershire, where he met the pioneering photographer Henry Fox Talbot. This led to Bridges' instruction in what was called the calotype process and, entrusted by Talbot with photographic paper, Bridges spent much of the next decade wandering the Mediterranean. The pro-slavery pariah took some of the first photographs of Greece, Turkey, and the Holy Land.[22]

Other men who owed their 'celebrity' to the defence of slavery now retreated into the darker corners of public memory. The star of Alexander McDonnell, the Irish chess player and pro-slavery economist, burned out quickly. In 1835, he succumbed to the chronic inflammation of the kidneys known as Bright's disease and died in a Bloomsbury boarding house. The Glaswegian journalist James MacQueen was forgiven his 'nasty jealousies & petty vanities' by Thomas Fowell Buxton, and they even joined forces to launch an expedition along the Niger River, but there was no serious resurrection of his fortunes. The poet Chauncy Hare Townshend later observed 'a considerable touch of pathos' when he heard MacQueen talk about 'bleakness and wildness'. His business ventures such as the Royal Mail Steam Packet Company failed, and MacQueen would die penniless in London at the age of ninety-two, leaving a wife – some thirty years his junior – to survive on the largesse of friends.[23]

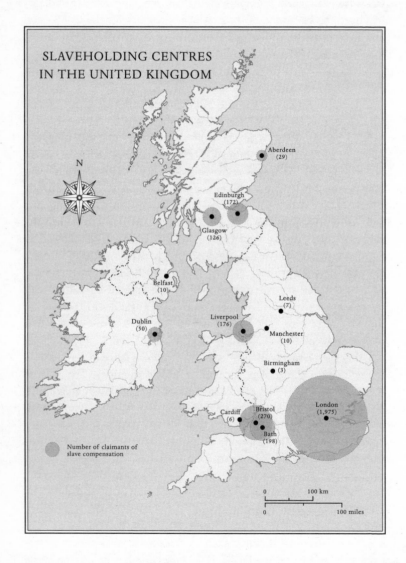

SLAVEHOLDING CENTRES
IN THE UNITED KINGDOM

N

Aberdeen
(29)

Edinburgh
(172)

Glasgow
(126)

Belfast
(10)

Leeds
(7)

Dublin
(50)

Liverpool
(176)

Manchester
(10)

Birmingham
(3)

Cardiff   Bristol
(6)   (270)   London
                         (1,975)
          Bath
          (198)

Number of claimants of
slave compensation

0   100 km

0   100 miles

In the mid-1830s, as compensation was doled out, debate began to turn on whether the apprenticeship system was working. 'The truth is,' confessed Buxton, 'that my spirits rise or fall according to the intelligence from that quarter.' Despite pockets of initial resistance, the apprenticeship system appeared to be successful in several key respects. On Monday, 1 August 1834, on the first day of the new regime, there had not been a single absentee on the Jamaican estate of Amity Hall that belonged to the former Chancellor of the Exchequer, Henry Goulburn. The apprentices were working less: whereas enslaved people had often suffered sixteen-hour days, apprentices were limited to forty-five hours in the week for their former master, with any overtime – and there was overtime on 70 per cent of Jamaican plantations – paid at a daily rate. With such wages, the apprentices were saving to buy early freedom for a stipulated price. Moreover, there were reports of leniency among some colonial judiciaries: when two apprentices in Guiana were caught stealing plantains, and when they threatened the arresting constable with a gun, a local magistrate let them off with a fine of a guinea each, a sentence that would have been unimaginable only a few years before. For some British observers, these early signs were extremely promising. When the Bishop of Jamaica reported to him, Buxton rejoiced to learn that 'the industry of the Negroes when working for wages, has so entirely belied the apprehensions of the planters here'.[24]

Scratching the surface, however, revealed a very different picture. For one thing, the living conditions 'enjoyed' by the apprentices were in some places materially worse than under slavery. In Jamaica, many planters stopped dispensing allowances of fish and meat, or gifts of clothes, rum, and oatmeal at Christmas and harvest-time. In Barbados, 14,000 children had been 'freed' in August 1834, from which point the planters simply refused to supply their parents with provisions for the starving infants. Planters also sought to scupper the apprentices' plans to buy early freedom by appraising their value – and therefore the price of manumission – at exorbitant, unrealistic rates. And for those apprentices who fell foul of the still-capricious law, there awaited all the horrors of the parish workhouse. For the inmates of these 'houses of correction', long days of cutting cane while bound in chains were bookended by punitive sessions on the infamous treadmills, the massive pedal-engines which ground grain and powered watermills.

Workhouse supervisors, who were 'men of hardened and brutal character', seemed to delight in forcing the weakest apprentices onto the treadmill including, in one recorded instance, a heavily pregnant woman. Other cases of brutality saw the sixty-year-old Mary James, who was 'weak and infirm', flogged so badly that she 'could not contain [her] urine', while for the crime of asking 'for a little food for her suffering child', one imprisoned apprentice was sentenced to solitary confinement.[25]

Nor could the apprenticeship system function properly without competent administration, a task that had been conferred in haste to dozens of stipendiary magistrates. Some of these men were white colonists already living in the West Indies, but most came out from Britain and this – really – was where their troubles began. Several died quickly from the 'seasoning fever' that greeted all visitors to the Caribbean; several more were lost to drink, with the governor of Jamaica complaining that two of the island's magistrates had 'died from habitual drunkenness, and that two or three others were expected to perish from the same cause'. Even where they survived, the magistrates had unenviable duties: one of them was charged with policing 7,000 apprentices across a sixty-mile stretch of Guiana, one-third of which was impassable on foot. Their pitiful salaries made the job even harder. Expected to meet their own expenses, the magistrates often ran up debts to planters whose conduct could not be assessed objectively thereafter. Indeed, the magistrates could not win. When they appeased the planters, the abolitionists damned them as the 'servile defendants and purchased instruments' of the colonists; yet when they upbraided the planters for mistreating the apprentices, they were persecuted as agents of the abolitionists. Besides burying four of his eight children in eastern Trinidad and incurring debts of more than £500, the magistrate Edward Dacres Baynes was arrested three times by the local police force.[26]

The major part of the apprenticeship system's problems stemmed from its genesis as a hastily concocted transition period between slavery and freedom. The abolitionists had hated the idea from the start but, in the summer of 1833, negotiators at Westminster had deemed the apprenticeship to be necessary: without the security of guaranteed labour, the Interest would not have consented to emancipation. But there was no reconciliation between the apprentice and the former slaveholder, nor any great sense of improvement in the colonies. Nor could the apprentices escape the unfortunate truth: for all the talk of eventually becoming a 'free black peasantry', they were performing the same dreadful work on the same estates for the same masters as they had done before emancipation. Apprenticeship was slavery in all but name.

Some abolitionists had understood this from the start. As early as October 1834, William Knibb had denounced the system in the starkest terms. 'Oh, this thrice-cursed apprenticeship!' he cried. '[It is] nothing but blood, murderous cells, and chains!' It followed that, after the briefest period of grace, and as soon as detailed reports on the apprenticeship arrived in Britain, the abolitionists pursued its early termination. Buxton made the first move in June 1835 when he called for a parliamentary inquiry into the end of the apprenticeship, but the Melbourne ministry refused him, and predictably so: as Lord Holland noted, any such inquiry would 'open the whole question of apprenticeships, alarm the West Indians about the compensation, and thereby discourage those who are *bona fide* exerting themselves at much trouble and expence to make the new system work'. There was a further, tactical problem with campaigning to abolish a system to which, only two years previously, the abolitionists had consented. As Buxton wrote, 'Gladstone, Lord John Russell, Grey, &c. would have it that I was a friend to the apprenticeship, because I sold [a] division on it, in Committee', and so Buxton was expected to stay 'friendly'. Though Buxton *eventually* secured a select committee on the apprenticeship, it did not deliver the expected results: following a series of optimistic dispatches from the governor of Jamaica, a committee populated by pro-slavery stalwarts such as William Gladstone and Patrick Maxwell Stewart suggested that the apprenticeship could survive intact until 1840, the date of its scheduled conclusion.[27]

Sitting on that committee with Daniel O'Connell and Stephen Lushington was one of Buxton's last acts as the abolitionist leader. Although he was now 'thoroughly liked and respected' and the object of 'constant urbanity' at Westminster, such 'kind feeling' was not automatically shared by his constituents. Despite the Anti-Slavery

Society organising another campaign to procure pledges against the apprenticeship, Buxton was sure that he would lose his seat in the 1837 election that was triggered by the death of William IV. On the day of nominations, Buxton knew the game was at hand, and he summoned George Stephen to the south coast to serve as an emergency campaign manager; Stephen travelled overnight from London, arriving 'unshaven [and] unbreakfasted'. Stephen and Buxton confronted a local Tory party that was well-oiled, ambitious, and schooled in all manner of trickery. 'The Tories had hired a stout mob from the adjacent county,' Buxton reported, 'and as they kept the beer going, our audience [at the hustings] was rather of the noisiest.' Buxton would not stoop to that level. 'It might or might not be my duty to get into Parliament,' he wrote, 'but it could not be my duty to corrupt the electors by beer and bank notes.' On the day of the vote, Buxton accepted his fate and paid tribute to 'the memory of my departed honours'. He declared himself 'glad that I have got a holiday', and confessed that 'I could not have stood the fatigues of Parliament many sessions more'.[28]

The fight against apprenticeship also went on without Zachary Macaulay, who succumbed at the age of seventy to the ravages of unceasing work and financial troubles. A statue was erected to his memory in Westminster Abbey, and even George Stephen refrained from cheap humour by remembering that Macaulay, 'like Atlas ... was useless except to carry a world; and to bear this burthen he was endowed with an industry that was marvellous'.[29]

In the absence of Buxton and Macaulay, the campaign against the apprenticeship system was led by Joseph Sturge, the Quaker merchant whose support had been essential to the formation of the Agency Society in the early 1830s. Although the late Macaulay had regarded Sturge as 'an extremely stupid person', he was an effective leader. After departing Britain in the autumn of 1836 for a six-month-long investigation of the West Indies, Sturge and the Barnsley chemist Thomas Harvey published *The West Indies in 1837*, a polemic which cast an unflinching, unflattering light on the apprenticeship. Quickly selling out its first edition, and bringing 'the battering ram of public opinion' to bear on Parliament, Sturge and Harvey preached that the West Indies were 'clouded by the Apprenticeship, which threatens, if not the ruin of the island, or the disorganization of the community, partial or complete loss of property, to those who now wantonly outrage the rights of their dependent bondsmen'. Moreover, they believed it 'undeniably established, that the Abolition of Slavery does not affect the safety of the state, nor the well-being of the community'. In November that year, a conference at Exeter Hall concluded with a ceremonial march to Downing Street. Echoing the scenes of April 1833, the abolitionists delivered a petition for the immediate end of coerced labour into the hands of the government.[30]

Now directed by the new Central Negro Emancipation Committee, the campaign against the apprenticeship was given greater weight – and a human face – by the *Narrative of Events Since the First of August, 1834*, a pamphlet that was dictated by the Jamaican apprentice James Williams. Aged eighteen at the time of writing, which meant that Williams was only twelve when the Christmas Rebellion shook his parish of St Ann, he narrated a post-emancipation nightmare that was full of vengeful planters, vicious magistrates, and cruel dungeon-masters, where working on the eternally revolving treadmill – known colloquially as 'dancing' – would either exhaust or mutilate the apprentices. 'I have been very ill treated,' Williams began, 'since the new law come in. Apprentices get a great deal more punishment now than they did when they was slaves.' The reason for this was simple malice: 'The master take spite,' he wrote, 'and do all he can to hurt them before the free come.' There was hunger, too. There was no salt, no bonus food at Christmas, and no mackerel. But there was plenty more pain. Williams described seven floggings by 'the Cat' and four spells of imprisonment, and he exposed the lunacy of a system which obliged Williams to compensate his master for the labour that was 'lost' while he was incarcerated. Just as Olaudah Equiano humanised the campaign against the slave trade, and just as Mary Prince gave a name to the campaign against slavery, Williams helped to turn the tide against the apprenticeship.[31]

There was 'but one remedy', claimed Williams's abolitionist allies. 'Half measures are worse than useless,' they wrote. 'It requires but a single, brief, simultaneous and energetic movement, and the struggle is over. Immediately re-organize your Anti-Slavery Societies,' they urged, and 'let the people, with one voice … demand the instant, the unconditional, and the everlasting annihilation of the accursed system.' From the spring of 1838, the end came quickly. In April, the Commons passed a bill to amend the 1833 Abolition Act by regulating working hours and appraisals, abolishing flogging entirely, and ensuring provisions for the apprentices, but it did not suffice. The Colonial Secretary, Lord Glenelg, feared that it was now impossible 'to possess the public mind with just and moderate views'. In May, the abolitionists sneaked a private members' bill in favour of immediate termination through a half-empty Commons, only for the government to secure a full majority in June for a counter-resolution committing the government to the full six years of apprenticeship. By now, though, whatever Parliament did or thought had almost ceased to matter, for as the news of the intensifying campaign against the apprenticeship made its way to the West Indies, many planters took the hint. They were also afraid that, when 'domestic' apprentices went free as scheduled on 1 August 1838, 'field' apprentices might riot in protest, since they had another two years to serve. By June, therefore, the legislatures of Barbados, St Vincent, and St Kitts arranged that *all* apprentices would be set 'free' on 1 August. Soon enough, the governors of Jamaica, Guiana, and Trinidad beseeched their colonies to do the same. The House of Assembly in Jamaica was insensibly angry. 'Our courts are never occupied with the obscenities which disgrace England,' it thundered, 'nor is it under our laws that wretches commit suicide to escape the refuge which is provided for worn-out and aged industry.' But they knew they were beaten. By late June, every colony had consented to end the apprenticeship entirely on 1 August.[32]

On the night of 31 July, the Baptist chapel in Falmouth, Jamaica, prepared for a special service. A large banner proclaiming 'FREEDOM' was stretched across the entrance to the chapel's yard and, underneath it, hundreds of Baptists streamed through to hear William Knibb preach. For almost an hour from eleven o'clock, Knibb led his congregation in 'some verses of a dirge' and 'devotional exercise' until, after a short silence, he spoke. Pointing to the clock in the chapel, he told them: 'The hour is at hand, the monster is dying.' Twelve notes later, he claimed victory: 'The monster is dead.' A few hours later, just before sunrise, Knibb prepared for slavery's funeral. A chain, a whip, and an iron collar were placed in a coffin, which was lowered into a grave. As the coffin disappeared into the dirt, the Baptists sang:

> Now, Slavery, we lay vile form in the dust,
> And, buried for ever, there let it remain:
> And rotted, and covered with infamy's rust,
> Be every man-whip, and fetter, and chain.

At ten o'clock, a thousand free Jamaican children gathered at the chapel. Setting out from the schoolhouse, they followed a carriage that was drawn by two 'gaily caparisoned' horses and draped with the motto, 'The Day of Jubilee'. Meandering through the streets of Falmouth, they came to the chapel-yard, which was 'decorated with flowers and branches of trees'. There, Knibb preached a sermon before leading everyone back to the schoolhouse. The playground was 'covered in boards, and adorned with boughs', and there was 'spread a banquet' for the thousand. 'Everyone having a glass of wine, the health of Queen Victoria was drunk with rapturous applause.' These celebrations, described in a triumphalist biography of William Knibb, would be a convenient place to finish a history of British colonial slavery; indeed, for nearly two hundred years, almost every history of slavery *did* finish here, or earlier. To stop in 1838, however, is to under-play how slavery continued to shape society in both the Caribbean and in Britain – as it does to this day.[33]

Epilogue: Who Else Must Fall?

Memory of slavery in the Caribbean is no sporting matter. Nearly one hundred [and] seventy years since general emancipation in the English-speaking sub-region, the immediacy of the recollection of slavery still angers many in the regional community. It also hinders movement towards ethnic conciliation, and serves to sustain the identity-consciousness that energizes the rapidly emerging reparations movement.[1]

Sir Hilary Beckles, 2007

I think [Churchill] would be very proud of the continuing legacy of Britain in those places around the world ... a stark contrast, of course, with other less fortunate countries that haven't had the benefit of British rule.[2]

Boris Johnson, while Mayor of London, 2014

In the second week of March 2014, the leaders of fifteen Caribbean countries made their way to the island of St Vincent. They came from the Bahamas off the coast of Florida, from Guyana in South America, from Belize on the border of Mexico, and from the islands in the East. Two hundred years ago, this was the kind of region-wide gathering where West Indian planters and merchants would have plotted resistance to plans for abolition. But in 2014 these Caribbean leaders came together for a very different purpose. The previous year, the Caribbean Community (CARICOM) had established its Reparations Commission (the CRC) with a mandate 'to prepare the case for reparatory justice for the region's indigenous and African descendant communities, who are the victims of Crimes against Humanity in the forms of genocide, slavery, slave trading, and racial apartheid'. Chaired by the Barbadian historian Sir Hilary Beckles, this meeting of the CRC would take a momentous decision: one hundred and eighty years after the abolition of slavery in the British colonies, and five decades after the majority of those colonies had secured their independence, these Caribbean nations would now pursue justice for the untold damage they had suffered at British hands. In December 2014, Beckles addressed the General Assembly of the United Nations in New York. Invoking the spirits of Toussaint Louverture, Nelson Mandela, Harriet Tubman, Malcolm X, Martin Luther King, and Maya Angelou, Beckles called upon the nations of Europe to rise to their responsibilities and account for 'the African Holocaust'.[3]

In the popular imagination there is an all-too-common tendency to regard emancipation in 1834, or even the end of the apprenticeship, as the final chapter in the history of colonial slavery. Neither case is true, not least because the legacies of slavery have continued to affect the Caribbean ever since. In the immediate aftermath of abolition, in the late 1830s and 1840s, 'free' black workers were beset by the same wage pressures and horrific power imbalances that affected British labourers at the same time: planters and their managers employed oppressive bargaining tactics, driving down wages, and imposing punitive levies on black workers who wished for 'the continued occupation of the cottages and provision grounds belonging to the estates'. And if absentee planters and merchants were 'ruined' by the 1846 sugar crisis, when all free-grown sugar was admitted to the British market on the same terms, it was the workers who suffered most. Poverty, unemployment, hunger, and disease became the occupational hazards of Caribbean life. As Natasha Lightfoot has shown for Antigua, which was the only colony where the authorities granted liberty *without* going through the apprenticeship, 'freedom rang hollow'.[4]

Nor were the former slaves and their descendants spared the state-led violence which characterised so much of life under the British Empire. In 1864, when the preacher Paul Bogle led several hundred black Jamaicans to the courthouse at Morant Bay to protest against extortionate taxes, food shortages, and deprivation more generally, the white militia opened fire upon them. And when black Jamaicans in the surrounding parish of St Thomas-in-the-East rose up in solidarity with their murdered brethren, the colony's governor, Edward John

Eyre, declared martial law. In the conflict that followed, euphemistically described as the Morant Bay Rebellion, British soldiers massacred 439 black Jamaicans. The British took 354 prisoners, executed many of them, and more than 600 men and women were flogged for their roles in the 'disturbance'.

Little had changed or improved by the turn of the century. When the stevedores of Georgetown went on strike and demanded higher wages, the white colonial forces again shot at unarmed black workers. In the first half of his majestic *Beyond A Boundary*, C.L.R. James describes a childhood in Trinidad that was riven by class disputes and racial antagonism. The Liberal statesman David Lloyd George would then describe the West Indies as 'the slums of the Empire', and the 1945 report of the West India Royal Commission depicted the Caribbean – in admittedly chauvinistic terms – as a region that was crumbling under the weight of disease, malnutrition, depression, and poverty. Most egregiously of all, hundreds of thousands of indentured Indian 'coolies' were shipped to the Caribbean to live and work in appalling conditions. When the *Empire Windrush* sailed in 1948, its passengers left a Caribbean region that, for more than two centuries, had been stewing in British colonial misrule. In other words, when they were released into 'liberty' in 1838, the freed black people of the British Caribbean became hostage to the same institutional cruelty, the same wanton violence, the same widespread deprivation, and the same rapacious greed with which the British were oppressing all other non-white peoples of the Empire.

This is the historical context of the CRC's campaign for reparatory justice, but its legal case for restitution is more complicated. For one thing, the descendants of British slaves have already failed in their claim against Lloyd's of London for financing and underwriting so many slaving voyages. For another, as the judgments of Lords Hardwicke (1749), Mansfield (1772), and Stowell (1827) made clear, slavery was *not* unlawful at the time of enslavement. Moreover, even if specific 'slave money' were claimed, it would never be found, having long since disappeared into the historical ether of the British economy. Further still, the British government does not accept the jurisdiction of the International Court of Justice at the Hague in cases from before 1974.

Even so, there are several helpful precedents. In 2008, the state government of Tasmania awarded AU $2.2 million to the 'stolen generation' of Aboriginal children who were abducted from their families and forcibly adopted by white Australian families. In 2010, the United States Department of Agriculture paid out US $4.5 billion to Native American and black American farmers who since 1887 had been denied access to loans and subsidies. In 2013, the German government made payments of nearly US $1 billion to survivors of the Holocaust. And in 2014, most relevantly for CARICOM's purposes, the British government announced a £19.9 million settlement with survivors of British atrocities during the Mau Mau Uprising in Kenya. The details of that case, and of the British government's attempt to cover up its actions, are truly shocking. Thousands of Mau Mau rebels were beaten, murdered, castrated, and sexually assaulted, and even though the colonial Attorney General deemed this abuse to be 'distressingly reminiscent of conditions in Nazi Germany or communist Russia', he had advised the colony's governor thus: 'If we are going to sin, we must sin quietly'. Indeed, upon decolonisation across the Empire, British officials had embarked upon a widespread mission to destroy evidence of these offences, and 'Operation Legacy' saw MI6 and the FCO burn, bury at sea, or hide millions of classified documents. Some of them dated back to 1662, and many of them concerned historical atrocities in the West Indies.[5]

Nonetheless, CARICOM's pursuit of justice does not involve a demand for financial restitution. There has been no attempt on CARICOM's part to reclaim the *value* of the damage done to the Caribbean, or of the wages that were not paid to African workers. The academic Robert Beckford has calculated this debt as being in the region of £7.5 trillion and, as the Indian politician Shashi Tharoor has remarked, 'no accurate figure is payable and no payable figure is credible'. Instead, politicians, academics, and diplomats from across the Caribbean, led by Hilary Beckles, have worked with a British law firm to craft a ten-point action plan which, they believe, will go some way to redressing the legacies of slavery and colonial misrule. Six of the ten points of action concern repatriation programmes, aid to indigenous Caribbean peoples, cultural and heritage institutions, technology transfer, 'bridges of belonging' to Africa, and psychological rehabilitation. The remaining four points address problems so vast, so pressing, and so endemic that even the most truculent apologist for Empire cannot dispute their relevance.[6]

First, the European nations who perpetrated the slave trade and slavery should dispense with the equivocal 'statements of regret' of the kind issued by David Cameron in 2015, or by Tony Blair in 2007. Upon the bicentennial of the abolition of the slave trade, Blair expressed 'deep sorrow for our nation's role in the slave trade and for the unbearable suffering, individually and collectively, [that] it caused'. The fact that Blair stopped short of apologising drew fire from several quarters. The Archbishop of York, Dr John Sentamu, said that Britain 'should have the sense of saying, "We are very sorry and we have to put the record straight"', and Hilary Beckles reflected that 'it was disgraceful to speak of regret rather than to apologise. That was a disrespectful act on Blair's part as it implied that nothing can be done about it – "Take our expression of regret and go away"'. As CARICOM explains, it is only with full and formal apologies that 'the healing process for victims and the descendants of the enslaved' can begin.[7]

Second, Britain and other former empires should recognise the endemic, pernicious, and long-lasting medical effects of sugar cultivation for what they are: a public health crisis. 'The African-descended population in the Caribbean has the highest incidence in the world of chronic diseases in the forms of hypertension and type-2 diabetes. This pandemic is the direct result of the nutritional experience, physical and emotional brutality, overall stress … associated with slavery, genocide, and apartheid.' CARICOM is really asking a simple question: if a centuries-long diet of sugar, abuse, and brutality have made a people sick, should the guilty not pay for the cure?

Third, Britain should remediate the widespread illiteracy that it bequeathed to Caribbean. The British planter's fear of literacy among the enslaved population was a defining feature of life before emancipation: a person like Samuel Sharpe who could read 'dangerous' parts of the Bible, or political reports in newspapers, was a threat to the stability of the plantation system. The nonconformist missionaries who might have taught the enslaved to read and write were treated as enemies of the Empire. It followed that, even in the 1960s, some 70 per cent of black West Indians were functionally illiterate; the consequent drag on economic development does not require explanation.

Finally, Britain should forgive the debts of its former colonies. As CARICOM relates, the 'Caribbean governments that emerged from slavery and colonialism have inherited [a] massive crisis of community poverty'. The need to 'carry the burden of public employment and social legacies designed to confront colonial legacies' has meanwhile caused Caribbean states to accumulate 'unsustainable levels of public debt that now constitute their fiscal entrapment'. Even more perversely, a great deal of that debt is owned by British institutions. Cancelling that debt, or at least supporting its repayment, is another vital aspect of reparatory justice.

The legacies of Caribbean slavery are many, clear, and dreadful but, rather than pursuing financial compensation, the CARICOM Reparations Commission has identified serious problems that the British government is under an historical, political, and moral obligation to solve. The enduring policy of Britain's governments, however, has been to deflect and deny. When the CARICOM campaign was announced in 2014, the Foreign Office issued this statement: 'We do not see reparations as the answer. Instead, we should concentrate on identifying ways forward, with a focus on the shared global challenges that face our countries in the 21st century. We regret and condemn the iniquities of the historic [sic] slave trade, but these shameful activities belong to the past. Governments today cannot take responsibility for what happened over 200 years ago.'

Yet when the Foreign Office made that statement, the British government was *still* repaying the loan that it raised in 1835 to fund compensation for West Indian slaveholders. This loan had been refinanced repeatedly in the century following emancipation, and it was not until 2015 that it was redeemed in full. This should have been the moment for reflection, consideration, and perhaps – at last – the full and sincere apology that Britain owes to the Caribbean. Instead, in February 2018, HM's Treasury tweeted the triumphalist 'Friday Fact' that, because it had taken so long to pay off the debt, millions of 'living British citizens helped pay to end the slave trade' [sic]. It was not lost on several readers that the British government had effectively invited black Britons to celebrate 'paying taxes to compensate those who enslaved [their] ancestors'.[8]

Enslavement has had long-lasting effects on the West Indies, but what were the legacies of slavery for Britain itself? One might begin with how Britons thought about the world, not least about race. Pro-slavery arguments about civilisation had bastardised stage-based Enlightenment theories, but it was in fact the end of slavery that truly accelerated the racist aspects of imperialist thinking. This might seem counter-intuitive but, after 1834, when imperial authorities could no longer regard Africans as slaves, skin colour became their defining feature. Debates about slavery and race had profound influence on prominent intellectuals, too. The eminent historian and essayist Thomas Carlyle's 'Occasional Discourse on the Negro Question' appeared in *Fraser's Magazine* in 1849 and it is arguably the most famous expression of nineteenth-century British racism. But Carlyle's essay was in fact the toxic imitation of pro-slavery writing from the 1820s and 1830s (much of which, of course, had first appeared in *Fraser's*). When he wrote that the black population of the West Indies was 'very happy', that Africans did not work because they could supply themselves 'by aid of sun and soil with as much pumpkin as will suffice', that 'British Whites are rather badly off', and that British philanthropists were members of a 'Sluggard-and-Scoundrel Protection Society', Carlyle emerged as the direct heir of the pro-slavery polemicists. More worry-ingly, it is not hard to see the descent of pro-slavery ideas about African peoples in the statement of Herbert Morrison, one of the major figures of mid-twentieth-century politics, that Britain's withdrawal from black colonies would be 'like giving a child of ten a latch-key, a bank account, and a shot-gun'.[9]

The defence of slavery had an equally profound influence on British theology. In December 1835, the Oxford clergyman John Henry Newman had preached a sermon entitled 'Slavery allowed not encour-aged under the Gospel' in which he alighted on 'a slave's Christian duty of allegiance and submission to his masters and to the established order'. Taking 1 Corinthians 7:21, a verse once beloved by West Indians, Newman argued that slavery was 'a condition of life ordained by God in the same sense [as] other conditions of life'. Newman might have conceded that the original slaving sin of 'men-stealing' was 'wicked and abominable', but it was 'not a duty to make slaves free and not a sin to have slaves any more than to have subjects'. For the future cardinal, the abolitionists who had claimed the authority of Christianity were 'the blind leading the blind', and 'both were going straight into the ditch'. This was not an isolated burst of pro-slavery bile: in an 1836 essay, Newman reiterated his position that 'everyone should remain in the place where he finds himself'. Even after apprenticeship ended in 1838, Newman maintained that Christians should not interfere with 'civil' institutions such as slavery and, in 1839, he simply repeated the 1835 sermon that called for slaves to be content with their situation. Newman was not the only 'Tractarian' thus inclined, and his editors have noted that his sermons articulated 'the typical Tractarian attitude towards slavery and ... the status quo'. He persisted in the belief that slavery was not 'intrinsically evil', writing in the 1860s that St Paul had tolerated slavery because it was not '*in se* a sin'. Newman went on to be the most important British clergyman of his century; in October 2019, he was canonised by Pope Francis.[10]

Slavery and emancipation were just as important to the development of British economics. For decades, historians have studied a sophisticated, intricate 'conservative' economics that upheld the merits of protective tariffs and imperial integration without realising that the economists who championed these policies – Alexander McDonnell, James MacQueen, Archibald Alison, and John Galt – were pro-slavery polemicists who wrote only to defend the West Indian colonies against plans for emancipation. Economic protectionism in Britain, insofar as it forms a coherent policy, owes much to the defence of slavery.

As the LBS project at UCL has shown,' slavery had a comparably long-standing effect on British writers such as Charles Kingsley, the theorist of 'muscular Christianity' and the author of *Westward Ho!* and *The Water-Babies*. The grandson of a Barbadian slaveholder, Kingsley told his friend and fellow novelist Thomas Hughes that emancipation was a disaster for his family. Such bitterness was evident when Kingsley defended the conduct of Governor Eyre after the Morant Bay Rebellion, blaming colonial tensions 'on congenital differences and hereditary tendencies [between the races] which defy all education'. This racial motif reappeared in *At Last*, Kingsley's 1871 account of his travels to the West Indies. Although he urged his readers to 'remember that we are very seriously in debt to the Negro', he returned with facility to the same shocking language that Peel and Canning once deployed in the House of Commons: 'If, like Frankenstein,' wrote Kingsley, 'we have tried to make a man and made him badly, we must, like Frankenstein, pay the penalty.' The spectres of a slaveholding past haunted other works of Victorian literature.

Theodora Elizabeth Lynch's 1847 novel *The Cotton-Tree* was her tribute to a lost world of colonial contentment and the once-happy bond that supposedly existed between noble white masters and their devoted slaves; her later *Wonders of the West Indies* was 'a poetic chronicle' of the gloried Antilles. The colonial tropes of white superiority and African inferiority were likewise embedded within Anthony Trollope's 1859 travelogue *The West Indies and the Spanish Main*. This was in stark contrast to *Jane Eyre*, where Charlotte Brontë used Bertha Mason to symbolise the degeneracy of white colonial society.[11]

The most dogged memorialist of slavery was Frederick Marryat, the sailor and children's novelist whose eponymous road in Wimbledon in south-west London stretches from the High Street to the walls of the All-England Tennis Club. In *Peter Simple*, Marryat ridiculed the 'mulattos, quadroons, sambos, and niggers of Barbados'. In *Perceval Keane*, the plucky young hero is captured by a brutal black pirate who hated and killed all white men that he met. These racist ravings did not exist in a vacuum. Joseph Conrad believed that Marryat had created priceless legends. 'There is an air of fable about his work,' wrote Conrad. 'Its loss would be irreplaceable, like the curtailment of a national story, or the loss of an historical document. His adventures are enthralling.' Conrad concluded without irony that Marryat was 'the enslaver of youth'. Dickens, too, was spellbound. While reading *Masterman Ready* he wrote that 'I have been chuckling and grinning and clenching my fists and becoming warlike for three whole days!' It was not perhaps coincidence that George Cruikshank, almost the West Indians' in-house cartoonist, was a friend and colleague of Marryat's and later the illustrator of *Oliver Twist* and *Sketches by Boz*.[12]

Nineteenth-century West Indian historians meanwhile embarked on what can only be described as a programme of whitewashing. William Mackinnon was a Tory MP and the heir to an Antiguan fortune, but his 1846 *History of Civilization*, a sweeping eight-volume account of human progress, held forth on the evils of slavery in Egypt, Greece, and Rome without once mentioning slavery in the West Indies. At the same time, Lord Holland's *Memoirs of the Whig Party* declared that emancipation had 'put an end to one of the greatest evils to which the human race has ever been exposed, or at least to our share in the guilt of it', but omitted the fact that Holland himself had possessed hundreds of enslaved people in Jamaica and worked with the West India Interest throughout the 1820s. Archibald Alison's ten-volume history of the French Revolution meanwhile maintained that Haitian independence was 'dreadful'. As he rivalled Thomas Carlyle in popularity, Alison regretted 'the dissimulation and cruelty of the savage character', the great malignance of 'unchained Africans', and their unfortunate relapse into 'savage life'.[13]

Even the great historian among the abolitionists, Thomas Babington Macaulay, found no room for Caribbean slavery in the five volumes of his 1848 masterwork, *The History of England from the Accession of James the Second*. Despite the development of the Royal African Company under the later Stuarts, and despite the massive flow of wealth from the sugar colonies to Britain, there was a 'startling silence' on slavery in Macaulay's pages. As Catherine Hall has related, his father, Zachary, might have had a lifelong preoccupation with Africa and the Caribbean but, after the passage of the Slavery Abolition Act in 1833, Thomas had no time for the 'impracticable, uncompromising reformer'. He disliked 'negrophiles' as much as 'nigger drivers'. The younger Macaulay hated even talking about slavery: he refused the vice-presidency of the Edinburgh Anti-Slavery Society and, once England had done its duty, he could not have cared less about the West Indies, peopled as they were – in his opinion – by 'stupid, ungrateful gangs of negroes'.[14]

There was a further cadre of white West Indians in journalism, not least at *The Times*. George Webbe Dasent was a long-serving assistant editor at the paper of record for twenty-five years and, more relevantly, the son of a St Vincent planter. He lamented that 'untutored Africans' had been 'liberated from restraint' and in his autobiography, *Annals of an Eventful Life*, he pined for a lost world of colonial order and civility, depicting the *planters* as the victims of emancipation. Thomas Chenery, who became editor in 1877, owed his inheritance to Barbadian plantations, while Mowbray Morris, the paper's long-serving manager, was the son of a Jamaican merchant.[15]

It is also notable – and perhaps unavoidable, given how widely slave money penetrated the British economy – that some of the great writers of the twentieth century descended from slaveholding families. Given the African and Caribbean contexts of several of his novels, it may not have been chance that Graham Greene's great-grandfather was Benjamin Greene, the brewer and St Kitts slaveholder who used his ownership of the *Bury & Suffolk Herald* to publish pro-slavery material and delighted in picking fights with Thomas Fowell Buxton. And while the slave-money had run out long before Eric Arthur Blair was born in Bengal, his great-grandfather had nonetheless received more than £4,000 as compensation for 218 enslaved people in Jamaica: that, of course, was a perversion of justice that would have fitted seamlessly into the Orwellian canon.[16]

British universities have their own problems to confront. The Codrington Library at All Souls College, Oxford, was financed by and named after the same Codrington dynasty which owned plantations on Barbados and slandered Buxton; appropriately, in 2017, All Souls launched an annual scholarship for Caribbean students and paid £100,000 to a college in Barbados. At Cambridge, a two-year investigation into the university's historical links to slavery and the slave trade was announced in April 2019, although – as some commentators pointed out at the time – the vast majority of the university's wealth is in fact held independently by the colleges. Three months later, Glasgow University, which is thought to have received the equivalent of £198 million in donations from slave traders and slaveholders, pledged £20 million towards a centre for developmental research that will be co-managed with the University of the West Indies.

Then there is finance. The names of Rothschild, Montefiore, and Baring are central to the history of slavery and emancipation and at least six of the Bank of England's directors in 1827 received slave compensation after 1834. A comparable heritage is shared by two of today's 'big four' accountancy firms: William Welch Deloitte's mother was the daughter of a West Indian planter, while Edwin Waterhouse – a founder of what is now PwC – was the son of a Liverpool cotton-broker who made a claim for enslaved people in British Guiana. Slaveholders played an even more important role in 'the formation and conduct of early insurance companies'. Two of the first five directors of Alliance were slaveholders, as were six of the original directors of Indemnity Mutual Marine, which now trades as Aviva. The slaveholder William Peat Litt was the first chairman of Life, whose business involved leading West Indians such as Thomas Moody and James Colquhoun, while the sugar trade was just as vital to the development of Phoenix. In fact, in the 1790s, some 63 per cent of capital in the marine insurance industry was invested in the West Indian trade.[17]

Legacies of slavery are correspondingly visible in other sectors of the British economy and, when it comes to 'both the City of London and other port cities, the story of slave-wealth's transmission into Britain is above all a story of mercantile capital'. The billion-dollar holding company the Man Group was founded in the 1780s as a sugar brokerage; coincidentally, the cash-and-carry retailer Booker, whose literary prize was once sponsored by Man, was chaired by the Labour peer Jock Campbell, whose family's wealth came from the Caribbean. Nor was the windfall of slave compensation coincidental to the railway boom. Nathaniel Snell Chauncy, the wealthy owner of several thousand enslaved people, willed his estate into the railways of Britain and the wider Empire. John Moss, the West Indian merchant who in 1833 conducted back-channel negotiations over slave compensation, was the inaugural chairman of the Liverpool & Manchester Railway; and George Gibbs, a Bristolian merchant who had major interests in Barbados and Jamaica, was a pioneer of the Great Western Railway that Brunel built from Bristol to Paddington.[18]

Between 1809 and 1874, a total of 592 Britons each died with a slave-earned fortune of more than £100,000, a sum worth over £6 million in today's money. Physical monuments to this wealth decorate the British landscape. Planters like John Gladstone poured their compensation windfall into the spider's web of railways that extended across Great Britain from the 1840s. The Lascelles family built Harewood House outside Leeds with wealth that stemmed from sugar plantations in Barbados. George Repton designed Camerton Court in Somerset for the Jamaican slaveholder John Jarrett. The red sandstone of Peckforton Castle in Cheshire, the family seat of the Tollemaches, was paid for by the sweat of Antiguan slaves. And Westport House in County Mayo, the seat of the Marquess of Sligo, was financed by slave money from Jamaica. Even the greatest monuments of Victorian architecture owe their construction, in part, to slavery. The Albert Memorial in Kensington Gardens, the Foreign Office building on Horse Guards Road, and the imposing Midland Grand Hotel at St Pancras are but three of the most celebrated designs of George Gilbert Scott, the pioneer of the Gothic Revival movement whose start in life owed much to the West Indian wealth of his mother's family. Elsewhere, slave money built entire communities. The seaside resort of Sidmouth was developed by the Jewish-Portuguese magnate Emanuel Lousada, whose family held extensive 'property' in Jamaica and Barbados. The harbour town of Larne in County Antrim owed its town hall, alms-houses, and cemetery to the Demeraran merchant Charles McGarel. And the island of Lundy in the Bristol Channel was purchased and developed in the 1830s by the former Jamaican slaveholder William Hudson Heaven.[19]

And there is a political legacy, for few leading members of the Interest or their allies suffered penalties. They reinvented themselves on the national stage, or at the very least persuaded others to forget this atrocious aspect of their histories. Robert Peel was the dominant political figure of the decade after emancipation. After founding the modern Conservative Party by means of the Tamworth Manifesto, in which he articulated his opposition to change for the sake of change, Peel's crusade against economic protectionism and the consequent repeal of the Corn Laws went a long way towards cultivating the small-government ideology that has defined conservatism ever since. Peel also had the gall, having opposed the abolitionists relentlessly, to claim that history had not recorded 'an act so disinterested, so sublime' as slave emancipation. 'In the progress of ages,' he declared, 'England's naval triumphs will shrink into a more and more narrow space in the records of our race – this moral triumph will fill a broader, brighter page.' Peel hoped 'that this "brighter page" [would] be not sullied by the admission of slave sugar into ... this country by our unnecessary encouragement of slavery and the slave trade'. It was quite the turnaround.[20]

Lesser figures in the pro-slavery resistance enjoyed success after emancipation, too. Peter Borthwick, the young Scotsman who had chased abolitionist lecturers across the country, became MP for Evesham in Worcestershire and then the editor of the *Morning Post*, an essential organ of the conservative press until it folded into the *Telegraph* in the 1930s. The Jamaican slaveholder Alexander Cray Grant retained enough popularity to unseat a Whig MP at the 1840 election for Cambridge, where a local paper described him as 'a most respect-able representative of the Tories, lay and clerical, gown and town, voters and non-voters, bullies, burghers, and bigots'. Other major antagonists in 'the West India Question' were equally untainted by their defence of slavery. After emancipation, the Duke of Wellington served as Foreign Secretary, Colonial Secretary, Leader of the House of Lords, commander-in-chief, and again as a caretaker prime minister. William Gladstone, whose father received compensation worth almost £14 million in today's money, and whose early political career was defined by the defence of Demeraran slavery, was the political giant of the later nineteenth century. Serving four times as prime minister, Gladstone became the paragon of the classical Liberal tradition. A pro-slavery past was no impediment to a political future.[21]

The historian Catherine Hall has observed that Britain's involvement in slavery and the slave trade is often 'marginalized and forgotten [as] something that happened "over there"', that was not part of 'here'. This is true. Britain has not been forced to deal with many legacies of slaveholding because, unlike in the United States, the enslavement of Africans was quarantined at a distance of several thousand miles. Even so, the scars of slavery in Britain itself are real. They are political, economic, and intellectual, but they are physical too: slaveholders and slave money built modern Britain, and this is why so many statues of slaveholders and their allies, and so many places and buildings named after them, are strewn across the land.[22]

Until the first weekend of June 2020, I had been convinced that the statues of men such as Edward Colston should remain in place – not as a means of celebrating whatever good they might have done in other walks of life, but of reminding Britons about their colonial past. I had believed that if making right the wrongs of Britain's past involves *remembering* what was done, then preserving historical artefacts and raising awareness of them were essential parts of the process. Indeed, removing those names and statues would risk obviating what little 'memory' Britons have of their slaveholding history; moreover, as this book has shown, if we were to remove every trace of slaveholding from the face of modern Britain, we would lose a great deal of it. However, the events of that weekend – not to mention the reaction of certain politicians, commentators, and organs of the press to the toppling of Colston and the Black Lives Matter protests more generally – have suggested two things to me.

First, statues of men such as Colston cannot have the effect on public thinking that I once desired without Britons of today possessing a comprehensive level of knowledge, which they often do not have, about the realities – not the mythology – of the British Empire; this book, I hope, will go some small way towards correcting this problem. It is only by white Britons understanding the systemic oppression and brutality with which Britain treated Africa and the Caribbean that white Britons can understand how black Britons may not feel 'at home' today.

Second, wrapping the statue of a Bristolian slave trader in chains and then dumping it into the harbour from which his slave ships had set sail was, as observed by Marvin Rees, the mayor of Bristol, a moment of historical poetry. The statues of Colston and other slavers are not contemporary representations of historical facts; rather, they are posthumous celebrations of those men and their deeds. What they represent is the fact that generations and centuries after the deaths of these men, the British public still deem it fit and proper to memorialise them, despite their role in perpetrating the slave trade and slavery. Now, the removal of these statues represents the fact that Britons of the 2020s – most of them young, many of them black – are prepared to declaim against not only the realities of historical colonialism, but also the unthinking readiness of Britons both historically and currently to celebrate that history.

After Colston, the epilogue to this book was overtaken quickly by events. The Greene King brewery apologised for its historical connections to slavery and announced that it would seek to make reparatory amends. The governing body of Oriel College, Oxford, agreed that its notorious statue of Cecil Rhodes should come down. The long-hidden histories of major banks, firms, universities, and families – many of them mentioned in the preceding pages – were dragged screaming into the spotlight shone at last by mainstream news outlets.

Now, perhaps, new histories can be written. This will not be flagrant revisionism or a national bout of self-loathing; instead, it will be a just and necessary corrective to centuries of self-congratulation. Previous 'histories' of slavery must shoulder the blame. The most influential account of the campaign against the slave trade was published in 1808 by Thomas Clarkson, but Clarkson was the hero of his own history. In the same way, George Stephen's memoirs provide the most colourful account of the campaign against slavery but, in Zachary Macaulay's words, Stephen was 'untrustworthy and self-interested, wanting to take the whole credit of the Abolition to himself'. Self-congratulation was the default reaction to the end of apprenticeship, too. When the children of Falmouth, Jamaica, celebrated the transition to 'freedom' in 1838, they were surrounded by portraits of Clarkson, Brougham, and Wilberforce. In a world where change was attributed to the deeds of 'Great Men', the abolitionists were presented as the white saviours of black Jamaicans; even more insidiously, freedom was their 'gift'. There was no room for Samuel Sharpe, or Mary Prince, or Quamina in those narratives.[23]

Consequently, the British 'remember' that Parliament abolished slavery, but not that Parliament had spent two hundred years encouraging and protecting slavery in the first place; they remember the selflessness of white abolitionists, but not the suffering – let alone the loves, lives, hopes, and dreams – of the enslaved and the sacrifices that they made in order to undermine the institution of slavery. Such selective amnesia is comprehensible: the idea of Wilberforce, Clarkson, and Buxton riding a wave of Christian sentiment to undo great evil is attractive, and every nationalist mythology needs a linear plot driven forward by heroic characters. Indeed, this narrative is much simpler to understand than the truth, which is that emancipation was entirely contingent upon the collapse of the Tories, the reform of Parliament, favourable Cabinet politics *and* slave rebellions in the Caribbean. Until those factors combined with abolitionist pressure in the early 1830s, defending slavery was a credible and often popular position in British society.

Of course, slave emancipation *was* a watershed moment in British history. It marked the culmination of nearly fifty years of abolitionist campaigning that was essential to the creation of the British culture of political voluntarism, and it inspired future generations of British campaigners who assailed the foreign slave trade. As Richard Huzzey has shown, 'Britain's enthusiasm for anti-slavery after [1833] ... did not collapse in the face of Victorian racism, imperialism, or indifference', but survived and flourished in 'chaotic and pluralist forms'. (More troublingly, of course, it became a core justification for the 'civilising' mission which informed the later colonisation of Africa.) The achievement of emancipation also inspired legions of American abolitionists who took

Clarkson and Macaulay as their role models, and who celebrated the anniversary of 1 August 1834 almost as vigorously as they celebrated 4 July 1776, their own Independence Day.[24]

Even so, the 'greatness' of abolition is celebrated for the wrong reasons. It was not 'great' because the British were the first to abolish slavery, since the histories of Haiti, Latin America, and the northern United States prove otherwise. It was not 'great' because it was an act of national altruism, since British slaveholders gave up their 'property' only after securing £20 million in compensation and years of apprenticed labour. Nor was abolition 'great' because the liberated peoples of the West Indies proceeded to enjoy the same rights, liberties, and privileges as white Britons: in reality, they were subjected to four years of apprenticeship, which was slavery in all but name, and then to the same violence, inequality, and rapacity that blighted the lives of the hundreds of millions of other victims of the British Empire.

Instead, abolition should be remembered as a 'great' moment in British history for this reason: when Thomas Fowell Buxton stood up in the House of Commons, when Elizabeth Heyrick boycotted slave-grown sugar, when Mary Prince told her story, and when Samuel Sharpe and Quamina rebelled, they confronted and eventually defeated an extraordinarily powerful enemy. The West India Interest was not just a handful of planters and merchants; it involved hundreds of MPs, peers, civil servants, businessmen, financiers, landowners, clergymen, intellectuals, journalists, publishers, soldiers, sailors, and judges, and all of them went to extreme lengths to preserve and protect colonial slavery. They were supported in these endeavours, fervently and viciously, by the ordinary white colonists of the West Indies and the rentable mobs of British cities. Those people, their money, their ideas, and their politics bequeathed the true and terrible legacies of British slavery, and those are the shameful legacies with which Britain and its former colonies must reckon even now.

Acknowledgements

This book really began in autumn 2010 as a proposal for doctoral research. During the intervening decade I have incurred a great many debts that I will now attempt to repay. First, I must thank John Robertson, Boyd Hilton, and the late Michael O'Brien for supervising my research; the Arts and Humanities Research Council, the Smuts Memorial Fund, and various funds administered by the Faculty of History at the University of Cambridge for financing that research; and Melissa Calaresu, Peter Mandler, and the other historians – both fellows and students – at Gonville & Caius College for making it such a welcoming home. I must also thank Jon Parry and Richard Huzzey for examining my dissertation, and Richard especially for being such a generous and supportive mentor in the years since graduation.

Much of this book was researched and written in libraries, and so I thank the librarians, staff, and archivists of the following institutions: in Cambridge, the University Library, the Seeley Historical Library, the Haddon Library, the Social and Political Sciences Library, the English Faculty Library, the Divinity Faculty Library, Gonville & Caius College Library, and the Cambridgeshire Records Office; in Oxford, the Bodleian Library, the Rhodes House Library, and Balliol College Library; in London, the British Library, the National Archives, the Senate House Library and the Institute of Commonwealth Studies at the University of London, and the Maugham Library at King's College; in Edinburgh, the National Library of Scotland; in Glasgow, the Mitchell Library; in Matlock, the Derbyshire Records Office; in Hawarden, the Flintshire Records Office and the Gladstone Library; in Liverpool, the Liverpool Records Office; in Bristol, the Bristol Records Office; in Belfast, the Public Records Office of Northern Ireland; in Trinidad, the Alma Jordan Library at the University of the

West Indies, St Augustine; in Jamaica, the National Library of Jamaica; and in Manchester, the Main Library of the University of Manchester and the Central Library. In particular, I must thank the Eccles Centre for American Studies at the British Library for granting me a Visiting Fellowship between 2019 and 2021 and for supporting several weeks of research.

Turning a dissertation into a book is not easy and it would have been a great deal harder without the guidance and assistance that I have received. I must therefore thank: my agent, Donald Winchester of Watson Little, for helping me to craft the proposal; my editor, Will Hammond at The Bodley Head, for taking a chance on an unpublished author and refining an occasionally byzantine manuscript into something much more readable; Bill Donohoe for creating this book's maps; Mary Chamberlain for copy-editing and Fiona Allen for proofreading the manuscript; Anneka Sandher for designing such a striking cover; Darren Bennett for designing the picture sections; and everybody else at The Bodley Head – Stuart Williams, Aidan O'Neill, and Lauren Howard – for making this such an enjoyable process.

I have also received the benefit of comments on both the proposal and successive drafts of the manuscript from Akbar Ansari, Mark Bennett, Alix Chartrand, Katie Donington, Allegra Fryxell, Richard Huzzey, Kennetta Hammond Perry, Murray Power, Jake Richards, Simon Skinner, and Felix Waldmann. The book is much better for their kindness and wisdom, and the mistakes that remain are my own.

Last, I thank my parents, to whom this book is dedicated. I owe them everything.

★

All maps © Bill Donohoe 2020. The following images are © the following organisations and individuals and/or reproduced with their permission:

First picture section, page 1 *top* and *bottom left*: Courtesy of the John Carter Brown Library; *bottom right*: Courtesy of the Library of Congress • page 2 *top*: Courtesy of the Henry Lillie Pearce Fund, Museum of Fine Arts, Boston; *bottom*: National Maritime Museum, Greenwich, London, Michael Graham-Stewart Slavery Collection. Acquired with the assistance of the Heritage Lottery Fund • page 3 *top* and *bottom*: Hakewill, A Picturesque Tour of the Island of Jamaica (London, 1825) • page 4 *top* and *bottom*: William Clark, Ten Views of the Island of Antigua (London, 1823). Courtesy of the John Carter Brown Library • page 5 *top left*: Reproduced in John Saunders, Portraits and Memoirs of Eminent Living Political Reformers (London, 1840); *top right*: Courtesy of Wilberforce House, Hull City Museums and Art Galleries / Bridgeman Images; *bottom left*: Frontispiece of Macaulay, Life and Letters (1900); *bottom right*: National Portrait Gallery, London • page 6 *top*: Courtesy of the John Carter Brown Library; *bottom*: Metropolitan Museum of Art. The Elisha Whittelsey Collection, The Elisha Whittelsey Fund, 1959 • page 7 *top left*: © Ickworth House, Suffolk / Bridgeman Images; *top right*: © PLA Collection / Museum of London; *bottom left*: Courtesy of The Baring Archive; *bottom right*: Copyright of Philip Mould Ltd / Bridgeman Images • page 8 *top left*: Courtesy of the Council for World Mission / SOAS Library; *top right*: Elizabeth Heyrick, *Immediate not Gradual Emancipation* [1824] (Philadelphia, 1836); *bottom*: Papers relative to the Wesleyan Mission, 31 (March 1828) •

Second picture section, page 1 *top left*: Yale Center for British Art, Paul Mellon Collection; *middle*: Courtesy of the Library of Congress; *bottom left*: The Ohio State University, Billy Ireland Cartoon Library and Museum; *bottom right*: Courtesy of University of Glasgow Library, Archives & Special Collections • page 2 *top*: National Portrait Gallery, London; *bottom*: Courtesy of Wikimedia Commons • page 3 *top*: Cassell's Illustrated History of England, Vol. V, p. 325. Out of copyright; *bottom*: © Bristol Museum & Art Gallery / Bridgeman Images • page 4 *top left*: Courtesy of the State Library of Victoria; *top and bottom right*: National Portrait Gallery, London; *bottom left*: Courtesy of the Birmingham Museum & Art Gallery • page 5 *top*: Wikimedia Commons; *bottom*: National Maritime Museum, Greenwich, London. Gift of the Executors of Mr and Mrs F H Boxer • page 6 *top*: Courtesy of the Birmingham Museum & Art Gallery; *bottom*: Courtesy of the Library of Congress • page 7 *top left*, *top right* and *bottom*: National Portrait Gallery, London • page 8 *top*: public domain; *bottom*: © Michael Graham-Stewart / Bridgeman Images.

Notes

Preface

1   Shashi Tharoor, *Inglorious Empire: What the British Did to India* (London, 2017), p. 235.
2   'British PM David Cameron arrives in Jamaica', *Jamaica Observer*, 29 September 2015; 'PM announces £300 million fund for Caribbean infrastructure', Gov.uk, 30 September 2015.
3   Caroline Davies, 'How do we know David Cameron has slave owners in family background?', *Guardian*, 29 September 2015.
4   Rowena Mason, 'Slavery reparations call overshadows Cameron's visit to Jamaica', *Guardian*, 30 September 2015; idem, 'Jamaica calls for Britain to pay billions of pounds in reparations for slavery', *Guardian*, 29 September 2015.
5   'PM's speech to the Jamaican Parliament', Gov.uk, 30 September 2015.
6   Mason, 'Jamaica calls'; 'UK signs deal to send prisoners home', Gov.uk, 30 September 2015.
7   David Cameron, *For the Record* (London, 2019); 'British values: article by David Cameron', Gov.uk, 15 June 2014; 'Full text: David Cameron's speech', *Guardian*, 24 August 2005.
8   Reginald Coupland, *The Empire in These Days: An Interpretation* (London, 1935), p. 268; Ian Cobain, *The History Thieves: Secrets, Lies, and the Shaping of a Modern Nation* (London, 2017), pp. 78–9; Toyin Agbetu, 'My protest was born of anger, not madness', *Guardian*, 3 April 2007; Robert Booth, 'UK government refuses to fund slavery memorial endorsed by Johnson in 2008', *Guardian*, 10 December 2019.
9   Dan Keenan, 'Two more held in Ballymena murder inquiry', *Irish Times*, 13 May 2006; 'Hurricane Katrina was sent to punish gays, says DUP man', *Belfast Telegraph*, 18 November 2005.
10 Michael Taylor, 'The ideas of the defence of British colonial slavery, 1823–33' (unpublished PhD dissertation, University of Cambridge, 2014).
11 For the division between 'pro-slavery' and 'anti-abolitionist', see Paula E. Dumas, *Proslavery Britain: Fighting for Slavery in an Era of Abolition* (Basingstoke, 2016). For professions of hatred for slavery 'in the abstract', see, *inter alia*: 'A Jamaica Proprietor', *Letter to the Duke of Wellington, on the subject of West India Slavery* (London, 1829) pp. 3–4; J.E. Alexander, *Transatlantic Sketches, comprising Visits to the Most Interesting Scenes in North and South America, and the West Indies, with Notes on Negro Slavery* (2 vols., London, 1833), 1:109; and Edward Irving, *A Statement of the Cause which Affects the Decrease or Increase of the Slave Population in the British Colonies* (London, 1833), p. 4.

Introduction: Demerara, 1823

1   Joshua Bryant, *Account of an Insurrection of the Negro Slaves in the Colony of Demerara, which broke out on the 18th of August, 1823* (Georgetown, 1824), v–vi.

2   Ibid., p. 1. The Demerara Rebellion of 1823 has been the subject of considerable scholarship. The most detailed study, to which this chapter owes much, is: Emilia Viotti da Costa, *Crowns of Glory, Tears of Blood: The Demerara Slave Rebellion of 1823* (Oxford, 1994). Other valuable works include: Michael Craton, *Testing the Chains: Resistance to Slavery in the British West Indies* (London, 1982) and Gelien Matthews, *Caribbean Slave Revolts and the British Abolitionist Movement* (Baton Rouge, LA, 2006).

3   Two excellent studies of death, disease, and the simple struggle for survival are: Vincent Brown, *The Reaper's Garden: Death and Power in the World of Atlantic Slavery* (Cambridge, MA, 2008) and Randy M. Browne, *Surviving Slavery in the British Caribbean* (Philadelphia, 2017).

4   'Unfinished letter of John Smith to the Secretary of the London Missionary Society, 21 August 1823' in *The London Missionary Society's Report of the Proceedings against the late Rev. J. Smith, of Demerara, Minister of the Gospel* (London, 1824), p. 184; John Smith, 'A Journal containing Various Occurrences at Le Resouvenir, Demerary, commenced in March, 1817' (Journal of John Smith), 15 March 1817, the National Archives, London (TNA), Records of the Colonial Office (CO), 111/46.

5   Bryant, *Account of an Insurrection*, p. 20.

6   Ibid., pp. 19, 20.

7   Pitt the Younger's quote and the examples of French cruelty in Saint Domingue are taken from Adam Hochschild's compelling history of the earlier British campaign against the slave trade, *Bury the Chains: Prophets and Rebels in the Fight to Free an Empire's Slaves* [2005] (New York, 2006), pp. 261, 258. In the author's estimation, the best single-volume history of the Haitian Revolution remains C.L.R. James's seminal *The Black Jacobins: Toussaint L'Ouverture and the San Domingo Revolution* (London, 1938).

8   Ibid., pp. 268, 257; for discussion of Zombi's role in the construction of 'the zombie', see: Raphael Hoermann, 'Figures of Terror: The "Zombie" and the Haitian Revolution', *Atlantic Studies*, 14 (2017), 152–73.

9   Viotti da Costa, *Crowns of Glory*, pp. 145, 182, 180.

10   Ibid., p. 181; Journal of John Smith, 22 October 1822; *Report of Proceedings against Smith*, p. 83.

11   The quotations in this and the subsequent twelve paragraphs are all taken from Bryant's *Account of an Insurrection* at, respectively, pp. 5; 7–9; 9–10; 7; 28–9; 13, 14; 53, 61, 83, 84.

12   Ibid., p. 90; Craton, *Testing the Chains*, p. 289.

13   Bryant, *Account of an Insurrection*, p. 18; *Morning Chronicle*, 20 October 1823.

14   Simón Bolívar, 'The Angostura Discourse' in *The Political Thought of Bolivar: Selected Writings*, ed. G.E. Fitzgerald (The Hague, 1971), p. 49.

1. An Evil of Our Own Creation

1   Olaudah Equiano, *The Interesting Narrative* [1789] *and Other Writings*, ed. Vincent Carretta (London, 2003), pp. 54–5.

2   The most accessible single-volume history of Barbados is probably Matthew Parker's *The Sugar Barons: Family, Corruption, Empire, and War* (London, 2012).

3   *The Narrative of General Venables, with an Appendix of the Papers relating to the Expedition to the West Indies and the Conquest of Jamaica, 1654–1655*, ed. C.H. Firth (London, 1900), pp. 136, 137.

4   Among the most compelling recent histories of the Atlantic slave trade is Marcus Rediker's *Slave Ship: A Human History* (London, 2008). The most strident account of how this process affected Africa remains: Walter Rodney, *How Europe Underdeveloped Africa* (London, 1972).

5   Eric Williams, *Capitalism and Slavery* (Chapel Hill, NC, 1944); Joseph E. Inikori, *Africans and the Industrial Revolution: A Study in International Trade and Economic Development* (Cambridge, 2002); James Wallace, *A General and Descriptive History of*

the Ancient and Present State of the Town of Liverpool (Liverpool 1796), p. 229; George III qu. in Peter Fryer, *Staying Power: The History of Black People in Britain* (London, 1984), p. 18.

6   For the Yorke–Talbot opinion, see: Travis Glasson, '"Baptist doth not bestow Freedom": Missionary Anglicanism, Slavery, and the Yorke-Talbot Opinion, 1701–30', *The William and Mary Quarterly*, 67 (2010), 279–318, at p. 279; for the second pronouncement, see: '*Pearne v Lisle*' in Charles Ambler, *Reports of the Cases Argued and Determined in the High Court of Chancery, with Some Few in Other Courts* (London, 1790), p. 84.

7   The seminal work on this moment in history is: Christopher Leslie Brown, *Moral Capital: Foundations of British Abolitionism* (Chapel Hill, NC, 2006).

8   The details of Sharp's biography are taken from: Hochschild, *Bury the Chains*, pp. 41–4.

9   *Morning Chronicle*, 23 June 1772; for the full text of Mansfield's judgment, see: *Somerset v. Stewart*, 14 May 1772 in Capel Lofft (ed.), *Reports of Cases Adjudged in the Court of King's Bench, from Easter Term 12 Geo. 3. to Michaelmas 14 Geo. 3.* (Dublin, 1790), pp. 51–74.

10   The details in this and the next two paragraphs are taken from the authoritative account of the Zong massacre: James Walvin, *The Zong: A Massacre, the Law, & the End of Slavery* (New Haven, CT, 2011).

11   Equiano, *Interesting Narrative*, passim. However, as Ryan Hanley has shown in the case of James Albert Ukawsaw Gronniosaw, 'black intellectuals, far from being solely concerned with abolitionism, participated in a broad array of political and social movements during the eighteenth century, occasionally even those that supported slavery': Ryan Hanley, 'Calvinism, Proslavery and James Albert Ukawsaw Gronniosaw', *Slavery & Abolition*, 36 (2015), 360–81.

12   Ottobah Cugoano, *Thoughts and Sentiments on the Evil and Wicked Traffic of the Slavery and Commerce of the Human Species* [1787] (Cambridge, 2013), p. 11.

13   Abingdon qu. in Judith Jennings, *The Business of Abolishing the British Slave Trade, 1783–1807* (Oxford, 1997), p. 80.

14   Norfolk qu. in Hochschild, *Bury the Chains*, p. 308. For these visual representations of abolition, see: John Coffey, '"Tremble, Britannia!": Fear, Providence and the Abolition of the Slave Trade, 1758–1807', *English Historical Review*, 127 (2012), 844–81.

15   Wilberforce in *Hansard*, House of Commons, 28 February 1805, 1st ser., III, 668–73; Peel, 18 March 1807, Add MS 40605, fo. 1, Papers of Robert Peel (Peel Papers), British Library, London; Reginald Coupland, *The British Anti-Slavery Movement* (London, 1933), p. 116.

16   Thomas Clarkson, *The History of the Rise, Progress, and Accomplishment of the Abolition of the African Slave Trade by the British Parliament* (London, 1839), p. 116; William Wilberforce, *An Appeal to the Religion, Justice, and Humanity of the Inhabitants of the British Empire* (London, 1823), p. 55; Ellen Gibson Wilson, *The Great Yorkshire Election of 1807: Mass Politics in England before the Age of Reform*, ed. Edward Royle and James Walvin (Lancaster, 2015), p. 280.

17   Clarkson, *History*, pp. 117, 615.

18   For this period in Sierra Leone's history, see: Padraic X. Scanlan, *Freedom's Debtors: Antislavery in Sierra Leone in the Age of Revolution* (New Haven, CT, 2017); *Report of the Committee of the African Institution, Read to the General Meeting on the 15th July, 1807* (London, 1807), p. 9.

19   *Hansard*, Commons, 6 June 1814, 1st ser., xxvii, cc1078–9; 'Definitive Treaty with France', *Parliamentary Debates from the Year 1803 to the Present Time* (London, 1816), 32:253

20   There was a brief 'pamphlet war' over the registry proposal involving, *inter alia*: James Stephen, *Reasons for Establishing a Registry of Slaves in the British Colonies* (London, 1815) and, on the other side, 'Colonist', *The Edinburgh Review and the West*

Indies: with Observations on the Pamphlets of Messrs Stephen, Macauley &c. and Remarks on the Slave Registry Bill (Glasgow, 1816).

21   Col. Edward Codd to James Leith, 25 April 1816, TNA, CO 28/85. Other details taken from: Andrea Stuart, *Sugar in the Blood: A Family's Story of Slavery and Empire* (London, 2012), pp. 273–83.

22   Qu. in Hochschild, *Bury the Chains*, p. 319; Michael Craton, 'Proto-Peasant Revolts? The Late Slave Rebellions in the British West Indies, 1816–1832', *Past & Present*, 85 (1979), 99–125, at p. 108.

23   One of the most detailed studies of Cropper's influence over the early anti-slavery campaign is: Mark Jones, 'The mobilisation of public opinion against the slave trade and slavery: popular abolitionism in national and regional politics, 1787–1838' (unpublished D.Phil dissertation, University of York, 1998); James Cropper to William Wilberforce, 3 May 1821, in Cropper, *Letters Addressed to William Wilberforce, M.P., Recommending the Encouragement of the Cultivation of Sugar in Our Dominions in the East Indies* (Liverpool, 1822), p. 9. See also K. Charlton, 'James Cropper and Liverpool's Contribution to the Anti-Slavery Movement', in *Transactions of the Historic Society of Lancashire and Cheshire*, 123 (1971), 57–80.

24   George Stephen, *Antislavery Recollections: In a Series of Letters Addressed to Mrs Beecher Stowe* (London, 1854), p. 84; Jones, 'Mobilisation', pp. 144, 154; Cropper to Zachary Macaulay, 21 October 1822, qu. in David Brion Davis, 'James Cropper and the British Anti-Slavery Movement, 1821–1823', *Journal of Negro History*, 45 (1960), 241–58, at p. 253.

25   Robert Isaac Wilberforce and Samuel Wilberforce, *The Life of William Wilberforce* (London, 1843), p. 506.

2. Hell and Paradise

1   *Lady Nugent's Journal: Jamaica One Hundred Years Ago* [1907] (Cambridge, 2010), p. 36.

2   Mary Prince, *The History of Mary Prince* [1831], ed. Sara Salih (London, 2004), p. 38.

3   For biographical details of Clarkson, see: Hochschild, *Bury the Chains*, pp. 88–92; Hugh Brogan, 'Thomas Clarkson', *ODNB*. For the 'box', see: Jane Webster, 'Collecting for the cabinet of freedom: the parliamentary history of Thomas Clarkson's chest', *Slavery & Abolition*, 38 (2017), 135–54, at pp. 135, 148.

4   Bryan Edwards, *The History, Civil and Commercial, of the British West Indies* (5th edn, 5 vols., London, 1819), 2:8.

5   Ibid., 1:8–12.

6   *Lady Nugent's Journal*, pp. 74, 2, 95.

7   James Robertson, 'Giving Directions in Spanish Town, Jamaica: Comprehending a Tropical Townscape', *Journal of Urban History*, 35 (2009), 718–42, at p. 725.

8   Charles Leslie, *A New History of Jamaica, in Thirteen Letters from a Gentleman to his Friend* (Dublin, 1741), p. 20; Christer Petley, *Slaveholders in Jamaica: Colonial Society and Culture during the Era of Abolition* (Oxford, 2009), p. 41; Margaret Williamson, 'Africa or old Rome? Jamaican slave naming revisited', *Slavery & Abolition*, 38 (2017), 117–34.

9   Parker, *Sugar Barons*, p. 260; Edwards, *History*, 2:206; Parker, *Sugar Barons*, p. 260.

10   Petley, *Slaveholders*, p. 54.

11   Studholme Hodgson, *Truths, from the West Indies* (London, 1838), pp. 101–2.

12   Christer Petley, *White Fury: A Jamaican Slaveholder and the Age of Revolution* (Oxford, 2018), pp. 64–6.

13   'Treatment of slaves in Barbadoes', *Christian Remembrancer*, 5 (1823), 406–8, at p. 408; James Franklin, *A Short View of the West India Question* (London, 1828), p. 39; 'Candidus', *A Letter, Addressed to Edward Bacon, Esq., upon his Sentiments Respecting Slaver in the West Indies* (2nd edn, Ipswich, 1830), p. 2.

14   J. Henry H. Holmes, *An Appeal to the Good Sense and Justice of the Inhabitants of the British Empire … in Respect to Slavery and the West Indies* (n.p., 1823), p. 53; *Barbadian*, 18 October 1823; *Address to the Electors of Great Britain, on the Condition of the Negroes in the British West Indies* (London, 1831), p. 5; Robert Hibbert, *Facts, Verified upon Oath, in Contradiction of the Report of the Rev. Thomas Cooper, concerning the General Condition of the Slaves in Jamaica* (London, 1824), p. 24; Henry de la Beche, *Notes on the Present Condition of the Negroes in Jamaica* (London, 1825), pp. 10–11.

15   John Gibson Lockhart, 'The West Indian Controversy II', *Blackwood's Edinburgh Magazine*, 14 (1823), 647–66, at p. 654; Franklin, *Short View*, p. 38; James MacQueen, 'Letters to the Right Hon. E.G. Stanley' [Letter I], *Blackwood's Edinburgh Magazine*, 34 (1833), 231–57, at p. 245; Franklin, *Short View*, pp. 38–9.

16   William Sells, *Remarks on the Condition of the Slaves in the Island of Jamaica* (London, 1823), *passim*; *Cheap Charity: A Dialogue on the Present Condition of the Negroes* (2nd edn, London, 1824); Henry Nelson Coleridge, *Six Months in the West Indies, in 1825* (London, 1826), p. 136; *The Voice of the West Indies, and the Cry of England* (London, 1832), p. 10.

17   *West Indian Reporter (WIR)*, 23 (1829), p. 141; J. Stewart, *A View of the Past and Present State of the Island of Jamaica* (Edinburgh, 1823), p. 220; Alexander, *Transatlantic Sketches*, p. 310; 'The Anti-Slavery Society', *Fraser's Magazine*, 1 (1830), 610–22, at p. 616.

18   Prince, *History of Mary Prince*, p. 3.

19   Ibid., pp. 19, 20–21, 25, 21.

20   Ibid., pp. 28, 19.

21   Poster in Jeffrey David Pardue, 'Agent of imperial change: James MacQueen and the British Empire, 1778–1870' (unpublished PhD dissertation, University of Waterloo, 1996), p. 82.

22   Prince, *History of Mary Prince*, pp. 15–16.

23   Trevor Burnard, *Mastery, Tyranny, & Desire: Thomas Thistlewood and His Slaves in the Anglo-Jamaican World* (Chapel Hill, NC, 2004), p. 104

24   Ibid., pp. 161, 82, 31.

25   Petley, *Slaveholders*, p. 44; *The Posthumous Works of the Late Rev. John Newton* (Philadelphia, 1809), 2:239; John Newton, *The Journal of a Slave Trader* [1750–54], ed. Bernard Martin and Mark Spurrell (London, 1962), p. 75; Equiano, *Interesting Narrative*, p. 104; Prince, *History of Mary Prince*, p. 24.

26   Burnard, *Mastery*, pp. 162–3; Prince, *History of Mary Prince*, pp. 59, 9–12.

27   *Anti-Slavery Monthly Reporter (ASMR)*, 2 (July 1825), p. 4.

28   Prince, *History of Mary Prince*, p. 38; Wilberforce, *Appeal*, p. 3; Thomas Clarkson, *Thoughts on the Necessity of Improving the Condition of the Slaves in the British Colonies, with a View to Their Ultimate Emancipation* (London, 1823), p. 5.

3. For All the Blood Spilt

1   *Hansard*, House of Commons, 15 May 1823, 2nd ser., IX, c358.

2   Walter Thornbury, 'The Poultry', in *Old and New London: Volume 1* (London, 1878), 416–24.

3   John Timbs, *Club Life of London with Anecdotes of the Clubs, Coffee-Houses, and Taverns of the Metropolis during the 17th, 18th and 19th Centuries* (2 vols., London, 1866), 2:139–41.

4   Catherine Hall, 'Anti-Slavery Society', *ODNB*; Jones, 'Mobilisation', p. 147.

5   J.R. Oldfield, 'Zachary Macaulay', *ODNB*; Catherine Hall, *Macaulay and Son: Architects of Imperial Britain* (London, 2012), pp. 3–4; Iain Whyte, *Zachary Macaulay, 1768–1838: The Steadfast Scot in the British Anti-Slavery Movement* (Liverpool, 2011), p. 191.

6   Patrick C. Lipscomb III, 'James Stephen (1758–1832) (ODMB)'; *The Memoirs of James Stephen, Written by Himself for the Use of His Children*, ed. Merle M. Bevington (London, 1954), pp. 12–13.

7   Coupland, *Anti-Slavery Movement*, pp. 118–20; Olwyn Mary Blouet, 'Sir Thomas
        Fowell Buxton (1786–1845)', *ODNB*; *Memoirs of Sir Thomas Fowell Buxton, Bart., with
        Selections from His Correspondence*, ed. Charles Buxton (London, 1848), p. 177; Stephen,
        Anti-Slavery Recollections, p. 224.

8   For this period in the Interest's history, see: Lillian M. Penson, 'The London West
        India interest in the eighteenth century', *English Historical Review*, 36 (1921), 373–92;
        Andrew O'Shaughnessy, 'The formation of a commercial lobby: the West India
        interest, British colonial policy, and the American Revolution', *Historical Journal*, 40
        (1997), 71–95.

9   M.H. Port, 'Isaac Gascoyne (c.1763–1841)', in *The History of Parliament: The House of
        Commons, 1790–1820*, ed. R.G. Thorne (London, 1986); Stephen Conway, 'Banastre
        Tarleton (1754–1833)', *ODNB*; Martin Lynn, 'The profitability of the early nineteenth-
        century palm oil trade', *African Economic History*, 20 (1992), 77–97. The surviving
        records of the Liverpool West India Association are patchy: Minutes of the Liverpool
        West India Association, Liverpool, Liverpool Record Office (LWIA), WES/380/1/2.

10   Stephen Farrell and David R. Fisher, 'Philip John Miles (1774–1845)', in *The History
        of Parliament: The House of Commons, 1820–1832*, ed. D.R. Fisher (Cambridge, 2009);
        Kenneth Morgan (ed.), *The Bright-Meyler Papers: a Bristol-West India Connexion, 1732–
        1837* (Oxford, 2007); 'A Friend to True Humanity', *An Appeal to Common Sense in
        Behalf of Justice, Humanity, and Religion, in a Letter Addressed to Henry Bright, Esq.,
        M.P.* (Bristol, 1823); Charles Payne to George Saintsbury, 26 July 1832, Minutes of
        the Bristol West India Association, Bristol Records Office, Bristol (BWIA),
        SMV/8/3/2/3; William Lloyd Garrison (ed.), *The Lectures of George Thompson, with
        . . . A Brief History of His Connection with the Anti-Slavery Cause* (Boston, MA, 1836), vii.

11   Minutes of the Glasgow West India Association, Mitchell Library, Glasgow (GWIA),
        TD1683/1/1–2; 'Colin Campbell of Colgrain (1782–1863)', *Legacies of British Slave-
        Ownership* [www.ucl.ac.uk/lbs] (*LBS*); 'James Ewing of Strathleven (1775–1853)', *LBS*.
        For MacQueen, see David Lambert, 'The "Glasgow King of Billingsgate": James
        MacQueen and an Atlantic Proslavery Network', *Slavery & Abolition*, 29 (2008),
        389–413, and *Mastering the Niger: James MacQueen's Map of Africa and the Struggle over
        Atlantic slavery* (Chicago, 2013); Michael Taylor, 'The British West India Interest and
        Its Allies, 1823–1833', *English Historical Review*, 133 (2018), 1478–1511, at p. 1494.

12   For details of the Interest's early meetings, see: David Beck Ryden, 'The Society
        of West India Planters and Merchants in the Age of Emancipation, c.1816–35'
        (unpublished paper given at the Economic History Society Annual Conference,
        27–29 March 2015), pp. 3–5; H.M. Stephens, 'Ellis, Charles Rose, first Baron Seaford
        (1771–1845)', *ODNB*; A. Aspinall, 'The Canningite party', *Transactions of the Royal
        Historical Society*, 17 (1934), 177–226, at p. 177. The original papers, minutes and records
        of the West India Interest (West India Committee Records) are now held at the
        Alma Jordan Library, University of the West Indies, St Augustine, Trinidad and
        Tobago (WICR); microfiche copies are held at the Institute for Commonwealth
        Studies, Senate House Library, University of London, London (ICS).

13   *Anti-Slavery Society Manifesto*, 13 February 1823, p. 3; Hochschild, *Bury the Chains*, p.
        323; Jones, 'Mobilisation', p. 158; James Walvin, *England, Slaves, and Freedom, 1776–1838*
        (University Press of Mississippi, Jackson, 1986), p. 151.

14   Jones, 'Mobilisation', p. 159.

15   Walvin, *England*, pp. 149–50; qu. in Jones, 'Mobilisation', pp. 165–6.

16   Jones, 'Mobilisation', pp. 157, 161; qu. in Whyte, *Macaulay*, p. 177.

17   *The Periodical Press of Great Britain and Ireland: or, An Inquiry into the State of the
        Public Journals, Chiefly as Regards Their Moral and Political Influence* (London, 1824),
        p. 1; Wilberforce, *Appeal*; James Stephen (I), *The Slavery of the British West India
        Colonies Delineated, as it Exists, both in Law and Practice* (2 vols., London, 1824–30);
        Zachary Macaulay, *Negro Slavery; or, a View of Some of the More Prominent Features
        of that State of Society* (London, 1823).

18   Jones, 'Mobilisation', p. 150.
19   Minutes of the West India Literary Committee, WICR, Boxes 5/1 and 6/7, 30 June 1823; ASMR 50:28, 6:52–3.
20   'To Wilberforce', Cobbett's Weekly Register, 13 December 1823; Literary Committee, 27 December 1823; An Official Letter from the Commissioners of Correspondence of the Bahama Islands, to George Chalmers, Esq., Colonial Agent, Concerning the Proposed Abolition of Slavery in the West Indies (London, 1823); Literary Committee, 1 and 8 December 1823; The Times, 17 December 1823; Joseph Sandars, A Letter Addressed to the Liverpool Society for the Abolition of that Society (Liverpool 1824); Literary Committee, 12 January 1824; W.P. Courtney, 'James Heywood (1788–1864)', rev. Bernard Nurse, ODNB; Minutes of the West India Standing Committee, ICS, M915/4, 10 May 1824; Coleridge, Six Months. For Markland's representation of Coleridge, see: Markland to John Murray II, 20 February 1826, Papers of John Murray (Murray Papers), National Library of Scotland, Edinburgh (NLS), MS 40778, fo. 5.
21   Blackwood's complicity in the pro-slavery moment has often been overlooked by historians. See, for example: David Finkelstein, The House of Blackwood: Author-Publisher Relations in the Victorian Era (University Park, PA, 2002); idem (ed.), Print Culture and the Blackwood Tradition, 1805–1930 (Toronto, 2006); R.S. Morrison and D.S. Roberts, eds., Romanticism and Blackwood's Magazine: 'An Unprecedented Phenomenon' (Basingstoke, 2013). Thomas C. Richardson, 'John Gibson Lockhart (1794–1854)', ODNB; John Gibson Lockhart, 'The West Indian Controversy', BEM, 14 (1823), 437–59; idem., 'West Indian Controversy II'; idem., 'The West Indian Controversy. No. III', BEM, 15 (1824), 68–82; and idem., 'The West Indian Controversy. No. IV', BEM, 16 (1824), 682–97. 'Controversy I', p. 442; John Gibson Lockhart to William Blackwood, September 1823, Papers of William Blackwood, NLS (Blackwood Papers), MS 4010, fo. 217; NLS, MacQueen to Blackwood, 1 April 1824, Blackwood Papers, MS 4012, fo. 267; MacQueen to Blackwood, 5 July 1833, Blackwood Papers, MS 4036, fo. 194; Literary Committee, 24 May 1828.
22   J.B. Cutmore (ed.), Conservatism and The Quarterly Review: A Critical Analysis (London, 2007), p. 15; ASMR (1829), 53:101; [Charles Rose Ellis and Robert Wilmot-Horton], 'West India Colonies', Quarterly Review, 30 (1824), 559–87; Joseph Lowe, 'Condition of the Negroes in Our Colonies', QR, 29 (1823), 475–508, in respect of which Lowe was paid £150 (UWI, WICR, Box 5/1, Literary Committee, 12 January 1824); John Miller and John Taylor Coleridge, 'West Indian Slavery', QR, 32 (1825), 506–44; Markland to Murray, 16 May 1831, Murray Papers, MS 40778, fo. 38; Stephen Isaacson, A Vindication of the West-India Proprietors, in a Speech Delivered at Mansion House Chapel, Camberwell, August 8, 1832 (London, 1832), p. 9; ASMR (1826), 11:175.
23   'Negro Slavery', Gentleman's Magazine, 96 (1826), 317–20, at p. 317; Ulrich Pallua, 'Images of Africans in British Slavery Discourse: Pro- and Anti-Slave Trade/Slavery Voices in The Gentleman's Magazine and The Monthly Review, 1772–1833', Stichproben, 16 (2009), 17–43, at pp. 37, 33; Memoirs of Buxton, p. 157; ASMR (1829), 45:429.
24   Anti-Slavery Manifesto, p. 3; A.G.L. Shaw, 'James Stephen (1789–1859)', ODNB; 'Letter from Lord Bathurst to the Duke of Manchester, Governor of Jamaica, concerning the Attitude of the Assembly to Slavery', 5 November 1823, National Library of Jamaica, Kingston, MS 724; James Stephen (II) to Zachary Macaulay, 16 June 1824, in The Life and Letters of Zachary Macaulay, ed. Viscountess Knutsford (London, 1900), p. 421.
25   Hansard, Commons, 18 March 1823, IX, cc624–9.
26   Biographical details for all the MPs mentioned here may be found in Fisher's volume of The History of Parliament that covers 1820 to 1832 and also on the Legacies of British Slave-Ownership website. Specific quotations have been taken from: J.A. Hamilton, 'Holmes, William (1779–1851)', rev. H.C.G. Matthew, ODNB; David R. Fisher, 'Joseph Marryat (1757–1824)' History of parliament, (HP), VI, 350–3;
27   Hansard, Commons, 15 May 1823, IX, cc257–75.

28 The foremost modern biography of Castlereagh is: John Bew, *Castlereagh: A Life* (Oxford, 2012).

29 *Hansard*, Commons, 15 May 1823, IX, cc275–87

30 Stephen, *Anti-Slavery Recollections*, p. 63; *Hansard*, Commons, 15 May 1823, IX, cc359–60.

31 George Canning to Robert Wilmot-Horton, 21 April 1826, Papers of Robert Wilmot-Horton, Derbyshire Records Office, Matlock (RWH Papers), D3155/WH/2760, fo. 13; Canning to Wilmot-Horton, 28 August 1825, RWH Papers, D3155/WH/2760, fo. 11; James Stephen (II) to Lord Bathurst, 16 October 1827, RWH Papers, D3155/WH/2941; George Hibbert, 13 June 1823, D3155/WH/2814, fo. 9.

4. The Ghosts of Bunker Hill

1 John Watt to James Watt, Kingston, 8 September 1823, Watt Family Correspondence, Public Records Office of Northern Ireland, Belfast (PRONI), MIC/135/1.

2 Edward B. Rugemer, *The Problem of Emancipation: The Caribbean Roots of the American Civil War* (Baton Rouge, LA, 2008), p. 84.

3 Charles C.F. Greville, *The Greville Memoirs: A Journal of the Reigns of King George IV, King William IV, and Queen Victoria*, ed. Henry Reeve (8 vols., London, 1899), 3:118. The official copies of Bathurst's circulars to the various colonial governors are found in *Papers ... In Explanation of the Measures Adopted by His Majesty's Government for the Melioration of the Condition of the Slave Population in His Majesty's Possessions in the West Indies* [Parliamentary Papers: 1824 (003)] (London, 1824), Schedule 1, pp. 7–14.

4 The evolution of the Interest's recommendations may be traced in the Minutes of the Standing Committee, 22, 25, 26, and 29 April 1823; Bathurst to Robert Wilmot-Horton, 20 January 1824, RWH Papers, D3155/WH/2939.

5 William Anderson to the President of the Council of Tobago, 30 May 1823, PP 1824 (003), Sch. 2, p. 104; *Jamaica Journal* qu. in Buxton, *Memoirs*, p. 138; *The Colonial Register and West India Journal* (1824), 1:108.

6 *Proceedings of the Honourable House of Assembly of Jamaica in relation to Those Which Took Place in the British House of Commons, on the 15th of May Last* (Kingston, 1823), pp. 9, 10, 14; Petley, *Slaveholders*, p. 91.

7 The most detailed study of Hibbert and his life is: Katie Donington, *The Bonds of Family: Slavery, Commerce, and Culture in the British Atlantic World* (Manchester, 2019); David Hancock, 'George Hibbert (1757–1837)', *ODNB*; Charles Ellis to George Hibbert, 8 October 1823, RWH Papers, D3155/WH/2939, fo. 4; Lord Bathurst to Robert Wilmot-Horton, 9 January 1824, RWH Papers, D3155/WH/2940.

8 *The Barbadian*, 20 September 1823; *Dominica Chronicle*, 29 March 1826.

9 *Cobbett's Weekly Register*, 1 June 1833; F.G. Smyth, *An Apology for the West Indians, and Reflections on the Policy of Great Britain's Interference in the Internal Concerns of the West India Colonies* (London, 1824), p. 3; Anthony Davis, *The West Indies: A Detail of Facts in Opposition to Theory* (London, 1832), p. 15; *John Bull*, 29 April 1833; *Barbadian*, 20 September 1823; *Voice of the West Indies*, p. 18.

10 'The Message of President James Monroe at the Commencement of the First Session of the 18th Congress', *National Archives Catalog* [catalog/archives.gov/id/306420].

11 Archibald Alison, 'The West India question', *BEM*, 31 (1832), 412–23, at p. 413; Franklin, *Short View*, p. 105; Lockhart, 'West Indian Controversy I', p. 450; *Hansard*, Commons, 16 March 1824, X, cc1164; Lt-Col. Evans to the Duke of Wellington, 9 April 1823, Papers of the Duke of Wellington, University of Southampton Library, Southampton (Wellington Papers), WP1/760/9; Major General Walpole to Lord Fitzroy Somerset, 22 February 1824, Wellington Papers, WP1/785/10. The author has already made

similar arguments about American expansionism, with Michael S. Kochin, in *An Independent Empire: Diplomacy & War in the Making of the United States* (Ann Arbor, MI, 2020).

12   John Barrow, 'The political importance of our American colonies', *QR*, 33 (1826), 410–29, at p. 411; John Barrow, *The Eventful History of the Mutiny and Piratical Seizure of HMS Bounty* (London, 1831); Barrow is also thought to have edited Joseph Lowe's 1823 pro-slavery article in the *Quarterly*: J.B. Cutmore, *Contributors to the Quarterly Review: A History, 1809–25* (London, 2008), p. 176; 'Colonial Policy', *Edinburgh Review*, 84 (1825), 271–303, at p. 297; Horatio Nelson to Simon Taylor, 10 June 1805, in *The Dispatches and Letters of Vice Admiral Lord Viscount Nelson*, ed. Sir Nicholas Harris Nicolas (London, 1846), 6:450–1

13   *The Times*, 13 October 1823; Buxton, *Memoirs*, p. 122.

14   'Abolition of the Slave Trade – And of Slavery', *Edinburgh Review*, 41 (1824), 194–228 at p. 209; *Christian Observer* qu. in Seymour Drescher, *Abolition: A History of Slavery and Anti-Slavery* (Cambridge, 2009), p. 259; *Hull Advertiser* and Parsons qu. in Jones, 'Mobilisation', pp. 171, 173.

15   Hibbert qu. in Petley, *Slaveholders*, p. 92; Wilberforce, *Life of Wilberforce*, 5:204; Buxton, 16 February 1824, *Memoirs*, p. 143.

16   The Duke of Wellington to Lord Bathurst, 14 October 1823, Wellington Papers, WP1/774/8; Canning to Wilberforce, 11 October 1823, qu. in Jones, 'Mobilisation', p. 167; Wilberforce, *Life of Wilberforce*, 5:201–2; Wilberforce to Macaulay, 13 October 1823, qu. in John Pollock, *Wilberforce* (London, 1977).

17   The two best studies of Huskisson's political career remain: Alexander Brady, *William Huskisson and Liberal Reform: An Essay on the Changes in Economic Policy in the Twenties of the 19th Century* [1928] (2nd edn, London, 1967) and C.R. Fay, *Huskisson and His Age* (London, 1951). Canning qu. in *A Biographical Memoir of the Right Honourable William Huskisson, Derived from Authentic Sources* (London, 1831), p. 40.

18   William Huskisson to John Gladstone, 2 November 1823, Gladstone Papers, Flintshire Records Office, Hawarden, GG MS 353; *The Times*, 27 April 1824; *Dominica Chronicle*, 22 June 1825.

19   Huskisson to John Bolton, 19 October 1823, Papers of William Huskisson, British Library, London (Huskisson Papers), Add MS 38745, fo. 58; Huskisson to Macaulay, 26 October 1823, Add MS 38745, fo. 69; Huskisson to Canning, 2 November 1823, qu. in *The Huskisson Papers*, ed. Lewis Melville (London, 1931), p. 168; Huskisson to Sandars, 22 January 1824, Add MS 38745, fos. 182–3; Huskisson to Charles Rose Ellis, 31 March 1823, Huskisson Papers, Add MS 38744, fos. 26–7.

20   'Petition of the London Missionary Society', *Hansard*, Commons, 13 April 1824, XI, cc403–4.

21   LMS *Report of the Proceedings against Smith*, p. 2.

22   *Report of the Trials of the Insurgent Negroes, Before a General Court-Martial Held at Georgetown, Demerara, on the 25th August, 1823* (Georgetown, 1824), pp. 186–7; Robert Wilmot-Horton to John Gladstone, 18 August 1824, GG MS 272; Wilmot-Horton to Gladstone, 16 March 1825, GG MS 272.

23   *Report of the Trials*, pp. 146, 148; LMS *Report of the Proceedings*, pp. 23, 26; *An Authentic Copy of the Minutes of Evidence on the Trial of John Smith, A Missionary, in Demerara* (London, 1824), p. 23.

24   *John Bull*, 27 October 1823; *Barbados Mercury*, 14 February 1824; Huskisson to Samuel Hope, 21 May 1824, Add MS 38745, fos. 297–8.

25   Wilberforce, *Life of Wilberforce*, 5:221.

26   *Hansard*, Commons, 1 June 1824, X, cc963–4; William Hazlitt, *The Spirit of The Age: or, Contemporary Portraits* (2nd edn, London, 1825), pp. 301–2; Buxton, *Memoirs*, p. 151.

27 Clarkson, *History*, p. 14; G.O. Trevelyan (ed.), *The Life and Works of Lord Macaulay* (10 vols., London, 1897–1908), 9:113.

5. Deliver Us from Evil

1 *Hansard*, House of Commons, 15 May 1823, c279.

2 *Memorials of the Rev. William J. Shrewsbury*, ed. John V.B. Shrewsbury (3rd edn, London, 1869), p. 3.

3 G.G. Findlay and W.W. Holdsworth, *The History of the Wesleyan Methodist Missionary Society* (5 vols., London, 1921–24), 2:59.

4 'West India Missions', *Edinburgh Review*, 40 (1824), 226–70, at p. 240.

5 *Hansard*, House of Commons, 23 June 1825, XIII, cc1290–1.

6 *Shrewsbury's Memorials*, pp. 92–3; David Lambert, *White Creole Culture, Politics and Identity during the Age of Abolition* (Cambridge, 2005), pp. 150–2.

7 *Hansard*, Commons, 23 June 1825, XIII, cc1292–3; Shrewsbury, *Memorials*, p. 145; Gov. Henry Warde to Lord Bathurst, 23 October 1823, in *Further Papers relating to the Slaves in the West Indies: (Demolition of the Methodist Chapel in Barbadoes)* [Parliamentary Papers 1825 (113)] (London, 1825), p. 3.

8 *Hansard*, Commons, 23 June 1825, XIII, cc1294–5; Shrewsbury, *Memorials*, pp. 140–2; Warde to Bathurst, in Further Paper's p. 3.

9 *Hansard*, Commons, 23 June 1825, XIII, cc1297–8.

10 Shrewsbury, *Memorials*, pp. 144, 147.

11 *Hansard*, Commons, 13 June 1825, XIII, c1298; 'Great and Signal Triumph over Methodism, and Total Destruction of the Chapel!!!', Bridgetown, 21 October 1823, in parliamentary Papers (PP) 1825 (113), p. 3; 'Counter-Proclamation', 23 October 1823, PP 1825 (113), p. 5.

12 'Instructions to the Wesleyan Missionaries' in *Memoirs of The Life and Writings of the Rev. Richard Watson, Late Secretary to the Wesleyan Missionary Society*, ed. Thomas Jackson (New York, 1834), p. 211; *Royal Gazette* (Jamaica), 13 November 1824; 'Minutes of a Meeting of the General Committee of the Wesleyan Missionary Society, 5 January 1825', in *The Evangelical Magazine and Missionary Chronicle*, 3 (1825), pp. 81–3.

13 Gad Heuman, 'William Knibb (1803–1845)', *ODNB*.

14 *Memoir of William Knibb, Missionary in Jamaica*, ed. John Howard Hinton (2nd edn, London, 1846), pp. 36, 44.

15 Ibid., pp. 45, 43, 49.

16 Ibid., p. 46; Catherine Hall, 'In the Name of Which Father?', *International Labor and Working-Class History*, 41 (1992), 23–28, at p. 23.

17 *Memoir of Knibb*, p. 46; Peter Duncan, *A Narrative of the Wesleyan Mission to Jamaica; with Occasional Remarks on the State of Society in That Colony* (London, 1849), p. 276.

18 PP 1824 (003), pp. 8–9; Alexander Barclay, *A Practical View of the Present State of Slavery in the West Indies; or, an Examination of Mr Stephen's "Slavery of the British West India Colonies"* (London, 1826), p. 127; *Some Account of the Society for the Conversion and Religious Instruction and Education of the Negroe Slaves in the British West India Islands* (London, 1823), p. 5; Minutes of the Standing Committee, M915/4, 21 November 1823.

19 Michael Craton, 'Christianity and Slavery in the British West Indies', *Historical Reflections*, 5 (1978), 141–60, at p. 147; Literary Committee, 15 July 1824; De la Beche, *Notes*, p. 28; S. Karly Kehoe, 'Colonial collaborators: Britain and the Catholic Church in Trinidad, c. 1820–1840', *Slavery & Abolition* (2019), 130–46, pp. 131, 133.

20 Lowell Joseph Ragatz, *The Fall of the Planter Class in the British Caribbean, 1763–1833: A Study in Social and Economic History* (London, 1928), p. 430; Elsa V. Goveia, *A Study on the Historiography of the British West Indies to the End of the Nineteenth Century*

(Mexico City, 1956), p. 106; G.W. Bridges, *A Voice from Jamaica; In Reply to William Wilberforce, Esq., M.P.* (London, 1823); idem., *Dreams of Dulocracy; or, The Puritanical Obituary: "An Appeal", Not to the Romantic Sensibility, But to the Good Sense of the British Public* (London, 1824); *Barbadian*, 3 August and 28 September 1824; G.W. Bridges, *Annals of Jamaica* (2 vols., London, 1828); *Royal Gazette* (Jamaica), 5 November 1825, 24 December 1825.

21   *Anecdotes of the life of Richard Watson, Bishop of Llandaff; written by himself at different intervals and revised in 1814* (London, 1817), pp. 454–5; '"Philalethes" [James Griffith] to the editor of the *Bath and Cheltenham Gazette*, 4 July 1823', National Library of Jamaica, Kingston, MS 723a, fo. 8. Much of the following passage is based on: Michael Taylor, 'British Proslavery Arguments and the Bible, 1823–33', *Slavery & Abolition*, 37 (2016), 139–58.

22   S. Tucker, 'On church establishments', *Imperial Magazine*, 2 (1832), 260–7, at p. 264; Rev. Cynric Williams, *A tour through the island of Jamaica, from the western to the eastern end, in the year 1823* (London, 1826), p. 70.

23   'To the Worthy and Independent Electors of the Borough of Newark', Gladstone Papers, GG MS 223, fo. 57; Watson, *Anecdotes*, p. 454.

24   'A West India Planter', *A Letter to the Most Honourable the Marquis of Chandos* (London, 1830), p. 14; 'Z', *Slavery – To the Editor of the English Chronicle and Whitehall Evening Post – To the West India Planters and Abolitionists – Negro Slavery* (Penzance, 1831), p. 4; Bridges, *Annals*, 1:461; Revd J.W. Wilkinson, *Thoughts on Negro Slavery* (London, 1833), p. 3; James MacQueen, *The West India Colonies: The Calumnies and Misrepresentations Circulated Against Them by the Edinburgh Review, Mr Clarkson, Mr Cropper, &c., Examined and Refuted* (London, 1824), pp. 137–8; Bridges, *Annals*, 1:464–5; 'Sermons on slavery', *Christian Remembrancer*, 13 (1831), 79–89, at p. 80.

25   *Barbadian*, 24 December 1823; Bridges, *Annals*, 1:462.

26   David Brion Davis, *The Problem of Slavery in the Age of Revolution, 1770–1823* (Ithaca, NY, 1975), pp. 526–7; *Glasgow Courier*, 16 August 1823.

27   Rev. R. Bickell, *The West Indies as they are; or a real picture of slavery: but more particularly as it exists in the island of Jamaica. In three parts, with notes* (London 1825), p. 179n; MacQueen, *West India Colonies*, p. 124.

28   'West India Planter', *Letter to Chandos*, p. 16; Alison, 'West India Question', p. 417.

29   *Morning Post*, 4 December 1832; *Proceedings at a Public Meeting of Persons Interested in the Preservation of the British West India Colonies, Held at the City of London Tavern, the 5th April, 1832* (London, 1832), p. 43.

30   'Sermons on slavery', p. 82; Dennis Reid, *An Address to the Right Hon. Geo. Canning, on the Present State of This Island, and Other Matters* (Kingston, 1823), p. 10; 'T.F.' to the *Liverpool Mercury*, 4 November 1823, in *The Correspondence between John Gladstone, Esq., M.P., and James Cropper, Esq., on the Present State of Slavery in the British West Indies* (Liverpool, 1824), ii; Lockhart, 'West Indian Controversy IV', p. 683.

31   Robert Young, *A View of Slavery in Connection with Christianity: Being the Substance of a Discourse Delivered in the Wesleyan Chapel, Stoney-Hill, Jamaica, Sept. 19, 1824* (London, 1825), p. 13; Henry Duncan, *Presbyter's Letters on the West India Question; Addressed to the Right Honourable Sir George Murray* (London, 1830), pp. 18–19.

32   'Vindex', *The Conduct of the British Government towards the Church of England in the West India Colonies: In a Letter to Viscount Goderich* (London, 1831), p. 6; Stephen, *Anti-Slavery Recollections*, p. 114.

6. Two Roads Diverging

1   William Huskisson to John Gladstone, 8 February 1824, Huskisson Papers, Add MS 38745, fos. 199–200.

2   *Hansard*, House of Lords, 3 February 1824, X, cci–5.

3   *Hansard*, House of Commons, 16 March 1824, X, cc1105–6.

4   Robin Blackburn, *The Overthrow of Colonial Slavery, 1776–1848* (London, 1988), p. 423. The abolitionists quoted this back to Canning repeatedly, e.g. *ASMR*, 6 (1825), 51; Buxton to Mrs Buxton, 9 February 1824, *Memoirs*, p. 142; Buxton's Journal, 14 February 1824, *Memoirs*, p. 143; Buxton to Mrs Buxton, February 1824, *Memoirs*, p. 144.

5   Gertrude Carmichael, 'Some Notes on Sir Ralph James Woodford, Bt.', *Caribbean Quarterly*, 2 (1952), 26–38, at p. 38; Ralph Woodford to Robert Wilmot-Horton, 6 August 1823, 1 April 1824, 7 May 1824, 10 January 1824, all in RWH Papers, D3155/WH/2901: Correspondence with Sir Ralph Woodford.

6   *Hansard*, Commons, 16 March 1824, X, cc1097–1101.

7   Woodford to Wilmot-Horton, 8 February 1824; *Hansard*, 16 March 1824, c1095, 1102.

8   Ibid., c1103.

9   James Colquhoun to Robert Wilmot-Horton, 4 July 1824, RWH Papers, D3155/WH/2769: Correspondence with James Colquhoun; Literary Committee, 22 March and 7 June 1824, printed as *The Speech of the Right Hon. George Canning ... on Wednesday, the 17th of March 1824* (London 1824); James MacQueen to William Blackwood, 1 April 1824, Blackwood Papers, MS 4012, fo. 267.

10 Buxton, *Memoirs*, pp. 143, 146, 143; William Allen to Buxton, 21 February 1824, in *The Life of William Allen, with Selections from His Correspondence* (3 vols., London, 1846), 2:376–7.

11 Macaulay to Hannah More, 24 March 1824, *Life and Letters*, p. 418; Wilberforce to Buxton, 17 March 1824, *Memoirs*, p. 149.

12 J.J. Gurney to Buxton, 10 March 1824, *Memoirs*, p. 145; 'Memoranda for Mr W Horton', RWH Papers, D3155/WH/3050: Papers by Major Moody, 1824 to 1826, fo. 2573.

13 Qu. in Jones, 'Mobilisation', pp. 172, 177.

14 Stephen, *Anti-Slavery Recollections*, p. 77; Isobel Grundy, 'Elizabeth Heyrick (1769–1831)', *ODNB*; Shirley Aucott, *Elizabeth Heyrick, 1769 to 1831: The Leicester Quaker who Demanded the Immediate Emancipation of Slaves in the British Colonies* (Leicester, 2007), p. 3; Elizabeth Heyrick, *Immediate, Not Gradual Abolition; or, An Inquiry into the Shortest, Safest, and Most Effectual Means of Getting Rid of West Indian Slavery* (London, 1824).

15 Heyrick, *Immediate*, pp. 14, 17, 18.

16 For the number of petitions, see Jones, 'Mobilisation', p. 209n3.

17 George Stephen, *A Memoir of the Late James Stephen, One of the Masters in the High Court of Chancery, in relation to Slave Emancipation* (Brighton, 1875), pp. 51–3; William Thomas, 'Thomas Babington Macaulay (1800–1859)', *ODNB*; Macaulay, *Life and Letters*, pp. 420–1.

18 Jones, 'Mobilisation', pp. 210–1, 212.

19 Ibid., pp. 213, 211–12, 216–17, 214.

20 *Report of the Committee of the Society for the Mitigation and Gradual Abolition of Slavery throughout the British Dominions, read at the General Meeting of the Society, held on the 25th Day of June 1824* (London, 1824): duties discussed *passim*.

21 Jones, 'Mobilisation', p. 175; Elizabeth Heyrick, *No British Slavery: or, An Invitation to the People to Put a Speedy End to It* (London, 1824); Jones, 'Mobilisation', p. 182.

22 *Gladstone–Cropper Correspondence*, p. 57; *Tropical Free-Labour Company: A Prospectus* (London, 1825).

23 For Wilberforce's collapse, see: William Hague, *Wilberforce: The Life of the Great Anti-Slave Trade Campaigner* (London, 2008), pp. 487–8; Wilberforce, *Life of Wilberforce*, 5:234; Hazlitt, *Spirit of the Age*, p. 325; Buxton, *Memoirs*, p. 152.

24 Wilberforce, *Life of Wilberforce*, 5:122, 5:234; Buxton, *Memoirs*, pp. 154–5.

25 *Life and Letters of Macaulay*, pp. 423–4; *Dominica Chronicle*, 28 September 1825; *Barbadian*, 18 June and 2 July 1823; *Life and Letters*, pp. 426–7; for a summary of the libel farrago, see Whyte, *Macaulay*, pp. 201–8.

26   Ibid., p. 440; Jones, 'Mobilisation', p. 217; Stephen, *Anti-Slavery Recollections*, p. 169; Whyte, *Macaulay*, xiii.

7. Am I Not a Man and a Brother?

1   'The West Indies', *Edinburgh Review*, 82 (1825), 464–88, at p. 480.

2   Most of Moody's biographical details are taken from, and this passage leans heavily on: Anita Rupprecht, '"When He Gets Among His Countrymen, They Tell Him That He Is Free": Slave Trade Abolition, Indentured Africans, and a Royal Commission', *Slavery & Abolition*, 33 (2012), 435–55.

3   Ibid., pp. 440, 454n43.

4   Ibid., pp. 446, 440, 447, 450.

5   Ibid., pp. 446–7.

6   Ibid., p. 447; Thomas Moody to Robert Wilmot-Horton, 25 June 1823, Wilmot-Horton Papers, D3155/WH/2849: Correspondence with Thomas Moody; Dougan's report was published as 'Separate Report of John Dougan' in *Reports by Commissioners of Inquiry into State of Africans apprenticed in W. Indies II. Further Papers relating to Captured Negroes* [PP 1825 (115)] (London, 1825), pp. 5–48.

7   Moody's separate reports are found in: PP 1825 (115), pp. 49–152; *Reports by Commissioners of Inquiry into State of Africans apprenticed in W. Indies: Part II of Major Moody's Report on Captured Negroes* (PP 1826 (81)) (London, 1826); Dougan's daughter sought to restore his reputation by submitting further reports to the Colonial Office, which Moody annotated extensively before permitting their publication: *Reports by Commissioners of Inquiry into State of Slaves in H.M. Colonies under Acts abolishing Slave Trade (Tortola)* (PP 1826–27 (462)). Quotes from: PP 1826 (81), p. 7; PP 1825 (115), p. 134. Moody's first letter from Baker Street is dated 9 January 1824: D3155/WH/2849.

8   Eric Richards, 'Sir Robert John Wilmot-Horton (1784–1841)', *ODNB*; J.C. Beaglehole, 'The Colonial Office, 1782–1854', *Historical Studies*, 1 (1941), 170–89, at pp. 182–3; Wilmot-Horton to Canning, 26 February 1824, RWH Papers, D3155/WH/2760: Correspondence with George Canning, fo. 19. The best study of Wilmot-Horton's political career is Stephen Peter Lamont, 'Robert Wilmot Horton and Liberal Toryism' (unpublished Ph.D dissertation, University of Nottingham, 2015).

9   Wilmot-Horton to Henry Drummond, September 1824, D3155/WH/2940, fo. 60; Ellis and Wilmot-Horton, 'West India Colonies'; D.J. Murray, *The West Indies and the Development of Colonial Government, 1801–1834* (Oxford, 1965), p. 123.

10   Qu. in Rupprecht, 'Countrymen', p. 449; Wilmot-Horton to Huskisson, 26 January 1824, D3155/WH/2940.

11   Edward Long, *The History of Jamaica* (3 vols., London, 1774), summarised by Silvia Sebastiani, *The Scottish Enlightenment: Race, Gender, and the Limits of Progress*, trans. Jeremy Carden (Basingstoke, 2013), pp. 107, 106; James Cowles Prichard, *Researches into the physical history of man* [1813], ed. George W. Stocking, Jr (Chicago, 1973); George W. Stocking, Jr., 'From chronology to ethnology: Prichard and British anthropology, 1800–1850', in Prichard, *Researches*, i–cxviii, at xx.

12   Bridges, *Annals*, 2:414; Rev. Benjamin Bailey, *The House of Bondage: A Dissertation upon the Nature of Service or Slavery under the Levitical Law* (London, 1824), p. 1; *Present State and Prospects of the West India Question, with Regard to its Final Adjustment* (London, 1830), p. 6; 'Physical Evidences of the Characteristics of Ancient Races among the Moderns', *Fraser's Magazine*, 6 (1832), 673–9, at p. 676.

13   *Correspondence, Gladstone–Copper*, p. 63; James Franklin, *The Present State of Hayti (Saint Domingo) with Remarks on its Agriculture, Commerce, Laws, Religion, Finances, and Population* (London, 1828), p. 362; PP 1826 (81), pp. 19, 20; H.P. Simmons, *Letter to the Right Hon. Earl Grey, on the West India Question* (Liverpool, 1833), pp. 5–6.

14   Hochschild, *Bury the Chains*, p. 314; Wilberforce, *Appeal*, p. 74; *ASMR*, 62 (1830), p. 299; Stephen, *Memoir of James Stephen*, p. 67; *Address to the Electors*, p. 6.

15   For the theory behind this: Catherine Hall and Keith McClelland, 'Introduction', and Karen O'Brien, 'Empire, History, and Emigration: From Enlightenment to Liberalism', in Hall and McClelland (eds.), *Race, Nation, and Empire: Making Histories, 1750 to the Present* (Manchester, 2010), pp. 6–7 and 15–35.

16   Bridges, *Annals*, 2:407; James MacQueen, *The Colonial Controversy, Containing a Refutation of the Calumnies of the Anti-Colonists* (Glasgow, 1825), p. 74.

17   Mungo Park, *Travels in the Interior Districts of Africa* (London, 1799), qu. in Henry William Martin, *A Counter Appeal in Answer to "An Appeal" from William Wilberforce* (London, 1823), p. 5; Alexander Gordon Laing, *Travels in the Timannee, Kooranko, and Soolima Countries, in Western Africa* (London, 1825), qu. in *WIR*, 37 (1830), pp. 393–4; Dixon Denham and Hugh Clapperton, *Narrative of Travels and Discoveries in Northern and Central Africa, in the Years 1822, 1823 and 1824* (London, 1826), qu. in Peter Borthwick, *A Report of Colonial Slavery and Gradual Emancipation, Delivered in the Assembly Rooms on Friday, March 1, 1833* (Edinburgh, 1833), p. 10; Bridges, *Annals*, 2:400, 399.

18   *A Reply to Mr Jeremie's Pamphlet, by an Inhabitant of St Lucia* (London, 1832), p. 109; Davis, *West Indies*, p. 88; Anthony Brough, *The Importance of the British Colonies in the West Indies* (London, 1833), p. 15.

19   *WIR*, 22 (1829), p. 125; Alexander McDonnell, *Considerations on Negro Slavery* (London, 1824), p. 223; Lockhart, 'West Indian Controversy II', p. 649.

20   RWH Papers, D3155/WH/3050, ff. 12–13; PP 1826 (81), p. 82; Lockhart, 'West Indian controversy II', pp. 652–3; Bridges, *Annals*, 2:430.

21   Holmes, *Appeal to the Good Sense*, p. 12; *Barbadian*, 5 June 1827; Lord Liverpool to Lord Bexley, July 1823, Papers of Lord Liverpool, British Library, London, Add MS 38295, fos. 102–8.

22   *Select Committee on Extinction of Slavery in British Dominions* (PP 1831–32 (721)) (London, 1832), pp. 189, 190, 199; *Marly; or, The Life of a Planter in Jamaica* (2nd edn, Glasgow, 1828), p. 87.

23   Catherine Hall, *Civilising Subjects: Metropole and Colony in the English Imagination, 1830–1867* (Cambridge, 2002), p. 107.

24   *ASMR*, 4 (1825), pp. 26–7; Jones, 'Mobilisation', p. 193; *ASMR*, 4:25 (1825), 6:54 (1825); James Colquhoun to Wilmot-Horton, 4 April 1823, RWH Papers, D3155/WH/2769; 'Britannicus', *A Reply to Article VII of the Edinburgh Review for October 1823, on T. Clarkson's Treatise on the Improvement and Emancipation of Slaves in the British Colonies* (London, 1824), p. 17.

25   *ASMR* (1830), 59:157; Borthwick, *Report of Colonial Slavery*, p. 15; *Barbadian*, 2 April 1830; Bridges, *Annals*, 2:249; James MacQueen, *A Fourth Letter to R.W. Hay, Esq., &c. &c. in Reply to Mr. Kenneth Macaulay's "Sierra Leone Vindicated"* (Edinburgh, 1827), p. 62.

26   *Morning Chronicle*, 20 October 1823; *Cobbett's Weekly Register*, 6 December 1823; 'The Colonial Crisis', *Fraser's Magazine*, 3 (1831), 625–30, at p. 629.

27   *Voice of the West Indies*, pp. 19–20; 'A Merchant', *An Attempt to Strip Negro Emancipation of its Difficulties as well as Its Terrors* (London, 1824), pp. 28–9; *Official Letter from the Commissioners*, pp. 15–16; Colquhoun to Wilmot-Horton, 4 July 1824, RWH Papers, D3155/WH/2769.

28   Thomas Babington Macaulay, 'Milton', *Edinburgh Review*, 42 (1825), 304–46, at p. 333; Vincent Carretta, 'Ignatius Sancho (1729?–1780)', *ODNB*.

29   Stephen, *Anti-Slavery Recollections*, p. 95; Tim Watson, 'Working the Edges of the Nineteenth-Century British Empire', *Literature Compass*, 13 (2016), 288–99; 'Louis Celeste Lecesne', *LBS*.

30   Gad J. Heuman, *Between Black and White: Race, Politics, and the Free Coloreds in Jamaica, 1792–1865* (Westport, CT, 1981).

31   *Nineteenth Report of the Directors of the African Institution, read at the Annual General
      Meeting, Held on the 13th Day of May, 1825* (London, 1825), p. 312; William Burge, *A
      Letter to the Right Honourable Sir George Murray . . . relative to the Deportation of Lecesne
      and Escoffery from Jamaica* (London, 1829), p. 469.

32   S.M. Waddams, 'Stephen Lushington (1782–1873)', *ODNB*.

33   *Hansard*, House of Commons, 21 May 1824, XI, cc796–804; *Hansard*, Commons,
      16 June 1825, XIII, cc1173–1205.

34   Richard Barrett, *A Reply to the Speech of Dr Lushington in the House of Commons on
      the 12th June 1827 on the Condition of the Free-Coloured People of Jamaica* (London, 1828),
      pp. 2, 48. See also, Hector Mitchel, *Two Letters to the Colonial Secretary . . . in Answer
      to the Yellow Book* (Kingston, 1828).

35   *Report of the Trial of Mr John Murray, in the Court of King's Bench, at Westminster-Hall,
      the 19th December, 1829, on an Indictment for a Libel on Messrs Lecesne and Escoffery*
      (London, 1830), pp. 7, 40.

36   *ASMR* (1831), 76:144; *Proceedings of the Old Bailey*, 'Thomas Fielder', 5 July 1832
      [oldbaileyonline.org].

37   Heyrick, *Immediate*, p. 5; *The Humming Bird, or Morsels of Information on the Subject
      of Slavery*, 7 (1825), 195; Minutes of the West India Merchants Sub-Committee,
      5 August 1828, ICS, M915/11; Alison Bashford and Joyce E. Chaplin, *The New Worlds
      of Thomas Malthus: Rereading the Principle of Population* (Princeton, 2016), p. 196.

38   The most authoritative work in this area remains Clare Midgley, *Woman against
      Slavery: The British Campaign, 1780–1870* (London, 1992), p. 48; Wilberforce to Macaulay,
      8 February 1826, in *The Correspondence of William Wilberforce*, ed. Robert Isaac
      Wilberforce and Samuel Wilberforce (2 vols., London, 1840), 2:494; Hochschild, *Bury
      the Chains*, p. 326; *WIR* (1829), 24:153.

8. Wages or the Whip

1   'Pan in Town' [1825], *The Poems of Thomas Love Peacock*, ed. Brimley Johnson (London,
      1906), pp. 291–2.

2   *Hansard*, Lords, 3 February 1824, X, cci–2. For an excellent summary of financial
      conditions in 1825 and the subsequent crash, see: Boyd Hilton, *A Mad, Bad, and
      Dangerous People? England, 1783–1846* (Oxford, 2006), pp. 300–4.

3   Huskisson qu. in Hilton, *Dangerous*, p. 301. For an account of these investments,
      see Frank Griffith Dawson, *The First Latin American Debt Crisis: The City of London
      and the 1822–25 Loan Bubble* (New Haven, CT, 1990), pp. 98–100.

4   For accounts of MacGregor's exploits, see: David Sinclair, *Sir Gregor MacGregor and
      the Land That Never Was* (London, 2004); Matthew Brown, 'Gregor MacGregor:
      Clansman, Conquistador, and Coloniser on the Fringes of the British Empire', in
      Colonial Lives across the British Empire: Imperial Careering in the Long Nineteenth Century,
      ed. David Lambert and Alan Lester (Cambridge 2009), pp. 32–57.

5   *On the Increasing Importance of the British West-Indian Possessions* (London, 1826), p.
      15; John Rock Grossett, *Remarks on West Indian Affairs* (London, 1824), p. 109;
      Memorandum of the Relative Importance of the West & East Indies to Great Britain
      (London, 1823), p. 7.

6   Gladstone to Huskisson, 31 December 1825, Huskisson Papers, Add MS 38747, fo.
      149; *The Journal of Mrs Arbuthnot, 1820–32* (2 vols., London, 1950), 1:428.

7   Ibid., pp. 427–8.

8   Alexander Baring [Lord Ashburton], *The Financial and Commercial Crisis Considered*
      (2nd edn, London, 1847), p. 13.

9   Ibid., p. 8.

10   'Notes from 1825', RWH Papers, D3155/WH/2939; Harriet Martineau, *Illustrations
      of Political Economy. Volume IV: Demerara* (London, 1832).

11   Thomas Seccombe, 'Alexander Macdonnell (1798–1835)', *ODNB*; William Greenwood
      Walker (ed.), *A Selection of Games at Chess, Actually Played in London, by the late
      Alexander McDonnell, Esq., the Best English Player, with his Principal Contemporaries*
      (London, 1836), iii; James MacQueen to William Blackwood, 1 January 1832,
      Blackwood Papers, MS 4034, fo. 42. Alexander McDonnell, *Considerations*; idem.,
      *The West India Legislatures Vindicated from the Charge of Having Resisted the Call of the
      Mother Country for the Amelioration of Slavery* (London, 1826), 'Compulsory
      Manumission or an Examination of the Actual State of the West India Question'
      [1827] in *Pamphlets on West India slavery* (Cambridge, 2010); and *A Letter to Thos.
      Fowell Buxton, Esq. M.P., in Refutation of his Allegations Respecting the Decrease of the
      Slaves in the British West India Colonies* (London, 1833); Alexander McDonnell, *Free
      Trade; or, an Inquiry into the Expediency of the Present Corn Laws, and the Relations of
      Our Foreign and Colonial Trade* (London, 1826); idem., *Colonial Commerce; Comprising
      an Inquiry into the Principles upon which Discriminating Duties Should be Levied on Sugar,
      the Growth Respectively of the West India British Possessions, of the East Indies, and of
      Foreign Countries* (London, 1828).

12   Memorandum for Mr W. Horton, n.d., RWH Papers, D3155/WH/3050, fo. 2567;
      Thomas Moody to Wilmot-Horton, RWH Papers, 18 Downing Street, 'Saturday',
      D3155/WH/2849; *Barbadian*, 6 July 1827; Moody to Wilmot-Horton, n.d., RWH
      Papers, D3155/WH/2849; Stephen, *Slavery Delineated*, 2:209, 25.

13   *Slaves: Berbice and Demerara. Minutes of Evidence taken before His Majesty's Privy Council,
      in the Matter of the Berbice and Demerara Manumission Order in Council – November
      1827* (Parliamentary Paper 1828 (261)) (London, 1828), p. 45; Charles MacKenzie, *Notes
      on Haiti, Made during a Residence in that Republic* (2 vols., London, 1830), II, 62;
      Thomas Jelly, *Remarks on the Condition of the White and Free Coloured Inhabitants of
      Jamaica, with Observations on the Causes which either Facilitate or Retard the Progress of
      Civilization amongst the Slaves of the West-Indies* (Montego Bay, 1826), p.13; Alexander
      McDonnell, *An Address to the Members of Both Houses of Parliament on the West India
      Question* (London, 1830), p. 15.

14   PP 1828 (261), p. 30; Memorandum by Major Moody, RWH Papers, D3155/WH/3050;
      3 March 1832. This debate about the *Code Rurale* was fuelled and informed by: *The
      Rural Code of Haiti; in French and English, with a Prefatory Letter to the Right Hon. the
      Earl Bathurst* (London, 1827).

15   'Substance of a Private Conversation with Mr Macdonnell, 25 Oct. 1827', RWH
      Papers, D3155/WH/2941, fo. 4.

16   Joseph Foster Barham, *Considerations on the Abolition of Negro Slavery, and the Means
      of Practically Effecting It* (2nd edn, London, 1823), p. 25; *Memorandum of the Relative
      Importance*, p. 3; *CWR*, 6 December 1823; Robert Wilmot-Horton, *The West India
      Question Practically Considered* (London, 1826), p. 56.

17   Seymour Drescher, *Econocide: British Slavery in the Era of Abolition* (Chapel Hill, NC,
      2010); *Address to Manufacturers, Traders, and Others, on the Importance of Preserving the
      Colonies* (London, 1826), pp. 14, 10; 'S.D.', 'Value of the West India colonies to the
      mother country', *GM*, 94 (1824), 224–7, at p. 225; *Marly*, p. 314.

18   Borthwick, *Report of Colonial Slavery*, p. 5; George Saintsbury, *East India slavery*, (2nd
      edn, London, 1829), pp. 4–5.

19   *WIR*, 41 (1831), p. 36; Alison, 'West India Question', pp. 413–4; McDonnell, *Colonial
      Commerce*, p. 12.

20   James Carmichael Smyth, *Reflections upon the Value of the British West Indian colonies,
      and of the British North American Provinces* (London, 1826), p. 10; Minutes of the
      GWIA, April 1823, fo. 440; C.A. Bayly, *Imperial Meridian: The British Empire and the
      World, 1780–1830* (London, 1989).

21   The first and most sophisticated analysis of conservative economics is: Anna
      Gambles, *Protection and Politics: Conservative Economic Discourse, 1815–1852* (Woodbridge,
      1999). The author exposed the pro-slavery nature of such economics in: Michael

Taylor, 'Conservative Political Economy and the Problem of Colonial Slavery, 1823–33', *Historical Journal*, 57 (2014), 973–95.

22 *ASMR* (1826), 9:81; Buxton, *Memoirs*, pp. 158–9; *Hansard*, Commons, 1 March 1826, XIV, cc968–1000.

23 *Hansard*, *Commons*, 1 March 1826, XIV, cc1007–75.

24 *Hansard*, *Commons*, 20 April 1826, XV, cc502–30.

25 Buxton, *Memoirs*, p. 159; *Life and Letters of Macaulay*, p. 434; 'State of Slavery in the Colonies', *Hansard*, Commons, 19 May 1826, XV, cc1284–1366.

26 Buxton's account of the election is taken from: Buxton, *Memoirs*, pp. 186–9.

27 Philip Salmon, 'Robert John Wilmot', *History of Parliament, Vol. 6*; Lamont, 'Wilmot Horton', p. 247; Colquhoun to RWH, 24 February 1826, RWH Papers, D3155/WH/2769; Hibbert to RWH, 25 February 1826, RWH Papers, D3155/WH/2814; RWH to Buxton, November 1827, RWH Papers, D3155/WH/2941.

28 For an overview of slavery in Mauritius, see: Anthony J. Barker, *Slavery and Anti-Slavery in Mauritius, 1810–33: The Conflict between Economic Expansion and Humanitarian Reform under British Rule* (Basingstoke, 1996).

29 Buxton, *Memoirs*, p. 184.

30 Details of Mauritian horrors may be found in: *ASMR* (1825) 3:20–2, (1829) 44:373–95; Stephen, *Anti-Slavery Recollections*, p. 102.

31 'Slave Trading, and the State of the Slaves at the Mauritius', *Hansard*, Commons, 9 May 1826, XV, cc1014–1501.

32 Buxton, *Memoirs*, pp. 189–90; Stephen, *Anti-Slavery Recollections*, p. 85.

9. The Centre Cannot Hold

1 Minutes of the Glasgow W.I.A., March 1827, fo. 540.

2 'Memoirs of the Right Hon. Robert Banks Jenkinson, Earl of Liverpool', in *The Annual Register, or A View of the History, Politics, and Literature of the Year 1828* (London, 1829), 449–63.

3 *Journal of Mrs Arbuthnot*, 5 March 1827, 2:85; Norman Gash, *Lord Liverpool: The Life and Political Career of Robert Banks Jenkinson, Second Earl of Liverpool, 1770–1828* (Cambridge, MA, 1984), p. 249.

4 Canning to Liverpool, 9 January 1824, in *George Canning and His Friends: Containing Hitherto Unpublished Letters, Jeux D'Esprit, etc.*, ed. Josceline Bagot (2 vols., London, 1908–9), 2:134; *Journal of Mrs Arbuthnot*, 15 February 1827, 2:79.

5 Boyd Hilton, 'The Political Arts of Lord Liverpool', *Transactions of the Royal Historical Society*, 38 (1988), 147–70.

6 *Journal of Mrs Arbuthnot*, 22 February 1827, 2:85.

7 Ibid., 2:102; Wendy Hinde, *George Canning* (London, 1973), pp. 441–2.

8 *Journal of Mrs Arbuthnot*, 10 May 1827, 2:108n1; Stephen Farrell, 'George Canning (1770–1827)', *History of Parliament: Volume VI*.

9 David Brown, 'John William Ward, Earl of Dudley (1781–1833)', *ODNB*; 'Slave Trade Abolition Bill', *Hansard*, Commons, 6 March 1807, IX, cc59–6; *ASMR* (1826), 11:174–6.

10 Hilton, *Dangerous*, p. 376; Eric J. Evans, *Britain before the Reform Act: Politics and Society, 1815–1832* (2nd edn, Oxford, 2008), p. 69. The '*ancien régime*' thesis was first put forward in J.C.D. Clark, *English Society, 1660–1832: Religion, Ideology and Politics during the Ancien Régime* (2nd edn, Cambridge, 2000).

11 *WIR* (1827), 1:1; Literary Committee, 24 March 1827.

12 Buxton, *Memoirs*, pp. 190–3.

13 Stephen to Macaulay, 1 June 1827, *Life and Letters*, p. 439; Buxton, *Memoirs*, p. 194.

14 Buxton, *Memoirs*, pp. 194, 192, 195; *ASMR* (1828), 39:277.

15 Greville, *Memoirs*, 1:91; Hinde, *Canning*, pp. 433–4.

16   Augustus Stapleton to Huskisson, 10 February 1827, in *Some Official Correspondence of George Canning*, ed. Edward J. Stapleton (2 vols., London, 1887), 2:258; Hinde, *Canning*, pp. 459–61; *Journal of Mrs Arbuthnot*, 8 August 1827, 2:134.

17   Hinde, *Canning*, p. 459.

18   *The Annual Register, or A View of the History, Politics, and Literature of the Year 1827* (London, 1828), p. 190; *The Times*, 17 August 1827; *Life and Letters of Macaulay*, pp. 443, 444.

19   Ibid, p. 445; Stephen, *Recollections*, p. 98.

20   John Gladstone to Wilmot-Horton, 19 January 1827, RWH Papers, D3155/WH/2939; Colquhoun to Wilmot-Horton, 29 March 1824, RWH Papers, D3155/WH/2769; Thomas Moody to Wilmot-Horton, 18 January 1826, RWH Papers, D3155/WH/2849.

21   The only dedicated biography of Goderich is: Wilbur Devereux Jones, '*Prosperity Robinson*': *The Life of Viscount Goderich, 1782–1859* (London, 1967).

22   J.C. Herries to Wilmot-Horton, qu. in *WIR* (1830), 31:279.

23   Goderich to Huskisson, 14 August 1827, Huskisson Papers, Add MS 38750, fo. 22; Huskisson to Wilmot-Horton, 7 November 1827, Huskisson Papers, Add MS 38752, fo. 26; Seaford to Huskisson, 14 August 1827, Huskisson Papers, Add MS 38750, fo. 28r; Gladstone to Huskisson, n.d., Huskisson Papers, Add MS 38750, fos. 257–8.

24   Seaford to Bagot, Dieppe, 3 October 1827, in *George Canning and His Friends*, 2:425–6; Stephen, *Recollections*, p. 105; *ASMR* (1827), 30:136.

25   For the narrative, see: Stephen Waddams, 'The Case of Grace James (1827)', *Texas Wesleyan Law Review*, 13 (2008), 783–94; Patricia Hagler Minter, 'The State of Slavery: Somerset, The Slave, Grace, and the Rise of Pro-Slavery and Anti-Slavery Constitutionalism in the Nineteenth-Century Atlantic World', *Slavery & Abolition*, 36 (2015), 603–17.

26   R.A. Melikan, 'William Scott, Baron Stowell (1745–1836)', *ODNB*. For the *Le Louis*, see: *Twelfth Report of the Directors of the African Institution, read at the Annual General Meeting held on 9th of April, 1818* (London, 1818), pp. 1–21.

27   *Reports of Cases Argued and Determined in the High Court of Admiralty, during the Time of the Right Hon. Lord Stowell*, ed. John Haggard (2 vols, London, 1833), 2:100, 132.

28   *WIR* (1828), 9:159; *Actual State of the Question between Our Colonial Slave Proprietors, and the Parliament and Abolitionists of This Country* (Glasgow, 1830), p. 21; Fryer, *Staying Power*, p. 131; 'A Briton', *Considerations on Certain Remarks on the Negro Slavery and Abolition Questions, in Lord Stowell's Judgment in the Case of the Slave 'Grace'* (Newcastle, 1827), p. 4.

29   Huskisson to Seaford, 25 January 1828, Huskisson Papers, Add MS 38754, fo. 234; *The Letters of King George IV, 1812–1830*, ed. A. Aspinall (3 vols., London, 1938), 3:346n1; A. Aspinall, 'The Coalition Ministries of 1827 (Continued)', *English Historical Review*, 42 (1927), 533–59, at p. 548; Jones, *Prosperity*, p. 169.

30   *Journal of Mrs Arbuthnot*, 10 January 1828, 2:157; *Life and Letters of Macaulay*, p. 445.

10. Before the Deluge

1   *ASMR* (1828), 40:294.

2   Qu. in Pardue, 'MacQueen', p. 81.

3   *Hansard*, Commons, 13 July 1830, XXV, cc. 1207–8; *Hansard*, Commons, 13 December 1830, I, cc. 1063–4; *WIR* (1831), 40:21; D.R. Fisher, 'Robert Peel (1788–1850)', *HP*, 6:703; *Hansard*, Commons, 3 June 1833, XVIII, cc. 341, 349; *The Speech of the Hon. John Dalzell, in the House of Assembly, Saint Vincent* (London, 1827), p. 17; John Gladstone, *Facts, relating to Slavery in the West Indies and America, Contained in a Letter Addressed to the Right Hon. Sir Robert Peel, Bart.* (2nd edn, London, 1830); William Burge to Robert Peel, 17 June 1831, Papers of Robert Peel, British Library, London, Add MS 40403, fos. 40, 42.

4   G.F.R. Barker, rev. David Eastwood, 'Henry Goulburn (1784–1856)', *ODNB*; Brian
    Jenkins, *Henry Goulburn, 1784–1856: A Political Biography* (London, 1996), p. 248; *Life
    and Letters of Macaulay*, p. 432.

5   *Journal of Mrs Arbuthnot*, 20 May 1828, pp. 187–8, and 23 June 1828, p. 195; *The Creevey
    Papers: A Selection from the Correspondence and Diaries of the late Thomas Creevey, M.P.*,
    ed. Herbert Maxwell (2 vols., London, 1903), 2:159.

6   Salmon, 'Robert Wilmot-Horton'; 'Saint Vincent', 30 December 1828, RWH Papers,
    D3155/WH/2936, 27r; James Colquhoun to Wilmot-Horton, 17 September 1827,
    RWH Papers, D3155/WH/2769.

7   S.G.P. Ward, 'Sir George Murray (1772–1846)', *ODNB*; MacQueen to Blackwood,
    1 August 1828; Blackwood Papers, MS 4022, fo. 120; *Arbuthnot Journal*, 2:188–9;
    MacQueen to Blackwood, 1 August 1828.

8   Blackburn, *Overthrow*, p. 437; Peter J. Kitson and Deborah Lee (eds.), *Slavery, Abolition,
    and Emancipation: Writings in the British Romantic Period* (8 vols., London, 1999), 3:xv;
    Walvin, *England*, p. 165; *Hansard*, Lords, 23 June 1828, XIX, 1465–7; *ASMR* (1826), 9:81.

9   MacQueen to Blackwood, 24 January and 30 April 1828, Blackwood Papers, MS
    4022; 'Confidential Memorandum by Major Moody', RWH Papers, D3155/WH/2940,
    fo. 256r; *WIR* (1828), 15:68; Garrison (ed.), *Lectures of George Thompson*, xxxii.

10 *Life and Letters*, p. 450; Stephen, *Recollections*, p. 105.

11 *The Speeches of the Duke of Wellington in Parliament*, ed. Col. Gurwood (2 vols., London,
    1854), 1:214; *Life and Letters of Macaulay*, p. 449; Wellington to Stephen, 25 July 1828,
    in *Despatches, Correspondence, and Memoranda of Field Marshal Arthur, Duke of Wellington,
    K.G.*, ed. The Duke of Wellington (10 vols., London, 1871), 4:556–7.

12 Wellington to Murray, 18 August 1828, in *Despatches*, 4:629–30; Murray to Wellington,
    19 August 1828, *Despatches*, 4:638.

13 For the metaphor, Jenkins, *Goulburn*, p. 72; 'Memorandum for George Murray',
    16 May 1829, Murray to Wellington, 17 May 1829, and Wellington to Murray, 31 May
    1829, *Despatches*, 5:604–9.

14 'Notes on Proposed Slave Laws', 10 October 1829, *Despatches*, 6:208; Wellington to
    Murray, 16 May 1829, 5:603.

15 *ASMR* (1828), 34:195; Buxton, *Memoirs*, p. 233.

16 Minutes of the Merchants Sub-Committee, 5 August 1828.

17 R.D. Fulton, 'Robert Stephen Rintoul (1787–1858)', *ODNB*; *Spectator*, 15 November
    and 20 December 1828, 28 March, 11 April, and 18 July 1829; Minutes of the Acting
    Committee, ICS, M915/6, 3 March 1830; *WIR* (1828), 18:47.

18 William Maginn, 'MS notes on the articles concerning Ireland, the West Indies, &c.
    in the last number of the Edinburgh Review', *Blackwood's Edinburgh Magazine*, 17
    (1825), 461–75, at p. 471; Literary Committee, 5 December 1830 and 29 January 1831;
    [Stephen Isaacson], 'The Colonists *versus* the Anti-Slavery Society (No. I)', *Fraser's
    Magazine*, 2 (1830), 334–41, and 'The Colonists *versus* the Anti-Slavery Society. Chap.
    II', *Fraser's Magazine*, 3 (1831), 114–26; Isaacson, *Vindication*; *Christian Remembrancer*,
    14 (1832), p. 622.

19 P.H. Scott, 'John Galt (1779–1839)', *ODNB*; 'Agricola' [John Galt], 'The Colonial
    Question', *Blackwood's Edinburgh Magazine*, 27 (1830), 455–62; idem., 'Letters on West
    Indian Slavery. By J. Galt, Esq. to Oliver Yorke, Esq. Letter I', 'Second Letter from
    John Galt, Esq., with Preliminary Observations, by Oliver Yorke', and 'Letters on
    West Indian slavery. By J. Galt, Esq.', *Fraser's Magazine*, 2 (1830), 440–49, 556–63,
    563–71; 'West Indian Slavery. By J. Galt, Esq. Letter III', *Fraser's Magazine*, 2 (1831),
    706–13; and 'The Whole West India Question, by John Galt, to Oliver Yorke, Esq.',
    Fraser's Magazine, 8 (1833), 81–90; idem, *Bogle Corbet; or, the Emigrants* (3 vols., London,
    1831), 1:311–12; John Galt to Robert Wilmot-Horton, 16 June 1825, RWH Papers,
    D3155/WH/2793, fos. 65–7.

20 Acting Committee, 3 March 1830; *WIR* (1829), 20:85n, 21:112; Stephen, *Recollections*,
    p. 117.

21 *WIR* (1828), 14:36–9.

22 Canning to Ellis, 27 May 1826, *Canning and Friends*, 2:351–2; Greville, *Memoirs*, 1:85; *ASMR* (1828), 40: 293; *Barbadian*, 11 May 1823; Moody to Wilmot-Horton, 18 January 1826, RWH Papers, D3155/WH/2849.

23 Standing Committee, 8 April, 8 May, and 13 May 1829; Seaford to Bagot, 3 October 1827; *London Gazette*, 26 April 1831; I.P.H. Duffy, *Bankruptcy and Insolvency in London during the Industrial Revolution* (New York, 1985), p. 22.

24 *WIR* (1829), 23:133; Standing Committee, 20 May 1829; William Burge to S.L. Giffard, 10 October 1831, Halsbury Papers, British Library, Add MS 56369, fos. 73–6; F.M.L. Thompson, 'Richard Temple-Nugent-Brydges-Chandos-Grenville (1776–1839)', *ODNB*.

25 One of the most recent histories of the 'Catholic Question' is: Antonia Fraser, *The King and the Catholics: The Fight for Rights, 1829* (London, 2018). Scholarly treatments include R.W. Davis, 'The Tories, the Whigs, and Catholic Emancipation, 1827–1829', *English Historical Review*, 97 (1982), 89–98; F. O'Ferrall, *Catholic Emancipation: Daniel O'Connell and the Birth of Irish Democracy, 1820–30* (London, 1985).

26 Ibid., pp. 203, 69, 70.

27 *Gentleman's Magazine*, 99 (1829), p. 165; *Arbuthnot Journal*, 9 October 1828, 2:213.

28 *ASMR* (1829), 46:441; Asa Briggs, *The Age of Improvement, 1783–1867* (2nd edn, Oxford, 2000), p. 201.

29 Briggs, *Improvement*, p. 201; *Hansard*, Commons, 4 February 1830, XXII, c. 93.

30 Hilton, *Dangerous*, pp. 408, 406.

31 Jones, 'Mobilisation', p. 245.

11. The Fall of the House of Liverpool

1   *ASMR* (1829), 53:97.

2   Buxton, *Memoirs*, p. 242; *Memoirs of Joseph Sturge*, ed. Richard Henry (London, 1865), p. 86; Buxton, *Memoirs*, p. 212; Jones, 'Mobilisation', p. 246.

3   Buxton, *Memoirs*, p. 228.

4   For this, see: Richard B. Sheridan, 'The West India Sugar Crisis and British Slave Emancipation, 1830–1833', *Journal of Economic History*, 21 (1961), 539–51.

5   Standing Committee, 9 February 1824; John Gladstone to Keith Douglas, 3 February 1830, Gladstone Papers, GG MS 328; *WIR* (1830), 31:278; 'Petitions and Correspondence with Government ... including Sugar & Rum', WICR, Box 9 Folder 1. This select committee's findings were eventually published as *Report from Select Committee on the Commercial State of the West India Colonies* (PP 1831–32 (381)) (London, 1832).

6   *The Times*, 9 April 1880.

7   *ASMR* (1830), 61:229, 241; Stephen, *Recollections*, p. 143; *ASMR* (1830), 61:257.

8   Stephen, *Recollections*, pp. 121–2.

9   Jones, 'Mobilisation', p. 259, 259n102; *Life and Letters of Macaulay*, p. 459; Jones, 'Mobilisation', p. 259n102.

10 Benjamin Godwin, *The Substance of a Course of Lectures on British Colonial Slavery, Delivered at Bradford, York, and Scarborough* (London, 1830); Jones, 'Mobilisation', p. 260; Buxton, *Memoirs*, p. 242n; *Memoirs of Sturge*, pp. 89–90.

11 Buxton, *Memoirs*, pp. 228, 230–1.

12 Christopher Hibbert, 'George IV (1762–1830)', *ODNB*; *Wellington and His Friends: Letters of the First Duke of Wellington to the Rt Hon Charles and Mrs Arbuthnot, the Earl and Countess of Wilton, Princess Lieven, and Miss Burdett-Coutts*, ed. Gerald Wellesley (London, 1965), p. 90; *Arbuthnot Journal*, 4 June and 29 June 1830, pp. 361, 364.

13 *The Times*, 29 June 1830; *Arbuthnot Journal*, 29 June 1830, p. 364.

14 'Debate in the Lords on the Abolition of the Slave Trade', 3 May 1792, in *Parliamentary Debates* (1817), 29:1349–50; Hochschild, *Bury the Chains*, p. 186; 'Debate in the Lords

on the Abolition of the Slave Trade', 11 April 1793, in *Parliamentary Debates* (1817), 30:659; *Life and Letters of Macaulay*, p. 221.

15   Simon Taylor to George Hibbert, 29 August 1804, on Dr Christer Petley's blog, *Slavery and Revolution*; Duke of Clarence to Samuel Hawker, 1807, *Georgian Papers Online*, GEO/ADD/44/10.

16   Jones, 'Mobilisation', p. 254; Robert Wilmot-Horton, *First letter to the freeholders of the county of York, on negro slavery* (London, 1830) and *Second letter to the freeholders of the county of York, on negro slavery* (London, 1830); *ASMR* (1830), 72:507; *ASMR* (1830), 65:366; Wilberforce to James Stephen, 7 August 1830, *Correspondence*, 2:522.

17   Terry Jenkins, 'Bristol', *HP*.

18   *ASMR* (1830), 65:363–4.

19   Jenkins, 'Bristol'; *ASMR* (1830), 65:362.

20   *Life and Letters of Macaulay*, p. 454.

21   Hilton, *Dangerous*, p. 416; Edward Royle, *Revolutionary Britannia? Reflections on the Threat of Revolution in Britain, 1789–1848* (Manchester, 2000), p. 84; *Arbuthnot Journal*, 29 November 1830, 2:405.

22   *Arbuthnot Journal*, 10 November 1830, 2:400; ibid., 7 November 1830, 2:398.

23   *Hansard*, Lords, 2 November 1830, I, cc. 52–3; Greville, *Memoirs*, 8 November 1830, 2:54.

24   *Arbuthnot Journal*, 20 November 1830, 2:402.

25   Greville, *Memoirs*, 16 November 1830, 2:62; Hilton, *Dangerous*, p. 420.

26   *Creevey Papers*, 1:336; E.A. Smith, 'Charles, second Earl Grey (1764–1845)', *ODNB*; H.R. Vassall, *Memoirs of the Whig Party during My Times*, ed. H.E. Vassall (2 vols., London, 1852–4), 1:98.

27   Smith, 'Grey'; *Letters of Dorothea, Princess Lieven, during Her Residence in London, 1812–34*, ed. Lionel G. Robinson (London, 1902), pp. 278–9; *Life and Letters of Sir James Graham, Second Baronet of Netherby, 1792–1861*, ed. Charles Stuart Parker (2 vols., London, 1907), 1:90; *Arbuthnot Journal*, 29 November 1830, 2:405.

28   The most compelling narrative of this episode is: Simon Garfield, *The Last Journey of William Huskisson: How a Day of Triumph Became A Day of Disaster at the Turn of a Wheel* (London, 2003).

29   Ibid., p. 155.

30   *Arbuthnot Journal*, 26 September 1830, 2:386; Garfield, *Huskisson*, pp. 161, 157, 163.

31   Huskisson, *Memoirs*, pp. 240–1; *ASMR* (1831), 74:31.

12. Reform, That You May Preserve

1   *Arbuthnot Journal*, 6 December 1831, 2:431.

2   For the Colonial Congress, see: B.W. Higman, 'The Colonial Congress of 1831', in Brian Moore and Swithin Wilmot (eds.), *Before & After 1865: Education, Politics, and Regionalism in the Caribbean* (Kingston, 1998), 239–48.

3   Ibid., pp. 243–4; Minutes of the Bristol W.I.A., 18 April 1832; Higman, 'Congress', p. 243.

4   *Arbuthnot Journal*, 16 January 1831, 2:411; Whyte, *Macaulay*, p. 227; Buxton, *Memoirs*, p. 255.

5   Buxton, *Memoirs*, p. 257.

6   'Negro Slavery', *Hansard*, Commons, 15 April 1831, III, cc. 1408–69, esp. 1415–16; Thomas Malthus, *An Essay on the Principle of Population; or, A View of its Past and Present Effects on Human Happiness* [1798] (6th edn, 2 vols., London, 1826), 1:15, 24. Major discussions of the relationship between slavery and demography include: B.W. Higman, *Slave Populations of the British Caribbean, 1807–1834* (Baltimore, 1984)

and Seymour Drescher, *The Mighty Experiment: Free Labor versus Slavery in British Emancipation* (Oxford, 2002), pp. 34–53.

7   *Hansard*, 15 April 1831, cc. 1418.

8   *The Times*, 16 April 1831.

9   Jones, 'Mobilisation', pp. 269'; Margaret Escott, 'Patrick Maxwell Stewart (1795–1846)', *HP*; Stephen, *Recollections*, pp. 113, 62; *Arbuthnot Journal*, 29 March 1831, 2:417.

10   Buxton, *Memoirs*, pp. 264–6.

11   *Memoirs of Sturge*, p. 98.

12   Leslie Stephen, rev. Peter Balmford, 'George Stephen (1794–1879)', *ODNB*; Stephen, *Recollections*, pp. 123–4, 129.

13   *Memoir of James Stephen*, pp. 70–2; Sturge, *Memoirs*, pp. 94–5; Stephen, *Recollections*, pp. 129–33.

14   Stephen, *Recollections*, p. 130–1; Sturge, *Memoirs*, p. 95.

15   Higman, 'Congress', p. 248.

16   Ibid., p. 241; Petley, *Slaveholders*, pp. 96, 98.

17   Petley, *Slaveholders*, p. 100.

18   PP 1831–32 (721), pp. 131, 130, 220; Frederick Marryat, *Newton Forster; or, The Merchant Service* (3 vols., London, 1832), 1:232.

19   Petley, *Slaveholders*, p. 100; *ASMR* (1830), 57:182.

20   Goderich to Earl Belmore, 1 March 1832, in *Despatches between Government and W. India Colonies, relative to Recent Rebellion among Slaves* (PP 1831–32 (285)) (London, 1832), p. 40; Belmore to Goderich, 2 May 1832, Colonial Office Papers, CO/137/182/22.

21   Philippa McDonnell, 'Why My Great-Great-Great Grandfather Defaced Ancient Egyptian Monuments', *The Guardian*, 3 August 2009; Hibbert to Belmore, 28 August 1828, Belmore Papers, PRONI, D3007/G/39/1.

22   Petley, *Slaveholders*, p. 98; PP 1831–32 (285), pp. 6, 12.

23   *Information from Jamaica respecting Inquiry into Treatment of Female Slave* (PP 1830–31 (231)) (London, 1831), pp. 9–10.

24   Ibid., pp. 10–11; Henry Bleby, *Death Struggles of Slavery: Being, A Narrative of Facts and Incidents, which Occurred in a British Colony, during the Two Years Immediately Preceding Negro Emancipation* (London, 1853), p. 122.

25   Petley, *Slaveholders*, pp. 96–7.

26   *Account of the Fatal Hurricane, by which Barbados Suffered in August 1831* (Bridgetown, 1831), i–ii, pp. 33–9.

13. A Most Extensive Conspiracy

1   *ASMR* (1830), 61:258.

2   Bleby, *Death Struggles*, i.

3   *Report from the House of Assembly, Jamaica, on Injury Sustained during Recent Rebellion* (PP 1831–32 (561)) (London, 1832), p. 20.

4   *Report from the House*, p. 20; Bleby, *Death Struggles*, p. 8; *Report from the House*, p. 20; *Despatches between Government*, p. 20.

5   *Despatches*, pp. 23, 22; Bleby, *Death Struggles*, p. 8.

6   Petley, *Slaveholders*, pp. 103, 101.

7   Knibb, *Memoir*, p. 103; *Despatches*, pp. 41, 4.

8   *Report*, p. 6; Bleby, *Death Struggles*, p. 4; *Despatches*, p. 19.

9   Bleby, *Death Struggles*, pp. 115, 114.

10   Ibid., p. 111.

11   Ibid., pp. 111–12; Mary Reckford, 'Jamaica Slave Rebellion of 1831', *Past & Present*, 40 (1968), 108–25, p. 117.

12 Bleby, *Death Struggles*, p. 113; Reckford, 'Jamaica', p. 117; Hochschild, *Bury the Chains*, pp. 340–1.

13 *Report*, p. 35; Bleby, *Death Struggles*, pp. 3, 114.

14 *Despatches*, p. 20; Knibb, *Memoir*, p. 118; Mary Turner, *Slaves and Missionaries: The Disintegration of Jamaican Slave Society, 1787–1834* (Kingston, 1998), p. 156; Bleby, *Death Struggles*, p. 7.

15 *Despatches*, pp. 22–3; Bleby, *Death Struggles*, p. 9.

16 *Despatches*, pp. 31–2.

17 Bleby, *Death Struggles*, pp. 9–10.

18 Ibid., p. 12; *Report*, p. 36.

19 *Despatches*, p. 27.

20 Ibid., pp. 15, 29–30.

21 Ibid., pp. 26, 29.

22 Bleby, *Death Struggles*, pp. 16–17.

23 Theodore Foulks, *Eighteen Months in Jamaica: with Recollections of the Late Rebellion* (London, 1833), p. 86.

24 Bleby, *Death Struggles*, p. 18.

25 *Report*, p. 17; *Despatches*, p. 50; Bleby, *Death Struggles*, p. 22; William Law Mathieson, *British Slavery and Its Abolition, 1823–1838* (London, 1926), p. 214.

26 *Despatches*, pp. 34, 38, 50, 37.

27 *Report*, p. 4; Bleby, *Death Struggles*, p. 21; *Despatches*, p. 51.

28 Abigail B. Bakan, *Ideology and Class Conflict in Jamaica: The Politics of Rebellion* (Montreal, 1990), p. 65; Foulks, *Eighteen Months*, p. 65; Petley, *Slaveholders*, p. 112.

29 Petley, *Slaveholders*, p. 117; Turner, *Slaves and Missionaries*, p. 161.

30 *Report from the House of Assembly*, p. 4; H.M. Waddell, *Twenty-Nine Years in the West Indies and Central Africa: A Review of Missionary Work and Adventure, 1829–1858* [1863] (2nd edn, London, 1970), pp. 65–6.

31 Bleby, *Death Struggles*, pp. 27–8.

32 Ibid., pp. 26–31.

33 Ibid., pp. 116–18.

14. Mere Anarchy

1 E.P. Thompson, *The Making of the English Working Class* [1963] (London, 1980), p. 901.

2 Diary of the Duke of Newcastle, 11–12 October 1831, Newcastle Papers, Ne 2 F 4/1, p. 6 [*Riots and Reform*, www.nottingham.ac.uk/manuscriptsandspecialcollections/learning/dukeofnewcastle/theme2/riotsandreform].

3 Ibid.; *Arbuthnot Journal*, 2:431, 414.

4 *The Holland House Diaries, 1831–1840: The Diary of Henry Richard Vassall Fox, Third Lord Holland, with Extracts from the Diary of Dr John Allen*, ed. Abraham D. Kriegel (London, 1977), 19 February 1832, p. 136; David Olusoga, *Black and British: A Forgotten History* (London, 2016), p. 230; Buxton, *Memoirs*, p. 286; *ASMR* (1832), 101:292; William IV to Viscount Goderich, 22 February 1832, Papers of the Earl of Ripon, British Library, London, Add MS 40682, fo. 318.

5 The rumour was put forth by Peter Borthwick and rubbished by Henry Bleby: *Death Struggles*, p. 41; George Hibbert to William Tharp, 3 May 1832, Tharp Papers, Shire Hall, Cambridge, R55/7/128/j.

6 Nicholas Draper, *The Price of Emancipation: Slave-Ownership, Compensation, and British Society at the End of Slavery* (Cambridge, 2013), pp. 23–7; *Holland House Diaries*, pp. 136–7; *Report from the Select Committee on the State of the West India Colonies* (PP 1831–32 (127)) (London, 1832), iii.

7 *ASMR* (1833), 105:473; Hibbert to Tharp, 3 May 1832.

8 Buxton, *Memoirs*, pp. 280–1; *ASMR* (1832), 95:135–6.

9   Jones, 'Mobilisation', p. 273; Stephen, *Recollections*, p. 181; *Life and Letters*, p. 466.

10   *Knibb, Memoir*, p. 175.

11   *Report from the House Assembly*, pp. 3–4.

12   Bleby, *Death Struggles*, p. 95; *Report from the House of Assembly*, p. 7;

13   *WIR* (1829), 16:9; Bridges to Belmore, 25 July 1830, Belmore Papers, D/3007/G/9/15, fo. 60; Bleby. *Death Struggles*, p. 139.

14   Bleby, *Death Struggles*, p. 140; Petley, *Slaveholders*, p. 99.

15   Petley, *Slaveholders*, pp. 120–2, 130.

16   'Attack on the Wesleyan Missionary Meeting-House', *Hansard*, Commons, 13 March 1827, XVI, cc1166–73.

17   Thomas F. Abbott, *Narrative of Certain Events Connected with the Late Disturbances in Jamaica, and the Charges Preferred against the Baptist Missionaries in that Island* (London, 1832), pp. 24–6.

18   Petley, *Slaveholders*, p. 83; W.J. Gardner, *A History of Jamaica: From Its Discovery by Christopher Columbus to the Year 1872* [1873] (3rd edn, London, 1971), p. 276; Bleby, *Death Struggles*, pp. 134–6.

19   Bleby, *Death Struggles*, p. 213; *Wesleyan-Methodist Magazine*, 56 (1832), p. 64; idem, *Death Struggles*, pp. 159, 148, 208.

20   Bleby's account of his ordeal may be found in *Death Struggles*, pp. 196–207.

21   Hilton, *Dangerous*, p. 426; Thompson, *Working Class*, p. 898.

22   *Royal Gazette, Guiana*, 1 May 1832; *Hansard*, Commons, 30 May 1833, XVIII, c. 113.

23   Buxton, *Memoirs*, p. 288.

24   Ibid., p. 289.

25   'Slavery in the Colonies', *Hansard*, Commons, 24 May 1832, XIII, cc. 37–49.

26   Ibid., cc. 65–6; Buxton, *Memoirs*, pp. 290–2; Stephen, *Recollections*, p. 177.

27   Ibid., p. 292.

28   Ibid.; *Life and Letters of Macaulay*, p. 466; William IV to Goderich, 5 June 1832, Ripon Papers, Add MS 40682, fos. 346–7.

29   Buxton, *Memoirs*, p. 243; *Life and Letters of Macaulay*, p. 470; Jones, 'Mobilisation', p. 271n176.

30   Mary Reckford, 'The Colonial Office and the Abolition of Slavery', *Historical Journal*, 14 (1971), 723–34, p. 733.

31   Howick to Belmore, early 1832, Akala, *Natives: Race and Class in the Ruins of Empire* (London, 2018), p. 133.

32   Goderich to Belmore, 1 March 1832, in *Despatches between Government*, pp. 45, 44.

15. The Condition of England

1   Charles Dickens, *Bleak House* (1852–3) (Oxford, 1996), Ch. XXXVIII, p. 563.

2   Literary Committee, 18 and 25 February 1832; Stephen, *Recollections*, p. 184.

3   Stephen, *Recollections*, pp. 184, 167–8; James Colquhoun to Charles Payne, 17 July 1832, Bristol W.I.A. Papers, SMV/8/3/3/3/24.

4   Stephen, *Recollections*, pp. 184–6.

5   Ibid., pp. 186–7.

6   Ibid., p. 169; Jones, 'Mobilisation', p. 275; Stephen, *Recollections*, p. 175.

7   Bleby, *Death Struggles*, pp. 154, 215; *Holland House Diaries*, p. 140; Belmore to Goderich, 30 April 1832, Colonial Office Papers, CO/137/182/17; Belmore Papers, D/3007/G/11/2, fo. 4.

8   Dispatch to Goderich, Colonial Office Papers, CO/137/182/37, 41; *New Monthly Magazine* (October 1832), p. 428; John Clark, W. Dendy, and J.M. Phillippo, *The Voice of Jubilee: A Narrative of the Baptist Mission, Jamaica, from its Commencement* (London, 1865), p. 225; Petley, *Slaveholders*, p. 124.

9   Richard Davenport-Hines, 'Constantine Henry Phipps, first Marquess of Normanby (1797–1863)', *ODNB*.

10   *Holland House Diaries*, p. 140; Dispatch from Mulgrave, 7 October 1832, Colonial Office, CO/137/183/31; Mulgrave to Goderich, 17 December 1832, qu. in Wilbur Devereux Jones, 'Lord Mulgrave's Administration in Jamaica, 1832–33', *Journal of Negro History*, 48 (1963), 44–56, p. 50; Mulgrave to Goderich, 5 August 1832, Ripon Papers, Add MS 40862, fo. 44; Mulgrave to Goderich, 23 February 1833, Ripon Papers, Add MS 40863.

11   Mulgrave to Goderich, 5 August 1832; Belmore Papers, D/3007/G/37/5; Bleby, *Death Struggles*, p. 224.

12   Petley, *Slaveholders*, p. 125; Bleby, *Death Struggles*, p. 256.

13   Jones, 'Mobilisation', p. 264;

14   Ibid., p. 265.

15   Stephen, *Recollections*, pp. 149–52.

16   Garrison (ed.), *Lectures of George Thompson*, xxxiv; Stephen, *Recollections*, p. 150; S.J. Morgan, 'George Donisthorpe Thompson (1804–1878)', *ODNB*.

17   Stephen, *Recollections*, p. 153; *Report of the Agency Committee of the Anti-Slavery Society, established in June, 1831* (London, 1832), p. 12.

18   Literary Committee, 30 and 23 June 1832; H.C.G. Matthew, 'Peter Borthwick (1804–1852)', *ODNB*; Stephen, *Recollections*, p. 154.

19   Literary Committee, 21 and 28 July 1832.

20   George Saintsbury to Charles Payne, 12 October 1832, Bristol W.I.A. Papers, SMV/8/3/3/3/28; *The Tourist: A Literary and Anti-Slavery Journal*, 5 November 1832, pp. 63–4; Stephen, *Recollections*, p. 154.

21   *Life and Letters of Macaulay*, p. 469.

22   Jones, 'Mobilisation', pp. 276, 250.

23   Stephen, *Recollections*, pp. 162, 165; *Memoirs of Sturge*, p. 100; Jones, 'Mobilisation', p. 256.

24   Jones, 'Mobilisation', p. 257; Stephen, *Recollections*, pp. 163, 167.

25   Stephen, *Recollections*, pp. 154, 158; *Memoirs of James Stephen*, p. 101.

26   *Black Dwarf*, 6 August 1823; see Carlile's *The Lion* and *The Republican*, passim; Alison Twells, *The Civilising Mission and the English Middle Class, 1792–1850* (Basingstoke, 2009), p. 152; Ryan Hanley, 'A Radical Change of Heart: Robert Wedderburn's Last Word on Slavery', *Slavery & Abolition*, 37 (2016), 423–45.

27   James Sambrook, *William Cobbett* (London, 1973), p. 61; William Cobbett, *Rural Rides* [1830], ed. Ian Dyck (London, 2001), p. 31; *CWR*, 4 August 1821, 13 December 1823; William Cobbett, *Eleven Lectures on the French and Belgian Revolutions* (London, 1830), p. 198; Literary Committee, 15 December 1823 and 5 December 1830.

28   PP 1832 (127) p. 780; PP 1828 (261), p. 30; *The Condition of the West India Slave Contrasted with that of the Infant Slave in Our English Factories, with Fifteen Illustrations from the Graver of Robert Cruikshank* (London, 1833); Simmons, *To Earl Grey*, p. 4; *The Factory-Child, A Poem* (London, 1831), pp. 19, 25.

29   [Henry Rondeau], *Anti-Negro Emancipation. An appeal to Mr. Wilberforce* (London, 1824), p. 8; John Foster, *Two Letters on the State of the Negroes in the West Indies* (Bedford, 1824), p. 15; 'A Member of the Assembly of Grenada', *A Few Remarks on Colonial Legislation, as Connected with the Communication from the Noble Secretary for the Colonies* (London, 1823), p. 47; Carlile, *Lion*, p. 29; 'Member … Grenada', *Few Remarks*, p. 47; Jelly, *Remarks*, p. 26.

30   *Voice of the West Indies*, p. 8; Bridges, *Voice from Jamaica*, p. 39; Nathaniel Sotham, *Plain Facts; or the Question of West India Slavery, Seriously Examined by the Test of Truth, and Real Observation* (3rd edn, Cheltenham, 1825), pp. 32–3.

31   PP 1831–2 (721), pp. 505–6; *The Times*, 25 April 1828; Thomas de Quincey, 'West India Property, 14 June 1828' and 'West India Property. 28 June 1828', in Stuart M. Tave, *New Essays by De Quincey: His Contributions to the Edinburgh Saturday Post and the Edinburgh Evening Post, 1827–1828* (Princeton, NJ, 1966), pp. 358–87, at pp. 360, 374; Carlile, *Republican*, 21 July 1826.

32 Carlile, *Lion* (1829), 4:741; Ryan Hanley, 'Slavery and the Birth of Working-Class Racism in England, 1814–1833', *Transactions of the Royal Historical Society*, 26 (2016), 103–23, at pp. 120–1.

33 Drescher, *Mighty Experiment*, p. 51.

34 Cecil Driver, *Tory Radical: The Life of Richard Oastler* (New York, 1946); Richard Oastler, *Facts and Plain Words on Every-Day Subjects, comprised in Two Speeches delivered at Wakefield on the Day of the First Election for the West-Riding of Yorkshire, December 20, 1832* (Leeds, 1833), p. 38; *Society for the Improvement of the Condition of Factory Children* (London, 1833), p. 13; Oastler, *Facts and Plain Words*, pp. 16, 38.

35 'A Methodist', *Rev. R. Watson, Mr. Macaulay, & Mr. Sadler* (Leeds, 1831), p. 1; *Condition of the West India Slave Contrasted*, p. 28; Driver, *Tory Radical*, pp. 200–1; *Leeds Mercury*, 15 December 1832.

36 Stephen, *Recollections*, pp. 248–9; *Life and Letters of Captain Marryat*, ed. Florence Marryat (2 vols., London, 1872), 1:204, narrated in: Tom Pocock, *Captain Marryat: Seaman, Writer, and Adventurer* (London, 2000), pp. 113–5.

37 'Notes on Slavery', Gladstone Papers, British Library London, Add MS 44649, fo. 31; Gladstone, 'Independent Electors' GG MS 223; *Hansard*, Commons, 17 May 1833, XVII, cc. 1345–7; Buxton, *Memoirs*, p. 304.

16. False Dawns

1   *ASMR* (1833), 105:533.

2   'List of West India Friends in Parliament, May 1833', Gladstone Papers, GG MS 2877; Standing Committee, 29 January 1833.

3   Garrison (ed.), *Lectures of George Thompson*, vii–viii; Literary Committee, 9 and 21 January, 2 and 30 March 1833.

4   James MacQueen, 'The Colonial Empire of Great Britain – Letter to Earl Grey, First Lord of the Treasury', *Blackwood's Edinburgh Magazine*, 30 (1831), 744–64, at pp. 744, 751.

5   Sue Thomas, '*Pringle v. Cadell* and *Wood v. Pringle*: The Libel Cases over *The History of Mary Prince*', *Journal of Commonwealth Literature*, 40 (2005), 13–35; Moody to Wilmot-Horton, 18 January 1826, RWH Papers, D3155/WH/2849; Thomas, 'Libel', pp. 126, 129; Lambert, *Mastering the Niger*, p. 138.

6   *Report from the Select Committee*, iv; *Abstract of the Report of the Lords Committees on the Condition and Treatment of the Colonial Slaves* (London, 1833), p. 2; *ASMR* (1833), 105:476–7, 523–4.

7   Petley, *Slaveholders*, p. 128.

8   Ibid., pp. 125, 129; Bleby, *Death Struggles*, pp. 271–3.

9   Buxton, *Memoirs*, pp. 300, 301.

10 Macaulay to Wilberforce, 26 November 1832, in *Correspondence*, 2:524–7.

11 *Holland House Diaries*, p. 207;

12 'King's Speech', *Hansard*, Lords, 5 February 1833, XV, cc. 86–90; *Three Early Nineteenth Century Diaries*, ed. A. Aspinall (London, 1952), p. 296.

13 Buxton, *Memoirs*, p. 302; *Memoirs of Sturge*, p. 101.

14 William IV to Goderich, 5 June 1832, and Herbert Taylor to Goderich, 5 June 1832, Ripon Papers, Add MS 40862, fos. 345–8.

15 Jones, 'Mulgrave', pp. 47–8; *Three Diaries*, pp. 291–2.

16 *Three Diaries*, p. 293.

17 Buxton, *Memoirs*, p. 308.

18 Ibid., pp. 308–10.

19 Ibid., pp. 301–11; William Gladstone to John Gladstone, 18 March 1833, GG MS 223, fo. 73.

20   Angus Hawkins, *The Forgotten Prime Minister, the 14th Earl of Derby. Volume 1: Ascent, 1799–1851* (Oxford, 2007), pp. 127–8.
21   E.A. Smith, *Lord Grey, 1764–1845* (Oxford, 1990), p. 302; *Three Diaries*, p. 316.
22   Buxton, *Memoirs*, pp. 311–12.
23   Henry Whiteley, *Three Months in Jamaica, in 1832: Comprising a Residence of Seven Weeks on a Sugar Plantation* (London, 1833), p. 2, Buxton, *Memoirs*, p. 312.
24   Michael Scott, *Tom Cringle's Log* (2 vols., Edinburgh, 1833); Catherine Hall, Nicholas Draper, Keith McClelland, Katie Donington, and Rachel Lang, *Legacies of British Slave-Ownership: Colonial Slavery and the Formation of Victorian Britain* (Cambridge, 2014), pp. 163–4.
25   Stephen, *Recollections*, p. 194; 'One of the Protestant Party', *Random Recollections of Exeter Hall, in 1834–1837* (London, 1838), pp. 5–10; Buxton, *Memoirs*, pp. 317–18.
26   Stephen, *Recollections*, p. 195; Buxton, *Memoirs*, p. 318.

17. The Price of Liberty

1   Buxton, *Memoirs*, p. 328.
2   Ibid., p. 321n.
3   *Three Diaries*, pp. 329–30.
4   Stephen, *Recollections*, p. 199; Hawkins, p. 437n60; *Three Diaries*, p. 330.
5   Buxton, *Memoirs*, pp. 320–1; 'Ministerial Proposition for the Emancipation of Slaves', *Hansard*, Commons, 14 May 1833, XVII, cc. 1193–1231.
6   Draper, *Price of Emancipation*, pp. 98–9. The clearest narrative of these parliamentary negotiations is probably still: Izhak Gross, 'The Abolition of Negro Slavery and British Parliamentary Politics, 1832–3', *Historical Journal*, 23 (1980), 63–85, to which the following paragraphs owe much.
7   Glasgow W.I.A., TD/1683/1/2, 13 May 1833; *Hansard*, Commons, 30 May 1833, XVIII, cc. 113–4; *Proceedings at a Public Meeting of Persons Interested in the Preservation of the British West India Colonies, held at the City of London Tavern, the 27th May, 1833* (London, 1833).
8   *Holland House Diaries*, pp. 213, 216; *Hansard*, Commons, 11 June 1833, XVIII, c. 581; *Holland Diaries*, pp. 218–9.
9   Buxton, *Memoirs*, pp. 298, 329; *The Debates in Parliament: Session 1833, on The Resolutions and Bill for the Abolition of Slavery* (London, 1834), p. 103.
10   Stephen, *Recollections*, pp. 204–5; *Memoirs of Sturge*, p. 106.
11   Gross, 'Abolition', p. 77.
12   Buxton, *Memoirs*, pp. 333–4; Gross, 'Abolition', pp. 77–8; William Gladstone to John Gladstone, 25 July 1833, GG MS 223, fo. 137.
13   Standing Committee, 10 July 1833; Petley, *Slaveholders*, p. 139–40.
14   George Hibbert to William Tharp, 4 July 1833, Tharp Papers.
15   William Gladstone to John Gladstone, 18 and 9 July 1833, GG MS 223.
16   William Gladstone to John Gladstone, 12, 13, 15, 16, 18, 19, and 22 July 1833, GG MS 223; Draper, *Price of Emancipation*, p. 139.
17   'Ministerial Plan for the Abolition of Slavery', *Hansard*, Commons, 31 July 1833, XX, cc. 196–221.
18   William Gladstone to John Gladstone, 7 August 1833, Gladstone Papers, GG MS 223, fos. 142–3.
19   Buxton, *Memoirs*, pp. 336–7; Stephen, *Recollections*, p. 206.
20   *Three Diaries*, pp. 330–1; *Holland House Diaries*, p. 208;
21   Timbs, *Club Life of London*, 2:179–80.
22   Buxton, *Memoirs*, p. 335.
23   Ibid., pp. 257–8; Stephen, *Recollections*, pp. 207–8.
24   Stephen, *Recollections*, pp. 207–8.

18. The Cat and the Mill

1   Hall et al, *Legacies*, p. 194.

2   Buxton, *Memoirs*, p. 339; Petley, *Slaveholders*, pp. 139–43.

3   Buxton, *Memoirs*, pp. 343, 342.

4   S.A. Skinner, *Tractarians and the 'Condition of England': The Social and Political Thought of the Oxford Movement* (Oxford, 2004). Froude to Newman, 25 January 1834, in *Hurrell Froude: Memoranda and Comments*, ed. Louise Imogen Guiney (London, 1904), p. 134; Froude to William Froude, 12 February 1834, *Memoranda*, p. 139; *Remains of the late Reverend Richard Hurrell Froude, M.A., Fellow of Oriel College, Oxford*, ed. John Keble and John Henry Newman (2 vols., London, 1838), 1:343; Hurrell Froude to Keble, 9 January 1834, in *Memoranda*, p. 132; Hurrell Froude to William Froude, 12 February 1834, in *Memoranda*, p. 139.

5   Rugemer, *Problem of Emancipation*, i; Carl Lawrence Paulus, *The Slaveholding Crisis: Fear of Insurrection and the Coming of the Civil War* (Baton Rouge, LA, 2017), pp. 80, 88.

6   Rugemer, *Problem of Emancipation*, pp. 191, 188–9, 191.

7   Buxton, *Memoirs*, p. 338; Petley, *Slaveholders*, p. 146; William A. Green, *British Slave Emancipation: The Sugar Colonies and the Great Experiment, 1830–1865* (Oxford, 1976), p. 131; James A. Thome and J. Horace Kimball, *Emancipation in the West Indies: A Six Months' Tour in Antigua, Barbadoes, and Jamaica, in the Year 1837* (New York, 1838), p. 144.

8   Thome and Kimball, *Emancipation*, pp. 144–5.

9   Buxton, *Memoirs*, pp. 353, 355.

10 Green, *Emancipation*, p. 131n4. The other formidable account of the apprenticeship and labour relations in the West Indies is: Thomas C. Holt, *The Problem of Freedom: Race, Labor, and Politics in Jamaica and Britain, 1832–1938* (Baltimore, 1992).

11 Thome and Kimball, *Emancipation*, pp. 137, 200, 203, 202–3.

12 Clare Taylor (ed.), *British and American Abolitionists: An Episode in Transatlantic Understanding* (Edinburgh, 1974), pp. 20, 21; Garrison (ed.), *Lectures of Thompson*, xi–xii.

13 Garrison (ed.), *Lectures of Thompson*, xxi, iv; *Messages of Gen. Andrew Jackson: with a Short Sketch of His Life* (Concord, NH, 1837), p. 350; *Niles' Weekly Register*, 31 October 1835, p. 145;

14 Taylor, *British and American*, pp. 40, 50–1; *Letters and Addresses by George Thompson, during His Mission in the United States* (Boston, MA, 1837), p. 124.

15 Ralph Waldo Emerson, *An Address in the Court-House in Concord, Massachusetts, on 1ˢᵗ August, 1844, on the Anniversary of the Emancipation of the Negroes in the British West Indies* (Boston, MA, 1844), p. 3; Alexander Crummell, *The Man, The Hero, The Christian! A Eulogy on the Life and Character of Thomas Clarkson, delivered in the City of New-York, December, 1846* (New York, 1847); Rugemer, *Problem of Emancipation*, p. 228; Larry E. Tise, *Proslavery: A History of the Defense of Slavery in America, 1701–1840* (Athens, GA, 1987).

16 Draper, *Price of Emancipation*, pp. 107–12, 270; L.G. Mitchell, *Lord Melbourne, 1779–1848* (Oxford, 1997), p. 198.

17 Draper, *Price of Emancipation*, pp. 114–5.

18 Ibid., pp. 117, 125, 136.

19 Ibid., pp. 127, 208, 128.

20 Ibid., pp. 215–6.

21 Ibid., pp. 211, 157, 160.

22 George Wilson Bridges, *Outlines and Notes of Twenty-Nine Years, 1834–1862* (n.p., 1862), pp. 10–11.

23 Lambert, *Mastering the Niger*, pp. 22–3.

24 Buxton, *Memoirs*, p. 374; Kenneth Morgan, 'Labour Relations during and after Apprenticeship: Amity Hall, Jamaica, 1834–1840', *Slavery & Abolition*, 33 (2012), 457–78, at p. 461; Buxton, *Memoirs*, p. 376.

25 Henrice Altink, 'Slavery by Another Name: Apprenticed Women in Jamaican Workhouses in the Period, 1834–81', *Social History*, 26 (2001), 40–59, at pp. 50, 46, 47.

26   Green, *Emancipation*, pp. 138, 143, 141, 139.

27   *Memoir of Knibb*, p. 228; *Holland House Diaries*, p. 307; Buxton, *Memoirs*, p. 427.

28   Buxton, *Memoirs*, pp. 385, 422–3.

29   Stephen, *Recollections*, pp. 50–1.

30   Anthony J. Barker, 'Distorting the Record of Slavery and Abolition: The British Anti-Slavery Movement and Mauritius, 1826–37', *Slavery & Abolition*, 14 (1993), 185–207, at p. 194; Alex Tyrrell, 'Joseph Sturge (1793–1859)', *ODNB*; Joseph Sturge and Thomas Harvey, *The West Indies in 1837; Being the Journal of a Visit to Antigua, Montserrat, Dominica, St. Lucia, Barbados, and Jamaica* (London, 1838), pp. 373–4, 375.

31   James Williams, *Narrative of Events, since the First of August, 1834* (London, 1837), pp. 8, 1, 18.

32   Ibid., p. 26; Green, *Emancipation*, pp. 156, 160.

33   Knibb, *Memoir*, pp. 256–9.

Epilogue: Who Else Must Fall?

1   Hilary McDonald Beckles, '"Slavery Was A Long, Long Time Ago": Remembrance, Reconciliation, and the Reparations Discourse in the Caribbean', *Ariel*, 38 (2007), 9–25, at p. 9.

2   Qu. in Akala, *Natives*, p. 123.

3   'Feature Address', Hilary McDonald Beckles, 10 December 2014 [www.un.org/pga/69/101214_address-beckles]. Beckles has explored reparations at length in *Britain's Black Debt: Reparations for Caribbean Slavery and Native Genocide* (Kingston, 2013).

4   For these early problems, see: Hilary Beckles and Verene Shepherd (eds.), *Caribbean Freedom: Economy and Society from Emancipation to the Present* (Princeton 1993); Natasha Lightfoot, *Troubling Freedom: Antigua and the Aftermath of British Emancipation* (Durham, NC, 2015), p. 9.

5   'Mau Mau: Sinning Quietly', *Guardian*, 6 June 2013; Cobain, *History Thieves*, pp. 101–35.

6   Shashi Tharoor, *Inglorious Empire: What the British Did to India* (London, 2017), p. 238.

7   Descriptions of the ten-point plan are taken from the website of the CARICOM Reparations Commission: [caricomreparations.org/caricom/caricoms-10-point-reparation-plan], accessed 29 December 2019.

8   'UK sternly resists paying reparations for slave trade atrocities and injustices', *Guardian*, 24 February 2014; David Olusoga, 'The Treasury's tweet shows slavery is still misunderstood', *Guardian*, 12 February 2018.

9   Thomas Carlyle, 'Occasional Discourse on the Negro Question', *Fraser's Magazine*, 40 (1849), 670–79; Morrison qu. in Timothy H. Parsons, *The Second British Empire: In the Crucible of the Twentieth Century* (Lanham, MD), p. 115.

10   J.H. Newman, 'Slavery Allowed Not Encouraged Under the Gospel', in Francis J. McGrath and Placid Murray (eds.), *John Henry Newman: Sermons, 1824–1843, Volume III: Sermons and Lectures for Saints' Days and Holy Days and General Theology* (Oxford, 2010), pp. 239–253, at pp. 239n, 241, 249, 250; J.H. Newman, 'How to Accomplish It' [1836], in *Discussions and Arguments on Various Subjects* [1872], ed. Gerard Tracey and James Tolhurst (Leominster, 2004), 1–43, at p. 32; Newman to Allies, 8 November 1863, in John Henry Newman, *Letters and Diaries*, ed. Charles Stephen Dessain (32 vols., London, 1961–77), 20:554–6.

11   Hall et al, *Legacies*, pp. 183–6, 189–92; 182, 192; 189, 181.

12   Ibid., pp. 176–8, 179–80, 166.

13   Ibid., pp. 170, 171, 172–3.

14   Hall, *Macaulay and Son*, pp. 321–2.

15   Hall et al, *Legacies*, pp. 173–4, 39.

16   Ibid., pp. 2, 196–7; 2, 3.

17   Ibid., pp. 98–100; 109, 110; 103–8, 239.

18   Ibid., pp. 79, 94, 91.

19   Ibid., pp. 58, 2, 40, 57, 59.

20   *Tamworth Election. Speech of Sir Robert Peel, June 28, 1841* (London, 1841), pp. 8–9.

21   Hall et al, *Legacies*, p. 62.

22   Catherine Hall, 'Thinking Reflexively: Opening "Blind Eyes"', *Past and Present*, 234 (2017), 254–63, at p. 261.

23   Idem, *Macaulay and Son*, p. 86.

24   Richard Huzzey, *Freedom Burning: Antislavery and Empire in Victorian Britain* (Ithaca, NY, 2012), pp. 5, 7.

Bibliography

MANUSCRIPT PRIMARY SOURCES

Papers of the Earl of Belmore, Public Records Office of Northern Ireland, Belfast.
  D/3007/G/9/15
  D/3007/G/11/2
  D/3007/G/37/5
  D/3007/G/39/1
William Blackwood Papers, The National Library of Scotland, Edinburgh.
  MS 4010
  MS 4012
  MS 4022
  MS 4034
  MS 4036
Bristol West India Association Papers, Bristol Records Office, Bristol.
  SMV/8/3/2/3
  SMV/8/3/3/3/24
  SMV/8/3/3/3/28
Colonial Office Records, The National Archives, London.
  CO 28/85
  CO 111/46
  CO/137/182/17
  CO 137/182/22
  CO/137/182/37
  CO/137/183/31
Papers of William Gladstone, British Library, London.
  Add MS 44649
Glasgow West India Association Papers, Mitchell Library, Glasgow.
  TD1683/1/1
  TD1683/1/2
The Glynne–Gladstone Papers, Flintshire Records Office, Hawarden.
  GG MS 223
  GG MS 272
  GG MS 328
  GG MS 353
  GG MS 2877
Halsbury Papers, British Library, London.
  Add MS 56369

The Papers of William Huskisson, The British Library, London.
  Add MS 38744
  Add MS 38745
  Add MS 38747
  Add MS 38750
  Add MS 38752
  Add MS 38754
The Papers of Lord Liverpool, The British Library, London.
  Add MS 38295
Liverpool West India Association Papers, Liverpool Records Office, Liverpool.
  WES/380/1/2
John Murray Papers, The National Library of Scotland, Edinburgh.
  MS 40778
National Library of Jamaica, Kingston, Jamaica.
  MSS 723a, 724.
Robert Peel Papers, The British Library, London.
  Add MS 40403
  Add MS 40605
Public Records Office of Northern Ireland, Belfast.
  MIC/135/1: Watt Family Correspondence
Papers of the Earl of Ripon, British Library, London.
  Add MS 40862
  Add MS 40863
Tharp Family Papers, Cambridgeshire Records Office, Shire Hall, Cambridge.
  R55/7/128/j
West India Committee Records (SC 89), Alma Jordan Library, University of the West
  Indies, St Augustine, Trinidad and Tobago.
  Box 5/1: Minutes of the Literary Committee, 1823–29
  Box 6/7: Minutes of the Literary Committee, 1830–39
  Box 9/1: Petitions and Correspondence with Government
West India Committee Records, Institute of Commonwealth Studies, Senate House
  Library, University of London, London.
  M915/4: Minutes of the Standing Committee, 1823–29
  M915/6: Minutes of the Acting Committee
  M915/11: Minutes of the West India Merchants Sub-Committee
The Duke of Wellington Papers, University of Southampton Library, Southampton.
  WP1/760/9
  WP1/774/8
  WP1/785/10
Robert Wilmot-Horton Papers, Derbyshire Records Office, Matlock.
  D3155/WH/2760: Correspondence with George Canning
  D3155/WH/2769: Correspondence with James Colquhoun
  D3155/WH/2793: Correspondence with John Galt
  D3155/WH/2814: Correspondence with George Hibbert
  D3155/WH/2849: Correspondence with Thomas Moody
  D3155/WH/2901: Correspondence with Sir Ralph Woodford
  D3155/WH/2936: Correspondence relating to the West Indies, 1825–28
  D3155/WH/2939: Confidential Papers on the West India Question
  D3155/WH/2940: Confidential Papers on the West India Question
  D3155/WH/2941: Papers on the West India Question
  D3155/WH/3050: Papers by Major Moody, 1824 to 1826

PRINTED PRIMARY SOURCES

Abbott, Thomas F., *Narrative of Certain Events Connected with the Late Disturbances in Jamaica, and the Charges Preferred against the Baptist Missionaries in that Island* (London, 1832).

'Abolition of the Slave Trade – and of Slavery', *Edinburgh Review*, 41 (1824), 194–228.

Abstract of the Report of the Lords Committees on the Condition and Treatment of the Colonial Slaves (London, 1833).

Account of the Fatal Hurricane, by which Barbados Suffered in August 1831 (Bridgetown, 1831).

Actual State of the Question between Our Colonial Slave Proprietors, and the Parliament and Abolitionists of This Country (Glasgow, 1830).

Address to Manufacturers, Traders, and Others, on the Importance of Preserving the Colonies (London, 1826).

Address to the Electors of Great Britain, on the Condition of the Negroes in the British West Indies (London, 1831).

Alexander, J.E., *Transatlantic Sketches, comprising Visits to the Most Interesting Scenes in North and South America, and the West Indies, with Notes on Negro Slavery* (2 vols., London 1833).

Alison, Archibald, 'The West India Question', *Blackwood's Edinburgh Magazine*, 31 (1832), 412–23.

Ambler, Charles, *Reports of the Cases Argued and Determined in the High Court of Chancery, with Some Few in Other Courts* (London, 1790).

Anecdotes of the life of Richard Watson, Bishop of Llandaff; written by himself at different intervals and revised in 1814 (London, 1817).

The Annual Register, or A View of the History, Politics, and Literature of the Year 1827 (London, 1828).

The Annual Register, or A View of the History, Politics, and Literature of the Year 1828 (London, 1829).

'The Anti-Slavery Society', *Fraser's Magazine*, 1 (1830), 610–22.

Anti-Slavery Society Manifesto (London, 1823).

An Authentic Copy of the Minutes of Evidence on the Trial of John Smith, A Missionary, in Demerara (London, 1824).

Bailey, Rev.Benjamin, *The House of Bondage: A Dissertation upon the Nature of Service or Slavery under the Levitical Law* (London, 1824).

Barclay, Alexander, *A Practical View of the Present State of Slavery in the West Indies; or, an Examination of Mr Stephen's "Slavery of the British West India Colonies"* (London, 1826).

Barham, Joseph Foster, *Considerations on the Abolition of Negro Slavery, and the Means of Practically Effecting It* (2nd edn, London, 1823).

Baring, Alexander, *The Financial and Commercial Crisis Considered* (2nd edn, London, 1847).

Barrett, Richard, *A Reply to the Speech of Dr Lushington in the House of Commons on the 12th June 1827 on the Condition of the Free-Coloured People of Jamaica* (London, 1828).

Barrow, John, 'The Political Importance of Our American Colonies', *Quarterly Review*, 33 (1826).

—, *The Eventful History of the Mutiny and Piratical Seizure of HMS Bounty* (London, 1831).

Bickell, Rev. Richard, *The West Indies as they are; or a real picture of slavery: but more particularly as it exists in the island of Jamaica. In three parts, with notes* (London 1825).

A Biographical Memoir of the Right Honourable William Huskisson, Derived from Authentic Sources (London, 1831).

Bleby, Henry, *Death Struggles of Slavery: Being a Narrative of Facts and Incidents, which Occurred in a British Colony, during the Two Years Immediately Preceding Negro Emancipation* (London, 1853).

Bólivar, Simon, *The Political Thought of Bolivar: Selected Writings*, ed. G.E. Fitzgerald (The Hague, 1971).

Borthwick, Peter, *A Report of Colonial Slavery and Gradual Emancipation, Delivered in the Assembly Rooms on Friday, March 1, 1833* (Edinburgh, 1833).

Bridges, George Wilson, *A Voice from Jamaica; In Reply to William Wilberforce, Esq., M.P.* (London, 1823).

—, *Dreams of Dulocracy; or, The Puritanical Obituary: "An Appeal", Not to the Romantic Sensibility, But to the Good Sense of the British Public* (London, 1824).

—, *Annals of Jamaica* (2 vols., London, 1828).

—, *Outlines and Notes of Twenty-Nine Years, 1834–1862* (n.p., 1862).

'Britannicus', *A Reply to Article VII of the Edinburgh Review for October 1823, on T. Clarkson's Treatise on the Improvement and Emancipation of Slaves in the British Colonies* (London, 1824).

'A Briton', *Considerations on Certain Remarks on the Negro Slavery and Abolition Questions, in Lord Stowell's Judgment in the Case of the Slave 'Grace'* (Newcastle, 1827).

Brough, Anthony, *The Importance of the British Colonies in the West Indies* (London, 1833).

Bryant, Joshua, *Account of an Insurrection of the Negro Slaves in the Colony of Demerara, which broke out on the 18th of August, 1823* (Georgetown, 1824).

Burge, William, *A Letter to the Right Honourable Sir George Murray . . . relative to the Deportation of Lecesne and Escoffery from Jamaica* (London, 1829).

'Candidus', *A Letter Addressed to Edward Bacon, Esq., upon his Sentiments Respecting Slaves in the West Indies* (2nd edn, Ipswich, 1830).

Carlyle, Thomas, 'Occasional Discourse on the Negro Question', *Fraser's Magazine*, 40 (1849), 670–79.

Cheap Charity: A Dialogue on the Present Condition of the Negroes (2nd edn, London, 1824).

Clark, John, W. Dendy, and J.M. Phillippo, *The Voice of Jubilee: A Narrative of the Baptist Mission, Jamaica, from its Commencement* (London, 1865).

Clarkson, Thomas, *Thoughts on the Necessity of Improving the Condition of the Slaves in the British Colonies, with a View to Their Ultimate Emancipation* (London, 1823).

—, *The History of the Rise, Progress, and Accomplishment of the Abolition of the African Slave Trade by the British Parliament* (London, 1839).

Cobbett, William, *Rural Rides* [1830], ed. Ian Dyck (London, 2001).

—, *Eleven Lectures on the French and Belgian Revolutions* (London, 1830).

Coleridge, Henry Nelson, *Six Months in the West Indies, in 1825* (London, 1826).

'The Colonial Crisis', *Fraser's Magazine*, 3 (1831), 625–30.

'Colonist', *The Edinburgh Review and the West Indies: with Observations on the Pamphlets of Messrs Stephen, Macauley &c. and Remarks on the Slave Registry Bill* (Glasgow, 1816).

The Condition of the West India Slave Contrasted with that of the Infant Slave in Our English Factories, with Fifteen Illustrations from the Graver of Robert Cruikshank (London, 1833).

The Correspondence between John Gladstone, Esq., M.P., and James Cropper, Esq., on the Present State of Slavery in the British West Indies (Liverpool, 1824).

The Correspondence of William Wilberforce, ed. Robert Isaac Wilberforce and Samuel Wilberforce (2 vols., London, 1840).

The Creevey Papers: A Selection from the Correspondence and Diaries of the late Thomas Creevey, M.P., ed. Herbert Maxwell (2 vols., London, 1903).

Cropper, James, *Letters Addressed to William Wilberforce, M.P., Recommending the Encouragement of the Cultivation of Sugar in Our Dominions in the East Indies* (Liverpool, 1822).

Crummell, Alexander, *The Man, The Hero, The Christian! A Eulogy on the Life and Character of Thomas Clarkson, delivered in the City of New-York, December, 1846* (New York, 1847).

Cugoano, Ottobah, *Thoughts and Sentiments on the Evil and Wicked Traffic of the Slavery and Commerce of the Human Species* [1787] (Cambridge, 2013).

Davis, Anthony, *The West Indies: A Detail of Facts in Opposition to Theory* (London, 1832).

de la Beche, Henry, *Notes on the Present Condition of the Negroes in Jamaica* (London, 1825).

The Debates in Parliament: Session 1833, on The Resolutions and Bill for the Abolition of Slavery (London, 1834).

Denham, Dixon, and Hugh Clapperton, *Narrative of Travels and Discoveries in Northern and Central Africa, in the Years 1822, 1823 and 1824* (London, 1826).

Despatches between Government and W. India Colonies, relative to Recent Rebellion among Slaves (PP 1831–32 (285)) (London, 1832).

Despatches, Correspondence, and Memoranda of Field Marshal Arthur, Duke of Wellington, K.G., ed. The Duke of Wellington (10 vols., London, 1871).

The Dispatches and Letters of Vice Admiral Lord Viscount Nelson, ed. Sir Nicholas Harris Nicolas (London, 1846).

Duncan, Henry, *Presbyter's Letters on the West India Question; Addressed to the Right Honourable Sir George Murray* (London, 1830).

Duncan, Peter, *A Narrative of the Wesleyan Mission to Jamaica; with Occasional Remarks on the State of Society in That Colony* (London, 1849).

Edwards, Bryan, *The History, Civil and Commercial, of the British West Indies* (5th edn, 5 vols., London, 1819).

Ellis, Charles Rose, and Robert Wilmot-Horton, 'West India Colonies', *Quarterly Review*, 30 (1824), 559–87.

Emerson, Ralph Waldo, *An Address in the Court-House in Concord, Massachusetts, on 1st August, 1844, on the Anniversary of the Emancipation of the Negroes in the British West Indies* (Boston, MA, 1844).

Equiano, Olaudah, *The Interesting Narrative and Other Writings* [1789], ed. Vincent Carretta (London, 2003).

The Factory-Child, A Poem (London, 1831).

Foster, John, *Two Letters on the State of the Negroes in the West Indies* (Bedford, 1824).

Foulks, Theodore, *Eighteen Months in Jamaica: with Recollections of the Late Rebellion* (London, 1833).

Franklin, James, *The Present State of Hayti (Saint Domingo) with Remarks on its Agriculture, Commerce, Laws, Religion, Finances, and Population* (London, 1828).

—, *A Short View of the West India Question* (London, 1828).

'A Friend to True Humanity', *An Appeal to Common Sense in Behalf of Justice, Humanity, and Religion, in a Letter Addressed to Henry Bright, Esq., M.P.* (Bristol, 1823).

Further Papers relating to the Slaves in the West Indies: (Demolition of the Methodist Chapel in Barbadoes) [Parliamentary Papers 1825 (113)] (London, 1825).

Galt, John ['Agricola'], 'The Colonial Question', *Blackwood's Edinburgh Magazine*, 27 (1830), 455–62.

—, 'Letters on West Indian Slavery … to Oliver Yorke, Esq. Letter I', *Fraser's Magazine*, 2 (1830), 440–49.

—, 'Second Letter … with Preliminary Observations, by Oliver Yorke', *Fraser's Magazine*, 2 (1830), 556–63.

—, 'Letters on West Indian slavery', *Fraser's Magazine*, 2 (1830), 563–71.

—, 'West Indian Slavery. Letter III', *Fraser's Magazine*, 2 (1831), 706–13.

—, *Bogle Corbet; or, the Emigrants* (3 vols., London, 1831).

—, 'The Whole West India Question, by John Galt, to Oliver Yorke, Esq.', *Fraser's Magazine*, 8 (1833), 81–90.

Garrison, William Lloyd (ed.), *The Lectures of George Thompson, with … A Brief History of His Connection with the Anti-Slavery Cause* (Boston, MA, 1836).

George Canning and His Friends: Containing Hitherto Unpublished Letters, Jeux D'Esprit, etc., ed. Josceline Bagot (2 vols., London, 1908–9).

Georgian Papers Online [http://gpp.rct.uk].

Gladstone, John, *Facts, relating to Slavery in the West Indies and America, Contained in a Letter Addressed to the Right Hon. Sir Robert Peel, Bart.* (2nd edn, London, 1830).

Godwin, Benjamin, *The Substance of a Course of Lectures on British Colonial Slavery, Delivered at Bradford, York, and Scarborough* (London, 1830).

Greville, Charles C.F., *The Greville Memoirs: A Journal of the Reigns of King George IV, King William IV, and Queen Victoria*, ed. Henry Reeve (8 vols., London, 1899).

Grossett, John Rock, *Remarks on West Indian Affairs* (London, 1824).

Hazlitt, William, *The Spirit of The Age: or, Contemporary Portraits* (2nd edn, London, 1825).

Heyrick, Elizabeth, *Immediate, Not Gradual Abolition; or, An Inquiry into the Shortest, Safest, and Most Effectual Means of Getting Rid of West Indian Slavery* (London, 1824).

—, *No British Slavery: or, An Invitation to the People to Put a Speedy End to It* (London, 1824).

Hibbert, Robert, *Facts, Verified upon Oath, in Contradiction of the Report of the Rev. Thomas Cooper, concerning the General Condition of the Slaves in Jamaica* (London, 1824).

Hodgson, Studholme, *Truths, from the West Indies* (London, 1838).

The Holland House Diaries, 1831–1840: The Diary of Henry Richard Vassall Fox, Third Lord Holland, with Extracts from the Diary of Dr John Allen, ed. Abraham D. Kriegel (London, 1977).

Holmes, J. Henry H., *An Appeal to the Good Sense and Justice of the Inhabitants of the British Empire ... in Respect to Slavery and the West Indies* (n.p., 1823).

Hurrell Froude: Memoranda and Comments, ed. Louise Imogen Guiney (London, 1904).

The Huskisson Papers, ed. Lewis Melville (London, 1931).

Information from Jamaica respecting Inquiry into Treatment of Female Slave (PP 1830–31 (231)) (London, 1831).

Irving, Edward, *A Statement of the Cause which Affects the Decrease or Increase of the Slave Population in the British Colonies* (London, 1833).

Isaacson, Stephen, 'The Colonists *versus* the Anti-Slavery Society (No. I)', *Fraser's Magazine*, 2 (1830), 334–41.

—, 'The Colonists *versus* the Anti-Slavery Society. Chap. II', *Fraser's Magazine*, 3 (1831), 114–26.

—, *A Vindication of the West-India Proprietors, in a Speech Delivered at Mansion House Chapel, Camberwell, August 8, 1832* (London, 1832).

'A Jamaica Proprietor', *Letter to the Duke of Wellington, on the Subject of West India Slavery* (London, 1829).

Jelly, Thomas, *Remarks on the Condition of the White and Free Coloured Inhabitants of Jamaica, with Observations on the Causes which either Facilitate or Retard the Progress of Civilization amongst the Slaves of the West-Indies* (Montego Bay, 1826).

The Journal of Mrs Arbuthnot, 1820–32 (2 vols., London, 1950).

Lady Nugent's Journal: Jamaica One Hundred Years Ago [1907] (Cambridge, 2010).

Laing, Alexander Gordon, *Travels in the Timannee, Kooranko, and Soolima Countries, in Western Africa* (London, 1825).

Leslie, Charles, *A New History of Jamaica, in Thirteen Letters from a Gentleman to his Friends* (Dublin, 1741).

Letters and Addresses by George Thompson, during His Mission in the United States (Boston, MA, 1837).

Letters of Dorothea, Princess Lieven, during Her Residence in London, 1812–34, ed. Lionel G. Robinson (London, 1902).

The Letters of King George IV, 1812–1830, ed. A. Aspinall (3 vols., London, 1938).

Life and Letters of Captain Marryat, ed. Florence Marryat (2 vols., London, 1872).

Life and Letters of Sir James Graham, Second Baronet of Netherby, 1792–1861, ed. Charles Stuart Parker (2 vols., London, 1907).

The Life and Letters of Zachary Macaulay, ed. Viscountess Knutsford (London, 1900).

The Life of William Allen, with Selections from His Correspondence (3 vols., London, 1846).

The Life and Works of Lord Macaulay, ed. G.O. Trevelyan (10 vols., London, 1895–1908).

Lockhart, John Gibson, 'The West Indian Controversy', *Blackwood's Edinburgh Magazine*, 14 (1923), 437–59.

—, 'The West Indian Controversy II', *Blackwood's Edinburgh Magazine*, 14 (1823), 647–66.

—, 'The West Indian Controversy III', *Blackwood's Edinburgh Magazine*, 15 (1824), 68–82.

—, 'The West Indian Controversy IV', *Blackwood's Edinburgh Magazine*, 16 (1824), 682–97.

The London Missionary Society's Report of the Proceedings against the late Rev. J. Smith, of Demerara, Minister of the Gospel (London, 1824).

Long, Edward, *The History of Jamaica* (3 vols., London, 1774).

Lowe, Joseph, 'Condition of the Negroes in Our Colonies', *Quarterly Review*, 29 (1823), 475–508.

Macaulay, Thomas Babington, 'Milton', *Edinburgh Review*, 42 (1825), 304–46.

Macaulay, Zachary, *Negro Slavery; or, a View of Some of the More Prominent Features of that State of Society* (London, 1823).

MacKenzie, Charles, *Notes on Haiti, Made during a Residence in that Republic* (2 vols., London, 1830).

MacQueen, James, *The West India Colonies: The Calumnies and Misrepresentations Circulated Against Them by the Edinburgh Review, Mr Clarkson, Mr Cropper, &c., Examined and Refuted* (London, 1824).

—, *The Colonial Controversy, Containing a Refutation of the Calumnies of the Anti-Colonists* (Glasgow, 1825).

—, *A Fourth Letter to R.W. Hay, Esq., &c. &c. in Reply to Mr. Kenneth Macaulay's "Sierra Leone Vindicated"* (Edinburgh, 1827).

—, 'The Colonial Empire of Great Britain – Letter to Earl Grey, First Lord of the Treasury', *Blackwood's Edinburgh Magazine*, 30 (1831), 744–64.

—, 'Letters to the Right Hon. E. G. Stanley', *Blackwood's Edinburgh Magazine*, 34 (1833), 231–57.

Maginn, 'MS notes on the articles concerning Ireland, the West Indies, &c. in the last number of the Edinburgh Review', *Blackwood's Edinburgh Magazine*, 17 (1825), 461–75.

Malthus, Thomas, *An Essay on the Principle of Population; or, A View of its Past and Present Effects on Human Happiness* [1798] (6th edn, 2 vols., London, 1826).

Marly; or, The Life of a Planter in Jamaica (2nd edn, Glasgow, 1828).

Marryat, Frederick, *Newton Forster; or, The Merchant Service* (3 vols., London, 1832).

Martin, Henry William, *A Counter Appeal in Answer to "An Appeal" from William Wilberforce* (London, 1823).

Martineau, Harriet, *Illustrations of Political Economy. Volume IV: Demerara* (London, 1832).

McDonnell, Alexander, *Considerations on Negro Slavery* (London, 1824).

—, *Free Trade; or, an Inquiry into the Expediency of the Present Corn Laws, and the Relations of Our Foreign and Colonial Trade* (London, 1826).

—, *The West India Legislatures Vindicated from the Charge of Having Resisted the Call of the Mother Country for the Amelioration of Slavery* (London, 1826).

—, *Compulsory Manumission or an Examination of the Actual State of the West India Question* [1827] in *Pamphlets on West India slavery* (Cambridge, 2010).

—, *Colonial Commerce; Comprising an Inquiry into the Principles upon which Discriminating Duties Should be Levied on Sugar, the Growth Respectively of the West India British Possessions, of the East Indies, and of Foreign Countries* (London, 1828).

—, *An Address to the Members of Both Houses of Parliament on the West India Question* (London, 1830).

—, *A Letter to Thos. Fowell Buxton, Esq. M.P., in Refutation of his Allegations Respecting the Decrease of the Slaves in the British West India Colonies* (London, 1833).

'A Member of the Assembly of Grenada', *A Few Remarks on Colonial Legislation, as Connected with the Communication from the Noble Secretary for the Colonies* (London, 1823).

Memoir of William Knibb, Missionary in Jamaica, ed. John Howard Hinton (2nd edn, London, 1846).

The Memoirs of James Stephen, Written by Himself for the Use of His Children, ed. Merle M. Bevington (London, 1954).

Memoirs of Joseph Sturge, ed. Richard Henry (London, 1865).

Memoirs of Sir Thomas Fowell Buxton, Bart., with Selections from His Correspondence, ed. Charles Buxton (London, 1848).

Memoirs of The Life and Writings of the Rev. Richard Watson, Late Secretary to the Wesleyan Missionary Society, ed. Thomas Jackson (New York, 1834).

Memorandum of the Relative Importance of the West & East Indies to Great Britain (London, 1823).

Memorials of the Rev. William J. Shrewsbury, ed. John V.B. Shrewsbury (3rd edn, London, 1869).

'A Merchant', *An Attempt to Strip Negro Emancipation of its Difficulties as well as Its Terrors* (London, 1824).

'The Message of President James Monroe at the Commencement of the First Session of the 18th Congress', *National Archives Catalog* [catalog/archives.gov/id/306420].

Messages of Gen. Andrew Jackson: with a Short Sketch of His Life (Concord, NH, 1837).

'A Methodist', *Rev. R. Watson, Mr. Macaulay, & Mr. Sadler* (Leeds, 1831).

Miller, John, and John Taylor Coleridge, 'West Indian Slavery', *Quarterly Review*, 32 (1825), 506–44.

'Minutes of a Meeting of the General Committee of the Wesleyan Missionary Society, 5 January 1825', in *The Evangelical Magazine and Missionary Chronicle*, 3 (1825).

Mitchel, Hector, *Two Letters to the Colonial Secretary . . . in Answer to the Yellow Book* (Kingston, 1828).

The Narrative of General Venables, with an Appendix of the Papers relating to the Expedition to the West Indies and the Conquest of Jamaica, 1654–1655, ed. C. H. Firth (London, 1900).

'Negro Slavery', *Gentleman's Magazine*, 96 (1826), 317–20.

Newman, John Henry, 'Slavery Allowed Not Encouraged Under the Gospel', in Francis J. McGrath and Placid Murray (eds.), *John Henry Newman: Sermons, 1824–1843, Volume III: Sermons and Lectures for Saints' Days and Holy Days and General Theology* (Oxford, 2010), pp. 239–253.

—, 'How to Accomplish It' [1836], in *Discussions and Arguments on Various Subjects* [1872], ed. Gerard Tracey and James Tolhurst (Leominster, 2004), pp. 1–43.

—, *Letters and Diaries*, ed. Charles Stephen Dessain (32 vols., London, 1961–77).

Newton, John, *The Journal of a Slave Trader* [1750–54], ed. Bernard Martin and Mark Spurrell (London, 1962).

Nineteenth Report of the Directors of the African Institution, read at the Annual General Meeting, Held on the 13th Day of May, 1825 (London, 1825).

Oastler, Richard, *Facts and Plain Words on Every-Day Subjects, comprised in Two Speeches delivered at Wakefield on the Day of the First Election for the West-Riding of Yorkshire, December 20, 1832* (Leeds, 1833).

An Official Letter from the Commissioners of Correspondence of the Bahama Islands, to George Chalmers, Esq., Colonial Agent, Concerning the Proposed Abolition of Slavery in the West Indies (London, 1823).

On the Increasing Importance of the British West-Indian Possessions (London, 1826).

'One of the Protestant Party', *Random Recollections of Exeter Hall, in 1834–1837* (London, 1838).

Papers . . . In Explanation of the Measures Adopted by His Majesty's Government for the Melioration of the Condition of the Slave Population in His Majesty's Possessions in the West Indies [Parliamentary Papers: 1824 (003)] (London, 1824).

Parliamentary Debates from the Year 1803 to the Present Time (41 vols., London, 1804–20).

Park, Mungo, *Travels in the Interior Districts of Africa* (London, 1799).

Peacock, Thomas Love, 'Pan in Town' [1825], in *The Poems of Thomas Love Peacock*, ed. Brimley Johnson (London, 1906).

The Periodical Press of Great Britain and Ireland: or, an Inquiry into the State of the Public Journals, Chiefly as Regards their Moral and Political Influence (London, 1824).

'Physical Evidences of the Characteristics of Ancient Races among the Moderns', *Fraser's Magazine*, 6 (1832), 673–9.

The Posthumous Works of the Late Rev. John Newton (Philadelphia, 1809).

Present State and Prospects of the West India Question, with Regard to its Final Adjustment (London, 1830).

Prichard, James Cowles, *Researches into the physical history of man* [1813], ed. George W. Stocking, Jr (Chicago, 1973).

Prince, Mary, *The History of Mary Prince* [1831], ed. Sara Salih (London, 2004).

Proceedings at a Public Meeting of Persons Interested in the Preservation of the British West India Colonies, Held at the City of London Tavern, the 5th April, 1832 (London, 1832).

Proceedings at a Public Meeting of Persons Interested in the Preservation of the British West India Colonies, held at the City of London Tavern, the 27th May, 1833 (London, 1833).

Proceedings of the Honourable House of Assembly of Jamaica in relation to Those Which Took Place in the British House of Commons, on the 15th of May Last (Kingston, 1823).

Proceedings of the Old Bailey, 'Thomas Fielder', 5 July, 1832 [oldbaileyonline.org].

Reid, Dennis, *An Address to the Right Hon. Geo. Canning, on the Present State of This Island, and Other Matters* (Kingston, 1823).

Remains of the late Reverend Richard Hurrell Froude, M.A., Fellow of Oriel College, Oxford, ed. John Keble and John Henry Newman (2 vols., London, 1838).

A Reply to Mr Jeremie's Pamphlet, by an Inhabitant of St Lucia (London, 1832).

Report from the Select Committee on the Commercial State of the West India Colonies (PP 1831–32 (381)) (London, 1832).

Report from the Select Committee on the State of the West India Colonies (PP 1831–32 (127)) (London, 1832).

Report from the House of Assembly, Jamaica, on Injury Sustained during Recent Rebellion (PP 1831–32 (561)) (London, 1832).

Report of the Agency Committee of the Anti-Slavery Society, established in June, 1831 (London, 1832).

Report of the Committee of the African Institution, Read to the General Meeting on the 15th July, 1807 (London, 1807).

Report of the Committee of the Society for the Mitigation and Gradual Abolition of Slavery throughout the British Dominions, read at the General Meeting of the Society, held on the 25th Day of June 1824 (London, 1824).

Report of the Trial of Mr John Murray, in the Court of King's Bench, at Westminster-Hall, the 19th December, 1829, on an Indictment for a Libel on Messrs Lecesne and Escoffery (London, 1830).

Report of the Trials of the Insurgent Negroes, Before a General Court-Martial Held at Georgetown, Demerara, on the 25th August, 1823 (Georgetown, 1823).

Reports by Commissioners of Inquiry into State of Africans apprenticed in W. Indies II. Further Papers relating to Captured Negroes (PP 1825 (115)) (London, 1825).

Reports by Commissioners of Inquiry into State of Africans apprenticed in W. Indies: Part II of Major Moody's Report on Captured Negroes (PP 1826 (81)) (London, 1826).

Reports by Commissioners of Inquiry into State of Slaves in H.M. Colonies under Acts abolishing Slave Trade (Tortola) (PP 1826–27 (462)) (London, 1827).

Reports of Cases Adjudged in the Court of King's Bench, from Easter Term 12 Geo. 3. to Michaelmas 14 Geo. 3., ed. Capel Lofft (Dublin, 1790).

Reports of Cases Argued and Determined in the High Court of Admiralty, during the Time of the Right Hon. Lord Stowell, ed. John Haggard (2 vols., London, 1833).

Rondeau, Henry, *Anti-Negro Emancipation: An Appeal to Mr. Wilberforce* (London, 1824).

The Rural Code of Haiti; in French and English, with a Prefatory Letter to the Right Hon. the Earl Bathurst (London, 1827).

'S.D.', 'Value of the West India colonies to the mother country', *Gentleman's Magazine*, 94 (1824), 224–7.

Saintsbury, George, *East India slavery*, (2nd edn, London, 1829).

Sandars, Joseph, *A letter Addressed to the Liverpool Society for the Abolition of that Society*, (Liverpool, 1824).

Scott, Michael, *Tom Cringle's Log* (2 vols., Edinburgh, 1833).

Select Committee on Extinction of Slavery in British Dominions (PP 1831–32 (721)) (London, 1832).

Sells, William, *Remarks on the Condition of the Slaves in the Island of Jamaica* (London, 1823).

'Sermons on slavery', *Christian Remembrancer*, 13 (1831), 79–89.

Simmons, H.P., *Letter to the Right Hon. Earl Grey, on the West India Question* (Liverpool, 1833).

Slaves: Berbice and Demerara. Minutes of Evidence taken before His Majesty's Privy Council, in the Matter of the Berbice and Demerara Manumission Order in Council – November 1827 (Parliamentary Paper 1828 (261)) (London, 1828).

Smyth, F.G., *An Apology for the West Indians, and Reflections on the Policy of Great Britain's Interference in the Internal Concerns of the West India Colonies* (London, 1824).

Smyth, James Carmichael, *Reflections upon the Value of the British West Indian colonies, and of the British North American Provinces* (London, 1826).

Society for the Improvement of the Condition of Factory Children (London, 1833).

Some Account of the Society for the Conversion and Religious Instruction and Education of the Negroe Slaves in the British West India Islands (London, 1823).

Some Official Correspondence of George Canning, ed. Edward J. Stapleton (2 vols., London, 1887).

Sotham, Nathaniel, *Plain Facts; or the Question of West India Slavery, Seriously Examined by the Test of Truth, and Real Observation* (3rd edn, Cheltenham, 1825).

The Speech of the Hon. John Dalzell, in the House of Assembly, Saint Vincent (London, 1827).

The Speech of the Right Hon. George Canning … on Wednesday, the 17th of March 1824 (London 1824).

The Speeches of the Duke of Wellington in Parliament, ed. Col. Gurwood (2 vols., London, 1854).

Stephen, George, *Antislavery Recollections: In a Series of Letters Addressed to Mrs Beecher Stowe* (London, 1854).

—, *A Memoir of the Late James Stephen, One of the Masters in the High Court of Chancery, in relation to Slave Emancipation* (Brighton, 1875).

Stephen, James (I), *Reasons for Establishing a Registry of Slaves in the British Colonies* (London, 1815).

—, *The Slavery of the British West India Colonies Delineated, as it Exists, both in Law and Practice* (2 vols., London, 1824–30).

Stewart, J., *A View of the Past and Present State of the Island of Jamaica* (Edinburgh, 1823).

Sturge, Joseph, and Thomas Harvey, *The West Indies in 1837; Being the Journal of a Visit to Antigua, Montserrat, Dominica, St. Lucia, Barbados, and Jamaica* (London, 1838).

Tamworth Election. Speech of Sir Robert Peel, June 28, 1841 (London, 1841).

Thome, James A., and J. Horace Kimball, *Emancipation in the West Indies: A Six Months' Tour in Antigua, Barbadoes, and Jamaica, in the Year 1837* (New York, 1838).

Three Early Nineteenth Century Diaries, ed. A. Aspinall (London, 1952).

'Treatment of slaves in Barbadoes', *Christian Remembrancer*, 5 (1823), 406–8.

Tropical Free-Labour Company: A Prospectus (London, 1825).

Tucker, S., 'On church establishments', *Imperial Magazine*, 2 (1832), 260–7.

Twelfth Report of the Directors of the African Institution, read at the Annual General Meeting held on 9th of April, 1818 (London, 1818).

Vassall, H.R., *Memoirs of the Whig Party during My Times*, ed. H.E. Vassall (2 vols., London, 1852–4).

'Vindex', *The Conduct of the British Government towards the Church of England in the West India Colonies: In a Letter to Viscount Goderich* (London, 1831).

The Voice of the West Indies, and the Cry of England (London, 1832).

Waddell, H.M., *Twenty-Nine Years in the West Indies and Central Africa: A Review of Missionary Work and Adventure, 1829–1858* [1863] (2nd edn, London, 1970).

Walker, William Greenwood (ed.), *A Selection of Games at Chess, Actually Played in London, by the late Alexander McDonnell, Esq., the Best English Player, with his Principal Contemporaries* (London, 1836).

Wallace, James, *A General and Descriptive History of the Ancient and Present State of the Town of Liverpool* (Liverpool, 1796).

Wellington and His Friends: Letters of the First Duke of Wellington to the Rt Hon Charles and Mrs Arbuthnot, the Earl and Countess of Wilton, Princess Lieven, and Miss Burdett-Coutts, ed. Gerald Wellesley (London, 1965).

'West India Missions', *Edinburgh Review*, 40 (1824), 226–70.

'A West India Planter', *A Letter to the Most Honourable the Marquis of Chandos* (London, 1830).

'The West Indies', *Edinburgh Review*, 82 (1825), 464–88.

Whiteley, Henry, *Three Months in Jamaica, in 1832: Comprising a Residence of Seven Weeks on a Sugar Plantation* (London, 1833).

Wilberforce, Robert Isaac, and Samuel Wilberforce, *The Life of William Wilberforce* (London, 1843).

Wilberforce, William, *An Appeal to the Religion, Justice, and Humanity of the Inhabitants of the British Empire* (London, 1823).

Wilkinson, Rev. J.W., *Thoughts on Negro Slavery* (London, 1833).

Williams, Rev. Cynric, *A Tour Through the Island of Jamaica, From the Western to the Eastern End, in the Year 1823* (London, 1826).

Williams, James, *Narrative of Events, since the First of August, 1834* (London, 1837).

Wilmot-Horton, Robert, *The West India Question Practically Considered* (London, 1826).

—, *First Letter to the Freeholders of the County of York, on Negro Slavery* (London, 1830).

—, *Second Letter to the Freeholders of the County of York, on Negro Slavery* (London, 1830).

Young, Robert, *A View of Slavery in Connection with Christianity: Being the Substance of a Discourse Delivered in the Wesleyan Chapel, Stoney-Hill, Jamaica, September 19, 1824* (London, 1825).

'Z', *Slavery – To the Editor of the English Chronicle and Whitehall Evening Post – To the West India Planters and Abolitionists – Negro Slavery* (Penzance, 1831).

NEWSPAPERS, JOURNALS, AND MAGAZINES

Anti-Slavery Monthly Reporter
Barbadian
Black Dwarf
Blackwood's Edinburgh Magazine
Christian Remembrancer
Cobbett's Weekly Register
Colonial Register and West India Journal
Dominica Chronicle
Edinburgh Review
Fraser's Magazine
Gentleman's Magazine
Glasgow Courier
Hansard
Humming Bird, or Morsels of Information on the Subject of Slavery
John Bull
Lion
Morning Chronicle
Morning Herald
Morning Post
New Monthly Magazine
Niles' Weekly Register
Quarterly Review
Republican
Royal Gazette, Guiana
Royal Gazette, Jamaica
Spectator

The Times
Tourist: A Literary and Anti-Slavery Journal
Wesleyan-Methodist Magazine
West Indian Reporter
Westminster Review

SECONDARY SOURCES

Akala, *Natives: Race and Class in the Ruins of Empire* (London, 2018).

Altink, Henrice, 'Slavery by Another Name: Apprenticed Women in Jamaican Workhouses in the Period, 1834–81', *Social History*, 26 (2001), 40–59.

Aspinall, A., 'The Coalition Ministries of 1827 (Continued)', *English Historical Review*, 42 (1927), 533–59.

—, 'The Canningite Party', *Transactions of the Royal History Society*, 17 (1934), 177–226.

Aucott, Shirley, *Elizabeth Heyrick, 1769 to 1831: The Leicester Quaker who Demanded the Immediate Emancipation of Slaves in the British Colonies* (Leicester, 2007).

Bakan, Abigail B., *Ideology and Class Conflict in Jamaica: The Politics of Rebellion* (Montreal, 1990).

Barker, Anthony J., 'Distorting the Record of Slavery and Abolition: The British Anti-Slavery Movement and Mauritius, 1826–37', *Slavery & Abolition*, 14 (1993), 185–207.

—, *Slavery and Anti-Slavery in Mauritius, 1810–33: The Conflict between Economic Expansion and Humanitarian Reform under British Rule* (Basingstoke, 1996).

Bashford, Alison, and Joyce E. Chaplin, *The New Worlds of Thomas Malthus: Rereading the Principle of Population* (Princeton, 2016).

Bayly, C.A., *Imperial Meridian: The British Empire and the World, 1780–1830* (London, 1989).

Beaglehole, J.C., 'The Colonial Office, 1782–1854', *Historical Studies*, 1 (1941), 170–89.

Beckles, Hilary, and Verene Shepherd (eds.), *Caribbean Freedom: Economy and Society from Emancipation to the Present* (Princeton 1993).

Beckles, Hilary McDonald, '"Slavery Was A Long, Long Time Ago": Remembrance, Reconciliation, and the Reparations Discourse in the Caribbean', *Ariel*, 38 (2007), 9–25.

—, *Britain's Black Debt: Reparations for Caribbean Slavery and Native Genocide* (Kingston, 2013).

Bew, John, *Castlereagh: A Life* (Oxford, 2012).

Blackburn, Robin, *The Overthrow of Colonial Slavery, 1776–1848* (London, 1988).

Brady, Alexander, *William Huskisson and Liberal Reform: An Essay on the Changes in Economic Policy in the Twenties of the 19th Century* [1928] (2nd edn, London, 1967).

Briggs, Asa, *The Age of Improvement, 1783–1867* (2nd edn, Oxford, 2000).

Brown, Christopher Leslie, *Moral Capital: Foundations of British Abolitionism* (Chapel Hill, NC, 2006).

Brown, Matthew, 'Gregor MacGregor: Clansman, Conquistador, and Coloniser on the Fringes of the British Empire', in *Colonial Lives across the British Empire: Imperial Careering in the Long Nineteenth Century*, ed. David Lambert and Alan Lester (Cambridge, 2009), 32–57.

Brown, Vincent, *The Reaper's Garden: Death and Power in the World of Atlantic Slavery* (Cambridge, MA, 2008).

Browne, Randy M., *Surviving Slavery in the British Caribbean* (Philadelphia, 2017).

Burnard, Trevor, *Mastery, Tyranny, & Desire: Thomas Thistlewood and His Slaves in the Anglo-Jamaican World* (Chapel Hill, NC, 2004).

Carmichael, Gertrude, 'Some Notes on Sir Ralph James Woodford, Bt.', *Caribbean Quarterly*, 2 (1952), 26–38.

Charlton, K., 'James Cropper and Liverpool's Contribution to the Anti-Slavery Movement', in *Transactions of the Historic Society of Lancashire and Cheshire*, 123 (1971), 57–80.

Clark, J.C.D., *English Society, 1660–1832: Religion, Ideology and Politics during the Ancien Régime* (2nd edn, Cambridge, 2000).

Cobain, Ian, *The History Thieves: Secrets, Lies, and the Shaping of a Modern Nation* (London, 2017).

Coffey, John, '"Tremble, Britannia!": Fear, Providence, and the Abolition of the Slave Trade, 1758–1807', *English Historical Review*, 127 (2012), 844–81.

'Colonial Policy', *Edinburgh Review*, 84 (1825), 271–303.

Coupland, Reginald, *The British Anti-Slavery Movement* (London, 1933).

—, *The Empire in These Days: An Interpretation* (London, 1935).

Craton, Michael, 'Christianity and Slavery in the British West Indies', *Historical Reflections*, 5 (1978), 141–60.

—, 'Proto-Peasant Revolts? The Late Slave Rebellions in the British West Indies, 1816–1832', *Past & Present*, 85 (1979), 99–125.

—, *Testing the Chains: Resistance to Slavery in the British West Indies* (London, 1982).

Cutmore, J.B. (ed.), *Conservatism and The Quarterly Review: A Critical Analysis* (London, 2007).

—, *Contributors to the Quarterly Review: A History, 1809–25* (London, 2008).

Davis, David Brion, 'James Cropper and the British Anti-Slavery Movement, 1821–1823', *Journal of Negro History*, 45 (1960), 241–58.

—, *The Problem of Slavery in the Age of Revolution, 1770–1823* (Ithaca, NY, 1975).

Davis, R.W., 'The Tories, the Whigs, and Catholic Emancipation, 1827–1829', *English Historical Review*, 97 (1982), 89–98.

Dawson, Frank Griffith, *The First Latin American Debt Crisis: The City of London and the 1822–25 Loan Bubble* (New Haven, CT, 1990).

Donington, Katie, 'The benevolent Merchant? George Hibbert (1757–1837) and the representation of West Indian Mercantile indentity' (unpublished dissertation, UCL, 2013).

Draper, Nicholas, *The Price of Emancipation: Slave-Ownership, Compensation, and British Society at the End of Slavery* (Cambridge, 2013).

Drescher, Seymour, *The Mighty Experiment: Free Labor versus Slavery in British Emancipation* (Oxford, 2002).

—, *Abolition: A History of Slavery and Anti-Slavery* (Cambridge, 2009).

—, *Econocide: British Slavery in the Era of Abolition* (Chapel Hill, NC, 2010).

Driver, Cecil, *Tory Radical: The Life of Richard Oastler* (New York, 1946).

Duffy, I.P.H., *Bankruptcy and Insolvency in London during the Industrial Revolution* (New York, 1985).

Dumas, Paula E., *Proslavery Britain: Fighting for Slavery in an Era of Abolition* (Basingstoke, 2016).

Evans, Eric J., *Britain before the Reform Act: Politics and Society, 1815–1832* (2nd edn, Oxford, 2008).

Fay, C.R., *Huskisson and His Age* (London, 1951).

Findlay, G.G., and W.W. Holdsworth, *The History of the Wesleyan Methodist Missionary Society* (5 vols., London, 1921–24).

Finkelstein, David, *The House of Blackwood: Author–Publisher Relations in the Victorian Era* (University Park, PA, 2002).

— (ed.), *Print Culture and the Blackwood Tradition, 1805–1930* (Toronto, 2006).

Fisher, David R. (ed.), *The History of Parliament: The House of Commons, 1820–1832* (Cambridge, 2009).

Fraser, Antonia, *The King and the Catholics: The Fight for Rights, 1829* (London, 2018).

Fryer, Peter, *Staying Power: The History of Black People in Britain* (London, 1984).

Gambles, Anna, *Protection and Politics: Conservative Economic Discourse, 1815–1852* (Woodbridge, 1999).

Gardner, W.J., *A History of Jamaica: From Its Discovery by Christopher Columbus to the Year 1872* [1873] (3rd edn, London, 1971).

Garfield, Simon, *The Last Journey of William Huskisson: How a Day of Triumph Became A Day of Disaster at the Turn of a Wheel* (London, 2003).

Gash, Norman, *Lord Liverpool: The Life and Political Career of Robert Banks Jenkinson, Second Earl of Liverpool, 1770–1828* (Cambridge, MA, 1984).

Glasson, Travis, '"Baptism doth not bestow Freedom": Missionary Anglicanism, Slavery, and the Yorke–Talbot Opinion, 1701–30', *The William and Mary Quarterly*, 67 (2010), 279–318.

Goveia, Elsa V., *A Study on the Historiography of the British West Indies to the End of the Nineteenth Century* (Mexico City, 1956).

Green, William A., *British Slave Emancipation: The Sugar Colonies and the Great Experiment, 1830–1865* (Oxford, 1976).

Gross, Izhak, 'The Abolition of Negro Slavery and British Parliamentary Politics, 1832–3', *Historical Journal*, 23 (1980), 63–85.

Hague, William, *Wilberforce: The Life of the Great Anti-Slave Trade Campaigner* (London, 2008).

Hall, Catherine, Hall, 'In the Name of Which Father?', *International Labor and Working-Class History*, 41 (1992), 23–28.

—, *Civilising Subjects: Metropole and Colony in the English Imagination, 1830–1867* (Cambridge, 2002).

— and Keith McClelland (eds.), *Race, Nation, and Empire: Making Histories, 1750 to the Present* (Manchester, 2010).

—, *Macaulay and Son: Architects of Imperial Britain* (London, 2012).

—, Nicholas Draper, Keith McClelland, Katie Donington, and Rachel Lang, *Legacies of British Slave-Ownership: Colonial Slavery and the Formation of Victorian Britain* (Cambridge, 2014).

—, 'Thinking Reflexively: Opening "Blind Eyes"', *Past and Present*, 234 (2017), 254–63

Hanley, Ryan, 'Calvinism, Proslavery and James Albert Ukawsaw Gronniosaw', *Slavery & Abolition*, 36 (2015), 360–81.

—, 'Slavery and the Birth of Working-Class Racism in England, 1814–1833', *Transactions of the Royal Historical Society*, 26 (2016), 103–23.

—, 'A Radical Change of Heart: Robert Wedderburn's Last Word on Slavery', *Slavery & Abolition*, 37 (2016), 423–45.

Hawkins, Angus, *The Forgotten Prime Minister, the 14th Earl of Derby. Volume 1: Ascent, 1799–1851* (Oxford, 2007).

Heuman, Gad J., *Between Black and White: Race, Politics, and the Free Coloreds in Jamaica, 1792–1865* (Westport, CT, 1981).

Higman, B.W., *Slave Populations of the British Caribbean, 1807–1834* (Baltimore, 1984).

—, 'The Colonial Congress of 1831', in Brian Moore and Swithin Wilmot (eds.), *Before & After 1865: Education, Politics, and Regionalism in the Caribbean* (Kingston, 1998), 239–48.

Hilton, Boyd, 'The Political Arts of Lord Liverpool', *Transactions of the Royal Historical Society*, 38 (1988), 147–70.

—, *A Mad, Bad, and Dangerous People? England, 1783–1846* (Oxford, 2006).

Hinde, Wendy, *George Canning* (London, 1973).

Hochschild, Adam, *Bury the Chains: Prophets and Rebels in the Fight to Free an Empire's Slaves* (New York, 2006).

Hoermann, Raphael, 'Figures of Terror: The "Zombie" and the Haitian Revolution', *Atlantic Studies*, 14 (2017), 152–73.

Holt, Thomas C., *The Problem of Freedom: Race, Labor, and Politics in Jamaica and Britain, 1832–1938* (Baltimore, 1992)

Huzzey, Richard, *Freedom Burning: Antislavery and Empire in Victorian Britain* (Ithaca, NY, 2012).

Inikori, Joseph E., *Africans and the Industrial Revolution: A Study in International Trade and Economic Development* (Cambridge, 2002).

James, C.L.R., *Beyond a Boundary* (London, 1963).

—, *The Black Jacobins: Toussaint L'Ouverture and the San Domingo Revolution* (London, 1938).

Jenkins, Brian, *Henry Goulburn, 1784–1856: A Political Biography* (London, 1996).

Jennings, Judith, *The Business of Abolishing the British Slave Trade, 1783–1807* (Oxford, 1997).

Jones, Mark, 'The mobilisation of public opinion against the slave trade and slavery: popular abolitionism in national and regional politics, 1787–1838' (unpublished D.Phil. dissertation, University of York, 1998).

Jones, Wilbur Devereux, 'Lord Mulgrave's Administration in Jamaica, 1832–33', *Journal of Negro History*, 48 (1963), 44–56.

—, *'Prosperity Robinson': The Life of Viscount Goderich, 1782–1859* (London, 1967).

Kehoe, S. Karly, 'Colonial collaborators: Britain and the Catholic Church in Trinidad, c. 1820–1840', *Slavery & Abolition* (2019), 130–46.

Kitson, Peter J., and Deborah Lee (eds.), *Slavery, Abolition, and Emancipation: Writings in the British Romantic Period* (8 vols., London, 1999).

Lambert, David, *White Creole Culture, Politics and Identity during the Age of Abolition* (Cambridge, 2005).

—, 'The "Glasgow King of Billingsgate": James MacQueen and an Atlantic Proslavery Network', *Slavery & Abolition*, 29 (2008), 389–413.

—, *Mastering the Niger: James MacQueen's Map of Africa and the Struggle over Atlantic Slavery* (Chicago, 2013).

Lamont, Stephen Peter, 'Robert Wilmot Horton and Liberal Toryism' (unpublished Ph.D. dissertation, University of Nottingham, 2015).

Legacies of British Slave-Ownership [www.ucl.ac.uk/lbs].

Lightfoot, Natasha, *Troubling Freedom: Antigua and the Aftermath of British Emancipation* (Durham, NC, 2015).

Lynn, Martin, 'The profitability of the early nineteenth-century palm oil trade', *African Economic History*, 20 (1992), 77–97.

Mathieson, William Law, *British Slavery and Its Abolition, 1823–1838* (London, 1926).

Matthews, Gelien, *Caribbean Slave Revolts and the British Abolitionist Movement* (Baton Rouge, LA, 2006).

McDonnell, Philippa, 'Why My Great-Great-Great Grandfather Defaced Ancient Egyptian Monuments', *The Guardian*, 3 August 2009.

Midgley, Clare, *Woman against Slavery: The British Campaign, 1780–1870* (London, 1992).

Minter, Patricia Hagler, 'The State of Slavery: Somerset, The Slave, Grace, and the Rise of Pro-Slavery and Anti-Slavery Constitutionalism in the Nineteenth-Century Atlantic World', *Slavery & Abolition*, 36 (2015), 603–17.

Mitchell, L.G., *Lord Melbourne, 1779–1848* (Oxford, 1997).

Morgan, Kenneth (ed.), *The Bright–Meyler Papers: A Bristol-West India Connexion, 1732–1837* (Oxford, 2007).

—, 'Labour Relations during and after Apprenticeship: Amity Hall, Jamaica, 1834–1840', *Slavery & Abolition*, 33 (2012), 457–78.

Morrison, R.S., and D.S. Roberts (eds.), *Romanticism and Blackwood's Magazine: 'An Unprecedented Phenomenon'* (Basingstoke, 2013).

Murray, D.J., *The West Indies and the Development of Colonial Government, 1801–1834* (Oxford, 1965).

O'Ferrall, F., *Catholic Emancipation: Daniel O'Connell and the Birth of Irish Democracy, 1820–30* (London, 1985).

O'Shaughnessy, Andrew, 'The formation of a commercial lobby: The West India interest, British colonial policy, and the American Revolution', *Historical Journal*, 40 (1997), 71–95.

Olusoga, David, *Black and British: A Forgotten History* (London, 2016).

The Oxford Dictionary of National Biography [www.oxforddnb.com].

Pallua, Ulrich, 'Images of Africans in British Slavery Discourse: Pro- and Anti-Slave Trade/Slavery Voices in *The Gentleman's Magazine* and *The Monthly Review*, 1772–1833', *Stichproben*, 16 (2009), 17–43.

Pardue, Jeffrey David, 'Agent of imperial change: James MacQueen and the British Empire, 1778–1870' (unpublished PhD dissertation, University of Waterloo, 1996).

Parker, Matthew, *The Sugar Barons: Family, Corruption, Empire, and War* (London, 2012).

Parsons, Timothy H., *The Second British Empire: In the Crucible of the Twentieth Century* (Lanham, MD, 2014).

Paulus, Carl Lawrence, *The Slaveholding Crisis: Fear of Insurrection and the Coming of the Civil War* (Baton Rouge, LA, 2017).

Penson, Lillian M., 'The London West India interest in the eighteenth century', *English Historical Review*, 36 (1921), 373–92.

Petley, Christer, *Slaveholders in Jamaica: Colonial Society and Culture during the Era of Abolition* (Oxford, 2009).

—, *White Fury: A Jamaican Slaveholder and the Age of Revolution* (Oxford, 2018).

—, *Slavery and Revolution* [https://blog.soton.ac.uk/slaveryandrevolution/].

Pocock, *Captain Marryat: Seaman, Writer, and Adventurer* (London, 2000).

Pollock, John, *Wilberforce* (London, 1977).

Ragatz, Lowell Joseph, *The Fall of the Planter Class in the British Caribbean, 1763–1833: A Study in Social and Economic History* (London, 1928).

Reckford, Mary, 'Jamaica Slave Rebellion of 1831', *Past & Present*, 40 (1968), 108–25.

—, 'The Colonial Office and the Abolition of Slavery', *Historical Journal*, 14 (1971), 723–34.

Riots and Reform, [https://www.nottingham.ac.uk/ manuscriptsandspecial collections/learning/dukeofnewcastle/theme2/riotsandreform].

Rediker, Marcus, *Slave Ship: A Human History* (London, 2008).

Robertson, James, 'Giving Directions in Spanish Town, Jamaica: Comprehending a Tropical Townscape', *Journal of Urban History*, 35 (2009).

Rodney, Walter, *How Europe Underdeveloped Africa* (London, 1972).

Royle, Edward, *Revolutionary Britannia? Reflections on the Threat of Revolution in Britain, 1789–1848* (Manchester, 2000).

Rugemer, Edward B., *The Problem of Emancipation: The Caribbean Roots of the American Civil War*, (Baton Rouge, LA. 2008).

Rupprecht, Anita, '"When He Gets Among His Countrymen, They Tell Him That He Is Free": Slave Trade Abolition, Indentured Africans, and a Royal Commission', *Slavery & Abolition*, 33 (2012), 435–55.

Ryden, David Beck, 'The Society of West India Planters and Merchants in the Age of Emancipation, c. 1816–35' (unpublished paper given at the Economic History Society Annual Conference, 27–29 March 2015).

Sambrook, James, *William Cobbett* (London, 1973).

Scanlan, Padraic X., *Freedom's Debtors: Antislavery in Sierra Leone in the Age of Revolution* (New Haven, CT, 2017).

Sebastiani, Silvia, *The Scottish Enlightenment: Race, Gender, and the Limits of Progress*, trans. Jeremy Carden (Basingstoke, 2013).

Sheridan, Richard B., 'The West India Sugar Crisis and British Slave Emancipation, 1830–1833', *Journal of Economic History*, 21 (1961), 539–51.

Sinclair, David, *Sir Gregor MacGregor and the Land That Never Was* (London, 2004).

Skinner, S.A., *Tractarians and the 'condition of England': The Social and Political Thought of the Oxford Movement* (Oxford, 2004).

Smith, E.A., *Lord Grey, 1764–1845* (Oxford, 1990).

Stuart, Andrea, *Sugar in the Blood: A Family's Story of Slavery and Empire* (London, 2012).

Tave, Stuart M., *New Essays by De Quincey: His Contributions to the Edinburgh Saturday Post and the Edinburgh Evening Post, 1827–1828* (Princeton, NJ, 1966).

Taylor Clare, (ed.), *British and American Abolitionists: An Episode in Transatlantic Understanding* (Edinburgh, 1974).

Taylor, Michael, 'Conservative Political Economy and the Problem of Colonial Slavery, 1823–33', *Historical Journal*, 57 (2014), 973–95.

—, 'The Ideas of the Defence of British Colonial Slavery, 1823–33', (unpublished PhD dissertation, University of Cambridge, 2014).

—, 'British Proslavery Arguments and the Bible, 1823–33', *Slavery & Abolition*, 37 (2016), 139–58.

—, 'The British West India Interest and Its Allies, 1823–1833', *English Historical Review*, 133 (2018), 1478–1511.

— (with Michael S. Kochin), *An Independent Empire: Diplomacy & War in the Making of the United States* (Ann Arbor, MI, 2020).

Tharoor, Shashi, *Inglorious Empire: What the British Did to India* (London, 2017).

Thomas, Sue, '*Pringle v. Cadell* and *Wood v. Pringle*: The Libel Cases over *The History of Mary Prince*', *Journal of Commonwealth Literature*, 40 (2005), 13–35.

Thompson, E.P., *The Making of the English Working Class* [1963] (London, 1980).

Thornbury, Walter, 'The Poultry', in *Old and New London: Volume 1* (London, 1878), 416–24.

Thorne, R.G (ed.), *The History of Parliament: The House of Commons, 1790–1820* (5 vols., London, 1986).

Timbs, John, *Club Life of London with Anecdotes of the Clubs, Coffee-Houses, and Taverns of the Metropolis during the 17th, 18th. and 19th Centuries* (2 vols., London, 1866).

Tise, Larry E., *Proslavery: A History of the Defense of Slavery in America, 1701–1840* (Athens, GA, 1987).

Turner, Mary, *Slaves and Missionaries: The Disintegration of Jamaican Slave Society, 1787–1834* (Kingston, 1998).

Twells, Alison, *The Civilising Mission and the English Middle Class, 1792–1850* (Basingstoke, 2009).

Viotti da Costa, Emilia, *Crowns of Glory, Tears of Blood: The Demerara Slave Rebellion of 1823* (Oxford, 1994).

Waddams, Stephen, 'The Case of Grace James (1827)', *Texas Wesleyan Law Review*, 13 (2008), 783–94.

Walvin, James, *England, Slaves, and Freedom, 1776–1838* (University Press of Mississippi, Jackson, 1986).

—, *The Zong: A Massacre, the Law, & the End of Slavery* (New Haven, CT, 2011).

Watson, Tim, 'Working the Edges of the Nineteenth-Century British Empire', *Literature Compass*, 13 (2016), 288–99.

Webster, Jane, 'Collecting for the Cabinet of Freedom: The Parliamentary History of Thomas Clarkson's Chest', *Slavery & Abolition*, 38 (2017), 135–54.

Whyte, Iain, *Zachary Macaulay, 1768–1838: The Steadfast Scot in the British Anti-Slavery Movement* (Liverpool, 2011).

Williams, Eric, *Capitalism and Slavery* (Chapel Hill, NC, 1944).

Williamson, Margaret, 'Africa or Old Rome? Jamaican Slave Naming Revisited', *Slavery & Abolition*, 38 (2017), 117–34.

Wilson, Ellen Gibson, *The Great Yorkshire Election of 1807: Mass Politics in England before the Age of Reform*, ed. Edward Royle and James Walvin (Lancaster, 2015).

Index